More praise for

NATURE WARS

"[A] sweeping and thoughtful work . . . there's a lot in *Nature Wars* for the reasoned and concerned human to learn about the changing natural landscape . . . [Sterba] paints a vivid and memorable portrait of these new ecosystems, where only one, plentiful species is capable of bringing balance and harmony among living things: homo sapiens."

—*Los Angeles Times*

"Fascinating . . . Sterba portrays the resulting conflicts not only between people and animals but also between hunters and activists, government officials and residents, and any number of other factions."

—*Washington Post*

"Written with considerable charm and more wit than commonly found in works that deal with ecosystems, [*Nature Wars*] includes extensive and often entertaining treatments of such common nuisances as beavers, Canada geese, and feral cats . . . For the denatured reader, there is a wealth of useful statistics."

—*The New York Review of Books*

"While advancing his brief that mankind has to do more to intervene as managers in the natural process, Sterba also ably documents how we influence wildlife without really trying or realizing it."

—*Christian Science Monitor*

"Jim Sterba's *Nature Wars* chronicles the dilemmas created by the resurgence of wildlife populations in much of the eastern United States . . . [A] thoughtful text."

—*Seattle Times*

"[Sterba] makes a provocative, controversial, but quite compelling case that we should not—and cannot—opt out of active management and stewardship of wildlife."

—*Pittsburgh Post-Gazette*

"In *Nature Wars,* Sterba, an award-winning journalist, examines how modern society is fighting a new war against the wildlife and nature that surround us . . . An interesting look at how man's attempt to control nature has created even more problems . . . Thoroughly researched."

—*DESERET NEWS*

"In his book *Nature Wars,* [Sterba] highlights nature's perils . . . nature has never been as idyllic as we think."

—EMMA BRYCE, *DISCOVER* MAGAZINE

"This is an excellent introduction to a 'problem' that is often one of human perception."

—*BOOKLIST,* STARRED REVIEW

"Jim Sterba employs humor and an eye for the absurd to document the sometimes bizarre conflicts that arise as a consequence of America's transformed relationship with nature . . . An eye-opening take on how romantic sentimentalism about nature can have destructive consequences."

—*KIRKUS,* STARRED REVIEW

"Sterba provocatively and persuasively argues that just at the moment when humankind has distanced itself irrevocably from nature, its behavior patterns have put people in conflict with a natural world that they don't know how to deal with . . . A valuable counternarrative to the mainstream view of nature-human interaction."

—*PUBLISHERS WEEKLY*

"An unusual feat of deep and sustained reporting, *Nature Wars* is full of surprises and marked, from first page to last, by uncommon sense, graceful writing, and precious wit."

—JOSEPH LELYVELD, AUTHOR OF
GREAT SOUL: MAHATMA GANDHI AND HIS STRUGGLE WITH INDIA

"Elegant and compelling . . . Jim Sterba uses wit and insight to reveal new and unintended consequences of human sprawl and the ways in which they have shaped today's relationships with Nature."

—JOHN H. ADAMS, FOUNDING DIRECTOR
OF THE NATURAL RESOURCES DEFENSE COUNCIL

"*Nature Wars* explores this marvelous story of environmental recovery and the opportunities and challenges that it brings to its residents and the entire globe in fascinating detail and with great insight by Jim Sterba. This is a great book and a story with lessons for us all."

"If there is one lesson to be learned from Jim Sterba's book, it is: Be careful what you wish for. Having decimated our planet's natural state, we are blithely overcompensating, overcorrecting, and overturning the balance of nature yet again. Read *Nature Wars* and weep. Or at least, stop and think."

"In *Nature Wars,* Jim Sterba lays out battle lines that emerged after populations of species that declined to near-extinction by the end of the nineteenth century came roaring back . . . This book is sure to initiate discussion about an issue that seems likely to move closer to the forefront in the years ahead."

"Jim Sterba has given us a fascinating, powerful, and important lesson in why we should be careful when we mess with Mother Nature."

"At last someone's grappling with the elephant in the room—or rather the deer, the coyote, the beaver, the bear, all these damn animals crowding into our living space. Sterba's book may strike some as observational comedy but he's deadly serious. Every word rings true. Nature is vengeful. All I can say is, he better not take a walk in his backyard without a shotgun."

"A wonderful, thought-provoking, important book that will overturn everything you thought you knew about wildlife in America. Jim Sterba confronts the shibboleths that make man-versus-beast conflicts so vexing, divisive, and fascinatingly complex."

"It's a truly original piece of work, often—I would say—inspired, told in a pitch-perfect voice, just north of sarcastic and south of appalled. At any event, a terrific read on a subject that is all around us yet largely unobserved."

—WARD JUST, AUTHOR OF *RODIN'S DEBUTANTE*

"Anything Jim Sterba writes is worth reading—and his latest, *Nature Wars,* is terrific. Sterba casts a reporter's sharp eye on a little noticed war unfolding under our noses, in our own backyards. We've messed with nature for way too long, and nature is getting even."

—JOSEPH L. GALLOWAY, COAUTHOR OF
WE WERE SOLDIERS ONCE . . . AND YOUNG AND *WE ARE SOLDIERS STILL*

"Brilliant . . . This informative and beautifully written book gives us the effect of civilization (often well-meaning) on the natural habitat, both flora and fauna. I loved the book and learned a great deal from it."

—PETER DUCHIN, MUSICIAN AND AUTHOR OF *GHOST OF A CHANCE*

"If you love animals and trees and other wonders of the natural world, this book will astonish you. Sterba's great gifts are reportorial energy, out-of-the-box thinking, and an easy, relaxed prose style that makes *Nature Wars* a pleasure to read, even as its counterintuitive discoveries explode on every page."

—DANIEL OKRENT, AUTHOR OF
LAST CALL: THE RISE AND FALL OF PROHIBITION

"Most Americans now live not in cities but in regrown forests, among at least as many deer as when Columbus landed. Jim Sterba tells us how this came to be and why it isn't all good. In graceful, clear-eyed prose, he explains why we need to relearn how to cut, cull, and kill to restore a more healthy balance to our environment."

—PAUL STEIGER, EDITOR IN CHIEF, PROPUBLICA

"*Nature Wars* is my favorite kind of read—a book that affectionately recasts much of what we thought we knew about our nation's past and our relationship to the American wild, while at the same time revealing how intimately we ourselves are a part of nature, but in the most surprising and unexpected ways. In Sterba's hands, your everyday notions about the creatures around you—whether pests, pets, or magnificent beasts—will turn into entirely new ways of seeing the world."

—TREVOR CORSON, AUTHOR OF
THE SECRET LIFE OF LOBSTERS AND *THE STORY OF SUSHI*

NATURE WARS

The Incredible Story of
How Wildlife Comebacks Turned Backyards
into Battlegrounds

JIM STERBA

B \ D \ W \ Y
BROADWAY BOOKS
New York

All rights reserved.
Published in the United States by Crown Publishers, an imprint
of the Crown Publishing Group, a division of Random House LLC,
a Penguin Random House Company, New York.
www.crownpublishing.com

BROADWAY BOOKS and its logo, B / D / W / Y, are trademarks
of Random House LLC.

Originally published in hardcover in the United States by Crown Publishers,
an imprint of the Crown Publishing Group, a division of Random House LLC,
New York, in 2012.

Grateful acknowledgment is made to Greg Mittman for permission to reprint
excerpts from *Reel Nature: America's Romance with Wildlife on Film* by Greg Mittman,
copyright © 1999 by the President and Fellows of Harvard College. A Weyerhaeuser
Environmental Classic edition published by arrangement with Harvard University

Portions of this book appeared in different form in the *Wall Street Journal*. Excerpts
from *Reel Nature* by Gregg Mitman are used with permission of the author, who
holds the copyright.

Library of Congress Cataloging-in-Publication Data
Sterba, Jim, 1943–
    Nature wars : the incredible story of how wildlife comebacks turned backyards
into battlegrounds / Jim Sterba.—1st ed.
        p. cm.
    Includes bibliographical references and index.
1. Nature—Effect of human beings on—United States. 2. Nature conservation—
Social aspects—United States. 3. Wildlife conservation—Social aspects—United
States. 4. Wildlife rehabilitation—Social aspects—United States. 5. United States—
Environmental conditions. I. Title.
    GF503.S74 2011
    304.20973—dc23

                                                              2012000296

ISBN 978-0-307-34197-6
eISBN 978-0-307-98566-8

Cover design: Megan McLaughlin
Cover photographs: © istock photo/Paul Tessier *(deer);* JFB/Getty Images
(businessman); Sascha Pflaeging/Getty Images *(background)*

First Paperback Edition

146028962

For Frances

CONTENTS

Wild turkeys roost in pines on the hill beside the house. Blue herons stalk the pond, stabbing at frogs and bass. Painted turtles sun themselves on floating barley bales. Ducks and geese fly in and out. Red-tailed hawks soar above. Crows are constant visitors. Vultures circle. Songbirds abound. Raccoons, red foxes, and opossums stop by. Spring skunks make their presence known. Plenty of woodchucks, rabbits, gray squirrels, and chipmunks share our little plot. Great horned owls keep us awake. Woodpeckers pound holes in the house siding. Beavers, muskrats, and bog turtles ply the marsh out back, and coyotes howl at dusk behind it. We've seen river otters, a fisher, and a long-tailed weasel. Bobcat sightings are credible, feral pigs are headed our way, a moose ambled to within a couple of miles as the crow flies. Last spring, a bear devoured our neighbor's birdseed, and a mountain lion turned up one state over.

My wife and I live, on weekends, in the northeast corner of Dutchess County, New York, on the edge of the country's largest metropolitan region. We rent a guest cottage on the remains of a 180-acre dairy farm that is a patchwork of meadows, marsh, and forest. That we share it with such a wild menagerie, just two hours north of New York City, is a source of some amazement, especially to people who live elsewhere.

Deer are everywhere. They have eaten out much of what grows on the forest floor. They graze in the field behind the house, sometimes in daylight. They snack in our yard and have salted it with ticks (I've had Lyme disease three times in eleven years). Turkeys are becoming less wild around us. They flock in the daytime beside busy roads, sometimes roaming in gangs through newly sown fields, pecking seed grain from the soil and causing farmers fits. Canada geese more than a thousand strong live more or less permanently within a radius of three miles from us, eating and defecating, eating and defecating. Their droppings are fouling local lakes and ponds, turning golf courses into obstacle courses, and rendering parks and athletic fields at times unusable.

Beavers engineered the eighty-acre marsh beyond our hill into a verdant habitat of ponds, streamlets, grassland, and brush. They built a dam and a big lodge behind it to raise a family. After two years of construction and procreation, they erected an estate worthy of *Architectural Digest,* but they took a toll on the hillside woods in doing so. During their second winter in residence, I surveyed that hillside and counted the stumps of forty-three trees they had chewed down—some of them eight inches in diameter. Beaver deforestation, we figured, was the price of a healthy marsh.

Coyotes have become commonplace. Normally nocturnal, they lope in fields near the house at dawn, searching for mice and rabbits. Village fire sirens set them to howling. People blame them (and fishers) for the disappearances of their cats. Hunters accuse them of preying on fawns. Road maintenance crews praise them for polishing off roadkill. Gray wolves, declared extinct in Massachusetts in 1840, are beginning to trickle east. One was shot near Shelburne, in the northern part of the state, in the fall of 2007 after killing sheep. It was thought to have wandered in from Canada or the northern Great Lakes, where the nearest breeding populations exist.

Cougars, too, are moving east. Their population, estimated at one hundred thousand, is mainly in the West. But as it grows and spreads, the big cats (also called mountain lions, pumas, panthers, and catamounts) are turning up in the Midwest, and sightings of them in the

Northeast have multiplied. Most have been dismissed as mistakes, but in June 2011 a young 140-pound male was hit by a sport utility vehicle in Milford, Connecticut, after cougar sightings had been reported near Greenwich. Studying DNA samples, researchers determined that the cat had made its way over three years more than 1,500 miles from the Black Hills of South Dakota.

Black bears in the Northeast have multiplied and moved in among us in recent years. Neighboring Massachusetts has an estimated 3,500 bears. Healthy bear populations in New Hampshire, Vermont, Pennsylvania, and New York have spread south into New Jersey, which is now home to perhaps four thousand bruins, along with lots of political and legal battles over hunting them. Connecticut bears were judged to be all but extinct after one was shot in 1819, the last known bear killing of the nineteenth century. By 1986, a few bears had ventured down from Massachusetts, hiding out in the hills and hollows in the northwestern corner of the state. The population has since grown to an estimated five hundred, and they have turned up as far south as Stamford and Greenwich.

Although moose were almost wiped out of Maine by 1935, the state's moose population is now estimated at twenty-nine thousand, and New Hampshire, Vermont, and New York have plenty, too. Massachusetts has nearly one thousand, and moose-vehicle crashes are mounting in the region, with often fatal consequences for both moose and driver. Moose are solitary creatures but are increasingly wandering into towns and suburbs from Boston to Burlington, where a recent headline in the *Free Press* read: "Urban Moose Here to Stay." Moose began infiltrating Connecticut in the 1990s, and more than one hundred now roam the state, which wildlife biologists believe is the southernmost extent of their range. However, just across the border in New York not long ago a six-hundred-pound female moose was spotted ambling near the town of Mahopac in Putnam County, north of New York City. The Big Apple itself hosts an increasing share of wild critters, including coyotes, deer, turkeys, beavers, raccoons, and, of course, the Canada geese famed for bringing down US Airways Flight 1549 after takeoff from LaGuardia on January 15, 2009.

. . .

The world is full of dire environmental reports. Many species of flora and fauna are threatened, nearly six hundred birds and animals are listed by the federal government as endangered, and everywhere you look their habitat is being carved up or paved over. Ominous threats loom, climate change being the latest and, perhaps, greatest. One study after another forecasts the extinction of more and more mammals, amphibians, and invertebrates as the human population soars above 7 billion.

Yet what is striking is how many wild species, large and small, have come back—from near extinction in some cases. They aren't all back, of course, but many animal and bird populations not only have been nursed back to health but have adjusted unexpectedly to life among people. This has happened nationwide, but it is especially true in the eastern third of the country, where the majority of Americans live. Along the East Coast, for example, a densely populated urban corridor stretches seven hundred miles from Portland, Maine, to Norfolk, Virginia. That corridor contains one city after another, with overlapping suburbs, and exurbs, splotches of rural sprawl, and growing populations of wild creatures.

It is very likely that more people live in closer proximity to more wild animals and birds in the eastern United States today than anywhere on the planet at any time in history.[1] This region's combination of wild ani-

---

1. This might sound preposterous, or at least very difficult to believe. It is a statement that, in the parlance of journalism, is weasel-worded. It requires some caveats. For example, there are greater concentrations of wildlife elsewhere in the world, and they have been even greater in the past—but with fewer people around them. Likewise, the variety of species, or biodiversity, is and has been much greater elsewhere. Human population densities are obviously higher in other places, but those densities have taken

mals, birds, and people is unique in time and place, the result of a vast but largely unnoticed regrowth of forests, the return of wildlife to the land, and the movement of people deeper into the exurban countryside.

People now share the landscape with millions of deer, geese, wild turkeys, coyotes, and beavers; thousands of bears, moose, and raptors; formerly domesticated feral pigs and cats; and uncountable numbers of small wild animals and birds. And more are on the way, moving in among us as their populations thrive and spread to regions where they haven't been seen for centuries—in some cases far beyond their historic ranges.

Before Columbus arrived, for example, several million Native Americans and perhaps 30 million white-tailed deer lived in the eastern forests—the heart of the whitetail's historic range in North America. Today in the same region there are more than 200 million people and 30 million deer, if not more. I have seen neighborhoods so fenced to keep out deer that their residents joke of living in prisoner-of-war camps.

This is a new way of living for both man and beast, and Americans haven't figured out how to do it. People have very different ideas regarding what to do, if anything, about the wild creatures in their midst, even when they are causing problems. Enjoy them? Adjust to them? Move them? Remove them? Relations between people and wildlife have never been more confused, complicated, or conflicted.

One reason for confusion and conflict is that Americans have become denatured. That is to say, they have forgotten the skills their ancestors acquired to manage an often unruly natural world around them, and they have largely withdrawn from direct contact with that world by spending most of their time indoors, substituting a great deal of real

their toll on the wildlife in their midst. There may be, or may have been, small patches of the planet with higher concentrations of wild fauna and people, but I doubt it. I have asked all sorts of demographers, geographers, and wildlife scientists to name a place and a time in which more people and wildlife aggregated in an area as large as the eastern third of the United States, and I have come up blank.

nature with reel nature—edited, packaged, digitized, and piped in elec-
tronically.

Over generations, hand-me-down knowledge of good stewardship
and the know-how of the working landscape were lost to many because
they were no longer needed. The arts of animal husbandry and farming were forgotten by most modern Americans, as were the woodsman
skills of logging, stalking, hunting, and trapping. Both the *Handbook for
Boys* and the *Whole Earth Catalog,* which passed along outdoor know-
how and subsistence skills and crafts to generations, seem charmingly
quaint. These skills weren't simply forgotten, they were forsaken. Not
only was managing the landscape something fewer and fewer people
wanted to do—it was something many of them didn't want done. They
became reluctant stewards. Indeed, they rebelled against the old stewardship. They came to see the working landscape as something that
needed protection from the very people who worked it.

Stewardship means making use of a resource and at the same time
leaving it to future generations in as good or better condition than before. But this wasn't happening. In the 1960s and 1970s, the environmental protection movement grew out of a widespread recognition that
the landscape had been abused and harmed. It fought the overuse of agricultural herbicides and pesticides; campaigned to clean up air, water,
and land fouled by those and other man-made pollutants; called for protections of wildlife threatened by overharvesting, pollution, and other
forms of human abuse; and pushed to curtail such extractive eyesore
industries as clear-cut logging and strip mining.

By the time the first Earth Day celebration took place in 1970, when
100 million people gathered around the globe to demonstrate their concerns for the environment, many people believed that the best way for
man to behave toward the natural world was to get out of it—to take his
chemicals, chain saws, and mining draglines and trucks, and go away,
to leave nature alone.

The idea that people had an obligation to be good stewards was replaced by the belief that if people weren't around throwing it out of kilter, a natural balance would prevail. This was an old conception that our first environmentalists, George Perkins Marsh and Henry David Thoreau, helped shape in the nineteenth century. They argued that human ignorance and exploitation were ruining the natural landscape. It followed, then, that without reform greater ruination was inevitable as human populations grew. "Ever since," Jan E. Dizard, a sociologist at Amherst, wrote, "nature writing has been framed by this narrative of loss." This was a powerful narrative for people who came of age in the era of environmental consciousness: Loss was the inevitable consequence of human meddling, regardless of intent.

A complicating extension of the idea of man the despoiler was a resurrected belief that the natural world was a benign place in which creatures lived in harmony with one another. This idea was in striking contrast to the amorality of a Darwinian nature that was indifferent and random, its creatures living in a world of predators and prey, struggling to eat, reproduce, and survive. In a benign natural world, wild animals and birds not only got along with one another but were often portrayed as tame and peaceable, with human habits and feelings.

This, in exaggerated form, was the world of faux nature packaged for delivery to people who wanted to believe that animals were just like us. In the late nineteenth century, this world came in books by the likes of Jack London, Charles Roberts, and William Long. Another nature writer, John Burroughs, called them "sham naturalists." His friend Theodore Roosevelt called them "nature fakers."

The motion picture camera allowed producers to present celluloid substitutes for nature that could be framed, cropped, segmented, distilled, condensed, themed, and staged to produce whatever distortions people were willing to pay to see. Increasingly, animals were portrayed, not only as being sentient, or having consciousness, but also as having perceptions, even intellectual thoughts. They didn't simply feel pain and pleasure, they had emotions too. Gradually in these productions, man emerged as the insensitive ogre. The classic example of this genre is Walt Disney's 1942 animated classic *Bambi,* in which man is the only bad guy. The anthropomorphic aspects of wildlife in early movies and TV spread to new generations after the Second World War in the form of sugar-coated educational films designed to show "unspoiled nature," that is, nature without people. In the 1950s, television's *Zoo Parade,* a wholesome runaway hit, turned zoo animals into friends, pets, and celebrities.

The postwar generation of baby boomers and their offspring lived in spreading clusters of suburban and exurban sprawl, for the most part, and they claimed that one of their reasons for moving deeper into the countryside was to live closer to nature. But their lifestyles had the opposite effect. They lived modern, comfortable, and busy lives and spent most of their time in houses, cars, and offices largely walled off from the sights, smells, temperatures, and sounds of the natural world around them. The landscape they occupied became a stage set for living. Stewardship for them wasn't raising crops, animals, and trees to harvest and create wealth sustainably, but rather preserving static surroundings, the manicured landscapes and vistas of property owners who made money elsewhere—back in the city, at an office park three exits down the freeway, or in front of a computer screen in a home study. Thus cocooned, they lost most hands-on contact with the natural world and, in the process, often lost the ability to contrast that world with the one that appeared on their screens.

Besides, until recent decades wildlife was more plentiful on film and TV screens than it was outdoors. Americans thought of wild animals and birds as being scarce and under threat, and they were right. Devastation of wild species by settlers and commercial hunters motivated conservationists in the late nineteenth century to begin a campaign to rescue wild populations by rebuilding habitat, creating refuges, and restocking deer, geese, turkeys, beavers, and other species in areas where they had been wiped out.

It is understandable that after generations of wildlife scarcity many people might be skeptical of the idea that many wild species are now not only plentiful but overabundant enough to cause serious problems for people and ecosystems. After decades in which wild populations had to be nurtured, the idea that creatures' numbers needed to be reduced, by lethal means if necessary, was disturbing to them. These animals had just as much right to live out their lives as we did, didn't they? Perhaps they needed the same rights as people. Debates over these questions and over what role, if any, people should play in dealing with people-wildlife conflicts turned into arguments that polarized society, divided communities, and set neighbor against neighbor. These arguments have spread all over the map. They aren't much different from divisive dustups over guns, abortion, and government's role in society, and they are often just as mean-spirited.

Americans can embrace saving the rain forest, the boreal forest, or some other pristine eco-remnant over the horizon. Writing a check for these causes, or to save wolves or wild horses, is easy when you are saving them from man. But saving a local ecosystem from animals is a different story. Saving a local flock of Canada geese might seem like the right thing to do, especially when the threat to them comes from people. Saving a local soccer field from Canada geese is a harder sell—unless your children play soccer.

American communities are full of what writer Paul Theroux calls "single species obsessives." I call them species partisans—people who choose a particular group or flock, or even individual animals, to defend. Each species has a constituency, be they geese, deer, bears, turkeys, beavers, coyotes, cats, or endangered plovers. Many people, of course, want to save all species. But often, advocates for one creature square off against the saviors of another. Feral cat defenders, for example, belittle arguments of bird defenders who assert that cats are an alien scourge on the landscape killing native songbirds just to exercise their killing skills. Strange alliances form. Bird lovers side with hunters and trappers on the need for lethal control of cats, foxes, and other bird predators. Deer lovers and bow hunters join hands to keep out sharpshooters. Trappers align with local governments and lobby statehouses to reinstate outlawed traps to limit mounting damage by beavers.

For species partisans, these battles can be exciting, and they are often fought with self-righteous conviction. Rational debate gives way to intransigence. Arguments become shouting matches or lawsuits. Fights get nasty.

When officials in Clarkstown, New York, decided to rid their village of hundreds of Canada geese a while back, demonstrators turned up with TV crews to protest against a pending "goose Holocaust." When Princeton, New Jersey, hired sharpshooters to cull its deer population, the mayor's car was splattered with deer guts and the township animal control officer began wearing a bulletproof vest after finding his dog poisoned and his cat crushed to death. When coyote sightings in Wheaton, Illinois, increased dramatically, and a resident's dog was mauled by a coyote and had to be euthanized, the town divided into procoyote and anticoyote factions. A nuisance wildlife professional, hired by the city council, discovered that a few residents were feeding the coyotes. He trapped and shot four of the animals, then began receiving voice-mail death threats. A brick was tossed through a city official's window, and council members received threatening letters. The FBI was called in.

Feeding wild animals is frowned upon by wildlife professionals. Ironically, doing so and thinking of them as pets stemmed, in part, from the pet industry itself. No one encouraged anthropomorphizing more than the purveyors of pets and products for pets. Since the 1980s, this multi-billion-dollar industry has burgeoned by encouraging people to see pets as companion animals, members of the family, and surrogate offspring; and reinforcing this pretense by creating a range of goods and services that mimic child care: toys and treats, sweaters and booties, pet sitters and day care, pet stress and mood medications, human-grade food, health insurance, and pricey veterinary care. For people who love pets or treat them like children, it doesn't take much persuasion to think of wild birds as "outdoor pets," as one seed company calls them, and to keep feeders full for them. Feeding wild birds is fun and an easy way to connect to wildlife, and its popularity created another multi-billion-dollar industry. Feeding other wildlife is, by extension, a small step. If a chickadee is an outdoor pet, why isn't a raccoon or a groundhog? Don't they warrant a cookie now and then? How about a little dog food for the coyote? Wouldn't the bear rifling the garbage can prefer a jelly dough-nut? Nuisance wildlife control operators know that putting out food for animals, say birds or stray cats, is asking for trouble from others, say raccoons and skunks—and fueling the growth of a sizable new wildlife mitigation industry. But many people don't make the connection, until it is too late and a professional has to be summoned. More than one thousand nuisance wildlife companies, and perhaps five thousand part-time operators, have sprung up since the 1980s. Critter Control Inc., for example, began franchising in 1987 and now has more than 130 opera-tions in thirty-eight states and Canada.

People who take up residence in the sprawl are often well educated, think of themselves as friends of the environment, and believe in help-ing wild animals and birds, or at least in doing them no harm. But the critters often refuse to reciprocate. They don't behave like furry friends or outdoor pets. They behave like wild animals.

Feeding wild creatures, whether this is done consciously or uncon-sciously, is one of the key reasons why many animals have done a far bet-ter job of accommodating to life among people than vice versa. While it is fashionable to say that most conflicts between people and wildlife are the result of human encroachment into wildlife habitat, make no mistake, critters have encroached right back. They have discovered that people maintain lush lawns; plant trees, shrubbery, and gardens; create ponds; put up bird feeders and "No Hunting" signs; and put out grills and garbage cans. These places offer up plenty of food, lots of places to hide and raise families, and protection from predators with guns.

Wildlife biologists call this enhanced habitat, meaning that for lots of species it has more and better amenities than can be found in the back-woods away from people. It is better, that is, until these creatures run in front of motor vehicles and are left to die beside the road. Or until they are judged to be criminal trespassers, rounded up, and trucked to a slaughterhouse. Or until they are seen as nuisances, caught, dispatched by bullet, injection, or gas chamber, and delivered to a landfill.

. . .

This book tells the story of how we turned a wildlife comeback miracle into a mess. It is history, in large part, and it begins with an early story that is familiar, however vaguely we remember it: of native peoples oc-cupying and managing the landscape and its bounty for centuries; of the arrival of Europeans with diseases that decimated Indian populations; of colonists with ideas about taming the wilderness and then waves of immigrant settlers who destroyed forests and killed off great popula-tions of wild birds and animals.

What happened next, in my experience, is much less familiar: slow, almost imperceptible forest regeneration and wildlife renewal playing out in overlapping waves. The forest comeback began in the nineteenth century with the abandonment of marginal land that had been cleared for farming in New England. Wildlife conservation and renewal began in the late nineteenth century and accelerated in the twentieth.

A crucial third wave—the dispersal of people out of cities—began in earnest after the Second World War and reached a milestone at the millennium's end when an absolute majority of the American people lived not in cities and not on farms but in the vast landscape in between. I have divided this story into three sections, beginning with forests be-cause the comeback of trees began first and set the stage for wildlife comebacks. In my experience few people are aware that most American forests were and are in the East and that they have been regenerating almost continuously for more than a century and a half in one of the greatest reforestations the planet has seen. The first chapter confronts an illusion at the heart of how many modern Americans think about forests. They think of them as being somewhere else, up north, or over the horizon, and saved from human destruction. The islands of Maine look exactly like a preserved north woods. They are, in fact, just the opposite, and as such they represent an early microcosm of the destruction and renewal of the entire eastern forest. In a history of sprawl, I show how the United States became, in essence, a nation of forest people.

The second section focuses on the early devastation of wildlife and how conservationists brought many species back not only to abundance but to overabundance with serious consequences. It begins with the beaver—North America's first commodity animal, the first to be systematically wiped off the map across much of the continent, and today, after a miraculous comeback, one of the most damaging wild creatures on the landscape. White-tailed deer, Canada geese, and turkeys followed similar trajectories of ruin, renewal, and abundance to the point of becoming nuisances to many people. Bears, like beavers, were wiped out early, not because they were valuable, but because they were perceived to be a menace. Out of sight in wild redoubts, bears were transformed over centuries in story and song into humanlike creatures. The Three Bears in Goldilocks lived as people. Bears became cuddly pillow toys. Even when real bears—large, powerful, and perpetually hungry—began turning up in backyards in recent years, old perceptions propelled misguided people to toss them a cookie or doughnut, the first step in creating a nuisance, then a menace, then a dead bear.

The third section explains how people over several generations have become disconnected from nature and how that disconnect allows them to use and abuse the landscape and its wild creatures in unthinking ways. For example, people inflict wholesale carnage on wildlife with their cars and trucks and dismiss roadkill as a ghoulish joke. They throw away pet cats as if they were last year's dresses and allow both pet and feral cats to prey on birds and other wildlife. They have turned feeding wild birds into the paramount means by which Americans now connect with wildlife.

Go back a few generations, and everyone was connected, everyone was a farmer or connected by family to a farm. Everyone knew how to kill and pluck a chicken. Most of these people endured a lot of hard, physical work, much of it out of doors, to eke out a living, and they certainly wouldn't have called their times the good old days. I explain how in just a generation or two, people went from hands-on interaction with the land, with its heat, dust, and barnyard smells, to an insular lifestyle of conditioned air, landscaped views, canned deodorants, and an industrial agriculture system that delivers a chicken in parts on a diaper in a foam tray wrapped in clear plastic. Exceptions abound, of course. Working the landscape on a small, local scale has become fashionable for some. In recent years, people in a growing movement have spread word of the importance of knowing where food comes from, how it is grown and raised, and why local and fresh is better than faraway and stale. Others want to do the same with trees, that is, harvest forest products locally and sustainably. Groups have come together to find ways to manage the natural space where they live for the good of the ecosystem as a whole and not simply one overabundant or problematic species within it.

On average, however, Americans now spend 90 percent of their time indoors, and they pay more heed to the nature conveniently packaged on their electronic screens than to the nature around them. Their direct experience with nature tends to be visual—a goldfinch on the bird feeder outside the living room window, or a deer in the road beyond a windshield that is about to be shattered.

PART ONE

FOREST PEOPLE

Many years ago I visited the International Rice Research Institute in Los Baños, the Philippines, where plant scientists work to improve the dietary staple of Asia and other parts of the world. To underscore the importance of rice, a geneticist working there told me this: If Martians arrived on our planet, observed its inhabitants closely for a while, and then flew home to report, they would tell their leaders that the primary occupation of the most intelligent form of life on Earth was growing rice. That is to say, more human beings devoted more time and energy and land to planting, growing, harvesting, transporting, and selling rice than to anything else. This sounded counterintuitive to someone from a nation that grew corn, wheat, and soybeans and spent far less effort farming than on other occupations.

I don't know whether that scientist was right or not. What made me think of his story, however, was a question that came up while I was researching this book: Where do most people in the United States live? The answer is just as counterintuitive: They live in the woods. We are essentially forest dwellers. Sure, tens of millions of people demonstrably don't live in a forest, and far more of them would not call where they do live a forest. Sure, they have trees in their yard or their neighborhood, or out in back of their house, or along their road or street, or around their cul-de-sac, or in back of the mall. But that isn't a "forest" forest. Nevertheless, if you draw a line around the largest forested region in the contiguous United States—the one that stretches from the Atlantic Ocean to the Great Plains—you will have drawn a line around nearly two-thirds of America's forests (excluding Alaska's) and two-thirds of the U.S. population. You could subtract the farmers living on patches of cleared cropland within, but they are few. You could subtract people who live in the downtowns of big cities, where concrete and asphalt prevail, but those places today have millions of trees. In any case, you end up with more people in this forest than out.

The modern American forest is a very unusual place, and forest dwellers of the past would find the ways we live in it to be bizarre. It is laced with roads and highways, power lines and drainage systems. It is splotched with parking lots, housing developments, office parks, golf courses, and shopping malls, and more of it is being chopped up every year. It covers or surrounds some of the most densely populated regions of America. The trees seem too obvious not to see, but amid this man-made jumble they can be overlooked, and the very vastness of the forested landscape can go unseen. But get up high, on a mountain ridge or up to the eighth floor of a high-rise, and you are likely to look out over an ocean of trees. It is a forest where an open landscape of family farms used to be, farms that once served as a buffer between people in cities and wildlife in the woods. No more. Today's forests extend not only to the edges of cities and towns but well into them. Several years ago, I asked Gordon Batcheller, a wildlife biologist with New York's Department of Environmental Conservation in Albany, to explain the comeback of beavers, an animal once virtually extinct in the Northeast, and the mounting conflicts between beavers and people.

"Simple," he told me, "the habitat is back, and it is now full of people." If you got in an airplane and flew from Albany to Boston during the day, he went on, you could look down and see almost nothing but trees from one downtown to the other. Fly the same route at night, and you see lots of lights—lights of people living in a huge forest.

How Americans became forest dwellers is the story of a vast regreening of the landscape, a regeneration of trees, particularly in the Northeast. David Foster, the director of the Harvard Forest, a three-thousand acre ecological research facility in Petersham, Massachusetts, told me that the regrowth of forests on such a scale had not been seen in the Americas since the collapse of the Mayan civilization 1,200 years ago, when millions of acres of once-cultivated land in Central America were left to the jungle. In the eastern United States over two and a half centuries, European settlers cleared away more than 250 million acres of forest. By the 1950s, depending on the region, nearly half to more than two-thirds of the landscape was reforested, and in the last half century, states in the Northeast and Midwest have added more than 11 million acres of forest.

These new forests grew back right under the noses of several generations of Americans. The regrowth began in such fits and starts that most people didn't see it happening. When it reached its apex in recent decades, many people didn't believe it had happened. That trees are still recolonizing land in some parts of the country, including the state of New York, is unimaginable to people I know. How is it possible, skeptics might well ask, for our little corner of the world to be regreening while so much of the rest of the planet is going in the opposite direction? We shall see.

Because it is very good news, the comeback of forests is greeted by a lot of people with skepticism amid the drumbeat of bad news about forests elsewhere. We are constantly reminded that the planet's wild places are besieged, old-growth trees threatened, boreal forests cut down at a horrendous rate, and rain forests stripped away. Report after report warns that delicate species of the globe's flora and fauna are disappearing by the score. This dire news isn't wrong, but it is incomplete. Forests aren't under assault *everywhere*. They have been regenerating in Russia and Europe for decades, but so far under the headlines that even environmental journalists are skeptical. In 2006, in what a *New York Times* reporter called "a surprising new analysis" published by the National

Academy of Sciences, researchers surveyed the fifty most forested countries on the planet and found that forests had expanded in twenty-two of
them—the richer, more developed, and less populated among them—
over the previous fifteen years.

But that is getting ahead of this story. First comes the saga of how
forests were cut down and how and why they grew back. The Europeans
who discovered America began their visitations and encampments on
slivers of terra firma. These were islands and tiny patches on the Atlantic coast, places called St. Augustine, Port Royal, Popham, Roanoke,
Jamestown, Plymouth, Massachusetts Bay, and Mannahatta. There they
clung to life and began a transformation of the landscape that would
spread across the continent. I begin with a look at the transformation
of such a place, Mount Desert and other islands on the coast of Maine,
over four centuries. The islands look like the North Woods, and today
they are. But hidden inside their thick spruce forests are the remains of
a very different world.

Chapter One

The Spruce Illusion

Water rushed below me. I could hear it but I couldn't see it. I was standing on a large granite stone eating an apple and swatting mosquitoes in the morning sun. The stone sat beside an asphalt road that marked the boundary of Acadia National Park. Before me was parkland. Directly in front of me, flanked by trees, was a small clearing covered with grapevines, their bright green leaves straining up toward the sun. The grapes covered the clearing like a blanket, and along its edges they had climbed up bushes and trees, curtaining them with vines and leaves. I stepped off the stone and down an embankment into the grapes and toward the noise. I bent down and pulled the interwoven vines apart with both hands, creating a small opening. Through it, I could see whitewater coursing down a brook bed, whooshing in little waterfalls over rounded stones and into a culvert under the road.

The covered brook and smothered trees so captured my attention that I didn't realize what the grapes were trying to tell me. The grapes looked unnatural, so out of place in a northern evergreen forest that I thought of them as intruders, and with each morning jog to the clearing the urge in me grew to clear away some of them so I could see the wonderful brook. I worried about a magnificent old birch tree on the edge of the meadow that the vines had climbed and appeared to be strangling. Three vines an inch thick hung from the birch like jungle swings, and eighty feet above, grape leaves spread across the birch's crown, soaking up its sunlight.

One morning I grabbed some long-handled pruning shears and jogged off to the clearing. I made my way down to the old birch and snipped the three vines. Their lower strands fell to the ground. Three upper strands hung straight, disconnected from their circulatory life-lines. Deprived of nutrient flows, they would shrivel and die. I had liberated the old birch. I felt a surge of pride and decided, right then, to go to war with the grapes. They were feral grapes, I thought, just like once-domesticated pigs or cats that had gone wild and multiplied on the landscape. I vowed to save all the surrounding trees from their deadly embrace and to uncover the brook for all to see. I was doing Acadia Park a favor, an unofficial volunteer working to save native species of trees, bushes, and plants from these alien invaders. I was helping to restore the park's wild state, to re-create in this one little clearing what Acadia and other national parks were supposed to be: natural landscapes.

This rationale propelled me morning after morning into battle with the grapes. After liberating the old birch, I cut vines that had climbed up every other tree around the edge of the meadow. Then I uncovered the brook. This wasn't easy because below the blanket of vines and leaves the grapes had formed root systems that crisscrossed each other in layers that resembled underground woven mats. Yanking on these roots caused some painful back strains and sore shoulders. The roots were tenacious. One morning I pulled on a dead tree branch hidden under some vines and a swarm of yellow jacket wasps attacked me, inflicting eight painful stings as I fled up to the road, the wasps in hot pursuit. Sometimes bikers pedaling along the road would spot me knee deep in grapevines and wave. Likewise, joggers and walkers would cast a curious glance and nod. Cars and trucks passed by all the time, but they were going too fast to catch more than a glimpse. I had no idea what these people thought. Perhaps they saw in my struggle with the grapes the quixotic quest of a madman best left in solitary derangement. I had no idea that

I was committing a federal crime punishable by up to six months in prison.[2]

Exploring the woods around the grapes, I found old bottles, broken dinner plates, slabs of concrete, and stone walls. One morning I unearthed half of a rusty 1927 Maine automobile license plate. This was a thrilling discovery because it was the first bit of evidence I had of the age of what I had come to think of as my personal archaeological site, with mysteries to uncover, artifacts to find, and stories to decode if I could only discover and unravel them. One day at the village library, I discovered an old island map that listed the land around the grapes as belonging to a "John Brown." My ruins were the old Brown family farm.

One day at the post office I asked Linda Hamor, the postmistress who knew everyone on the island and pretty much everything that had happened on it since the last Ice Age, who might know about the Brown farm. "Call George Peckham," she said.

George Peckham, a seventy-eight-year-old retired engineer, had grown up on the island and now lived a quarter mile up the road from the grapes with his wife, Marion. He offered me a tour. The ruins were overgrown with big old trees. "I'd guess that ash there is at least seventy-five years old," he said. Then he added something startling.

"Except for a couple trees in front, this was all cleared land when I was a kid—pasture and hayfields. It was clear enough for a small traveling carnival to set up every summer. And I remember coming here with my mother to pick wild strawberries. Over that way was Murphy's gravel operation—there were big open pits." Now it was thick forest.

---

2. I had violated part 2 (Resource Protection, Public Use and Recreation) of the general Federal Code provisions governing the National Park Service; specifically section 2.1 (Preservation of Natural, Cultural and Archeological Resources), subsection (a): "Except as otherwise provided in this chapter, the following is prohibited: (1): Possessing, destroying, injuring, defacing, removing, digging, or disturbing from its natural state: (ii): Plants or the parts or products thereof." The penalties section of this statute reads: "(a) A person convicted of violating a provision of the regulations . . . of this section shall be punished by a fine as provided by law, or by imprisonment not exceeding 6 months, or both."

At the archives of Acadia National Park, Mike Blaney and Brooke Childrey helped me find a land deed that included the Brown property. It began:

"History of this Parcel from the grant of Louis XIV, King of France, to the ownership of the estate of William Bingham . . ." It listed owners of the property over 241 years. Beginning in 1845, John Brown and his descendants operated a small subsistence farm, gravel pit, and granite quarry for nearly a century. In 1947 the family sold their holdings to John D. Rockefeller Jr., who in 1961 donated the land to the park. By the time I arrived on the scene, the forest had swallowed up the Brown farm so completely that passersby got no glimpse of the ruins within. The only hint of their existence was the grapevines, which clung to their clearing, tenaciously fending off the trees. It came as a shock when I finally realized what the grapes were trying to tell me: "We were here first." The trees were the newcomers. The grapes were a remnant of a very different civilization that had existed not that long ago. They were like a hand reaching out of a grave in a last, desperate signal of an old way of life about to be snuffed out by the new forest.

· · ·

Mount Desert looks as if it is very much part of the "North Woods"—a thick forest of evergreens interspersed with mixed hardwoods and dotted with ponds and cedar swamps, with villages, cottages, boatyards, and lobster pounds perched along a rocky seashore. Visitors can drive or climb to the summit of Cadillac Mountain, at 1,530 feet above sea level the highest point on the island, and look out upon a landscape created by glaciers that advanced and receded for a million years. Like a sculptor with chisels and sandpaper, the glacial ice cut and smoothed bedrock, creating twenty-six mountains of pink granite arranged side by side, north to south, many elongated like baguettes of French bread. The mountains, some of them bald on top, are cloaked in white and red spruce trees, balsam fir, hemlock, and red and white pines, and are splotched with a mix of hardwoods, mainly oak, maple, and birch. The ice created a fjord, seven miles long, up the middle of the island, and gouged out other valleys that contain lakes, ponds, bogs, and dense cedar swamps. People are concentrated along the island's coastal fringes. There, too, are the commercial trappings of a tourist industry fed mainly by Acadia National Park, the island's primary attraction.

The island and the park attract almost 3 million visitors annually. Guidebooks say that at 108 square miles, Mount Desert is the third-largest island off the continental United States, after Long Island and Martha's Vineyard, and, with its mountains seeming to lurch up out of the sea, it is certainly the most physically arresting of the three. For newcomers and visitors, it is easy to find here confirmation that if people just leave nature alone it will be fine. It is easy to imagine Indians and then Europeans discovering a pristine natural wilderness so beautiful that they made up their minds in turn to save it from the despoliations of man. But such imaginings would be wrong. Only small patches of the island were saved more or less in their natural state. Today what visitors see is a North Woods forest. What they are looking at, however, is natural beauty re-created, protected, and managed by man—a kind of "wilderness" theme park rebuilt by nature under human supervision.

Newcomers like me had difficulty believing that in 1880 this island was a pastoral countryside of hay meadows, livestock pastures and cropland, trees here and there, and forest hugging the steep sides of mountains off in the distance. It was hard to imagine bustling hubs where the commerce of logging, fishing, shipbuilding, and milling had taken place; villages with blacksmiths, shoemakers, wool carders, shingle makers, sawyers, and carpenters; the storefronts of merchants; factories producing lumber, barrels, ice, bricks, stones, and salted fish for market; and wharves where ships loaded materials for export and unloaded goods from afar. But that's what Mount Desert looked like after the Civil War and well into the twentieth century.

Old-timers like George Peckham fondly recounted the days when the island had been much more manicured and refined. When Peckham was born in 1927, Mount Desert was a radically different place. Much of the island—that is, land flat enough and with soil enough to farm—had been cleared of trees by the late nineteenth century. The trees were used for fuel and lumber or were simply burned to get them out of the way for pasture, hay, and cropland. The lowland landscape and the patchwork of family farms and homesteads that occupied it were still very much in evidence when Peckham was growing up, although some of that farm acreage had already been bought up, given to Acadia National Park, and left to the trees to take back. Peckham grew up in the tail end of an era in which well-heeled vacationers turned the island into one of society's most fashionable resorts. The island's villages—Bar Harbor, Northeast Harbor, Southwest Harbor among them—bustled in the summer with people "from away."

"When I was growing up, this island was more civilized than it is now," he told me. "Northeast Harbor was booming back then. It had four garages for cars, and lots of chauffeurs, butlers, and cooks. It had four hotels, six grocery stores, two drugstores, a high school, and a summer theater. The whole island was more developed and less wild than it is now."

. . .

Mount Desert Island has been under human supervision for almost two thousand years. Scholars don't know exactly when Indians first arrived (graves dating back to 3000 B.C. have been found elsewhere on the Maine coast), but they are believed to have established their first settlement around 1000 B.C. at the west entrance to Somes Sound, at a place now called Fernald Point—a gently sloping hillside, with freshwater springs and protected coves. They used it and a place now called Manchester Point across the sound off and on for the next twenty-six centuries, coming and going with the seasons. Because they were hunter-gatherers and their populations were small, these people managed the land and waters of Mount Desert with a light touch—but they did manage them for their own purposes.

The first Europeans to arrive in the Gulf of Maine in the 1490s were cod fishermen—mainly Bretons, Basques, and Portuguese. Looking for fresh water and places to dry their fish, they came ashore and met the local Indians. These visits evolved into barter trade: fur garments and freshly killed meat, for example, for cloth and small metal tools. Explorers and traders followed, exchanging manufactured goods for Indian furs, mainly beaver, but for Europeans in the fifteenth and sixteenth centuries Maine was a cod-fishing paradise. By the 1620s, hundreds of fishing vessels were sailing annually from European posts to catch cod in the Gulf of Maine.

Europeans broke ground on Mount Desert in 1613, when the first settlers—forty-eight Frenchmen led by a Jesuit priest named Father Pierre Biard—arrived at Fernald Point and decided, among other survival tasks, to try a little farming. Long before their crops could come in, however, they were discovered, captured, and driven off by an English privateer based in Virginia named Captain Samuel Argall. His job was to expel all Frenchmen he found along the coast.[3] It would take another 148 years for farming to be taken up in earnest on the island, this time by the English—and only after the French and Indian Wars had finally sputtered to an end. The transformation of Mount Desert into a working landscape began in the fall of 1761, when a twenty-nine-year-old cooper named Abraham Somes arrived from Gloucester, Massachusetts, and took up residence at the north end of the fjord that would be named in his honor.

---

3. Earlier that year in Virginia, Captain Argall kidnapped Pocahontas, the seventeen-year-old daughter of the Potomac chief, Powhatan, to exchange for English captives, property, and food. Six years earlier Pocahontas had "rescued" Captain John Smith, leader of the Jamestown Colony, from her father.

Over the next 150 years, settlers, fishermen, loggers, farmers, ship-builders, and ice and granite cutters would exploit the landscape, eventually stripping away the trees on virtually all the land that was flat enough to farm. Trees on mountainsides too steep for farming and too far from water-powered sawmills were spared—for the time being. But the loggers were rapacious. They moved rapidly across the island, cutting roads in the woods, hauling out trees, and leaving brush to dry and catch fire.

At the height of the logging boom, ten water-powered and two steam-powered sawmills were working at full capacity on the island, and much of the harvested wood was shipped to the mainland. By 1870, the historian Samuel Eliot Morison wrote, most of the island's first-growth forest was gone. The settlers of Mount Desert and their offspring had created a pastoral countryside of small farms and industries not unlike the English landscape their ancestors had left behind. Some 34,000 of the island's 73,000 acres were classified in government records as "improved," meaning they were no longer "wild," by the prevailing definition, but had been put to some use and not left as forest. If you subtract the 2,638 acres of lakes and ponds that dotted the island, nearly half the island's acreage had been "improved." In 1871, in a revealing book titled *Mount Desert on the Coast of Maine,* a travel writer named Clara Barnes Martin described the island landscape this way: "Except in one or two inaccessible valleys, the forest primeval is all gone; but huge stumps and scathed trunks show what the axe and the fires have done."

One of the great historical ironies of Mount Desert Island was that its natural beauty was being destroyed just as it was being "discovered." Until the mid–nineteenth century, the idea that "wilderness" could be appealing was bizarre to most people. But Thomas Cole, the landscape artist, and other painters of the Hudson River school, helped change that notion. Cole visited the island first in 1844. Other painters followed. They glorified the island's rugged beauty and its people's simple life, portraying in their brushstrokes both the raw landscapes and the lives of farmers and fishermen who lived by the sea. These paintings inspired "rusticators" to flock to the island in summer in what would eventually become a booming tourism industry, called "excursionism" at the time.

The tourism industry helped fishermen and farmers alike. Horses pulling tourist carriages needed hay, and the rusticators and tourists wanted seafood, needed milk and meat, and would take all the berries and vegetables islanders could grow. Big dairy farms were established, but there weren't enough farmhands to do the growing and milking, so hundreds of summer farm jobs were filled by laborers from the mainland. Labor was in such short supply that workers were recruited from England, Scotland, Sweden, and Germany.

Fishermen and farmers weren't the only ones at work. In the 1880s, parts of Somes Sound, at the very heart of the island, looked more like Pittsburgh than wilderness as quarrymen cut slabs of pink granite and shipped them to construction sites in Washington, D.C. (Library of Congress), Philadelphia (U.S. Mint), Springfield (Illinois State Capitol), New York (Ellis Island), and other cities. More than seven hundred men worked the granite and lived in boardinghouses at Hall Quarry. In the winter, when the freshwater ponds were frozen over, men worked cutting out blocks of ice which were stored in sawdust and loaded on ships bound for Boston, New York, and the West Indies.

By the beginning of the twentieth century, the island was about as "tame" as it could be. But worse was yet to come in the minds of a few like-minded rusticators. Real estate speculation was rampant, so-called "cottages" with forty or sixty rooms were under construction in Bar Harbor, and, perhaps more ominous, the gasoline-powered portable sawmill was making inroads—meaning the remaining trees on the mountains were increasingly vulnerable. In 1901, Charles W. Eliot, the president of Harvard University, wrote to another prominent summer resident, George Dorr, who contacted others, including John S. Kennedy and George Vanderbilt, about creating a group to protect what natural landscape was left on the island. Dorr would spend much of his inheritance buying up land to protect it, and he would become known as the chief founder of Acadia National Park. Later, John D. Rockefeller Jr. and others joined the effort. By 1913, this group had patched together six thousand acres of mountains and coastline (less than 10 percent of the island), and three years later they persuaded President Woodrow Wilson to name it Sieur de Monts National Monument. In 1919, it became Lafayette National Park, the first such park east of the Mississippi. Between 1913 and 1940, Rockefeller designed and built fifty-seven miles of gravel carriage roads through the park and on private land that would eventually be donated to the park.

The people who pieced together the park, however, made no pretense that it was "wilderness" by any definition of the times. By 1928, Lafayette Park, and land acquired for it but not yet officially donated, stood at 10,500 acres. In that year, Charles W. Eliot II, a landscape architect and son of the Harvard president, presented to the Bar Harbor Village Improvement Association a report, *The Future of Mount Desert Island,* discussing future acquisitions for the park. In it he wrote

> The whole Island has been "manhandled," cut, and burned in the past so that the wilderness aspect of parts of the future park is entirely a matter of the extent, recentness, and evidentness of man's interference with the processes of nature. This is not to deny the beauty of some parts of the Island which are characterized by solitude and which are apparently wild and untouched or far from what most of us associate with civilization. This character of area is the most precious and most easily destroyed feature of the Island, and should therefore be guarded and administered as such.

In 1929, Lafayette was renamed Acadia National Park. It eventually encompassed nearly half of Mount Desert Island and parts of nearby Isle au Haut and the Schoodic Peninsula.

. . .

Mount Desert is the largest of more than three thousand islands along the Down East coast of Maine, and the other islands share its history of deforestation. Reforestation was accelerated on Mount Desert by the creation of Acadia National Park, which put the land within it off limits to development. Reforestation of the other islands was mainly the result of passive neglect. Still, it is difficult today to imagine those islands as the commercial and agricultural hubs they once were. To sail among them, as thousands of boaters do each year, is to commune with the sea and the North Woods. Island after island, crowded with spruce trees and cedar, fir and pine, creates an evergreen vista easily mistaken for virgin wild. The vista is punctuated by snug harbors full of lobster boats and yachts, and dotted with summer homes, vacation houses, and tourist venues, but whole stretches of the 250-mile-long coastline are uninhabited, and it is easy for visitors to assume that they have been this way forever, untouched by man. However, as Philip W. Conkling wrote in 1981:

> Like many other outwardly satisfying ideas, there is a notion that here in Maine, at relatively short distances from the mainland, are inaccessible pieces of New England landscape that have remained untouched, untrammeled, and unchanged since the white man arrived. Unfortunately, this does not hold up to closer scrutiny. The appearance of most of the islands is the result of nearly four centuries of human occupation and alteration. In fact, they are some of the oldest, continuously utilized pieces of landscape in eastern North America. Upwards

of 15 generations of European boat-borne people—not to mention the 4,000 to 5,000 years of previous Indian use—have altered island ecologies, in some cases subtly, in other cases dramatically.

The "uninhabited look" of many Maine islands today is caused by decades of declining populations—essentially in the half century before Conkling's book was published. The "unspoiled look," in other words, is relatively new. For 350 years before this new look came along, the islands of Maine were beehives of industrial and agricultural activity. Before trains and roads, ships were the only transport available to get to Maine. The islands were relatively safe havens from the natives on the mainland, so they were settled first by Europeans who set up way stations for ships, trading posts, lumbering and shipbuilding concerns, and farms.

· · ·

George Peckham was in college in Orono in 1947 when a fire swept Mount Desert Island, burning one-fourth of its forests and destroying hundreds of houses and hotels. He sped home to fight it—his last hands-on experience on the island for decades. In 1950, he married Marion Schurman of Northeast Harbor and moved off the island to work for General Electric in Burlington, Vermont, and the Great Northern Paper Company in Millinocket, Maine. They returned home to stay twenty-three years later.

"I couldn't get over how mature the forest was when we got back," he said. "There was hardly any new growth—no room for it."

By 2005, when I first talked with George and Marion Peckham, they had been living on Mount Desert Island for thirty-two years, and I asked him what had changed during that time. Obvious, he said, the trees had had thirty-two more years to grow.

"Today, it's worse than when we came back. In my mind, this

whole island is a big overgrown forest, and that's dangerous during dry spells. The trees keep closing in. Heck, today I live in a hole in the woods."

By the summer of 2010, when President Barack Obama and his family paid a weekend visit, Mount Desert's trees had had more than a quarter of a century to grow since my first visit in 1983. They had gotten thicker and taller. They had colonized meadows that weren't regularly cleared of seedlings and saplings by human labor like the ones at Fernald Point and Little Long Pond.[4] Of the original 34,000 acres of "improved" land, only 3,341 acres (less than 10 percent) remained cleared. Those acres made up thirty-five land parcels classified as "farms," but only fourteen of those were actually farmed, mostly by hobbyists and budding locavores. Today the transformation of Mount Desert Island from working landscape to scenic landscape is all but complete. A few boatbuilders survive, but the island's boatyards are mainly maintenance and storage facilities for the yachts of summer people. The one holdout is lobstering. Big, loud lobster boats ply the waters, hauling up and setting their traps. Thousands of colorful buoys, connected by ropes to the traps on the sea bottom, dot the waters of Mount Desert, perhaps the last remnants of the island's "working" way of life. For visitors, of course, they are part of the scenery.

. . .

Mount Desert and the other islands on the Maine coast aren't unique in being valued more today for scenery than for the resources they

---

4. Perhaps nothing on the island looks more "natural" than Little Long Pond, a thirty-five-acre former salt marsh surrounded by one thousand acres of grassy meadows owned by the Rockefellers and managed by the Greenrock Company. In fact, it takes hundreds of man-hours cutting back alders, spruce, and other trees to keep them from swallowing up the meadows; Doug Hopkins, the property superintendent, told me: "There's no great science to it. You want it to be neat but not look manicured—wild but neat. If you didn't do anything, I bet you wouldn't have no field here in ten years."

once provided. As we shall see, what happened there also happened across the northeastern United States. In many ways, Mount Desert is a microcosm of what happened on much of America's original forested landscape—the vast region stretching from the Atlantic coast to the Great Plains that settlers called "wilderness."

Chapter Two

An Epidemic of Trees

In 1635, a few of the more adventurous settlers of the Massachusetts Bay Colony decided that the time had come to move out. They felt squeezed. A census conducted the previous year showed that the coastal settlements contained some 4,000 people, 1,500 head of cattle, 4,000 goats and sheep, and free-ranging pigs too numerous to count.

It had been fifteen years since William Bradford stepped off the *Mayflower* at Plymouth and pronounced the new home of his Pilgrims to be "hideous and desolate wilderness, full of wilde beasts and wilde men." And it had been six years since John Winthrop arrived to begin his "holy experiment" with Puritan settlers around the shores of what became Boston Harbor. The Pilgrims and Puritans brought with them the old-country idea that they were on a mission of God to tame this foreboding new land, which in the classic view was the opposite of the Garden of Eden, an ordered place. And in the face of much adversity they tamed it and ordered it. They established farms, many of them on meadows and fields created by "wilde beasts and wilde men," namely beavers and Indians, and they planted crops, some of them introduced to them by Indians. They surrounded their fields and gardens with zig-zag split-rail wooden fences to keep livestock out. Pigs, and sometimes cattle, were allowed to roam freely to forage (and provide meals for such forest predators as wolves and cougars). The Puritan colony was becoming a pastoral clone of the old country. And it was getting crowded.

So a group of more than a dozen families set off to establish a settlement in the western wilderness. They were led by a fur trader named Captain Simon Willard and by the Reverend Peter Bulkeley. They were headed for an expanse of grassy meadow near the confluence of rivers that Willard knew about, where they might find ready feed for their cattle. To get there they headed west and north, sometimes following Indian trails. Their journey, as imaginatively described by Edward Johnson in *Wonder-Working Providence,* published in 1654, was fraught with difficulty and peril. They got lost. They climbed up and down hills. They tramped through woods and thickets "where their hands are forced to make way for their bodies passage." They traversed swamps, climbing across fallen logs and wading up to their knees. Brush scratched their legs badly, "even to wearing their stockings to the bare skin in two to three houres." By the time they found the meadow, according to Johnson, they had penetrated "further into this Wildernesse than any formerly had done." They were, in fact, only ten miles from a spot on the Charles River where Atlantic Ocean tidewater lapped up from Boston Harbor. Their trek probably took no more than a day.

They named their new place Concord. It was the first inland settlement of the Massachusetts Bay Colony. To the Englishmen back on the coast, it may have seemed like howling wilderness, but it wasn't a wilderness at all, even by the loosest definitions of the word. Concord had been a relatively civilized place for thousands of years—a great expanse of forest shaped and improved by Indians alongside a meadow left in the wake of a retreating glacier and occupied and fashioned by beavers. The Indians called it Musketaquid (Grass-Ground River). This landscape had fallen into disrepair relatively recently, after epidemics of European diseases in 1616 and 1633 killed off most of the Indians. As Brian Donahue wrote in *The Great Meadow: Farmers and the Land in Colonial Concord*:

Concord was not entirely covered with mature trees (although it had plenty of those), but in many places entangled by the surge of adolescent growth that had followed recent abandonment. Large stretches of the sandy lands that had been kept open by the Native people were no doubt overgrown by impassable thickets of brush and brambles. . . . [It was] land in a feral state.

I mention the settlement of Concord because it illustrates two common misperceptions about America's forests: where they were and how wild they were.

First, in my experience many people perceive the nation's forests, past and present, as concentrated in the West. This is understandable, since most of our national forests and other federally owned lands are in the West, and our best-known national parks are to be found there. For much of the late twentieth century, popular attention focused on the timber industry in California and the Pacific Northwest. That's where the giant redwoods are, Douglas fir, and Sitka spruce and where environmentalists enlisted the northern spotted owl to save the old-growth forests of hemlocks, cedars, and firs where the owls lived, and where the term *tree-hugger* was transplanted from the Chipko movement in India.[5] Some historical accounts reinforce the misperception by referring to the great "western wilderness," which is correct only in the sense that the forests that the settlers ventured into were, by and large, located to the west of where they had started—only a few miles to the west in the case of Concord (and in the case of Maine they headed east). The first and foremost "western wilderness" was, in fact, the Great Eastern Forest. When the first European settlers arrived, three-quarters of all the

---

5. The Chipko—meaning "embrace" in Hindi—movement began in 1973 in the Indian state of Uttarakhand, a region of mountains and forests bordering Tibet, to stop commercial loggers from cutting down trees. One tactic was for local village women to surround a tree holding hands in an effort to keep contractors from felling it.

forests in what would become the continental United States were in the eastern third of the country, mostly east of the Mississippi River.

Second, *wilderness* is a loaded word. It fits nicely into the founding mythology, conjuring up a vision of a forest primeval full of formidable creatures and humans who were not civilized enough to be called anything but savages. Demonizing the landscape and its occupants helped justify their conquest and destruction, which was the first step in the creation of a new Eden.

In fact, the eastern forest was nothing like that. It was not a continuous blanket of old trees, a so-called climax forest. It was a giant patchwork of ancient stands, young thickets, swamps, and meadows undergoing continual change over centuries. Nature assaulted it with lightning fires, tornados, hurricanes, insects, floods, and droughts. By some accounts, Indians regularly burned untold millions of acres to clear away forest understory of brush, fight insects, or create sight lines for defense and to grow wild berries. They essentially farmed the forest to encourage productive mast (nut) species such as oaks, hickories, and chestnuts, and to enhance habitat to attract the wild animals and birds they depended upon for food, clothing, and tools. Scholars debate how much Indian manipulation occurred and where. Indian populations varied in time and place, but were relatively small in relation to the vast expanses of landscape.

In any case, the arrival of Europeans in the fifteenth century changed Indian lifestyles enormously. Some populations moved to the coast, built permanent settlements and fortified villages, expanded cropland, and became farmers and traders. Some populations all but died out from European diseases—against which Indians had little immunity. Nobody knows how early the epidemics began—perhaps in the late 1400s, when the first cod fishermen in the Gulf of Maine came ashore for fresh water and brought viral infections with them. Smallpox was reported on Hispaniola in 1518, jumping to Mexico with Hernán Cortés in 1520. Around 1525, Spaniards brought a terrible smallpox plague to the Incas in Ecuador. Hernando de Soto arrived near Tampa in 1539 with an army of more than six hundred men, two hundred horses, a pack of dogs, and a herd of pigs and wandered west across the South for four years—after which whole Indian cultures disappeared. Some scholars theorize that subsequent labor shortages meant huge swaths of the Indian-managed landscape went "wild." Or, as historian Francis Jennings put it, instead of finding "virgin land," colonists found "widowed land."

This landscape may not have been impenetrable, but to settlers it was certainly intimidating. For the first hundred years after Columbus discovered the Bahamas, while cod fishermen and explorers plied the coastal waters and traders began to establish trading relationships with Indians, the interior of North America was known to few Europeans (most of them gold-seeking Spaniards in the South). William Cronon, the environmental historian, described the toehold Europeans clung to in the Northeast: "For the entirety of the sixteenth century, maps of New England consisted of a single line separating ocean from land, accompanied by a string of place-names to indicate landmarks along the shore; the interior remained blank."

. . .

Just how much forest covered what is now the United States before the Europeans arrived isn't known. Why? Because there was too much of it to measure. In his 1989 history, *Americans and Their Forests*, Michael Williams, a historical geographer at Oxford University, asserts that it wasn't valued enough to measure:

> Initially, the forest was so common that no one bothered to write about it, let alone collect statistics, and the extent of the forest and the amount of the clearing went unrecorded. The very use of the word "lumber" in North America for rough-cut wood and felled trees rather than "timber" was indicative of attitudes, for these materials were something that

"lumbered the landscape"; they were useless and cumbrous. Standing timber was regarded as a waste material, of which there was an over-abundance; in many places it had a value of less than zero. Bare land was worth more than land and trees.

The federal government commissioned studies and surveys in the nineteenth century, but it didn't even take an educated guess at how much forest there was until the twentieth century, after so much lumber had been cut that the nation appeared to be running out of trees. The first known map of American forests wasn't produced until 1873. It was drawn by William H. Brewer, a botanist at Yale College.

The first official estimate of forest cover prior to the settlement by Europeans was published in 1909, by Royal S. Kellogg, an assistant to Gifford Pinchot, the head of the U.S. Department of Agriculture's Forest Service. It was titled *The Timber Supply of the United States*. Kellogg assembled what historic land-clearing data he could find, surveyed how much forest was left in 1907, and estimated, state by state, how much forest had probably existed in the year 1630. Kellogg used 1630 to mark the "original forests" before Europeans began cutting them down. And that was fair, since European settlers before 1630 were relatively few, were confined to the coast, and had minimal impact beyond their immediate settlements.

Kellogg's report and Brewer's map of 1873 are astonishing to anyone who thinks great expanses of forest covered the West. The Rocky Mountain forests were relatively small blotches on his map. From western Montana and northern Idaho, the original forest looped westward across northern Washington and then down the Pacific coast into northern and eastern California. But the western forest, while containing lots of harvestable timber in much bigger trees, was dwarfed in acreage by the vast size of the forest that covered the East. The eastern forest stretched solidly in the north from Maine through Michigan, Wisconsin, and northern Minnesota. It skirted northern Illinois but blanketed middle states and the southern tier west through most of Missouri, eastern Oklahoma, and the eastern half of Texas.

Kellogg estimated that in what became the contiguous United States, 71.7 percent of the nation's forested lands in the year 1630 were in the East. That is, they extended from the Atlantic Ocean westward, petering out in the prairie, or Great Plains. By Kellogg's estimate, the twelve states along the Atlantic coast out to and including the Appalachian Mountains were, on average, 93 percent forest covered in 1630.

The geographical West—that is to say the Great Plains, the Rocky Mountains, and the Pacific coast—was plenty wild. The arresting peaks of the Rockies made eastern mountains seem like foothills in comparison. Western forests, however, were relatively small in terms of the landscape they occupied, and their time for "taming" didn't come until well after the Civil War. Indeed, lumbering didn't begin in earnest on the Pacific coast until the beginning of the twentieth century. By then, Europeans had been wrestling the eastern "wilderness" into submission for at least 250 years.

· · ·

The first task for any settler was tree removal—that is, unless he was lucky enough to find and pay a premium for a beaver-created meadow good for growing hay and pasturing or an Indian-cleared field for planting crops. Trees were an impediment. They stood in the way of survival. They blocked sunlight from reaching the ground to energize the growth of the edible plants settlers cultivated. In the short run, settlers could avoid starvation by packing basic foodstuffs into their home site and by hunting and gathering. But survival in the long run meant transforming patches of forest into hospitable terrain for the practice of European-style subsistence agriculture, with its domesticated animals, pastures, crop fields, and hay meadows.

The preferred method of tree removal in many places was girdling, a technique that involved stripping away a ring of bark from around the trunk. Without the innerbark, through which nutrients flowed, the tree died, leaving a leafless skeleton that slowly dried out and decayed over ten to twenty years.

Standing trees were a scourge, but the wood in them was a cheap luxury. The wood could be turned into lumber to build cabins, fences, and barns, and it could be cut and burnt as fuel for heating and cooking. One of the forgotten appeals of the New World for immigrants from England was that every family, rich or poor, could enjoy a luxury denied all but the well-to-do back home: warmth. In the old country, where forests in 1600 covered less than 10 percent of the landscape, fuel for cooking and heating was costly. Cost was not an issue in the New World. Hearth fires could burn around the clock.

Eventually, settlers could sell the wood products their forests provided, or trade them for manufactured goods. The potash that resulted from burning had value as a material for making soap and fertilizer. Hemlock bark was used in tanning leather. Demand for these materials grew in Europe as well, and selling them for export helped propel subsistence farmers into a commercial economy that spanned the Atlantic.

White pine (*Pinus strobus*) was the wood of choice for building materials for both ships and homes. Because they grew tall, straight, and strong and because they were relatively free of knots, white pines made excellent masts for sailing ships and were also cut into cross yards and bowsprits.[6] For houses and barns, they were sawed into boards for siding and flooring and cut into timbers and framing studs. One of white pine's virtues is that it floats better than other conifers and most hardwoods. That meant it could be cut down, skidded over snow or ice in winter to the nearest river, and then, come spring, floated downstream to a

---

6. The British Admiralty attempted to reserve the best mast pines for its ships, sending hatchet-wielding surveyors into New England forests to chop a symbol called a "board arrow" to mark them. Colonists ignored the marks and later rules outlawing the cutting down of big pines.

sawmill. Settlers used white pines to build their homes, barns, schools, churches, corncribs, chicken coops, pigsties, and just about every other structure they required. (White pine was eventually used to construct the boxes in which most goods were shipped before cardboard.)

The deforestation of the New World began very slowly, and forested lands didn't reach their historic low point in the Northeast until the 1880s, when nearly half of them had been lost to agriculture.[7] As the population grew and pioneers moved west, the pace of tree cutting accelerated. The colonial population stood at 3 million when Independence was declared in 1776, and people were already trickling across the Appalachians. By the time the Treaty of Paris was signed in 1783, in which Britain ceded to the new United States control of all lands south of Canada, north of Florida, and east of the Mississippi River, that trickle grew as word spread of the rich soil in the Ohio Valley and beyond. This expansion westward gradually shifted the focus of deforestation for farmland and logging for lumber to the Midwest.

Two developments undoubtedly did more to usher in a new era of forest exploitation in the Great Lakes than any other. The first was the invention of the steamboat in the 1790s by John Fitch, in combination with Robert Fulton's sailing of his model of it, the *Clermont,* from New York City to Albany in 1807, thereby demonstrating that commerce could go upstream easily. The second was the opening in 1825 of the Erie Canal from the Hudson River at Albany to Lake Erie at Buffalo. Forty feet wide, four feet deep, and 363 miles long, the canal allowed boats and barges to move crops and goods to and from farmers and settlers along its route. It also meant that New York was now commercially connected to Detroit, and it would eventually be connected to Chicago. Suddenly, the Great Lakes region was easy to get to, and commerce could flow east to west and west to east as never before.

---

7. In the parlance of the forester, *deforestation* means taking land out of tree growing. Land on which trees are removed for wood over time continues to be regarded as forested even if it takes trees many decades to regrow on it.

In 1830, the first sawmill opened in Flint, Michigan, to process logs from the swampy mixed-conifer and hardwood forests of the Saginaw Valley. A year later, Alexis de Tocqueville visited Saginaw and wrote: "We are perhaps the last travelers allowed to see its primitive grandeur." When Michigan became a state in 1837, Detroit still was a small port town of eight thousand, but 435 sawmills were already in operation in the southern third of the state. The plunder of Great Lakes forests was under way. Markets expanded quickly. Detroit needed homes and buildings. They were built with Michigan trees. The Erie Canal provided access to ready markets on the East Coast. And on the west side of Lake Michigan, the construction of Chicago was under way.

Something else happened in 1837 that would fuel the exploitation of Great Lakes forests. An Illinois blacksmith named John Deere invented the steel-tipped plow. Before it came along, farmers had used wooden plows with cast-iron edges to turn the ground. But those venturing into the Great Plains found that these old plows could not break tough prairie sod. The sod broke them. With John Deere's new plow, professional prairie breakers hired themselves out to cut and turn the sod. Farmers who could afford the new plows used them behind a team of horses to break two acres a day. The land could be readied to plant corn and wheat many times faster than forested land elsewhere. The next few years saw the birth of the American "bread basket." But the Great Plains had one big drawback: virtually no trees. The Great Lakes had plenty, and as railroad lines expanded, Chicago would grow and prosper by funneling wood west. With 2,500 wooden crossties required for each mile of track, the railroads consumed whole forests themselves.[8]

By 1850, the U.S. population had grown to 23.3 million, and wood

---

8. By 1910, more than 350,000 miles of rail lines had been built—up from only 10,000 miles in 1850. Crossties wore out (they weren't treated with creosote until 1900). They had to be replaced on 50,000 miles of track annually, which meant cutting down 5 to 20 million acres of trees a year.

supplied 90 percent of the nation's energy needs. Most of this wood was cut locally and burned in homes for heat and cooking. Demand for lumber exceeded its production. A U.S. census in that year introduced new categories for classifying land. Land cleared of forest for farm or other uses was called "improved." Forested land was "unimproved." The 1850 Census estimated that 100 million acres of former forest had been "improved." This meant that roughly one-fourth of the original eastern forest had been cleared for other uses.

That was just the beginning.

The timber barons were rapacious. They had government encouragement and could count on corruption to get their way. The public was essentially silent—people generally supported tree cutting to clear land for farming and help build the economy. Americans depended on forests in ways that are often overlooked in retrospect, according to Douglas W. MacCleery, a longtime policy analyst for the U.S. Forest Service and one of the reigning experts on the history of American forests. He wrote

> Wood was virtually the only fuel used in this country for most of its history. It warmed its citizens, produced its iron, drove its locomotives, steamboats, and stationary engines. Lumber, timbers and other structural products were the primary material used in houses, barns, fences, bridges, even dams and locks. Such products were essential to the development of rural economies across the nation, as well as to industry, transportation, and the building of cities. American forests—the products derived from them and the land they occupied—were, in a very real sense, the economic foundation of the nation.

The forests, of course, paid a price. Loggers not only plundered magnificent stands of white pine across the Great Lakes region but left environmental devastation in their wake. Tree trimmings called slash were left on the landscape to dry and burn in some of the worst fire disasters in American history.[9]

In 1929, two U.S. Department of Agriculture economists, William Sparhawk and Warren Brush, surveyed Michigan and estimated that in less than one hundred years 92 percent of the state's original forests had been cut down. They estimated that for every two trees that had been cut and harvested during the boom another tree had been lost to fire or otherwise wasted. Nowhere else in the nation had a state's forest resources been as thoroughly plundered and the landscape so scarred. Huge tracts of the old pine forest were dubbed "lands nobody wants."

In the late nineteenth and early twentieth centuries, with the forests of the Northeast and Midwest commercially exhausted, the timber barons turned their saws and axes to the pine forests of Georgia and the Southeast and the giant conifers of the Pacific Northwest. Logging across the South exploded between 1880 and 1920. In 1919, the region produced 37 percent of the lumber consumed in the United States. And as in the Great Lakes, the timber barons left behind the making of devastating fires and soil erosion. By 1910, the Pacific Northwest was outproducing the Great Lakes region, and by 1920, it supplied 30 percent of the nation's timber.

White pine had been thought to be inexhaustible, but by the beginning of the twentieth century, it clearly wasn't. The same was true for other valuable tree species. James Defebaugh, a timber industry historian, wrote in 1905 that the country had been harvesting timber by "drawing on the surplus" but that now, like a badly run business, it

---

9. In October of 1871, at the same time the Great Chicago Fire killed two hundred people, burned down 17,450 buildings, and got the attention of the national press, the worst fire disaster in U.S. history was under way up near Green Bay, Wisconsin. Known as the Peshtigo Horror, for a small town incinerated in its path, this fire burned 1,280,000 acres in Wisconsin and northwestern Michigan, killing nearly 1,500 people and maiming many more. Fires in Lower Michigan that same fall burned another 2.5 million acres. These fires burned away organic matter and baked nitrogen from the sandy soil, taking away what little fertility it had originally. With little or no cover to hold the soil in place, wind and rain carried much of it away.

had started to "draw down on the capital funds." Government officials painted startling pictures of the demise of "virgin" forests and projected a bleak future for American trees and the wood supply.

In his 1907 forest census, Royal Kellogg estimated that the nation had lost 43 percent of its forest, with anywhere from 40 to 70 percent stripped away in the Northeast and Midwest, depending on the state. The assault on southern forests was just beginning, and in the West it had barely begun. He ended his report on an ominous note: "We are cutting our forests three times faster than they are growing. There is menace in the continuance of such conditions."

White pine harvests were dwindling, and hardwoods, including oak and yellow poplar, were in serious decline. Although the environmental damage was great, the words *environment* and *ecology* were not familiar at the time and weren't in any case a big concern. Far more important was the scary idea that the country might run out of trees.

"It was an alarming prospect that struck at the very heart of America's self-image as the storehouse of boundless resources," Michael Williams wrote. "The nation might be reduced to the state of some impoverished and denuded Mediterranean country."

By the time officials in Washington sounded the alarm that the nation was running out of virgin stands of trees to harvest, another phenomenon had been under way for decades but went largely unnoticed: Forests were regenerating in New England.

. . .

There were lots of reasons to quit farming in New England in the nineteenth century, but one early event stands out: the most violent explosion in recorded history halfway around the world. On the island of Sumbawa in the Dutch East Indies (now Indonesia) near the equator, a volcano named Tambora began to rumble and cough on the evening of April 5, 1815. On April 11 and 12, eruptions shook houses and boats hundreds of miles away. Over ten days, Tambora belched twenty-four cubic miles of lava and pulverized rock (try to imagine a cubic mile of anything), and created a crater more than three miles wide and nearly a mile deep. Flowing lava, flying rocks, and deadly gases killed thousands of people on Sumbawa and nearby islands. Earthquakes and tsunamis killed tens of thousands more. Hundreds of millions of tons of ash filled the sky, turning days into nights and blanketing the nearby island of Bali in a foot of volcanic soot. The ash smothered vegetation on islands for hundreds of miles around, and carpets of floating pumice covered the seas. An estimated 117,000 people in the region eventually died, many from starvation caused by crop failures and epidemics.

Tambora's explosive power dwarfed subsequent and more familiar volcanic eruptions. Because news in those days traveled by ship, word of the volcano's devastation spread slowly in comparison to the better-known and better-documented eruption of Krakatoa sixty-eight years later (after the invention of the telegraph in 1837). But Tambora was much bigger (24 cubic miles of ejected debris) than Krakatoa (3.5 to 11 cubic miles), or the famed eruptions of Vesuvius (1.4 cubic miles) and Mount Saint Helens in Washington (less than 1 cubic mile). The 2010 eruption of Eyjafjallajokull in Iceland, with a dust plume that grounded airlines across Europe, was, by comparison, a planetary popped zit.

Like a giant cannon, Tambora blew ash and an estimated 400 million tons of sulfurous gases some twenty-seven miles straight up into the stratosphere, high above the weather. This material blew up and through the troposphere—the layer nearest earth's surface, where clouds, wind, rain, and 75 percent of the weight of the atmosphere (nitrogen, oxygen, trace gases, and water vapor) reside. The troposphere is 4.8 miles thick at the North and South Poles and 9.6 miles thick at the equator. Tambora blew its load more than seventeen miles beyond it, up where the air is thin and a layer of ozone protects the earth from the sun's ultraviolet rays. There, the ash and gases spread, circling the globe and cloaking it like a veneer, the biggest ash particles sinking quickly, the smallest lingering. The sulfurous gases reacted with water vapor and ozone to create an aerosol layer of sulfuric acid that reflected the sun's warming rays back into space. This layer stayed up for months and years until the stratosphere's gentle circulation gradually brought it back down into the troposphere, where the weather grabbed it and deposited it on earth in the form of mineral ash and nature's acid rain.

In the meantime—the summer after the eruption—crop failures dotted the Northern Hemisphere. Rice failed in parts of China, wheat and corn in Europe, potatoes in Ireland (where it rained nonstop for eight weeks and triggered a typhus epidemic that killed sixty-five thousand and spread to England and Europe).[10] Famine spread across Europe and Asia. Food riots and insurrections swept France, which had already been caught up in chaos following Napoleon's 1815 defeat at Waterloo.

Tambora may not have been the sole cause of these disasters. Smaller eruptions of volcanoes had taken place in the Caribbean (La Soufrière on Saint Vincent in 1812) and the Philippines (Mayon on Luzon in 1814). The planet, beginning in the fifteenth century, had been going through periods of intense climatic change—sharp cooling and warming now collectively known as the Little Ice Age. In the coldest periods, mountain glaciers advanced around the world and the Thames River in London froze over in winter. But the most severe periods of cold seemed to be abating by the time Tambora came along. Its effects came as a jolt. In New England, 1816 was called "the year without a summer" because there were crop-killing frosts every month, including normally frost-free months of summer, across the region. It snowed in Virginia in June and again on the Fourth of July. At Monticello, Thomas Jefferson, the retired president, had such a poor corn harvest that he had to borrow $1,000 to make up for lost income. In New Haven, Connecticut, the

---

10. At Lake Geneva in Switzerland, vacationers from England sat out gloomy June storms reading ghost stories and composing their own. Lord Byron wrote a narrative poem, "Darkness," in which there was no sun, "no day." His personal physician, Dr. John Polidori, wrote "The Vampyre," and Mary Shelley began her novel *Frankenstein*.

last frost of spring was on June 11, and the first frost of autumn on August 22—shortening the normal growing season by 55 days. Corn, the staple crop of New England, couldn't mature under such conditions. Crop failures were widespread. In Connecticut, three-quarters of the state's corn crop was too unripe, soft, or moldy to make cornmeal.

While New Englanders faced food shortages and price hikes, they did not experience famine. But the hardship may have set Yankee farmers to thinking about where they farmed or whether they should try something else. In their elegant 1983 book, *Volcano Weather: The Story of 1816, the Year without a Summer,* Woods Hole oceanographer Henry Stommel and his wife, Elizabeth, wrote: "The summer of 1816 marked the point at which many New England farmers who had weighed the advantages of going west made up their minds to do so."

The trickle westward had already begun, but Tambora and the Erie Canal made it a stream. They not only accelerated westward settlement and the transformation of the Midwest from forests to farms but also helped begin a transformation of New England from farms back to forest.

. . .

Settlers in the Ohio Valley and the lower Midwest found land with clear advantages over that farmed by their eastern counterparts. Much of the farmland in New England was hilly, rocky, subject to erosion, and as Michael Williams, the forest historian, noted, "climatically marginal for many crops." In the Midwest settlers found that land was relatively flat and free of stones, and the soil unimaginably rich—so fertile that it required no fertilizer initially. These characteristics gave grain farmers there an enormous economic advantage over grain farmers in the East. They also made Midwest land suitable for the use of newly invented farm machinery on a large scale. Harvests burgeoned, and with the opening of the Erie Canal, shipping costs plummeted (from $100 a ton by road to less than $10 a ton by boat). Midwest farmers could pay to ship their corn, wheat, and other grains to the East and still make a handy profit.

New England farmers couldn't compete by growing these crops. Some of them quit farming altogether, or they moved to the Midwest to farm there. Others stayed put, adopted new practices and crops, and prospered. Even if the land wasn't as naturally fertile as settlers found in the Midwest, there was plenty of livestock in New England, and that meant lots of available manure for fertilizer to grow other things. Farmers in the East had the advantage of being close to burgeoning cities that were markets for virtually everything they raised. They would prosper by providing farm products too bulky or perishable to ship from the Midwest. They could import cheap Midwest grain and feed it to chickens, hogs, sheep, and cattle to produce eggs and meat. Some became dairymen, supplying milk, butter, and cheese. They expanded orchards and truck gardens to supply a growing populace with fruits and vegetables. They grew hay to supply the horses, mules, and other draft animals that supplied power for agriculture and manufacturing and pulled the trolleys and wagons in the cities. For those who quit, jobs could be had in southern New England towns that were filling up with mills and factories and were accessible by rail. Others made their way to New Bedford and other coastal ports to sign on as crewmen on whaling ships headed for the South Seas.

The first trees began growing on abandoned farmland in parts of Massachusetts not long after the canal opened. By 1840, reforestation was clearly evident in parts of New England. In western Massachusetts, perhaps half the farmland was abandoned within twenty years after 1850, and much of it was colonized by native white pines.

By around 1880, the return of trees was evident in New York, Pennsylvania, and New Jersey. But very few people—Thoreau was a notable exception—saw reforestation happening while it was happening. The question is why. One answer is that as old farms gave way to new forests Americans looked the other way, and for good reason. Through four hundred years of European discovery, exploration, colonization, and settlement of the North American landscape, the act of removing trees was considered to be virtuous. It was progress celebrated by landscape painters who captured pastoral scenes of the New England country-side. Some of the paintings show landscapes full of the tree stumps. The stumps were symbols of progress and points of pride. The advent of popular photography in the late nineteenth century, particularly the development of film by George Eastman in 1884, coincided with the peak years of deforestation in the Northeast, and photographs taken during this period likewise documented the progress evident on rural landscapes largely devoid of trees.

So imagine what happened when farmland began to be abandoned to forest in the nineteenth century. To let precious land, cleared by backbreaking labor, go untended, unprotected from an invasion of trees, was the opposite of progress. As Michael Williams interpreted it, the process was "retrogressive, difficult to comprehend, and even sinful to contemplate." It was an abdication of a farmer's responsibility to be a good steward of the working landscape (although farmers themselves didn't mind giving up scrub acreage), and as such it was largely ignored by government statisticians.

. . .

As new trees were taking root on untended farmland to create new for-ests, old forests continued to be destroyed. The idea that forests should be studied and managed was novel, but by midcentury people had begun thinking about saving the old forests, or at least slowing the destruction of what was left of them. A few of them suggested that trees had more than just economic value. Some also worried aloud about the environ-mental consequences of removing them. What effect did clearing have on climate, on health? Would it affect the changing seasons?

George Perkins Marsh, widely called America's first environmentalist, was an attorney, scholar, and diplomat who studied the effects of clearing forests in Europe and the Mediterranean region. While serving as ambassador to Italy in 1864 he published his monumental book, *Man and Nature; or, Physical Geography as Modified by Human Action.* In it, Marsh wrote at length about the role of forests in nature and the injurious impacts of their clearing on all sorts of other natural systems. The book sparked an awakening of interest in the environmental consequences of man's destructive ways and set the stage for what became known as the conservation movement.

In the eighteenth and early nineteenth centuries, a few thinkers and writers started an intellectual revolution by suggesting that forests and other wild places were gifts from God and not venues that God willed man to subjugate. The idea that living a primitive life in a wild place might be wholesome was suggested in Daniel Defoe's *Robinson Crusoe* in 1719 and Jean-Jacques Rousseau's *Emile* in 1762. In the nineteenth century, writers such as Washington Irving in *The Legend of Sleepy Hollow* (1820) and James Fenimore Cooper in the *Leatherstocking* novels (1823–41) created appreciation of forests and affection for the noble backwoodsman. Instead of thinking of the forest as the embodiment of evil that settlers were duty bound to vanquish, Thoreau and other transcendentalists wrote that experiencing wild nature brought awareness and enhanced man's perfection. Others argued that forests had aesthetic value and that wild nature was wholesome. Landscape painters began to capture the beauty of wilderness undisturbed by man. In the 1830s and 1840s, Thomas Cole and other artists of the Hudson River school painted scenes of wild landscapes in the Catskill Mountains in New York and beyond and sold them to collectors for handsome sums. John Muir discovered the Yosemite Valley and campaigned for wilderness preservation.[11] By century's end, with supplies of untamed

---

11. Among the requirements for creating a national park were that an area be unique geologically and a pristine wilderness—that is, uninhabited by man. In the Yosemite Valley, where the idea of national parks was born, Major James D. Savage led the

lands dwindling, appreciation of wilderness had grown into an unlikely national passion. By then, of course, more and more people were living not on a rugged landscape but in comfortable cities and villages and on previously tamed landscapes. Undisturbed nature was somewhere else. Entrepreneurs began to capitalize on the idea that people would pay to go and see it, building railroads to get them there. Agents sold trips to wilderness areas, offering vacation packages at nearby hotels and guided tours to see the charms of the wild—charms that had escaped the attention of their forebears. The historical flip-flop was described by William Cronon this way: "For Muir and the growing number of Americans who shared his views, Satan's home had become God's own temple."

Two ideas grew and spread in tandem, and later in opposition to each other. The first, advanced by Muir, was that since wilderness was valuable for its own sake, saving it was a good idea. The second, promoted in Washington, was that the forests in these areas provided valuable resources and should be kept and managed sustainably. These ideas helped to create the political will to begin efforts to conserve forests, create preserves, and bring back wildlife. No one had more willpower for the task than President Theodore Roosevelt. He spread the alarm that the United States was running out of forests and pushed for new legislation to save them. By 1906, which was the peak year for national wood production and consumption, it had become good politics to talk about a looming wood shortage. But a deep rift opened over how to solve it and why forests should be preserved. Gifford Pinchot, Roosevelt's forestry chief, was a "wise use" conservationist who sought to protect forests from rapacity but also make use of them and manage them wisely. Muir, in contrast, campaigned for preservation of wild places undisturbed by

---

Mariposa Brigade on an 1851 expedition that killed or relocated the Ahwahneechee Indians who lived there—mainly to get them out of the way of the Gold Rush. In 1864, President Abraham Lincoln signed a bill protecting the valley. Two years later, John Muir arrived and fell so in love with Yosemite's unspoiled (and peopleless) grandeur that he founded the Sierra Club and devoted his life to "saving" wilderness.

man. Arguments over wise use versus no use lasted a century and go on today. Some people, then and now, argued for doing both.

When loggers began to realize they were running out of forests to cut, they slowly learned to be tree farmers. Michael Williams estimated that trees were replanted on one million acres annually during the 1930s.

Because of the laws in place at the time, only publicly owned lands could become national forests, and most of those lands were in the West. As a result, national forests were set aside first in western states: By 1909, at the end of the Theodore Roosevelt presidency, some 172 million acres of public land in the West had been designated as national forests. The East lagged because most land was in private hands.

Reforestation started later in the South and took longer than it did in the Northeast. Some trees, such as loblolly and shortleaf pine, regenerated naturally in some areas. But a great deal of deforested land would have to be replanted. After the Civil War, many cotton and rice plantations went into decline. They had thrived on slave labor and, for a while, indentured former slaves. But as that cheap labor supply dwindled, cotton and rice production moved west to Louisiana and Texas and machines took over. In their wake, many of the South's plantations planted and farmed longleaf and loblolly pine trees. Many were bought for a song by rich northerners and turned into quail-hunting preserves.

While the total amount of lumber and fuel wood consumed continued to rise with population growth until the peak year of 1906, per capita lumber consumption had by then already begun to drop. Growing use of coal, oil, natural gas, and electricity reduced demand for wood as fuel. Also, aluminum, steel, and, later, plastics began to be substituted for wood in building construction. In the 1920s, oil production began to revolutionize the ways Americans lived and fed themselves. Oil ushered in the era of modern agriculture, high-yield monocultures of corn and soybeans, and, eventually, factory farms.

According to Douglas W. MacCleery, the U.S. Forest Service analyst, 27 percent of the nation's cropland in 1910 was devoted to growing food for draft animals—the horses, mules, and oxen that provided transportation and did the heavy work on farms and in towns and cities. Crude oil, pumped out of the ground and refined into gasoline to fuel cars, trucks, and tractors, made draft animals obsolete. And that, in turn, freed some 70 million acres of land that had grown hay, oats, and corn for draft animals to instead grow food for people. Then, after 1935, another product of the petroleum era, chemical fertilizer, gradually came into widespread use to nourish new hybrid seeds and greatly increase yields. The result was that it took less land and labor to grow more food. In 1990, farmers grew five times more food per acre than farmers in 1930 had grown, and they farmed fewer acres.

All the while, trees were recolonizing land. In the eastern third of the country between 1910 and 1959, an estimated 43.8 million acres of farmland reverted to forest, mainly in the Northeast. In the next two decades the process accelerated, with farmland returning to forest at a rate of 1,180,000 acres per year.

Who noticed?

Nigel Williams, the British humorist, for one. In his witty 1995 book, *From Wimbledon to Waco*, Williams (no relation to Oxford's Michael Williams) takes his family on a trip to the United States. They fly to Los Angeles, tour the West, and hop a plane to New York. They rent a car and drive north. They are new to New England.

"I had never expected there would be quite so many trees in New England," Williams wrote in a chapter entitled "The Great New England Tree Conspiracy." The contrast with the desert hills of the West Coast was startling. This was a "tree epidemic."

> The trees were the ones in charge around here. There was no horizon. There was no way of telling whether you were going up or down or north or south or east or west. There was only a mysterious green corridor. And when you did finally reach a settlement of some kind, it seemed to be laid out in deference to the trees. There was no vil-

lage green, no pub, no break in the forest, just a brief, hesitant line of shops that reminded me of the kind of thing you might see in Surrey or Hampshire—and then another few billion trees.

The houses in Darien, Connecticut, Williams wrote, "hid, like the witch's place in Hansel and Gretel, in an all-embracing forest."

Why did these forests seem to be so much more obvious to Williams than to Americans who resided in them? One reason, of course, is that trees grow slowly, probably too slowly for busy people to notice. Modern Americans didn't stay in one place long enough to watch slow changes in the landscape—if they were watching at all. They moved around, plopping into an exurb in one part of the country that pretty much replicated one somewhere else.

But there was something else at work: changed attitudes about progress. For many Americans, *progress* had become a dirty word. Much of the American "wilderness" had been methodically destroyed in the name of progress. Forests of the twenty-first century were being destroyed across swaths of the planet by a human population no more rapacious but far larger than in the past. This, too, was happening in the name of progress. Each new assault on forests elsewhere on the planet reinforced the notion that assaults were happening everywhere, including here. Each new gouge into the rural landscape for a housing tract or parking lot served to confirm this. Battles over the old-growth forests in the Pacific Northwest focused attention on continuing loss. Into this mind-set—a kind of mental narrative of loss—a counterintuitive notion did not easily fit: that a giant forest had regrown in our midst.

To see this new forest required looking beyond a mental picture of forest destruction. Some people couldn't see it, including newcomers to northwestern Connecticut or "anyone who has moved here in the last 30 or so years," wrote Cynthia Hochswender, the editor of the *Lakeville Journal* in December of 2007: "In town meetings and in coffee shop conversation . . . folks often refer to the primeval forests that are fast disappearing from the local hills and valleys. The fact is, as anyone knows who takes the time to learn about these things, that the forests are actually aggressively re-growing in a region that was stripped of all its trees a century ago. Those were the days of the iron industry, when trees were what kept the fires burning in the blast furnaces in Lakeville, Lime Rock, Sharon and on Mt. Riga."

From around 1730 to end of the Civil War, local trees were cut to make charcoal that was burned in furnaces to produce a malleable wrought iron in the form of bars or rods that local forgers or farmers could heat and fashion into horseshoes, pickaxes, sledgehammers, axes, sickles, and knives. They also made munitions.

In his 1991 book *Second Nature: A Gardener's Education,* Michael Pollan wrote of moving his family to Cornwall, Connecticut, not far from Lakeville, where he discovered a "post-agricultural hardwood forest," as he called it. Walking in the woods near his house one spring afternoon, he stumbled upon the ghostly ruins of an abandoned nineteenth-century settlement named Dudleytown.

"What makes Dudleytown spooky is the evident speed and force and thoroughness with which the forest has obliterated the place," he wrote. "In the space of a few decades it has erased virtually every human mark. . . . The forest, I now understood, is 'normal'; everything else— the fields and meadows, the lawns and pavements and, most spectacularly, the gardens—is a disturbance, a kind of ecological vacuum which nature will not abide for long."

Sometimes the forest isn't what it seems to be. All sorts of outdoor entrepreneurs offered forays into the "wilderness" beginning in the 1980s. There were wilderness encounters, wilderness adventures, wilderness treks, wilderness weekends, wilderness camping, wilderness climbing, wilderness canoeing, and a host of other programs that got people off the asphalt, out of their cars, and into the wide world of nature. This wasn't bad. It was just deceptive—the equivalent of restaurants that offer "wild" game that was farm raised because, as we shall see, it is illegal in the United States to sell real wild game. In this case, what was often passed off as wilderness was once an old farm.

Sometimes it took a little exploring to tell the difference. In 1977, for example, a Connecticut College graduate decided to spend that summer in the woods of northern Vermont by himself, communing with nature and reading Thoreau. That part of Vermont had the feel of the North Woods, an ideal setting for studying the works of America's great naturalist. He hiked into "deep forest" and began cutting down trees to build a little cabin. Exploring the woods around him, he found "some surprises." Only a hundred yards from his building site, he came upon a wall of stones covered with ferns and moss that marched up a hillside. Beside it was an overgrown lane, and nearby a spring and an old hole that might have once been a cellar. Later he wrote: "The woods most certainly had a history that I had been quite unaware of, a history of people working and transforming the land, and creating a landscape very different from the one I now occupied. Despite the steep and rocky nature of the land, and the dark extent of the current forest that nearly obscured its history, this whole area had once been inhabited, cleared of trees, and farmed."

The student was David R. Foster, now director of the Harvard Forest. He wrote about his Vermont discovery in a 1999 book, *Thoreau's Country: Journey Through a Transformed Landscape*. Because Thoreau wrote about nature, and because Walden, where he lived from 1845 to 1847, is today called "the birthplace of the American conservation movement," many people think he lived in "a largely natural world." Foster wrote: "However, this nostalgic vision is quite incorrect. Walden was just one of many New England woodlots that supplied fuel to households, each of which consumed 10 to 30 cords of wood per winter to heat a drafty house with an inefficient fireplace or stove. Concord was a commercially thriving agricultural community and regional cross-roads in which cows and chickens greatly outnumbered native wildlife and meadows overwhelmed forests."

The cabin Thoreau built on Walden Pond in 1845 was situated on the edge of Concord in a fourteen-acre second-growth woodlot owned by Ralph Waldo Emerson. Thoreau lived through what Foster calls the peak of New England's "agrarian splendor," when it was a landscape of small farming villages and a population composed of people who for the most part made their living from the land.[12] His journals, however idyllic, are full of "the sights and sounds and natural history of an open, vibrant, and quite domesticated landscape."

The Fitchburg Railroad line had reached Concord the year before Thoreau arrived. It ran along the south side of Walden Pond, and its locomotives burned wood for fuel. Some of that wood was cut nearby, and in the decade that followed Thoreau's arrival, trees were stripped from the land to power the trains. By 1854, when *Walden Pond, or Life in the Woods* came out, forests in the area had been cut down to almost their low point. In other words, the region was more deforested than at any time before or since.

But that was already changing. By the end of Thoreau's life, New England's landscape was, in his words, "returning to a wilder state," many of its citizens having moved on to the Ohio Valley or to industrializing cities nearby. Foster offers a marvelous description of what happened when they were gone:

> As people left the land, pines and birches and blackberries crowded into the neglected pastures and forest sprang up in old corn fields. Many of the homes, barns, schoolhouses, and wooden fences collapsed, leaving only their more durable remnants in woods that are now crisscrossed with trails descended from an abandoned network of rural roads. The fields that I grew up in, like those of the few other farm landscapes of modern New England, were the meager remains of a once vast countryside of pasture and hay fields and barns that extended from Long

---

12. Farmers who worked eighteen-hour days would not use the word *splendor*.

Island Sound through Connecticut, Rhode Island, and Massachusetts to northern Vermont, New Hampshire, and southern Maine. Since Thoreau's day, most of the land has reverted to forest, like the one where I was retreating to build my cabin.

Most of the eastern forest that grew back in the nineteenth and twentieth centuries remained forest in the twenty first century, including 79 percent of the landscape in New England. That's no reason for complacency. Asphalt never sleeps. But it is a giant woods nonetheless, however difficult it is for people to perceive it as such. The "woods" in our minds is still the place Grandma lived, or that "dark and creepy" place on the way to the Emerald City, or the sylvan glade where Bambi grew up. The "forest" we think of today is home to redwoods and spotted owls, or government-designated "wilderness" preserves and national parks. The forest is a long way away, over the horizon, or way up north.

Only it isn't. It's right outside your window. See those beech trees? They weren't there fifty years ago. What about that big old oak? In 1825, it was an acorn. As for the patch of saplings and scrub brush up that hill? That was a hay field ten years ago.

Chapter Three

Sprawl

On April 9, 2000, the *New York Times* devoted the entire issue of its Sunday magazine to suburbs, asserting on its front page, "There's nothing 'sub' about the suburbs anymore." Data collected for the 2000 Census had revealed a demographic tipping point: For the first time an absolute majority of the American people lived not in cities, not on farms, but in an ever-expanding suburban and exurban sprawl in between.[13] Never in history have so many people lived this way.

In historical terms, sprawl blossomed overnight. Until 1950, suburbs had so few people that the Census Bureau hadn't even created a category for them. But that changed quickly when a severe housing shortage after the Second World War led Washington to stimulate a home-building boom where land was available on the urban fringe. Suburbanites sprouted like crabgrass. By 1960, the census found Americans to be 34 percent urban, 33 percent rural, and 33 percent suburban, and in the next ten years suburbanites would tip the balance.

"In 1970, for the first time in the history of the world, a nation-state

---

13. Some dictionaries define *sprawl,* the verb, as "to spread out awkwardly." Earle Draper, the planning director for the Tennessee Valley Authority, was credited with being among the first to use the word *sprawl* in a 1937 speech in which he said, "Perhaps diffusion is too kind a word. . . . In bursting its bounds, the city actually sprawled and made the countryside ugly . . . uneconomic [in terms] of services and doubtful social value." *Sprawl* later became a noun as well. William Whyte defined it in 1958 as leapfrog development.

counted more suburbanites than either city dwellers or farmers," Kenneth T. Jackson wrote in his authoritative 1985 history, *Crabgrass Frontier: The Suburbanization of the United States*. By 1980, some 40 percent of the population was living in what author James Howard Kunstler would label "the geography of nowhere."

. . .

Ancient cities had suburbs of a sort. They were slums on the fringes, outside the walls built around cities at enormous expense to fend off attackers. People lived outside the walls because they were unwelcome inside them. Downtowns were for genteel people—professionals and merchant classes—who lived in townhouses. People on the edges or outside the walls were of the working and underclasses, sometimes craftsmen, such as carpenters and tailors, and sometimes undesirables—outcasts, slaves, prostitutes, and lowly laborers in slaughterhouses, leather tanneries, soap making and other industries not wanted in town. "Even the word suburb suggested inferior manners, narrowness of view, and physical squalor," wrote Professor Jackson.

That all changed with the industrial revolution, when the squalor moved downtown. At first a few wealthy urbanites sought relief from it by building estates or mansions (which they sometimes called "cottages") in the country, where they spent summers or weekends. Then came planned suburban communities to help people who could afford them escape cities. In 1868, Frederick Law Olmsted and Calvert Vaux began the creation of Riverside on the western edge of Chicago. It was the first of sixteen suburbs around the country that they would design for the relatively wealthy. Their idea was to combine greenery, clean air, and rural tranquillity with such urban comforts as piped-in water, sewer lines, paved roads, and gaslights. Riverside was a success, but it was Chicago's great fire of 1871 that triggered an explosion of suburban growth and an expansion of commuter railroads. Affluent residents of secluded new homes could commute to work by rail and live far removed from the stink of stockyards and slaughterhouses and the pollution, crowds, and noise of the downtown factory and warehouse areas.

In the Northeast, Olmsted created Chestnut Hill and Brookline, west of Boston, and Yonkers and Tarrytown Heights, north of New York City. The wealthy found these new developments idyllic retreats, with both urban amenities and country clubs, far removed from the raucous, smelly, and dirty downtowns. These communities were only the beginning.

Because almost no new housing had been built between the beginning of the Great Depression and the end of the Second World War, the United States faced an acute housing shortage. More than 14 million soldiers and sailors had been demobilized. They went home, or anywhere else where they could find a bed, and started having babies. Between 1946 and 1964 they had 76 million babies. The beginning of this baby boom made the housing shortage worse. As Jackson described the situation in a PBS documentary: "By 1947, you have millions of husbands and wives and children living together, bunched up, crunched in with their in-laws. That was my situation; four kids. I remember sleeping in a dining room. People would take any kind of a place that had a roof over it and a wall around it as a place to live."

On June 22, 1944, President Roosevelt signed into law the Servicemen's Readjustment Act to provide benefits for returning veterans. Besides fifty weeks' worth of unemployment compensation and free college tuition, the act guaranteed low-interest loans to buy homes with no down payment, and that touched off a house-building boom. Developers took over. They set loose their bulldozers on cheap land on the urban fringe, flattening almost everything in their paths. They leveled hillsides, removed trees and brush, and filled in swamps. They created streets and put in drainage, water pipes, and electric lines.

Veterans and the so-called Silent Generation, born during the Depression and the war years, loved the new suburbs. Farmers' children liked them, too. To move into suburbia and get a day job was to escape farm work. Besides, the mechanization of crop production made a lot of farm labor superfluous. With city jobs plentiful, many didn't mind leaving the family farm for a new way to live, working regular hours, getting weekends off, and doing something unheard of on the farm: taking a vacation.

Homes in the new suburbs were new, relatively spacious, affordable, safe, and comfortable places for veterans to get on with their lives and raise their children. Those children—the first generation of baby boomers—grew up, by storied accounts, bored to tears. The freestanding, single-family home, however, became part of the national ethos, said Jackson, and by the mid-1980s, two-thirds of Americans owned one.

Farmers, meanwhile, quit in droves. The agricultural landscape, which peaked in 1940 with 31 million people living on 6.1 million farms, emptied out. By 1990, the number of farms had dropped to 2.1 million and the farm population had plummeted to less than 3 million. A lot of land went out of production. In the meantime, however, demographers had their eye on a countertrend. Kenneth M. Johnson, a Loyola University–Chicago demographer and sociologist, called it "the rural rebound" in a 1999 report. Newcomers were invading the countryside but not farming it. They were sprawling out.

"The new arrivals are a mixed lot of retirees, blue-collar workers, lone-eagle professionals, and disenchanted city dwellers; all see a better way of life in rural areas," wrote Johnson. These people moved into areas that were nice places to live: the Mountain West, the upper Great Lakes, the Ozarks, parts of the South and the rural Northeast. They moved into areas with forested lakes, winter sports, mountain vistas, golf courses, or some combination of them.

Most people didn't migrate very far. They simply moved out beyond postwar suburbs into once-rural areas that came to be called exurbs. As highways improved, real estate developers could leapfrog farmland on a city's edge and build new housing units farther down the highway or off the next exit ramp. Buyers would get more house and land for less money if they were willing to commute farther to work. Some farmers carved out roadside lots for their offspring to build on, or sold an acre or two to young couples wanting to build affordable starter homes. Developers bought land along rights-of-way and or beside newly constructed highways and built strip malls. Between 1963 and 1999, so many people sprawled into these areas that 412 rural counties were reclassified as metropolitan counties, or what Johnson called "edge cities."

"These quasi-urban agglomerations of office parks and shopping centers make it easier for people to reside in rural areas without severing their links to the metropolitan economy," he added. "The newcomers, moreover, have few ties to the traditional rural economy or way of life; they are in rural America but not of it."

In 2004, *Times* columnist David Brooks wrote: "We're living in the age of the great dispersal" into outer suburbs, or "to the suburbs of suburbia." This vast decentralization, he continued, was creating "a tribe of people who not only don't work in cities, they don't commute to cities or go to the movies in cities or have any contact with urban life." You now had, he went on, "booming exurban sprawls that have broken free of the gravitational pull of the cities and now float in a new space far beyond them."

Untethered from old cities, some of these new developments weren't on the edge of anything but an interstate. Cities, suburbs, exurbs, sprawl, and countryside got mixed together. One city's suburbs bumped into suburbs from the city down the highway, but in between to each side were still a few farms. These areas, such as the one between Chicago and Milwaukee, were dubbed "urban corridors." They fit together, sort of, and they didn't, sort of. However they fit, they had one thing in common: trees, lots of trees.

· · ·

But is America a nation of forest dwellers? That depends, of course, on how *forest* is defined and where people live in proximity to it. The Great Eastern Forest was the largest tree-covered landscape in the contiguous United States when Europeans arrived. It wasn't completely forested then, and it certainly isn't now. Remarkably, however, trees have grown back on roughly two-thirds of the land that forest researchers believe was forest covered in 1630.

How many people live in it? Nearly 204 million, or two-thirds of the population of 308.7 million in 2010. That number includes everyone, rural and urban. If you subtract the 23 million people who live in the twenty largest eastern cities, you are left with about 179 million, or 58.2 percent of the total U.S. population—still a clear majority. Most of those people live among a lot of trees but not in what would traditionally be called a forest. Sprawl, for example, can include suburbs, exurbs, golf courses, cropland, pasture, parks, highway median strips, parking lots, McMansions, Burger Kings, and people. It obviously isn't officially defined forest. Yet areas of sprawl, particularly in the East, are so covered with trees that they have the feel of a forest, and, as we shall see, for many wild creatures they have all the comforts of forest—and more.

The phrase *urban forest* might seem oxymoronic. Yet a lot of trees grow in what the Census Bureau officially defines as urban areas. For example, 24 percent of New York City's land area is covered by the canopies of 5.2 million trees. Nationally, tree canopy covers about 27 percent of the urban landscape, on average. Not surprisingly, it is heaviest in the East.

In the most heavily populated region of the United States, the urban corridor that runs from Norfolk, Virginia, to Portland, Maine, with eight of the ten most densely populated states, forest cover varied from a low of 30.6 percent in Delaware to a high of 63.2 percent in Massachusetts. The corridor runs straight through Connecticut, the fourth most densely populated state, and one that is more than 60 percent forested.

Three out of four residents live in or near land under enough trees to be called forestland if they weren't there. John C. Gordon, the former dean of the Yale School of Forestry in New Haven, made a similar observation in speeches.

"If you looked down at Connecticut from on high in the summer, what you'd see was mostly unbroken forest," he said. "If you did the same thing in late fall after the leaves have fallen from those trees, what you'd see was stockbrokers."

PART TWO

WILD BEASTS

For millennia before Europeans found the New World, Native Americans depended on wild animals, birds, and aquatic life for their survival and well-being. They harvested this bounty for food, clothing, shelter, tools, decorations, and spiritual symbols. They established trading relationships between cultures and regions, bartering what they had for what they lacked. Indians were omnivores, and most tribes were the most significant predators of the wild animals and birds in their domains. However, because their numbers were relatively small, and because they practiced various forms of habitat management on behalf of the wild creatures they killed, some historians don't believe that the negative impact they had on wild populations was great.

The arrival of Europeans changed that, and the consequences were eventually catastrophic to wildlife. The fishermen, explorers, and traders who came in the sixteenth century established barter relationships with Indians eager to exchange beaver pelts, deer hides, and other furs they had in abundance for an array of manufactured products: metal knives and ax heads, brass kettles and other cooking utensils, fishhooks and sewing needles, woven cloth and blankets. These items may seem basic, but to Indians they were technological advancements as eagerly sought as the latest digital touchpad is today. What began as simple barter grew into what history books called "the fur trade," a feeble euphemism for the massacre of animals that grew and spread across the landscape to supply voracious markets across the Atlantic, and a phrase that belittles the enormous economic importance of furs, skins, and hides in New World discovery and settlement.

Like Indians, European colonialists hunted and gathered wild bounty to feed and clothe their families as a supplement to the livestock and seed they brought with them to establish pastoral communities. Often, pioneer settlers existed on deer, turkeys, fish, and other wildlife, along with meager provisions packed in, while they cleared forest to grow crops. As their numbers grew, these settlers—so-called pot hunters because they harvested wildlife for the family pot—exacted a toll on the wild animals and birds around them. But that toll was dwarfed by the fur trade and by a budding corps of professionals called market hunters who sold their bounty for profit.

Market hunters killed anything they could sell as meat, hides, fur, and feathers. They operated under no rules except those of free marketplace supply and demand, and demand for their harvests soared in the first half of the nineteenth century as the westward expansion accelerated and European immigrants poured into the newly created United States of America. Between 1810 and 1850, the population tripled to more than 23 million, and the hunters found ready markets for deer, turkeys, geese, and ducks at local meat markets, restaurants, and households. If they had ice, they could pack their bounty in it and send it off to more distant buyers. The markets for fish, fur, and feathers were international. Market hunters killed whooping cranes, ibises, pelicans, terns, plovers, swans, and other birds with unique or colorful feathers and sold their plumage to milliners in New York and London who turned them into women's hats and feather boas.

The last half of the nineteenth century, when the U.S. population tripled again to 76 million, became known as the era of wildlife extermination. Railroad construction boomed after the Civil War, opening up new territories to exploitation and settlement. Repeating rifles became plentiful and inexpensive, and they made the killing cheaper and easier. Railroad-building crews and logging camps took plenty of cheap wild protein. By 1867, refrigerated railcars could keep meat fresh for ten days in the summer, thus expanding markets for game to faraway restaurants and meat markets in Chicago, St. Paul, Boston, Omaha, New York, and Philadelphia. As a result, populations of deer, turkeys, bison, elk, and many other edible or otherwise valuable species were wiped out across huge tracts of the landscape. Songbird eggs were looted to sell for food or to collectors. Species once considered to be so plentiful as to be inexhaustible were decimated. Some were threatened with extinction. Some, including the passenger pigeon, became extinct.

. . .

For more than 350 years, the exploitation of wild animals and birds in North America grew slowly but steadily, reaching a crescendo in the late nineteenth century. By then, the carnage had become so egregious that it, combined with forest destruction, triggered a backlash called the conservation movement. A few men—a handful of wealthy eastern big-city aristocrats, really—began to talk about putting an end to the slaughter. Editorials in *Forest and Stream,* a weekly magazine, by editor George Bird Grinnell, and books and articles by the young outdoorsman and politician Theodore Roosevelt, among others, gave voice to a small movement intent on stopping it. The movement's initial focus was on saving wild birds from plume hunters and hatmakers, and protecting what was left of big game and habitat in the West. It eventually expanded to develop broad goals for the natural landscape, including the preservation of remaining forests and the reforestation of cutover lands, saving threatened wild species and restoring healthy wild bird and animal populations. These efforts took more than one hundred years and involved state agencies, private groups, and the federal government. Laws were enacted outlawing market hunting, but adequate enforcement took decades. And it took even longer to convince most farmers, ranchers, and government agents to stop killing off predators such as cougars, wolves, and bears.

State and federal governments set aside wild habitat by creating refuges, publicly owned forests and parks. In place of market and pot hunting, they adopted what became known as the North American model of wildlife conservation, in which wild creatures were managed by governments on behalf of all citizens. It gave everyone access to wild bounty under rules designed to propagate wild populations on a sustainable basis. To allow wild populations to rebound, states imposed moratoriums on hunting and trapping, some lasting for many years. They also set limits on the number and sex (males only) of birds or game animals that could be killed and the times of year they could be pursued. Just as important were ambitious programs to catch birds and animals from remnant populations in isolated areas and move them back into places where they had been wiped out in hopes that they would reproduce and proliferate.

What the founders of the conservation movement didn't think about was sprawl. When the first federal and state wildlife agencies were established in the late nineteenth and early twentieth centuries, sprawl didn't exist. In its place were family farms that made up a vast agricultural landscape, largely devoid of trees except for small woodlots. This was a working landscape that held at its peak some 31 million people living on 6.1 million farms. Both wild flora and fauna were very much controlled. Pheasants, for example, were encouraged. Weasels weren't. This control was sometimes benign, such as putting up a scarecrow to deter crop damage, and sometimes lethal, such as injecting a chicken's egg with strychnine to kill the proverbial fox in the henhouse. Guns and traps were kept handy as well. This farm acreage amounted to a huge doughnut of managed land around big cities, towns, and villages. It separated most people from the forest, or what was left of it, and its wild inhabitants. The doughnut, however, began to shrink from the 1940s on.

Early postwar suburbs weren't very friendly to wildlife. But that didn't matter because, except for the odd squirrel and a few birds, there were precious few wild creatures around. Turkeys, bears, beavers, geese, and other wildlife were just beginning to recover. They were in distant redoubts and refuges. Eventually, however, the conservation movement produced miraculous comebacks of many wild species across a landscape of regrown forests filling up with sprawl dwellers. And that is when relations between man and beast began to go awry.

Growing populations of wild animals and birds became habituated to life with or near people. Sprawl became their home. To be sure, many species showed little or no appetite for sprawl, which fragments habitat, disrupts migration and travel patterns, reduces species diversity, and adversely impacts native habitats in other ways. For many species, however, sprawl had all the things that they needed to thrive, foremost among them being food, protection, and hiding places. Even species known to be people-shy—wild turkeys and bears, for example—accommodated as their numbers grew.

In fact, the living arrangements of many Americans today amount to a vast wildlife management regime, although most people in my experience don't think of it that way. Sprawl dwellers planted grass, trees, shrubs and bushes, and flower and vegetable gardens. They created backyard habitats with ponds and native plants, and put out food so they and their children could observe, firsthand, any wild creatures that might turn up. Sprawl institutions, including malls, corporate campuses, food outlets, schools, and hospitals, installed Dumpsters that became cafeterias of wild creatures.[14] Local governments adopted rules to protect residents from practices thought to be unsafe, such as discharging a firearm,

---

14. In 1935, George R. Dempster conceived of a large detachable container to use on construction sites that didn't have to be emptied often. Patented as the Dempster Dumpster, this cost-cutting container revolutionized the garbage and waste-hauling industry. It also allowed food waste to pile up for days.

or inhumane, such as trapping. Across this landscape, a menagerie of so-called subsidized species proliferated. This was, in the minds of many residents, wonderful. For others, the results weren't difficult to foresee. Conflicts between people and wildlife mounted. People began to argue about what to do and who to blame.

Chapter Four

The Fifty-Pound Rodent

Don LaFountain pulled his white Ford Ranger off the highway, hopped out of the cab, walked around back, and lowered the tailgate. He grabbed a pail of tools and two contraptions that looked like wire-mesh suitcases, which he dropped down the road embankment beside murky water in a flooded woodlot. Then he drove his pickup sixty yards to a convenience store parking lot and walked back to his job site.

LaFountain, a barrel-chested fifty-year-old with a neatly trimmed beard and a gentle manner, tried not to call attention to his work. That wasn't easy on a highway full of morning commuters in central Massachusetts on a snowy spring morning. We were on Route 12 near Oxford, across the road from a Walmart. I was there trying to get a feel for what it was like to be a soldier in one of the more bizarre battles in America's new wars over wildlife—this one playing itself out in the Bay State, over beavers.

The state's beaver population was burgeoning, and so were complaints about beaver damage. They were gnawing down prized ornamental trees in expensively landscaped yards. They were building dams that were backing up water and creating swamps and ponds and flooded roads, driveways, basements, backyards, wells, septic systems, sewers, railroad culverts, utility line towers, and all sorts of other structures that had been built in low-lying areas in an era when people gave no thought to an animal they had never seen. Why should they? There was no reason to think about a creature that hadn't existed in the state for two and a half centuries.

Beavers had been wiped out of Massachusetts by 1750, and the only beavers residents could remember were Bucky Beaver, the 1950s TV star of Ipana toothpaste commercials ("Brusha brusha brusha, get the new Ipana"), and an eight-year-old named Theodore "Beaver" Cleaver in the 1957–63 TV sitcom *Leave It to Beaver*. But by 2002, real beavers were very much back—an estimated seventy thousand of them, and counting. That meant more people and beavers living together than at any time in the state's history. The same was true across much of the nation, and as beaver populations grew they became one of the most problematic wild animals Americans have had to deal with. According to the Wildlife Services Division of the U.S. Department of Agriculture, "Many experts believe that the cost of beaver damage is greater than that caused by any other wildlife species in the United States."

People and beavers were sharing the same habitat as never before. They had similar tastes in waterfront real estate. Both liked to live along brooks, streams, rivers, ponds, and lakes with lots of nice trees nearby. They did, however, have different tastes in landscaping. People liked to plant trees. Beavers liked to chew them down to build dams. "Compulsive damming disorder," LaFountain quipped.

The wire-mesh traps he took out of his truck were designed to catch the beavers alive. When we walked back to them, LaFountain pointed across the water to a large pile of gray sticks. That was the beaver lodge, he said, and it had been built the previous fall or earlier by the beavers in residence. They had also dammed a culvert, backing up water into the woodlot that would have flowed under the road, creating a swamp. Going in several directions from the lodge were water trails used frequently enough by the beavers to keep them clear of grasses, weeds, or debris. One of these trails came along the edge of the swamp near the road. LaFountain said that was a good place to set one of his traps. He took out a knife and cut a six-inch branch from a wild cherry tree nearby, opened a can from his tool bag, and dipped the stick into the brown paste inside. This goop was a mixture that included the secretions of beaver castor gland. He pulled the trap open like a suitcase and, using a piece of wire, fastened the scented cherry stick to the inside top half of the mesh trap. He cocked the trap's trigger and attached a safety ring so it couldn't spring shut while he was handling it. Then he carefully lowered the baited and cocked trap into the swamp and, with another stick, pushed away the safety ring. The trigger, which was now three to four inches below the surface of the water, was set to go off. The cherry stick coated with scent was several inches above the water.

The idea was to fool the resident beavers into believing another beaver had come into the swamp. To challenge the intruder, a resident beaver would follow the scent of the castor gland at night to the trap. To rise out of the water and sniff the cherry stick, the beaver would have to step with a hind leg on the trigger below, tripping it and causing the bottom half of the suitcase to spring out of the water and close with the top half like the jaws of a giant clam. The beaver would be trapped inside but held far enough above water to prevent it from drowning. LaFountain repeated the process with his second trap about thirty yards up the edge of the swamp. When he finished, we walked back to the truck and drove to another work site, near Boxboro, where beavers had flooded a family's backyard and were stealing firewood logs from the stack beside their house to expand their dam in the woods out back.

Don LaFountain was born in Northampton, in western Massachusetts, and began learning how to trap in the early 1960s, trapping raccoons when he was ten years old. He devoured magazines and books about animals and trapping, and spent hours at a time watching predators and prey in the wild. He learned how to skin his catches, remove their flesh and fat, stretch their fur over racks to dry and preserve, and sell the pelts for pocket money.

LaFountain first tried trapping beavers in 1994. Beaver pelts were bringing about $27 at the time. It was interesting work but no way to earn a living. By the time I caught up with him, he had taken all sorts of courses in furbearer trapping and nuisance wildlife mitigation and was the owner-operator of Integrated Wildlife Control, one of hundreds of new companies springing up to resolve people-wildlife conflicts. He carried a Trapper Registration number and a Problem Animal Control permit, both issued by the state. He had been president of the Massachusetts Association of Problem Animal Controllers and an officer of the National Wildlife Control Operators Association. He handled all sorts of complaints about wildlife—squirrels in the attic, raccoons in the chimney—but he specialized in beavers. The wire-mesh live-catch traps he was using during my visit are called Hancocks and Baileys after their inventors.

Don LaFountain knew what he was doing. He also knew that being too obvious about it invited trouble. Sometimes people would stop and ask him, in an accusing kind of way, what he was up to. He didn't blame them, he said. Most people in Massachusetts grew up in cities and suburbs and didn't know much about the natural world.

"Funny," he said, "man's the bad guy and nature's all balanced until something turns up in their attic. Then they need me." Modern suburbanites, he said, were understandably concerned and often frightened by the sound of thrashing in their attic or by the sight of a furry creature in the backyard trying to get into the grill. At that point they needed someone with practical knowledge of wild creatures and their habits that they lacked. As if to illustrate his point, LaFountain's cell phone began to chirp as we were cruising up Route 495.

"Hello, Integrated Damage Control," he answered. He listened to the frantic voice of a woman. "So what exactly is the skunk doing in your yard now, ma'am?" He listened. "No, no. No need to be alarmed. You're perfectly safe. It's not a big problem. I can handle it quickly, usually without any spraying. I'll call tomorrow."

LaFountain said people either loved him for solving their problems or loathed him for trapping and removing cute, furry animals. On occasion, people would confront him as he was carrying a live beaver in a trap back to his truck. He was too imposing a figure to threaten, but they sometimes said, "You're not going to kill it, are you?" It was a question he tried to deflect by saying that the beavers were being captured alive in cage traps, treated humanely, and that his methods not only were legal but had won the praises of animal protection groups. His customers, on the other hand, usually didn't ask. Asking would result in an answer they didn't want to hear. They wanted to assume that the animals causing their problems would be removed by LaFountain and then relocated to some place where they could live happily ever after.

. . .

Castor canadensis is the largest rodent in North America. It is a much bigger animal than most people imagine, with an adult male typically weighing forty to sixty pounds and measuring four feet in length from the tip of its nose to the end of its tail. It has the girth of a Labrador retriever. By comparison, the beaver's aquatic cousin, the muskrat, is about the size of a small rabbit and typically weighs no more than four pounds.

On land, beavers lumber around awkwardly, waddling on their short front legs and dragging their long flat tails behind them. In water, they are torpedoes. Using their tails and hind legs, they propel and maneuver with the speed and agility of seals and sea lions.

Beavers need running water and trees to build a dam and create a pond that serves to protect them from predators. In doing this, they create and maintain their own habitat by impounding water behind the dams, which look like loose piles of sticks but are surprisingly strong and largely watertight. They usually start by pushing sediment, rocks, and sticks into a ridge perpendicular to the stream flow. They anchor tree branches to the ridge and to the bank of the stream, push other sticks through the ridge parallel to the stream and, on this foundation, layer leafy branches and more sticks, twigs, and aquatic plants to form a tight mesh. To stop leaks, they push in mud, sand, corncobs, stones, and whatever else they can find. They gather dam-building materials from as close to the stream as possible to limit their time out of water when they are most vulnerable to predators.

Beaver dams create swamps, or wetlands, which are beneficial to countless other species of fauna and flora. These wetlands are lodes of species diversity, the "rain forests of the North." By chewing down trees and maintaining their dams to keep the water level behind them fairly constant, beavers slow moving water, allowing sediments in it to fall out to create rich layers of soil and, eventually, broad lowland meadows that serve as breaks from the surrounding forest. Beaver dams filter pollutants, help control seasonal flooding, and reduce erosion. Because the beaver is one of the few animals (man is another) capable of engineering the landscape for their own purposes, biologists call it a "keystone species."

In the pond created by their dam, beavers build their homes, or lodges, using the same materials gathered to build the dam. Lodge entrances are underwater. A beaver swims under the pond water to a hole that rises into the dry part of the lodge, a nesting area for sleeping and procreation. The nest is covered with a thick layer of sticks and mud, with small holes for air circulation. Its floor inside is padded with soft grasses and wood chips to absorb moisture. The lodge is home to a monogamous pair of adult beavers; their offspring, called kits, up to two years old; and another litter on the way. Litters typically contain two to four kits, occasionally six. Females usually get pregnant in winter and give birth in the spring.

In late autumn, beavers gather tree branches and other bark-covered brush and store them underwater near the lodge entrance hole so that when the pond freezes over in the winter the family has access to food without having to venture on top of ice and be more vulnerable to predation. The beaver's main predators are man and wolves. Otters, coyotes, and foxes prey on kits, but adult beavers are usually bigger than these predators and can easily outmaneuver them in the water.

. . .

The last glacier of the Pleistocene Epoch was melting away twelve thousand years ago, leaving in its wake a North American landscape full of lakes and rivers—perfect habitat for beavers except for one missing requirement: trees. At first, the terrain was tundra dotted with lichens, moss, and some small cold-weather plants. As the tundra warmed, seeds of woody plants invaded from the south (so did mammals, including man) and within a few centuries—a mere snap of the fingers in geologic time—a vast forest appeared.

Beavers, including bear-sized behemoths, inhabited most of North America where water and wood were available. They ranged north all the way to the edge of the tree line in the Arctic, southeast to peninsular Florida (where alligators are a predator), and southwest to all but the dry, treeless deserts.

The eastern third of the United States, along with the eastern half of Canada, full of glacial lakes, rivers, and forests, was a beaver paradise. Paleo-Americans and Indians made use of fur-bearing mammals going back at least eleven thousand years, and archaeologists found that beavers were important sources of food, clothing, and tools for tribes in the Northeast. Their teeth became cutting and gouging tools, and beaver bones had many uses, including divining the future.

Beavers were relatively easy to find. Their lodges stood out in ponds. Algonquians and other tribes often divided hunting territory into units controlled by families and marked individual beaver lodges to signal that their occupants belonged to a particular family. Catching and killing beavers was more difficult. Indians used a variety of weapons and tools, including bows and arrows, axes, spears, clubs, nets, snares, deadfall traps, and leg and body traps. Sometimes they breached the dams and drained the ponds so the lodge access hole was exposed. Eventually they used guns.

Nobody knows how many beavers existed in North America before Europeans arrived, or, for that matter, how many of them Indians killed for their needs annually. One noted naturalist, Ernest Thompson Seton, made a guess that in the year 1600 anywhere from 50 million to 400 million beavers lived over most of the continent. Even he called it speculation, but these numbers turn up as crude benchmarks in books and research papers on the subject to this day.

Trade between Indians and Europeans along the Atlantic coast and up some rivers went on for a century before the first settlers arrived at Jamestown in 1607. Cod fishermen were the first to discover the bountiful furs the Indians possessed. The furs, of mink, ermine, otter, and sable, could be sold back home for prices that dwarfed what they got for their fish. Indians were eager to exchange furs for the wondrous European tools and fabrics. Indians along the Gulf of St. Lawrence were so eager to trade that when the French explorer Jacques Cartier arrived in 1534 he found them on shore holding up beaver pelts on sticks in an effort to lure him and his crew to land and trade. Cartier's reports on subsequent voyages up the St. Lawrence River, where beavers abounded, got the attention of European hatmakers.

While the beaver's fur was valued among Indians and, later, Europeans for its comfort and warmth, it was especially prized by the makers of felt hats. Beaver felt hats were already fashionable among Europeans by the sixteenth century—so much so that the rodents became extinct in western Europe and nearly extinct in Russia and Scandinavia. The arrival of North American beaver pelts kept the industry going for another three hundred years.

By the time Henry Hudson arrived in 1609, the Indians along the Hudson River had become well practiced at the barter drill with Europeans. On one of his first visits ashore on the western side of the river, Hudson and his men were invited into a roundhouse made of bark where

Indians had laid out an array of furs to trade. Dutch traders quickly discovered what fishermen and explorers had learned in previous decades: that the Indians could supply great quantities of fur of excellent quality. Soon, colonists at Fort Orange (Albany) and New Netherland (New York) were making trading deals with various Indian groups who brought furs down rivers in their canoes. These furs, overwhelmingly beaver pelts, would be used by colonists to pay investors back home who had staked their voyages and settlements.

Thomas Weston had the same arrangement in mind when he helped organize the Merchant Adventurers of London and raise a reported seven thousand pounds sterling to stake the voyage of the *Mayflower* and the settlement of its Pilgrims in 1620. But when the *Mayflower* returned to England the next year empty, the investors were chagrined. Malnourished, sick, periodically squabbling with Indians, the Pilgrims were preoccupied with survival. In November 1621, on another ship, named *Fortune,* they managed to send five hundred pounds sterling's worth of beaver pelts, dried sassafras for curing syphilis, and split oak for making barrel staves, but it was seized by French privateers and its cargo lost. Trade with the Indians came to a complete halt in 1622 after Myles Standish's disastrous raid at Wessagusset in which two Indian leaders were savagely stabbed to death and others killed. Word of the "massacre" spread among nearby tribes. Fearing they were next, the Indians fled their villages. Suddenly the Pilgrims had lost their chief source of income. In 1625, some of them went on a trading mission up the Kennebec River at what became Augusta, Maine, and returned with four hundred beaver pelts. Later, the Pilgrims established a highly successful trading outpost there. But in 1626, the Merchant Adventurers, figuring they'd never get paid back, let alone make a profit, cut their losses and sold their shares to eight Pilgrim leaders for £1,800. The fur trade picked up in the 1630s, when the *Mayflower* Pilgrims shipped more than two thousand beaver skins to England. Wrote Nick Bunker in *Making Haste from Babylon: The Mayflower Pilgrims and Their World*: "Without the fur trade, the colony would have failed, and the name of the ship would have faded into oblivion."

A much different story unfolded in what became New York City. It is ironic that the city today is a focus of protests against sellers and wearers of fur because New York City owes its very existence and location to fur in general and to the beaver in particular. Indeed, the rodent was deemed so important that the city's official seal, created in 1686, depicts five living creatures: an eagle, a European sailor, an Algonquian Indian, and *two* beavers.

Manhattan Island, Dutch explorers quickly realized, was an ideal place for a colonial settlement. In 1625, New Netherland traders bought some five thousand beaver pelts and 460 otter skins from Indians and shipped them home. On May 24, 1626, only twenty days after he arrived to see it for the first time, Peter Minuit, the new military commander of the colony, "bought" Manhattan from some local Indians for sixty guilders' worth of European-made goods (later calculated to be worth $24 at the time of sale). News of the purchase arrived in Amsterdam four months later aboard the ship *Arms of Amsterdam*. Waiting for it on the dock was a Dutch official named Pieter Schaghen. When Schaghen heard the news, he wrote a letter to his bosses in The Hague. Because other documentation of the purchase hasn't been found, wrote Russell Shorto in *The Island at the Center of the World*, the Schaghen letter "is, in effect, New York City's birth certificate."

The importance of colonial fur was obvious from the letter:

High and Mighty Lords
My Lords the States General
At The Hague
High and Mighty Lords:
Yesterday, arrive here the Ship the Arms of Amsterdham, which sailed from New Netherland, out of the River Mauritius, on 23rd September. They report that

our people are in good heart and live in peace there; the Women also have borne
some children there. They have purchased the Island Manhattes from the Indians
for the value of 60 guilders; it is 11,000 morgens in size. They had all their grain
sowed by the middle of May, and reaped by the middle of August. They send
thence samples of summer grain; such as wheat, rye, barley, oats, buckwheat,
canary seed, beans and flax. The cargo of the aforesaid ship is

> *7246 Beaver skins*
> *178½ Otter skins*
> *675 Otter skins*
> *48 Mink skins*
> *36 Wildcat skins*
> *33 Minks*
> *34 Rat skins [muskrat]*
> *Considerable Oak timber and Hickory*

Herewith, High and Mighty Lords, be commended to the mercy of the Almighty,
In Amsterdam, The 5th of November Ao. 1626

Your High Mightinesses' obedient,
P. Schaghen

Americans who think trapping is inhumane and wearing fur is repugnant might be astonished to learn how important a role beavers played in North American history: The exploration and conquest of the northern United States and Canada were propelled in large part by the economic rewards of finding, catching, killing, eviscerating, and skinning these fifty-pound aquatic rodents. The reason was that Dutch, French, and English explorers to the New World, unlike the Spanish, found no gold and treasure. But they did find a paycheck. The beaver became America's first commodity animal. Beaver pelts became a currency. Trade in them created an economic network that spanned the Atlantic Ocean from the New World wilderness to the royal courts of Europe and lasted for 300 years. The network's tentacles connected Indian hunters and trappers to frontier trading posts, middlemen, transporters, exporters, processors, and sellers.

The fur trade kick-started trans-Atlantic capitalism, built fortunes in Europe and America, fueled the economic development of western Europe, and lay at the heart of relationships, good and bad, between Europeans and Indians. Yet its importance was largely overlooked by nineteenth- and twentieth-century historians and was relegated in large part to writers of pulp novels about brave men and adventurers out on the frontier. In reality, beaver fur was at the heart of "the struggle for dominion in America," Paul Chrisler Phillips asserts in *The Fur Trade*. The furs of mink, otter, ermine, and sable were considered to be more luxurious, but it was the beaver pelt that dominated the trade by far. Beavers were plentiful, easy to find, and so relatively easy to kill that conservationists would later liken their exploitation to mining.

Beaver fur itself was made into coats and robes, attached to collars and cuffs of other garments, and turned into fur wraps and scarves. But its primary use was to make felt for hats, a fashionable and expensive necessity for men and many women. These hats show up in the paintings of Rembrandt, Rubens, Vermeer, and other artists. They were sturdy, flexible, and water resistant, lasted a lifetime, and came in many shapes and styles, including top hats, bonnets, ornate wide-brimmed military covers, and other formal headgear. In 1641, Samuel Pepys, the London diarist, paid the equivalent of three months' wages for his.

By 1650—more than a century before the thirteen colonies became the United States—the beaver populations in the streams from the lower St. Lawrence Valley in the north down through the coastal plain from Maine to the Carolinas had been all but eliminated. As beavers dwindled and competition for them grew, Indian traders had to push deeper into territory controlled by other Indian traders, and European traders began to court their competitors' suppliers. These tactics fractured alliances, set off rivalries, and touched off tribal wars. As more and more

Europeans arrived, both upstart and established traders pushed inland, seeking direct access to remote beaver-catching tribes in order to trade for furs directly, cut out Indian middlemen, and, in so doing, increase profits.

With beavers largely extirpated east of the Appalachians, English traders and their Indian partners moved west into the Ohio Valley and the Great Lakes region, alarming the French and their Indian partners in Canada. The French responded by building forts on Lake Champlain, the Niagara River, and other places and sending troops into the Ohio Valley. The French moves, in turn, alarmed Indian trading partners of the English—the six nations of the Iroquois League (Mohawk, Seneca, Cayuga, Oneida, Onondaga, Tuscarora). The League accused the English of reneging on agreements to protect them. Tensions peaked in 1753, when an angry Mohawk chief named Theyanoguin came to Manhattan, then in English hands, to make the accusation face to face. According to the Revolutionary War historian Richard M. Ketchum, the chief stomped out with his braves, saying in parting, "So, brother, you are not to expect to hear of me anymore, and, brother, we to hear no more of you."

With that, a very fruitful century-old agreement between the colonists and the Iroquois League was imperiled, and so was the continuing supply of the most lucrative commodity from the New World. Now, in turn, the London colonial administrators were alarmed, and they ordered the governor of New York to negotiate a new treaty. The governor sent invitations to the other colonies—Massachusetts, New Hampshire, New Jersey, Pennsylvania, Maryland, and Virginia—to a meeting in Albany. It convened with twenty-four delegates on June 19, 1754.

Benjamin Franklin was one of Pennsylvania's delegates. Little more than a month before, on May 9, he had published in his *Pennsylvania Gazette* a political cartoon: a drawing of a snake cut into eight pieces representing the colonies and a caption that read, "JOIN or DIE." Franklin tried to enlist support for what became known as the "Albany Plan of

Union." He failed, but the delegates did vote unanimously to establish a committee of colonies to study "whether a Union of all the Colonies is not at present absolutely necessary for their security and defense." The seed of the idea of union was planted. Franklin's plan, in turn, guided the First Continental Congress in 1774 and became the essence of the union adopted by the Constitutional Convention of 1787. As Ketchum wrote: "Improbable it may seem, but an industrious, aquatic, fur-bearing rodent deserves a share of the credit for the first real effort at unifying Britain's American colonies."

Before the English lost the thirteen colonies, however, they had conquered New France (Canada) and with it a continuing stake in the fur trade. With the 1763 Treaty of Paris, ending the French and Indian Wars, the French turned their Montreal trading operations over to the English.

In 1803, Thomas Jefferson, the third president of the United States, bought the Louisiana Territory from Napoleon Bonaparte for $15 million, doubling the size of the United States. In 1806, Captain Meriwether Lewis and William Clark returned from their two-year exploration of the Missouri and Columbia rivers, confirming the abundance of beavers west of the Mississippi River, the tastiness of roasted beaver tail, and the passage to beat the English to western furbearers. Beavers, however, were dwindling. As early as 1821, in response to a decline in beaver pelt production continent-wide, the Hudson's Bay Company in Canada tried to implement a conservation policy. It failed. This was still the golden age of wildlife exploitation in North America. Profits and greed ruled. By the 1830s, the beaver population of North America had been reduced to an estimated 9 million, and those animals were concentrated in the isolated Northern Rockies and western reaches of the continent. However, before trappers could push into those regions to extract them, the market for beaver pelts collapsed.

In the early 1830s, three things came along just in time to keep the beaver from being completely wiped out: nutria, silk, and cholera. The nutria, or coypu, is an aquatic rat (*Myocastor coypus*) found in South America. Smaller than a beaver but larger than a muskrat, it has webbed feet and a long round tail. The fur of nutria mimics the beaver's in many ways, and it was, at the time, plentiful and much cheaper than beaver. With this big economic advantage, nutria fur exports from South America to Europe soared, and felt made from nutria gradually replaced beaver felt. At around the same time, inexpensive silk from China was making its way to European hatmakers, and silk hats, with their different color and feel, became highly fashionable and affordable. Asiatic cholera reached Europe in 1830, and people blamed its spread in part on contaminated clothes. They stopped buying fur and started throwing out or burning what they had. According to James B. Trefethen, author of *An American Crusade for Wildlife*, in 1831 beaver pelts were selling for $6 a pound in St. Louis. Two years later, the price had dropped to $3 a pound.

From roughly 1500 to 1900—a period nearly double the time the United States of America has existed as a nation—tens of millions of beavers were killed across the continent, until only remnant populations survived in isolated regions of Canada and the United States. By 1894, New York's Adirondack Mountains, the largest wild forested landscape in the eastern United States, was down to a single colony of five beavers. By some estimates, only one hundred thousand or so beavers were left on the entire continent, most of them in the Canadian outback.

· · ·

One of the motivations conservationists had for restoring healthy populations of beavers was so they could build dams and re-create the rich wetland ecosystems that had long been regarded as useless swamps to be drained and destroyed. Actually bringing beavers back wasn't difficult. Canada could supply the beavers. The question was, Where to put them? Huge swaths of old beaver habitat had been destroyed. If transplanted beavers were to survive, they needed plenty of streams, lots of trees, and no predators. The Adirondacks were one logical choice. In 1892, New York created Adirondack Park and vowed in its state constitution to keep it "forever wild." The park had lots of trees but, by then, no wolves. They had been destroyed as vermin.

Between 1901 and 1907, state wildlife agents released thirty-four Canadian beavers into the Adirondacks and outlawed trapping them. By the end of 1907, the population had grown to an estimated one hundred animals. Eight years later, in 1915, the Adirondacks had an estimated fifteen thousand beavers, and in 1923 New York State authorized an annual trapping season, not for fear of overpopulation, but because wildlife agencies in those days believed in consumptive use of wild resources and saw their role as providing controlled citizen-trapper access to a plentiful, renewable resource. Nonetheless, with no other major predators, beavers thrived and expanded their habitat. From one family of five in 1895, New York's beaver population grew to some eighty-one thousand in 1995. Long before that, in 1928, they spilled into western Massachusetts.

The idea that beavers could become a scourge didn't arise, and the potential seriousness of conflicts between people and beavers went largely unforeseen. Remember, beavers were gone from the landscape before colonists settled it. Europeans and beavers never lived together. Settlers found lush beaver-engineered lowland meadows but no beavers. During the nineteenth and twentieth centuries there was no reason to think about beavers either but every reason to think about building the nation's infrastructure efficiently and cost-effectively. That meant you didn't build a road over a mountain when you could go around it. That meant laying out railroad tracks, roads, highways, water pipes, and drainage systems in valleys, beside rivers, and in relatively flat lowlands. Along these same routes went utility poles, electricity lines, and telephone wires. Planners laid out these arteries with periodic flooding in mind, but not flooding caused by beavers. Yet much of the vast grid that keeps America moving and humming was built on prime beaver habitat. So were a lot of homes. As people sprawled out, beavers sprawled in, and with populations of both growing and spreading, conflicts were inevitable. Young beavers, tossed out by their parents in their second year, go off looking for a mate and flowing water to dam up for a new homestead. Sometimes this means simply moving a little ways upstream or downstream. Sometimes it means traveling many miles and discovering a nice little creek in someone's backyard where a fireplace woodpile offers ready-cut construction materials.

By the mid-1980s, Massachusetts was the third most densely populated state in the Union, behind New Jersey and Rhode Island (New York was seventh), and much of its population had sprawled far beyond Boston into distant exurbs and rural areas. The state's beaver population had grown to an estimated eighteen to twenty thousand, and although damage complaints hadn't grown to levels deemed unacceptable, wildlife officials believed that the beaver population's *social* carrying capacity was near. In contrast, *biological* carrying capacity means the point at which the beaver population (or any other species) reaches the limit of food and other resources that its habitat can sustain. Its adjunct, *ecological* carrying capacity, is the point beyond which a species adversely affects its habitat and the flora and other fauna within it. *Social* carrying capacity is more subjective. The phrase was coined to designate the point at which problems or damage caused by a wild population outweigh its benefits in the public mind.

Massachusetts wildlife biologists decided that an ecologically beneficial and socially acceptable population of beavers was around twenty thousand. To maintain that number meant eliminating population increases. Trappers were logical population control surrogates. They would pay the state for an annual trapping license and recoup some of their costs by selling beaver pelts on the commercial fur market. The rationale for trapping was quite straightforward and spelled out many times. Here is how state and federal wildlife biologists from New York and Massachusetts put it in 1998:

> Management of beaver for sustained yield provides the benefits of wetlands creation and enhancement, while holding populations to socially acceptable levels. The fur trapper has been the instrument for management. In both New York and Massachusetts, wildlife managers at the sub-federal level balance the benefits that beaver produce with the costs that they impose on society. This is done through the annual establishment of trapping seasons to balance their populations with the social and biological carrying capacity of their habitat.

Because their dams, lodges, and woodpiles are predictably located in lowlands and along waterways, beavers are relatively easy to count. Aerial and other surveys can be very effective in estimating their numbers accurately. The ability to compile comparatively accurate population estimates made the beaver a terrific species for measuring the effectiveness of a state's management program. That is, wildlife regulators could measure in beaver colony numbers the effect of a change in trapping rules. By tweaking the rules slightly—raising or lowering the number of beavers that each trapper is allowed to take, say, or increasing or decreasing the length of the trapping season—and requiring trappers to report their harvests, state wildlife managers could maintain the beaver population at agreed-upon levels.

The system worked well for a while, with the beaver population growing modestly. Around one thousand licensed trappers were removing a few thousand beavers a year. But problems lay ahead. For one thing, trapping was a slowly dying skill practiced as a hobby by dwindling numbers of lower-income, aging rural men, and young people weren't taking it up. Beavers were turning up increasingly in suburban sprawl, where more and more people lived as well, and where trappers didn't like to go. One of the joys of the hobby for trappers was that it got them out into the woods away from people.

Prices for fur pelts fluctuated at international auctions, but synthetic substitutes for fur had tempered demand, as had campaigns against trapping and wearing fur coats conducted by animal protection groups who said doing so was inhumane. Antitrapping sentiment had sprung up and grown in relatively affluent parts of the world. In 1991, the European Union decided to ban fur imports from countries allowing traps that caught animals by the leg, mainly the foot. Foot-hold traps were the most common traps used in the United States and Canada, which exported three-fourths of their $1.5 billion in annual sales to Europe. The ban would have all but ended the North American fur industry, which was fine with animal protection groups but worrisome to wildlife managers. The ban's implementation was postponed repeatedly over the years, but anti-trapping and anti-fur-wearing campaigns in Europe succeeded in lessening the demand for fur. By 1990, fewer than one hundred sixty thousand trappers were left in the United States (compared with 35 million fishermen and 14 million hunters), and most of them were part-timers. The typical trapper, according to the American Trappers Association, earned $18,000 a year in nontrapping income and about $2,000 from trapping after work or on weekends.

By 1996, the Massachusetts beaver population was estimated at twenty-four thousand and damage complaints were growing. The only beaver predators in the state were a dwindling group of about four hundred people who bought trapping licenses annually, and the system for controlling beavers was breaking down. And at that point, animal protection groups stepped in to save beavers from that very system.

The Humane Society of the United States (HSUS) is the largest nonprofit animal protection pressure group in the country. Headquartered in Washington, D.C., it is often confused with local humane societies that run animal shelters. Established in 1954, HSUS grew rich and powerful over the years with campaigns against cockfighting, clubbing of baby seals, caging of livestock, and puppy mills, and, in general, for ending many forms of animal abuse, a category in which it included hunting and trapping. Since 1990 it has used ballot initiatives as a tactic to change laws in states in which legislators were reluctant to do so. Ballot initiatives involve collecting signatures from enough voters in a state—an often costly process—to force the state to put a question directly to the voting public.

HSUS brought its antitrapping campaign to the Bay State in 1996 and, in conjunction with the Massachusetts Society for the Prevention of Cruelty to Animals (MSPCA), helped organize and fund an animal welfare coalition called Protect Pets and Wildlife (ProPAW). The coalition's theme was "Ban Cruel Traps," both the foot-hold and a body-gripper called the Conibear. It easily collected enough voter signatures to put on the fall ballot a referendum entitled the Massachusetts Wildlife Protection Act, or "Question 1." The measure sought to prohibit the use of body-gripping and foot-hold traps except when public health officials decided that their use would end a health or safety risk. It would require trappers to use only live-catch cage traps. The ProPAW coalition spent $1.2 million, most of it from HSUS, in a campaign of television advertising depicting "cruel traps." One of its eight TV spots showed a dog with one leg missing—the victim of a leg-hold trap. Another showed a cat writhing in a trap—implying that pets were also at risk, and possibly even children. The trap shown in the ad had jaws with teeth, like the traps once used to catch bears but outlawed by the state more than seventy years before. Another trap used in an ad had smooth steel jaws but no rubber pads as required by Massachusetts law. Wildlife scientists and researchers routinely used padded foot-hold traps to catch, tag, and release animals without harm.

State officials called the ads distortions. They said that there had been only one documented case in Massachusetts of a pet getting caught in a legally set trap and that that pet had been released unharmed. No child had ever been caught in such a trap. The Massachusetts Division of

Fisheries and Wildlife (MassWildlife) put out one press release in June, five months before the election, asserting that the approval of Question 1 would greatly hamper state efforts to manage beaver, muskrat, and coyote numbers. Increased populations would lead to increased conflicts with people and, in the end, would turn what were valuable resources harvested for fur into pests to be eradicated at taxpayer expense. The press release noted that Massachusetts had forty two trapping laws and regulations—some of the most restrictive in the country—requiring traps and trapping standards that had been validated as humane by the state's Supreme Judicial Court as recently as 1995. Those standards mandated that traps in use must either capture an animal alive and unharmed or kill it quickly. The agency said Question 1 was based on bad science and should be rejected. HSUS protested that the press release amounted to lobbying, which government officials were legally barred from doing. In response, the state's Office of Campaign and Political Finance accused MassWildlife of using state funds in a partisan political way to influence voters and ordered it to stop. MassWildlife, composed of the very people tasked with managing wildlife in the state—the biologists, wardens, and agents with the most knowledge and experience in keeping wild bird and animal populations healthy and minimizing their conflicts with people—was silenced.

The *Boston Globe* came out against Question 1, calling it "misguided." In an editorial, it said that banning body-gripping traps "would result in unchecked breeding of beaver, coyote and muskrat," which "are already a nuisance in many communities and cannot be effectively controlled with the box or cage traps called for in the referendum." It concluded: "Voters shouldn't be asked to fix what isn't broken."

On November 5, about 1.4 million voters (64 percent) approved the Wildlife Protection Act and some 800,000 voted against it.

"Emotion ruled over science, and that's a real problem for wildlife management in this country," Rob Deblinger, an assistant director of MassWildlife, later told Fen Montaigne in the *Wall Street Journal*. "In the city and suburbs, people have a disconnection with the land, so their relationship is basically what they see on television. But in a rural area, you are used to living on the land. You know how to deal with these things because you've been doing it forever."

"The majority of the voting public was very well intentioned but very misinformed," Bill Davis, spokesman for MassWildlife, told the *Chicago Tribune* in 2001. "I think this is what happens when you take a wildlife management issue and make it a political one." Opponents of ballot initiatives said they amounted to "ballot box biology." An HSUS spokesman told the *Tribune*, "The people clearly supported the end of these inhumane practices. There are other methods besides trapping and killing. Whether it is beavers or cougars or bears that are in conflict with humans, the question is: Do we pull out a trap and a gun, or do we deal with it in a modern way?" The "modern way" meant a nonlethal way.

One of the ironies of the Massachusetts ban was that few if any voters knew that one of the traps they had banned, the body-gripping Conibear, had been invented and celebrated as a humane alternative to leg-hold traps. It was named after its inventor, Frank Ralph Conibear, who had spent thirty-two years trapping in Canada's Northwest Territories using unpadded leg-hold traps that he thought were inhumane and inefficient. Conibear decided to try to build a trap that killed instantly, one based on the motions of kitchen eggbeater blades that would snap into an animal's neck and chest and crush it. In 1929, he had a prototype. But nothing came of it until the 1950s, when, in Vancouver, an Association for the Protection of Fur-Bearing Animals was formed, and its vice president, an animal welfare activist named Clara Van Steenwyck, encouraged Conibear to tinker with it again. In 1953, the association funded the manufacture of fifty more prototypes for field testing. These were further refined and went on the market in 1958. The Canadian Association for Humane Trapping and the Canadian Provincial Wild Life Services were so smitten with the new traps that they offered trappers a swap: old leg-holds for new Conibears—free. In 1961, the American

Humane Association awarded Conibear its first Certificate of Merit. In 1970, Queen Elizabeth II, on a tour of the Canadian North, met him to celebrate his achievement. In 1981, the Humane Trapping Committee of the British Columbia government gave Conibear and two others a $24,000 prize for "outstanding creativity in the development of more humane animal traps."

In Massachusetts, however, the Conibear had been lumped into the antitrapping catchall of "cruel traps." But Mark Folco, an outdoors writer for the *Standard-Times* in New Bedford, Massachusetts, called it "the most humane and effective device used by fur trappers in wetlands, set underwater to trap and thus control large rodents like beavers and muskrats. Like a common mouse trap, it breaks the animal's neck or spine when it swims through it, killing instantly, and it's approved by the American Veterinary [Medical] Association."

Ted Williams, a columnist for the National Audubon Society magazine, which generally favored trapping as a way of controlling predators of rare or endangered birds, argued that cruelty was relative: "The 'cruel' Conibears, which cost $18 each, weigh two pounds, and kill instantly, have been replaced by 'humane' 25-pound live traps that cost $250 each and hold the terrified animals for hours until they can be bashed on the head and thrown away."

Bashed on the head and thrown away? He's right, but that's not what voters I talked to thought they had approved. The clear message of the antitrapping forces was: Vote for this initiative and animals won't die. Saving beavers and other animals from the "cruel" traps meant saving their lives. If you were philosophically against killing animals, against killing wildlife for sport or economic gain, against killing furbearers with traps, then relative cruelty probably wouldn't have mattered. You would not be interested in quibbling over what amounted to humane killing or inhumane killing. It would be killing either way, and that's what you would be against.

After the vote, trappers could legally use only the mesh suitcase–like traps that caught animals alive, not their old favorites. Most of them quit. The few who converted caught fewer than one hundred beavers a year. Muskrats went largely untrapped, too. Cranberry farmers complained about burgeoning muskrat populations and the damage they caused by burrowing into the dikes built around their cranberry bogs to keep them flooded for part of the year.

By 1998, as beaver populations grew, Massachusetts wildlife agents claimed they were spending so much time investigating beaver damage complaints that other management duties suffered. The state legislature responded in 2000 by passing a law delegating beaver problems to the state's 351 municipal boards of health, but it didn't give them any money to do the job. The boards normally worried about such issues as measles outbreaks and polluted water. Now they became responsible for deciding if beavers were causing damage and, if so, issuing permits to trap them. Many of them didn't know how to decide. Some faced pressure from residents for or against doing anything. Some boards responded as best they could, some didn't. In some areas, especially in the rural parts of western Massachusetts, residents didn't bother with the health boards. They simply took out their shotguns or rifles and killed problem beavers—a solution dubbed "high-speed lead poisoning." Most suburbanites, however, had to go through the health board procedures and hire a nuisance-wildlife company. By 2002, state wildlife officials estimated that Massachusetts had some seventy thousand beavers. Beaver damage complaints ballooned.

"Beavers Driving Ipswich Batty: Roads, Backyards, Trails Being Flooded," read a headline in the *Boston Globe* in the fall of 2001. By then, residents all over the state were grousing about beavers flooding driveways, chewing down valuable trees, inundating septic tanks and basements, contaminating wells, and threatening town water supplies. Beavers were damming up culverts and causing water in swamps to rise to levels threatening the integrity of the foundations of towers holding electricity and communication lines. Their dams were flooding low-lying commercial forests, damaging timber crops. Backed-up water in beaver ponds soaked into railroad beds, saturating them, causing them to soften, and increasing the threat of train derailments. Beaver dams disrupted the water flows around electric power generation facilities and saturated toxic waste sites, causing leaching.

Beaver damage wasn't restricted to Massachusetts, of course. As populations of the industrious rodent grew, similar problems were reported nationwide. Solving them was a growing expense for taxpayers.

It was around this time when Don LaFountain stopped calling himself a "recreational trapper" and started calling himself a "professional wildlife damage controller." The difference? As a weekend hobbyist, he could sell the pelt of each dead beaver he trapped for $20, more or less depending on the vagaries of the fur auction market. As a licensed professional, he could charge $150 for removing a "problem beaver," $750 for removing a typical family of five, and $1,000 and more for installing "beaver deceivers."[15] By 2012, LaFountain had enough business to restrict clientele to large landowners, railroads, watersheds, and utilities, doing consulting and beaver problem-solving for $75 an hour and up.

Animal protection groups discounted press reports that the beaver population was spiraling out of control. They called them "highly relative and subjective," adding, "What looks like 'damage' in the first stages of return is actually just an adjustment of the vegetation around streams and lakes to the presence of beaver after a long period of absence." They said that trapping doesn't work because new beavers move in and that beaver populations will stabilize themselves at levels dependent on available habitat and forage. For Don LaFountain, whether beaver populations were growing or stabilizing—and it varied across Massachusetts—was beside the point. The fact was that beavers were

---

15. The more expensive "beaver deceiver" or "beaver baffler" systems of pipes and screens would keep the pond below flood stage and allow the beavers to stay. But this way wasn't perfect either. Beavers are clever. Sometimes they find the water intake pipe and plug it, allowing water to rise.

causing a lot of damage that all sorts of residents, businesses, corporate campuses, schools, railroads, electric companies, and local governments would not tolerate. His business was booming.

Voters assumed that trapping beavers alive would spare their lives because the animals could be relocated: that is, transported to a new life in a new habitat, free of the pressures and complaints of modern, suburban man, to live out their lives. It's a nice thought. The problem with it is that relocating wild animals in Massachusetts is illegal, as it is in many other states, for several reasons. While relocation sounds good, live-trapping and moving animals puts them under a lot of stress, and their survival rate is relatively low. The creatures arrive in a strange new environment and find themselves competing with animals already there. They may bring diseases with them. The unstated bottom line is this: Under the laws of Massachusetts and many other states, it doesn't matter whether wild animals are captured in traps judged to be humane or not, they end up just as dead. After they die, they are skinned and fleshed, and their pelts are dried.

Though Conibears had been banned from use by recreational trappers during trapping seasons, municipal health boards now issued emergency permits for their use any time of the year for removing nuisance beavers. The boards didn't have to report how many permits they issued, but state wildlife officials believed that far more beavers were killed this way than during the trapping season. It just happened out of voters' sight and out of mind.

What happens after they catch animals in live-catch traps is called "humane euthanasia." One preferred method is to place the animals in a gas chamber of carbon monoxide or carbon dioxide and asphyxiate them. Another, LaFountain's preference, was to shoot them in the back of the head with a .22 caliber pistol. It was a quick death.

On the last day I spent with him, LaFountain shot four captured beavers, loaded them into his pickup, drove them home, and threw them in a freezer. Later, he trucked the frozen carcasses to an old friend, a former trapper himself, who skinned and pelted them as a hobby. He eventually sold the pelts to another man who resold them at a fur auction. Just as before, the pelts ended up on the international fur market and wound up in China and Russia, where they were made into fur coats and other products. The old trapper gave LaFountain scents from the castor glands he had extracted as payment. LaFountain used them for trapping more beavers.

Chapter Five

The Elegant Ungulate

Each fall some 10 million Americans take to forest and field carrying rifles, shotguns, pistols, old-fashioned muzzle-loaded long guns, cross-bows, or longbows and arrows in a display of armed might that would send jittery potentates scrambling for the barricades in less stable parts of the world. Not here. Here, civic-minded leaders issue proclamations closing schools so kids can join their fathers in this autumn ritual of fellowship and firepower known as deer season.

Here is an informal army equal to the manpower in the ten largest armed forces in the world—China, United States, India, North Korea, Russia, South Korea, Pakistan, Iran, Turkey, and Vietnam—combined. Pennsylvania alone fields a force of deer hunters twice the size of the U.S. Army. These people go off in pursuit of what has been called "the most widely-distributed terrestrial big game animal in North America and perhaps the world," an ungulate scientifically named *Odocoileus virginianus.*

If the goal is to have a good time in the outdoors, then deer season is a success. Although hunters are declining, hunting remains one of the top forms of outdoor recreation, and an overwhelming majority of hunters hunt deer. If the goal is to spur the economy, then deer season is also a success. Deer hunters pump more than $12 billion into the economy annually. They spend more on gear than do fishermen and golfers combined. Besides weaponry, they outfit themselves with night

vision devices for scouting, heat-seeking scopes and trail cameras to lo-
cate deer, global-positioning satellite modules to know where they are,
and all-terrain vehicles to get places fast. They dress up in camouflage
clothing treated to hide the human scent. They buy mineral attractants
and bottles said to contain potent estrus urine taken from female deer in
heat to lure amorous bucks.

If, however, the goal is to reduce a burgeoning population of white-
tailed deer, then deer season is a colossal failure. Licensed hunters kill
more than 6 million whitetails each fall, but that's not nearly enough to
do the job. Deer population densities are so high in some places that it
would take kill ratios several times higher just to stabilize local herds.

A century ago, whitetails had been wiped out of many areas by
uncontrolled hunting. They reached a historic low around 1890 of an
estimated 350,000 animals in isolated pockets of the country. Ernest
Thompson Seton in 1909 put the figure for 1900 at 500,000 in all of
North America. Conservation efforts after that allowed whitetail populations to revive slowly and spread. Yet as late as the 1960s, seeing a deer
was a remarkable event in many areas. By the 1970s, whitetails were
beginning to turn up in places they hadn't been seen before, poking
into suburbs and small towns. In the 1980s, their populations began to
explode, doubling and tripling in the next twenty years. In the 1990s,
whitetails in the United States were variously estimated at from 25 million to 40 million, and in many places their populations were growing
unchecked.

When they were scarce, whitetails were seen almost universally as
elegant creatures, a thrill to watch leaping a fence, tail high. As their
numbers grew, perceptions changed. They became nuisances, even menaces. Some people called them defoliation machines, long-legged rats,
or, as some Pennsylvanians dubbed them, mountain maggots.

By 2006, deer had collectively become a mass transit system for ticks
carrying Lyme disease. Deer damage to farm crops and forests topped
$850 million, and whitetails were eating their way through more than

$250 million worth of landscaping, gardens, and shrubbery. Deer, by their browsing habits, had degraded forest ecosystems all over the East. They were preventing forests from regenerating by eating the plants, woody shrubs, and small trees that grew under the canopies of large trees from ground level to as high up as their mouths could reach when they stood on their hind legs. This essentially removed the habitat of creatures that lived in that forest understory, putting some populations of songbirds, for example, at risk. But threats to forests and songbirds paled in comparison to the whitetail's menace to people in the form of collisions of deer and motor vehicles, which were occurring at a rate of three thousand to four thousand per day. The toll of cars crumpled, people killed and injured, Lyme disease contracted, gardens destroyed, crops eaten, and forests damaged resulted in something of a milestone on March 20, 2005, when the *New York Times* editorialized: "Forgive us if you are among the millions of gardeners, farmers, bird-watchers, drivers, fence builders, claims adjusters, body-shop operators, roadkill scrapers, 911 dispatchers, physical therapists and chiropractors who know this already. White-tailed deer are a plague."

How did such beautiful creatures become so much trouble? Why did the mechanisms devised by nature and man to control the deer population go wrong? Was it a lack of predators, a decline in hunting, changes in habitat, or mismanagement by state wildlife agencies? The answers are surprisingly simple: yes to all. But they are not complete without another factor in which they all play a part: human sprawl.

To look at maps on which deer density is estimated is to see that whitetails live in places where people live: across the eastern third of the country for the most part. Deer biologists say whitetails are quick studies: that is, it doesn't take long for them to discover that the people who have sprawled across the landscape aren't the predators they used to be. The dispersal of a majority of Americans into the countryside in the last decades of the twentieth century, and the attitudes they brought with them, created ideal conditions for a whitetail population explosion. Whitetails are an "edge" species; that is, they flourish in those transition zones where one type of vegetation ends and another begins. Sprawl—including exurban subdivisions, big-box houses on multiacre plots, weekend places, second homes, hobby farms, and even semiworking farms—multiplied the edges and created a mosaic of hiding places, open places, feeding places, watering places, bedding places. Unlike the farmers who preceded them, sprawl dwellers grew all sorts of plants that they didn't eat or otherwise harvest and make use of. With prodigious amounts of fertilizer, water, and hired labor, they grew plants mainly to look at. They created, in the words of Dr. William McShea, a wildlife biologist at the National Zoo in Washington, D.C., "deer nirvana. It's one big edge."

Sprawl dwellers made one more crucial adjustment to this "nirvana." They removed from the landscape the only major predator of whitetails left: themselves. As we shall see, *Homo sapiens* have been one of the top killers of deer since the last Ice Age. But in just a few recent decades, sprawl dwellers got out of the predation business. They papered their property with "No Hunting" signs and, unlike their farmer-predecessors, didn't hunt deer themselves. They passed laws restricting or banning the discharge of firearms, sometimes across whole townships and counties. Those laws, designed for human safety, had the effect, intended or not, of putting large chunks of the landscape off limits to hunting. Many states outlawed the discharge of firearms near homes and roads, and some localities enacted more stringent rules. Suddenly, for the first time in eleven thousand years, hundreds of thousands of square miles in the heart of the white-tailed deer's historic range were largely off limits to one of its biggest predators. Suddenly, an animal instinctively wary of predators, including *Homo sapiens,* found itself in a lush habitat where major predators—drivers being the exception—didn't exist.

In Massachusetts, for example, it is not legal to discharge a fire-arm within 150 feet of a hard-surfaced road, or within 500 feet of an occupied dwelling without the owner's written permission, not easily obtained because sentiment against hunting is high. Because the Bay State is densely populated and has a lot of roads, these rules have the effect of making huge sections of the landscape off limits to hunting with guns. One house, for example, makes eighteen acres around it a no-hunting zone. If you add up the land covered by these two restrictions alone, as Tom O'Shea, Mike Huguenin, and Dave Szczebak of the Massachusetts Division of Fisheries and Wildlife, did for me, you find that they put about 60 percent of the state's 5.2 million acres off limits to hunting using guns.[16]

Sprawl, thus, with its enticements and restrictions, acts as a kind of petri dish for whitetail propagation. In rural forests, although conditions vary widely, deer biologists say a rule of thumb is that ten to fifteen deer per square mile is ideal, forty-five per square mile is too many. In parts of the eastern sprawl, it is not uncommon to have sixty whitetails per square mile, even one hundred. If ever there was a place that needed competent deer management, it is sprawl. But state wildlife managers got used to ignoring sprawl when deer were scarce, and they continued to do so when deer invaded. They preferred to tend to deer management in rural areas where hunters hunted and hunting was popular. Sprawl was messy. Residents usually divided into factions. Some people didn't want deer managed at all. Too many of them sided with the deer. Over and over, arguments broke out about what to do, or not do, about deer. And those arguments, as we shall see, often turned ugly.

· · ·

The ancestors of today's deer crossed into North America from Asia beginning about 3.5 million years ago and evolved into at least thirty regional subspecies in North and Central America. Among them, white-

---

16. In addition, nearly half the state's 351 municipalities impose restrictions on firearms and/or hunting with guns or bows and arrows.

tails established a range across the eastern half of the continental United States and the southern tier of Canada and into Mexico and Central America.

Like cows and camels, deer are ruminants with four stomachs, the first of which—the rumen—is full of microorganisms that break down plant tissue. Deer forage on a wide variety of plant materials, including grasses, leaves, acorns, twigs, bark, and fungi, but will eat pretty much any vegetation when hungry. They eat roughly five to nine pounds of plant matter per day. Whitetails are named for the undersides of their tails, which when raised expose white hair—a flag used to signal danger to deer around them. Graceful, quick, and wary, they can run thirty-five miles per hour but usually scamper only for short distances, until they find shelter from what alerted them. They drop their tails, the white disappears, and they become much more difficult to see. Their coats are a marvel of premicrofleece engineering: Hair fibers on them are hollow, or tubular. These provide insulation to hold in body warmth and to allow deer to sleep in snow without melting it. The hollow hairs give deer natural buoyancy when swimming. Whitetails have keen hearing and an acute sense of smell. Their big brown eyes can spot movement, but they are color blind—so the bright orange worn by many hunters goes unnoticed. They can live ten years or more and attain weights as adults of 110 pounds to more than 225 pounds, with big bucks weighing even more.

As the most plentiful large herbivore, whitetails are prey for a variety of meat-eating animals and birds, and more so when they are weak or young. All sorts of carnivores and scavengers feed on deer, including cougars, wolves, bears, bobcats, wolverines, coyotes, foxes, domestic dogs, fisher, lynx, eagles, even ravens. Fawns are especially vulnerable. Besides man, only dogs, bobcats, coyotes, bears, cougars, and wolves kill enough deer to have any influence on populations. Of those, only wolves and cougars depend on killing deer for food.

Paleo-Americans began preying on whitetails as soon as they arrived from Asia, and they and Native Americans continued to do so as hunter-gatherers in the eleven thousand years after the last glacier of the last Ice Age retreated. Some modern researchers think man was not only a major predator of deer but the top predator. Human populations and their eating habits varied widely over the whitetail's range, but with few exceptions early Americans were omnivores and meat eaters, and for numerous Indian cultures venison was the most important component in their diet. Indians were not the ecologically invisible people living in idyllic harmony on the landscape that back-to-nature writers from the late nineteenth century on portrayed them to be. Eco-Indians became fashionable again in the 1970s, but the idea was subsequently challenged by modern scholars, most notably in the 1999 book *The Ecological Indian: Myth and History* by Shepard Krech III, professor of anthropology at Brown University. Indians were wildlife managers. Indians held spiritual beliefs and followed certain ecological principles in harvesting wild birds and animals because their survival depended on a regular harvest of them. Theirs may have been a relatively primitive lifestyle, but it was a successful one. With the arrival of European traders, Indians abandoned their lifestyle and became earnest fur traders. As with beaver pelts, what the Europeans offered them was an insatiable market for deer hides across the Atlantic. The trade began in sixteenth-century Spanish Florida and spread over the next century west across the Gulf of Mexico, up the Atlantic coastline, and into the southern interior. All sorts of goods and commodities were traded between Europe and the American Southeast, but, according to Krech, by the eighteenth century two were supreme: deerskins and slaves.

Three stages of exploitation would over four centuries reduce whitetails to remnant, isolated populations. Competition for deerskins intensified in the seventeenth and eighteenth centuries as traders from Virginia, Charleston, Savannah, Pensacola, Mobile, New Orleans, Augusta, and other places pushed inland to make deals with Indians. The trade in hides led to extirpation of deer populations in one area after the next. Krech estimated that annual exports of up to eighty-five thousand deerskins in the late 1600s grew to over five hundred thousand skins in the middle 1700s before declining. "The deerskin trade was as good as over after 1800," he wrote. After three centuries of slaughter "inveigled by the white tradesman and underwritten by the European buying public," Indians and traders "left the land [in the East] nearly barren of certain wildlife and the Indians themselves destitute of subsistence and cultural options." But that did not mean an end to deer killing.

A second stage of whitetail exploitation began after Independence as settlers moved west of the Appalachians and the treaties enforced by the U.S. Cavalry pushed Indians further west. Deer in the heartland were still relatively plentiful, but settlers and commercial hunters quickly took their toll. A swell of immigrants created vast new markets for professionally shot venison. Market hunters killed deer by the tens of thousands, supplying venison to Great Lakes logging camps and sending hides to Philadelphia, where domestic tanning and leather goods industries were growing. Factories there turned out leather stockings, hats, caps, gloves, breeches, aprons, waistcoats, doublets, entire suits, coats, belts, shoe uppers, and boot linings. Deerskin could be used to make opaque window coverings, wall covers, snow shoe netting, upholstery fabric, bellows, harnessing, saddles, handbags, book bindings, and bull whips. Antlers were used to make such items as hat racks, knife handles, and buttons. Deer hair was used to stuff saddles and furniture. Deer tallow was used to make candles.

The third stage, the so-called era of extermination in the last half of the nineteenth century, was the worst, and not just for deer. All wildlife suffered, from bison to songbirds. Demand for wild products soared as immigrants poured in and the U.S. population grew to 76 million. Any wild species with any value was killed for meat, fur, or feathers. Money flowed.

"Trains that ran on the labyrinth of tracks across whitetail range were important vehicles, both figuratively and literally, in the species' nearly total demise," wrote Richard and Thomas McCabe. "By rail, millions of immigrants flooded the continent's interior, and millions of pounds of deer hides and venison were drained out."

Across most of the United States by the end of the nineteenth century white-tailed deer were so scarce that market hunters no longer bothered with them. Deer had been wiped out of New England except for northern Maine and Cape Cod (where a herd of two hundred had survived since colonial days). A few thousand roamed the isolated parts of the Adirondack and Catskill mountains in New York. Pennsylvania, New Jersey, Delaware, Maryland, and Ohio had virtually none. In the swampy redoubts of the Carolinas and Georgia, along the Gulf Coast and down the Mississippi Valley, remnants held out. By 1900, white-tailed deer had been reduced to 1 percent of their estimated pre-Columbian numbers.

· · ·

In the first four hundred years of European occupation, the wild animals and birds of North America were killed without regulation or under rules that were spotty, difficult to enforce, and easy to ignore. How could it be stopped? If outlawing the killers didn't work, what would?

The answer, as it turned out, was a scheme to give all the wildlife to all the people, so that each person would, in theory, have a vested interest in looking after it—the so-called North American model. The model evolved from Greek and Roman ideas that some things in the natural world should not be owned, or bought and sold, by anyone. Rather, they should be part of a commons and shared equally. Common rights to water for commerce and navigation, for example, go back to Roman law. In England under common law, the king owned all wild game and other public resources. The Magna Carta, issued in 1215, required the monarch to grant commoners access to royal land for foraging, grazing, fishing, and hunting. As lands privatized through grants to the king's loyal supporters, however, they became the private domain of this new nobility, and commoners were squeezed out. Wildlife on these estates was essentially privatized, too, and the penalties for poaching were severe.

At the heart of the North American model was the idea that wild birds and animals could not be privatized. They should be held in public trust for the benefit of all citizens, not special interests, managed by government as renewable resources, and harvested sustainably or otherwise enjoyed with equal access by all on public lands. This idea evolved out of court cases, state laws, and, eventually, federal laws. The court cases placed the welfare of most wildlife in the hands of states to manage; migratory birds later became subject to an international treaty under federal jurisdiction.

Much commercial trafficking in wild meat, furs, and feathers crossed state lines, and this trade went unregulated despite state prohibitions. Traffickers simply killed wildlife in a state where it was illegal to sell, then smuggled it into another state where sales weren't restricted. Enforcement coordination between states was weak, so conservationists called for a federal law to provide a legal umbrella over state efforts.

In 1900, a U.S. representative from Iowa, John F. Lacey, chairman of the House Public Lands Committee and a staunch conservationist, introduced a bill in Congress making it a federal crime to poach game, fish, and plants and sell them across state lines. The bill was primarily aimed at curbing illicit trade in feathers for women's hats. The bill passed, and later that year President William McKinley signed into law the Lacey Game and Wild Birds Preservation and Disposition Act—the first federal law protecting wildlife and a clear signal that market hunting would no longer be tolerated.

Hunting to feed your family was a different story both before and after the Lacey Act. Early settlers initially lived off the land and whatever bulk commodities they could pack with them. Plentiful wild turkeys, deer, and other game and fish could be relied upon to get them through months or years of clearing the forest and building a house. Before their first crops could be harvested and domestic livestock arrived, they lived much like hunter-gatherers. Even after a farm was firmly established, game birds and animals were hunted to supplement the family larder. These people were poor subsistence farmers, so every bit of free food helped. It was part of the American identity from the beginning that all citizens had equal rights to hunt wild game—rights that were enshrined in some early state constitutions. When rural people needed venison, they went out and killed a deer. In their minds, the right to put meat into the family pot preempted any claims the state made for the same wildlife, and it didn't matter who owned the land on which the meat was taken. This view prevailed into the late 1800s, even though it had become rare for families to subsist completely on what they could raise, gather, or hunt. While supplies of game were plentiful and seemingly inexhaustible, both pot hunting and market hunting continued unquestioned. But as game dwindled, competition for what was left increased.

Into this competition marched the nineteenth-century American version of European aristocrats. In New York, they had names such as Rockefeller, Morgan, Roosevelt, and Vanderbilt, and these men had counterparts in every city. They were wealthy urban gentlemen who wanted wild game not to kill for food but to hunt for sport. They had both time and money to spend pursuing wildlife under "sporting" restraints of fair play and fair chase. To foster their sport, these men sought to conserve deer and other species to ensure a plentiful supply for future hunts. Some of them were rich enough to buy up huge tracts of land. In the second half of the nineteenth century, communing with unspoiled nature became a fad, and upper-class city people flocked into rural areas to find it. What they found was a countryside already occupied. No matter how remote the landscape, people lived on it or at least near it. At the time, the vast majority of Americans lived in rural areas, and among these people were poachers and rural outlaws—or at least that's the way the sportsmen viewed them. Country people didn't think of themselves as outlaws, of course, and didn't like city slickers ramming game laws down their throats. Laws enacted at the behest of outside sportsmen were, in their view, little more than reversions to monarchy.

Rich sportsmen from New York and Boston invaded the Adirondacks, bought up land, and created private hunting and fishing preserves. The land was cheap. It had been stripped of its pine trees by loggers who then moved on. By 1893, large tracts of abandoned timber land—some 940,000 acres (an area the size of Rhode Island)—were held in more than sixty private preserves by rich urbanites. These men stocked their streams and lakes with fish, fed deer to keep them around, and even imported exotic species to hunt. To many locals this didn't seem right, and they took their grievances to Albany, the state capital. In 1899, a committee of the state legislature reported: "The poor, as well as the men of moderate means, are complaining that our forest lands are rapidly being bought up by private clubs, and not without some reason, our [woods] are all being monopolized by the rich; that we are apeing the English plan of barring the poor man from the hunt." As old hunters and guides saw it, said the committee, private guarded preserves as well as regulations on state-owned lands "deprive them of the rights and privileges they have freely enjoyed since birth, all of which some of them claim are un-American and wrong."

By the late nineteenth century, the Adirondacks were home to only a remnant population of whitetails, but it was the largest herd left in New York and the Northeast, and the competition over who got to hunt the deer fell between local poachers, preserve owners and members, and outside sport hunters. Historian Karl Jacoby, in his 2001 book *Crimes Against Nature: Squatters, Poachers, Thieves, and the Hidden History of American Conservation*, described how this competition turned in favor of the sportsmen and conservation: Essentially sport hunters convinced some local residents that they could make more money guiding outsiders on their hunts than they could make poaching deer. Guides realized that their growing business depended on a ready supply of deer to hunt. So, quite naturally, they turned against locals who poached and sided with sportsmen and the need for regulations and enforcement, even turning in their poaching neighbors. The poachers fought back, often out of spite. They set fires in private preserve forests and burned down the barns of neighbors who fingered them to the authorities.

· · ·

By the late nineteenth century, huge parcels of the American landscape—including some entire states, such as Illinois, Indiana, Ohio, and Vermont—had no deer at all, and conservationists realized that limiting the deer kill with regulations, however vigorously they were enforced, would not be enough to rebuild herds. Deer had to be brought in for restocking, provided that suitable habitat could be found to ensure their survival. Fortunately, by this time abandoned cropland was reverting to forest, and logged-out forests were regenerating. These budding forests had lots of seedlings, bushes, and ground vegetation for deer to eat.

Restocking became the proactive phase of the whitetail's comeback. The first recorded effort took place on April 27, 1878. Ten deer were captured from the grounds of the state prison near Dannemora, New York, in the northern Adirondacks, and taken 116 miles southeast to Rutland, Vermont, and released nearby. It would take many decades of restocking to bring back healthy whitetail populations in most states, but not in Pennsylvania and Michigan.

In 1906, fifty whitetails from Michigan's remnant herd were delivered to Pennsylvania and released in specially created refuges there. Eleven years later, Pennsylvania's deer managers were being blamed by commercial foresters, farmers, and orchard owners for crop damage from "too many deer." Aldo Leopold, a U.S. Forest Service conservationist, asserted that in 1931 Pennsylvania had an estimated 800,000 deer but a habitat carrying capacity for only 250,000. In the winter of 1935–36, one biologist reported, anyone who wanted to take a walk along some mountain streams could see fifty to one hundred dead deer in less than a mile. They had starved to death.

· · ·

Michigan's whitetail saga is a bizarre and instructive example of how deer hunter groups and friendly politicians in the state capital, Lansing, fostered overabundance—and then how sprawl dwellers made problems worse.

For my parents' generation, deer hunting was a rare treat, a few days off work to camp out in the North Woods in early winter and a chance to rope a big buck to the fender for the proud drive home. For me, deer hunting was proof that there was a fine line between recreation and deprivation. We camped in a big, cold, damp canvas tent lit by kerosene lanterns, slept on army surplus cots, huddled around a smoky woodstove, and ate burnt eggs at four in the morning. We bundled into prickly woolen underwear and thick red plaids, trudged through snow deep into the woods, and sat motionless on a stump, rifle cradled in an elbow, as day broke and fingers and toes turned to Popsicles.

We went up north because that's where the deer were. I assumed that's where they belonged. I associated them with the pine forest and cedar swamps up there, a place that looked natural and unspoiled, certainly wilder than the open country where we lived in the southern third of the state. Down there deer were rarely seen.

As it turned out, my assumptions about Michigan deer and the North Woods were haywire. The idea that the North Woods was one of nature's wild places where deer lived away from man's intervention, except during hunting season, was fantasy. What I learned later was that whitetails were up north because people had put them there. For centuries, the historic heart of Michigan deer country had been in the south—in a region below a line that ran more or less between Bay City in the east and Muskegon in the west—the so-called Mason-Quimby line. The line delineated two very different forest regimes. Below was a deciduous forest of oak, hickory, elm, ash, beech, and maple trees on a patchwork landscape of forest, swamps, meadows, and ever-changing edges. The vast conifer stands above the line, in contrast, were inhospitable places for whitetails. At their densest, these forests had little undergrowth for deer to browse. Long winters, deep snow, and little food made the region marginal deer country, but it was a good place to be a moose, wolf, or bear.

In the nineteenth century, the Michigan deer population underwent a colossal, man-made, geographical flip-flop. Europeans moved in and rearranged the landscape, and deer populations were "drastically reversed," in the words of Ralph I. Blouch, a state wildlife historian. In the south, European settlers cut down the forest, drained the swamps, killed off the wildlife, including whitetails, and created farms. In the north, pine forests were plundered and the scarred landscape left in logging's wake was slow to recover. On lands nobody wanted, the state designated forest preserves and game refuges. Slowly, this landscape sprouted an array of herbaceous plants, followed by woody plants. A patchwork of bushes and saplings emerged, then a mosaic of open spaces and young trees with edges of brush and other vegetation in between. Fire suppression campaigns and erosion controls helped. Depression-era workers planted hundreds of millions of tree seedlings. The result was new habitat with plenty of food, plenty of places to hide, and few predators, and it would produce an explosion of white-tailed deer where few had existed before.

Hunting restrictions and their enforcement helped whitetails along. The most important of these, by far, was the so-called buck law, which decreed that hunters could kill only males, or bucks. Females were to be spared. Bucks are serial breeders. They inseminate as many cooperative females as they can find during the rutting season. Thus the more does available, the more fawns, and the deer population grows. Michigan adopted a buck law in 1921. It was easy for hunters to understand, and the results—more deer—quickly became obvious. Michigan would turn its old conifer forests into a new paradise for white-tailed deer and their hunters, one that became increasingly important to the economic vitality of the North Woods.

State wildlife agencies were originally established at the behest of conservationists and sport hunters. The commissions that oversaw them were most often appointed by governors. These political appointees, usually hunters and fishermen themselves, were subject to pressure from other hunters, who were also voters. From the beginning of restocking efforts into the postwar era, state wildlife managers generally saw their role as one of producing more deer to hunt while keeping deer populations healthy. States sold hunting licenses and used the money to run management programs. Hunters paid the state to become its surrogate deer managers. Sometimes state biologists would argue that whitetail overpopulation could lead to starvation or habitat degradation and thus that the herd needed to be thinned out. But these recommendations had to be weighed by political appointees who also listened to the hunters who paid their salaries. Too many hunters believed that the more deer, the better. Surveys of deer hunters had long shown that what satisfied a majority of them most was going into the woods on the hunting season's opening morning and seeing plenty of deer.

The specter of whitetail overpopulation was first raised in Michigan in 1937 by the state's first deer biologist, Ilo Bartlett. He estimated the state herd at 1.125 million animals and talked for the first time about a "deer problem." The most obvious way to trim the herd was to end the buck law and start killing does. But most hunters had become enamored with the buck law and the large whitetail numbers it helped create. They had come to believe that killing does wasn't sporting, wasn't fair, and wasn't manly. Men hunted bucks, and the quest was to bring home the wiliest old buck with the biggest set of antlers out there. In reality, the overwhelming numbers of bucks killed were less than two years old, and often scrawny. It took Bartlett four years to convince his bosses that deer overpopulation was real and had to be dealt with. Their first timid step came in 1941, when they opened thirty-seven square miles of Allegan County to a special doe-killing hunt after the regular season ended, allowing camps of four or more hunters to kill one deer of either sex for camp meat. The hunter-campers killed 17,100 deer, most of them females—a great success in herd trimming. But hunters elsewhere in the state were outraged. Even nonhunters railed at the notion of killing females. Under pressure, the game commission promptly canceled the experiment.

Through the Second World War, hunting pressure was relatively light, and deer populations continued to rebound. By the 1960s, white-tail populations had grown to 1.5 million, and it was so easy in the North Woods to kill deer that hunters were informally dividing themselves by skill levels and hunting techniques, by the choice of weapon they used to hunt and the quality of deer they sought to kill. They could choose a rifle with a telescope or a bow and arrows made by hand.

Then something strange happened. The deer population crashed. Michigan deer biologists reported that it had plummeted by 1970 to five hundred thousand animals. For many hunters, this was confirmation that killing females was wrong, although some people blamed vacation home building, road construction, or pollution for the drop.

The real reason, however, was too obvious to see: trees. The trees in the North Woods had grown big and old, a second generation of white pines, cedars, firs, and hardwoods that had grown for half a century largely undisturbed by nature or man. As trees mature, their canopies spread and get dense, blocking the sun's rays from penetrating to the forest floor. The North Woods had become its old inhospitable self. Whitetails had less food. And, of course, deer managers couldn't control the weather. When northern hard winters arrived and snow got deep, the sheltered cedar swamps in which hungry whitetails huddled together in so-called deeryards became death traps.

What to do? There were two ways to stop deer from starving: grow more food for them in place or truck food in. State wildlife managers had long opposed supplemental feeding. They knew hunting clubs and private groups were illicitly feeding corn and hay, but they were loath to allow supplemental deer feeding on public lands. In 1961, however, a severely cold winter changed their minds and they consented to feeding deer surplus government corn "for emergency purposes." That decision, popular with hunters, opened the door to emergency supplemental feeding in the winters of 1964, 1968, and 1970.

The first option—growing more deer food—made more sense to deer biologists, who in the early 1970s persuaded state game managers to launch a $20 million "deer habitat management" program. It was, essentially, a "kill trees to save deer" scheme in which workers tore into the forest with bulldozers, chain saws, and axes to create "ideal mixtures of tree species, age classes of trees, forest openings, and winter cover." Edges, in a word. When the timber prices went up, the state invited commercial loggers to do the work for them. Between 1972 and 1987, loggers and state agents created more than seventy thousand acres of "forest openings"—holes in the woods created to help a creature that had historically lived someplace else. The holes allowed growth of the same young, ground-level vegetation that had fed the whitetail proliferation in the North in the first place and, as a result, created a deer-hunting industry on which northerners now depended.

Growing more local whitetail food, however, didn't stop hunters from trucking in supplemental food. Indeed, putting out food piles became a standard hunting strategy, even though many hunters likened the practice to "putting garbage in the woods" and labeled it unethical and unsportsmanlike. It doesn't take a trained wildlife manager or veterinarian to understand what happens when you aggregate wild animals by drawing them together with food. Any kindergarten teacher will tell you that if you put thirty five-year-olds in a room and one of them has a cold, pretty soon they'll all have colds—and they will bring those colds home to their families. The same thing happens at feeding stations on deer farms and bait piles set out for wild whitetails. One diseased deer leaves a little mucus behind, another deer picks it up.

Michigan wasn't alone: Baiting was permitted in twenty-eight states. Michigan did become unique, however, when in 1994 the first case of bovine tuberculosis was diagnosed in a local deer. Spread by nose-to-nose feeding at bait piles, the virus infects lungs and weakens and then kills its host. By 1999, the disease had turned up in 228 tested deer and six cows. The U.S. Department of Agriculture said it was the only sustained outbreak of bovine TB among free-ranging wildlife ever documented in North America. Baiting was banned in the affected areas.

By mid-1990s, Michigan's whitetail population had exploded in the southern third of the state, where millions of acres of cleared cropland had gone out of production, grown up with trees, and been converted to deer-friendly sprawl. By 2005, more than half the state's deer herd lived in forty-one counties in the southern half of the Lower Peninsula, with densities of fifty to one hundred deer per square mile in some counties. This amounted to a historic realignment of whitetails back to their historic range as well as serious whitetail overabundance. Besides deer, this region now held 8 million people, or 80 percent of the state's population. The suburban counties around metropolitan Detroit—Oakland, Livingston, and Washtenaw—were being overrun by whitetails. The *Detroit News* reported that in some parts of Oakland County there were one hundred deer per square mile. State deer managers said half of them needed to die just to stabilize their populations. They showered these counties with permits to kill does and to kill deer in parks. They lengthened the hunting season and offered landowners tax breaks if they allowed hunting. But most of the special permits weren't used because most deer hunters didn't like to hunt where they lived. For generations,

Michigan deer hunters had gone up north, and the North Woods beck-oned still—now replete with Indian gambling casinos and strip clubs to occupy a hunter's downtime. Observed the *Detroit Free Press:* "The cachet of the trip north apparently still matters more than where the deer are—unless, of course, they get your car first."

. . .

Well before the turn of the twenty-first century, the North American conservation model had broken down as a deer population control regi-men in many areas, and the reasons it no longer worked would have shocked the conservationists who had put it in place a century before: Both the advent of sprawl and a decline in the popularity of hunting were undreamed of back then. Veteran hunters aged and died, and not enough young people wanted to fill their shoes. Youngsters preferred chasing aliens on video screens indoors to stalking whitetails in the au-tumn woods. At the same time, many more people had come to believe that killing deer or any wildlife for sport was inhumane, or, in the case of hunting and killing in sprawl communities where most Americans now lived, unsafe. Thus deer populations across wide swaths of the North American landscape could no longer be controlled by hunting.

. . .

One of the first battles between people who wanted to control excess deer and people who wanted to protect deer from harm played out in western Massachusetts in the late 1980s when those responsible for maintaining a safe, clean water supply for some 2.5 million people in and around Boston realized that they could no longer ignore the fact that the proliferation of white-tailed deer in the woods around the Quabbin Reservoir was putting that water supply at risk. Formerly a farming hin-terland, the region had filled with new residents from cities and suburbs, and when reservoir managers made a decision to do something about the deer, "they stepped into the vortex of conflicting values, definitions, and attitudes that characterize our sense of nature," in the words of Jan E. Dizard, a professor at nearby Amherst College and author of a 1994 book about the Quabbin deer battle entitled *Going Wild: Hunting, Animal Rights, and the Contested Meaning of Nature.*

Amherst, the town, was not only home to Amherst College but also the main campus of the University of Massachusetts. Students and teachers there, and others who lived nearby, enjoyed walking, biking, and fishing in a small section of the Quabbin watershed that was open to the public, and, as Dizard wrote, "they were not about to sit passively by while remote bureaucrats ran roughshod over the pastoral landscape." Many people viewed the Quabbin forests as a wild place unspoiled by people, even though it was obviously a product of human construction.

While concern over the mounting deer population had been expressed earlier, the idea of deer control was not broached until 1988, when the herd within the reservoir watershed was estimated at from 1,500 to 3,000 animals, or twenty to fifty deer per square mile—two to five times more than the statewide average.

A typical forest in the region would have trees of all ages and many species, bushes, tangles of bramble, and other underbrush. The Quabbin deer had eaten away oak and other hardwood seedlings and had cleaned out much of the underbrush and ground vegetation. The landscape under the canopy of old trees looked like a park, and visitors could see through it for hundreds of yards. The trouble was that understory vegetation was vital to the watershed's ability to hold and filter the rainwater that replenished the reservoir. The deer were creating a forest with trees the same age, sparse ground cover, and increasing erosion—all threatening to the drinking water supply. "It looked like the Serengeti Plain, with herds of deer running around like antelopes," David Kittredge, a forester at the University of Massachusetts, told me later.

The public battle over what to do about the deer was loud and angry and lasted two years during which the whitetail population grew to an estimated seventy per square mile. The Metropolitan District Commission, the body in charge of managing the reservoir at the time, considered and rejected several nonlethal options, including birth control, the solution favored by most people against lethal control. It was a pipe dream then, and it still is. More than two decades later, injecting females with fertility-control drugs remains too expensive and ineffective for use on free-roaming deer. The commission also looked at chemical repellents, plastic tree tubes, fencing, and a catch-and-relocate strategy. All these options, favored by those against killing the deer, were flawed and too costly, the commissioners decided.

The commission studied deer predators. Already present were bobcats and coyotes, but they alone couldn't control the deer population. Quabbin was too small to contain the mountain lions and wolves that some people suggested be introduced. Would people nearby with children, pets, or livestock really tolerate wolf packs and cougars? Obviously not. The only viable option, the commission decided, was the least well liked: hunting. Hundreds of people turned up at workshops, open forums, and public hearings in 1989 and 1990. Some carried placards reading "Killing for fun is obscene" and "Stop the war on wildlife." The most radical antihunters were advocates of animal rights who argued that it was morally wrong to kill a deer for sport and that the lives of individual animals mattered. Others argued that since man's mismanagement was the cause of the problem, the obvious solution was for man to get out and leave nature alone. In interviews with Professor Dizard, these people used phrases such as "Let nature heal herself," "Nature knows best," and "Nature provides." Deer and forest would work things out if only man stopped meddling.

While the battle raged, the commission considered three options for killing deer: hiring of sharpshooters, a recreational hunt open to licensed hunters, and a controlled hunt with a limited number of hunters following strict rules. The first option, sharpshooters, was ruled out because

Massachusetts had no government program to certify their competence. Besides, the Massachusetts Division of Fisheries and Wildlife opposed them because the public (hunters) would thereby be denied access to a public resource. A recreational hunt was likewise ruled out because the commission felt it couldn't be adequately controlled and because it would draw the most protest. A controlled hunt was agreed to for the autumn of 1991. While protesters demonstrated and antihunting groups filed lawsuits, hunters killed 576 deer over nine days.

Opponents called the hunt a "slaughter." The leader of Citizens to End Animal Suffering and Exploitation (CEASE) said the hunters had "wiped out the deer population." A few days before Christmas, demonstrators in Belchertown, near Quabbin, lit 576 candles to commemorate each of the dead deer.

"Two weeks ago I lost 576 of my closest friends there," said one.

. . .

I hadn't realized just how contentious whitetails had become for suburbanites until my wife and I went to visit a friend at the Institute for Advanced Study, in Princeton, New Jersey. The institute, where Albert Einstein had worked for twenty-two years and where other geniuses are hired to think and write, had twenty-three permanent faculty members, eleven emeritus professors, 150 visiting research scholars, and no students. It also had 640 acres of woods and corn and soybean fields that neighbors said were a haven for deer. Princeton Township, also home of Princeton University, had watched its whitetail population grow steadily since 1972, when it banned the discharge of firearms as a safety measure and thus ended deer hunting with guns. With lots of lush landscaping and no predators, the deer herd grew from an estimated population of 220 in 1972 to more than 1,000 in 1989. Lyme disease was spreading and deer-car crashes were on the rise. The institute quietly took the lead in culling the herd in 1984 by allowing selected bow hunters onto its property during deer season. Each fall, a memorandum went into faculty and staff mailboxes announcing the hunt.

Days before our visit in 1989, a copy of the memo turned up in one mailbox with a drawing of a deer's head with an arrow through it, and blood, in red ink, dripping from the wound. It was followed by another memo about a Harvard study asserting that a deer "bristling with arrows and plunging about in a vulgar display of agony will effect more damage [to foliage and property] per square foot than a normal, unpunctured and unstimulated deer." The memo contained a graph showing increased damage in square-foot increments as a rising S-curve for each arrow in a deer. "Note: behavior of deer containing more than 36 arrows tended to level off," the memo tweaked. It was signed, "Prof. Nomo Mentum." A few years earlier, an anonymous "interested party" had suggested bringing onto the premises a breeding pair of timber wolves to limit both the deer population and the supply of children and dogs on institute premises. Then there was the "In Defense of Hunting" memo, which argued that the woods were already so dangerous because of Lyme disease ticks, poison ivy, bikers, joggers, dogs, the "occasional flasher," and "some ferocious Princeton students" that a few days of hunting weren't so terrible. Someone also submitted an "eyewitness account" memo: "The arrow went through the doe's neck. We all saw it strike. . . . We came to several pools of blood with prints of her knees beside them." One treatise, attributed to a visiting anthropologist, compared the no-waste deer-killing and skinning ways of the noble Navajo to the wasteful savagery of the white man.

It was all great fun, and in that spirit I decided to call institute members and get their opinions on the deer hunt. Astrophysicist John N. Bahcall said his children "deeply opposed" the hunt. Physicist Freeman Dyson laughed. Historian George F. Kennan had no comment. Emeritus professor Albert O. Hirschman, the economist, noted that in

1984 he hadn't received a hunt memo and reasoned wryly that this was a clever design by the administration to cull the ranks of the professors emeriti who might stroll innocently into the woods.

"I like them. I let them eat the plants in my garden," said Enrico Bombieri, the IBM von Neumann Professor of Mathematics. "The population is too large, but I don't think bow and arrow is a very effective way of reducing it."

"After seeing *Bambi* nobody wants to kill a deer," said Prof. Luis A. Caffarelli, whose major interest was free-boundary problems in differential equations. He suggested catching and moving them. But John Kuser, who teaches forestry at Rutgers and heads Princeton Township's ad hoc deer committee, said that would cost $300 per deer. You'd need to catch and move five hundred township-wide, and since the deer population can double annually you'd have a yearly bill of $150,000. Plus, he said, nobody wanted them.

Princeton Township was similarly divided. Stan Waterman, the underwater filmmaker who shot sharks with a movie camera, walked two black poodles in the institute woods most afternoons and made plenty of noise, which didn't sit well with the camouflaged hunters he occasionally spotted in tree notches. "I find it appalling," he told me. "It's the Rambo mentality." Fellow resident and diver Peter Benchley, author of the bestseller *Jaws,* was all for culling. A deer had wrecked his wife's car a few years back. "If only they didn't have those saucer eyes and Walt Disney behind them," he said. "The Bambi complex seems to have taken over around here."

The Institute's culling had minimal impact on the deer herd in Princeton Township, an area of seventeen square miles. By 2000, the deer population was estimated at 1,600, or ninety-four deer per square mile, and deer-vehicle collisions had climbed to 338. Bow-hunting groups were lobbying to be let in to kill deer, and animal protection groups wanted deer kept alive. Caught in the middle, Phyllis Marchand, the mayor, called Anthony J. DeNicola, a Yale graduate with a Ph.D.

in wildlife ecology from Purdue, who in 1995 had founded a nonprofit company called White Buffalo Inc. and had quickly become a very busy man. He specialized in deer population control, mainly by putting together teams of sharpshooters to cull deer in suburbs. He agreed to take the job. DeNicola's team began by studying the movements of both deer and people and scouting for ambush sites. They set piles of corn to lure deer to sites with clear shooting lanes from tree stands.

Protests began immediately. A group called the Mercer County Deer Alliance was formed to protect deer. It went to court and staged demonstrations and candlelight vigils. Two dozen property owners had given permission to White Buffalo to use their land for baiting stations and shooting sites. One deer-loving resident offered $1,000 to any property owner who rescinded permission. None did.

The sharpshooters used relatively small-caliber .223 rifles with infrared telescopes and silencers to kill deer with single shots through the head. From elevated stands, they aimed down at the deer so that any errant bullets would go safely into the ground. The shooters worked at dawn, at dusk, and at night, virtually unseen by residents. With, say, a dozen deer feeding at a bait pile, shooters aimed at dominant deer (leaders) first, then adult does and the rest (often confused and hesitant) in rapid succession, aiming to kill them all in a matter of seconds. Afterward, they gathered up the carcasses, along with bloody leaves and other debris, leaving no evidence of the cull. Over a ten-day period in February 2001 they killed 324 deer at a cost of about $350 per deer. Mayor Marchand pronounced the effort, the first in a five-year deer reduction program, a success.

In January and February 2002, in the second phase, White Buffalo killed 303 deer by sharpshooting and a technique called the net and bolt method, which involved dropping a net on feeding deer and then quickly killing them with a special bolt gun typically used in abattoirs. Opponents called that method cruel. Demonstrations commenced again. Lawsuits were filed. Opponents hired private investigators to shadow

White Buffalo workers. Mark Johnson, the township animal control officer, started wearing a bulletproof vest after his cat was found crushed to death and his dog was poisoned. One morning, Lucien Marchand, the mayor's husband, went out front to get the newspaper and found deer guts splattered over the hood of his wife's Honda. In a letter to the *New York Times*, the mayor called the program "safe and effective" and said it was "bringing the township's residents much-needed relief from the deer." The cull continued.

. . .

Over the years, I have watched suburban deer wars play out in community after community across the country. Different casts, same characters, same anger, same arguments, same questions, same certainty, same ignorance, same grief. In a 1997 issue of the *Wildlife Society Bulletin,* Jay F. Kirkpatrick and John W. Turner Jr., wildlife contraception researchers, wrote a hilarious satire of the squabbles over deer problems in the fictional town of East Overshoe, based on dozens of such meetings they had attended over the years. They begin with a town gathering attended by at least ten factions: (1) save-the-deer people, (2) people against hunting, (3) people against any management, (4) people who hate deer, (5) officials who want to be reelected, (6) a state fish-and-game representative, (7) shotgun hunters, (8) bow hunters, (9) representatives from animal-rights and/or animal welfare groups, and (10) the media.

Having attended many such meetings myself, I know the drill. Someone rises to say that there are more and more deer around, perhaps too many. Another resident asks, How many deer are there? Another asks what "too many" means. Someone says that "too many" means that deer are causing problems. Officials decide to hold a special town meeting on the "deer issue." It quickly turns into a shouting match.

"My wife hit one and totaled the car last month. Deer are a menace. I say kill 'em all!" says one man.

"They ruined my garden!" says an elderly woman.

"The ticks are so thick I'm afraid to let my kids play outside."

"How can you talk about killing such majestic creatures?"

"We love seeing deer."

"Why can't we leave nature be?"

"Deer have as much right to be here as we do."

"This is a people problem, not a deer problem. We encroached on their habitat."

"Why can't people plant things deer don't like to eat, drive more carefully, and check themselves and their children for ticks!"

At this point, town board members sense they have a political hot potato on their hands and decide to hire an "expert" to find a solution for which they won't be blamed. They task the expert with submitting a report after the next election. The community, meanwhile, is breaking up into factions. Citizens Against Murder is formed and reported on in the local paper. The head of the bow-hunting club in a nearby town reads about it. The local TV station shows a herd of fifteen deer grazing on a local football field and interviews residents for and against deer. A second public hearing is packed with loud and angry residents and lasts five hours. Finally, the expert submits a professional-looking inch-thick study that confirms a "deer problem," and the reason for it is—you guessed it—too many deer. Instead of five to fifteen deer per square mile, as might be found in a rural setting, this lush exurban landscape supports an estimated sixty-five deer per square mile, and there's enough food to support many more.

What to do? Remove deer, the expert opines. How? Lethally or nonlethally? Most sprawl people are against killing deer—at first. Instead, they have gone on the Internet and found all sorts of wonderful ways to solve the problem without killing the deer:

Catch the deer and spray or wash them to remove their ticks. Catch the deer and move them. Sterilize them. Animal rights people speak in glowing terms about how wonderfully birth control works—in limited tests. Lots of people at the meeting have heard about someplace over the horizon where a deer contraception program has been a great success.[17]

Once these techniques are shown not to be panaceas, sober community members, including some initially against killing deer, agree to support lethal removal—but not before someone suggests bringing in natural predators, that is, 150-pound mountain lions and packs of wolves. This person is shouted down.

Now, the path is clear to cull the deer herd. But how?

The representative of a local bow-hunting group has an answer: Give us exclusive permission to hunt deer in your community and we'll solve your problems safely and economically. This is a bow hunter's dream come true: a township full of deer and no hunting competition. The lady from the local gardening club reacts: I don't want deer eating my flowers, but my friend Marsha over in North Ungulate, where they let in bow hunters, says there are deer running around with arrows sticking out of them. It's pitiful, and so cruel. How could we allow that?

An official representing the state game board says screened hunters using short-range shotguns can solve the problem, and they'll pay to do it. Oh my God, says a young mother, guns! Deer hunters are yahoos. They'll kill people, kids, and dogs. We can't have guns in our community. An older gentleman points out that it was fifteen years ago when the community banned the discharge of firearms in West Salt Lick, thereby eliminating gun hunting and creating the current problem.

Then how about sharpshooters? That, as it turns out, is what the consultant recommends. The township could contract them to solve the deer problem for about $350 a deer. Of course, these are taxpayer dol-

---

17. In 2006, the president of the Garden Club of Mount Desert (Maine) and a self-described "gardener and deer lover" told a hearing on the town deer problem that she knew birth control salt licks had worked on elk at Rocky Mountain National Park. When I asked her about this a few days later, she told me she had toured the park and had been told about the salt licks by a ranger there. Kyle Patterson, the park's spokesman, told me: "We are unaware of any use of salt licks distributing contraceptives to elk." Sharpshooters began culling the elk herd in 2008.

lars and they might have to be paid annually to keep the problem under control. The room is abuzz.

"Mercenaries!" shouts a man who turns out to be a bow hunter. Both the bow hunters and gun hunters in the crowd applaud the outburst, eschewing hired guns. The antihunters don't want them either. Now an uncomfortable alliance is forming. Animal rights people, antihunting people, bow hunters, and the gun hunters against the mercenaries are on the same side. This makes a lot of people uncomfortable. Years pass.

That is almost exactly the story that unfolded over eight years in Lower Makefield Township, an affluent, built-up suburb of Philadelphia in Bucks County. A whitetail "problem" was demonstrated in 2002. In 2007, the township's board of supervisors hired Bryon P. Shissler to tell them what to do about this problem, paying him $14,000 to come up with a plan in six months. Shissler, a wildlife biologist, had become an expert on deer issues in Pennsylvania, especially as they arose in the suburbs. Indeed, by 2007 he was among the best in the country and had started Natural Resource Consultants, Inc., to advise communities on how best to solve their deer problems. Selling deer-problem advice and solutions had become a thriving niche business in the suburbs and exurbs. Shissler believed that the deer management model formulated on an agricultural model of growing deer as a crop and estimating sustainable yields for hunters was broken. Hunters had declined in Pennsylvania to just 8 percent of the population, but a new paradigm of managing entire ecosystems for the benefit of all inhabitants, including people and trees, was slow to sink in. Suburbs and exurbs weren't natural ecosystems, of course, but they were ecosystems nonetheless, and they aggregated suburbanites and deer in an increasingly troubling mix.

Shissler knew from previous studies that the residents of Lower Makefield had strong opinions on nature and wildlife in general, and deer in particular, and knowing how to thread one's way through them meant being careful and wording statements and reports delicately. *Kill* is not a delicate word. So when Shissler submitted his report to the supervisors, he opted to recommend "human directed mortality" in the form of hired professional sharpshooters to reduce the deer population.

A year passed. In the meantime, the Pennsylvania Game Commission, backing bow hunters, adopted new regulations for suburban deer control. The commission would not issue the necessary permit for a sharpshoot unless recreational hunting was allowed first. In early 2009, the board voted to award White Buffalo Inc. a $59,000 contract to conduct a sharpshoot. A bow-hunting group, Big Oak Whitetail Management Association (BOWMA), would conduct a recreational archery shoot. In August, Deer Friends, an alliance to stop the culling, was formed with help from Sarah Speed, the state director of the Humane Society of the United States, and Roy Afflerbach, a former state senator turned animal rights lobbyist.

The bow hunters went first, hunting in a three-hundred-acre nature preserve called the Five Mile Woods over fifty-four days and killing only twenty-nine deer. Protesters showed up, police were called three times, a security guard was hired. Costs were estimated at more than $7,000, or $240 per deer killed. Shissler had predicted that the bow hunters would educate the deer by their presence to stay away. That's what happened. When the bow hunters departed and the sharpshooters arrived, the deer were skittish. Most stayed well clear of shooting sites, and only eleven were killed.

Outside the preserve, White Buffalo had asked for twenty baiting and shooting sites. The board, however, feeling pressure from antikilling residents, eventually gave them six sites. Despite heavy snow, the sharpshooters killed 83 deer outside the preserve in two weeks. In all, the sharpshooters and bow hunters had expected to kill 300 deer. Their combined total was only 123—a result supervisor Pete Stainthorpe called "not acceptable."

· · ·

The extended deer kerfuffle in Lower Makefield played out in one form or another in thousands of towns, suburbs, townships, counties, government preserves, and other entities over the years. And because these fights are local, there is virtually no learning curve from one place to another, from one community to the next. The vested interests, on the other hand, long ago honed their arguments and march them from one fight to the next. Local bow hunters can solve the problem, cheap, if only given the chance. Fertility control is just around the corner.[18] Meanwhile, the magnificent white-tailed deer, a visual treasure to behold, becomes a long-legged rat.

18. Most fertility control experiments have been expensive and conducted on deer in relatively confined areas. The first effort, on New York's Fire Island, began in 1993, and its effectiveness is still debated. Besides sharpshooting, White Buffalo conducts such experiments, but its website in 2011 reported that problems and a cost of $600 to $1,000 per female deer "suggests that use of contraceptives will be limited to small insular herds."

Chapter Six

Lawn Carp

Shortly before 3:30 A.M. on a chilly June morning in 1999, Tom Maglaras pulled his Chevy pickup into a parking lot next to the maintenance shed beside Lake Carmel, doused its lights, and cut the engine. Soon, another man pulled up with a truck and trailer filled with forty wooden and wire-mesh poultry crates. By 4 A.M., half a dozen men and two women had arrived at the parking lot. One of the women, Annmarie Baisley, was the ranking politician in Kent, a town of fourteen thousand residents that surrounds the lake in the Hudson Highlands, sixty miles north of New York City. The other, Kathy Doherty, was chairwoman of the town's Lake Carmel Park District.

Maglaras, a licensed wildlife control contractor, and his crew had been hired to round up the Canada geese that lived around the lake. They fanned out in the dark, checking the nylon-mesh fencing and three temporary corrals they had set up on the lakeshore the day before. One side of each corral was left open. Informal polling had indicated that the people who lived around the lake, swam and fished in it, and used its beaches, playgrounds, and walking paths were in favor of removing the geese. The geese were depositing feces and dropping feathers everywhere, creating unsightly and uninviting messes, and, residents claimed, lowering their property values. In 1997, a questionnaire was sent to residents, and 180 of them responded; 80 percent favored removal of the geese and 16 percent were opposed. This was a tiny sample but, officials believed, indicative of the sentiment of residents around the lake. The big problem, as they saw it, was opposition from organized outsiders. The roundup and killing of 452 geese in nearby Clarkstown in 1996 and 1997—the first to occur in the eastern United States after an initial culling project in Minneapolis–St. Paul in 1995—had touched off loud demonstrations by animal protection advocates who came from as far away as New York City and Washington, D.C. Kent officials had spent five years debating, researching, and arguing about the geese and getting state and federal permits to remove them. None of the people now gathered in the dark wanted to be confronted by protesters and television cameras. So only Maglaras, Baisley, and Doherty knew the date they had picked for the roundup until Maglaras briefed his crew a few days before and swore them to secrecy. Maglaras wanted to begin the job in the cool early-morning hours. Town officials agreed because an early start would help ensure that the roundup would be finished before any buses carrying children drove by. They said they didn't want children to see what was happening or to have the town accused by their parents of traumatizing them.

At dawn, some of the men boarded two small boats and cruised out onto the 201-acre lake as slowly and quietly as their outboard motors allowed. Other men climbed into canoes and paddled out onto the water. The boats made wide arcs out and around the back of a flock of about 150 geese roosting on the water. Then the men began moving toward the flock at creep speed. The birds began to stir, honk, and swim slowly toward shore. This was a delicate time. June, in this part of the country, is molting season, when Canada geese lose their feathers and grow new ones over several weeks and are unable to exercise their primary means of escape, which is to take flight. Still, the men had to move carefully to prevent the geese from spooking and perhaps diving underwater to escape. On shore, they could simply run away. The idea this morning was to keep the flock together and moving toward the makeshift fences that would funnel the big birds up out of the water and into the corrals.

All went well. Once the geese were corralled, some of the men waded into a maelstrom of thrashing honkers, grabbing them by their wings and legs and passing them to other men, who stuffed them into the poultry crates, five or six birds to a crate. In all, 125 geese were rounded up and crated. Two dozen escaped. The entire operation was over by 7 A.M., with the crated geese en route to a slaughterhouse in Hempstead, on Long Island. There, they were "breasted," that is, their breasts—the meatiest part of a goose—were cut out of the carcasses, frozen, and eventually delivered to the food pantry operated by the United Way of Sullivan County.

The phone in the Kent town office began to ring around 9 A.M. Word of the roundup had gotten out. For authorizing $8,000 for goose removal, Annmarie Baisley was denounced as "an assassin" and worse. Baisley was a chain-smoking, no-nonsense administrator, but as the number of calls mounted, some coming from far away, and as they began to include threats, she shut down the office early. The first protesters, along with crews from local TV stations, arrived shortly thereafter, one with a placard reading "Baisley the butcher."

Some Kent residents and outsiders never forgave her, but others in the days and weeks that followed the roundup thanked her for removing most of the geese, noting that the lake's picnic grounds, walking paths, and public beaches were, for the first time in years, largely free of goose feces. With far fewer geese defecating, water in the lake became clearer, and tests showed that its quality improved, making swimmers feel safer.

A year later, Baisley was still getting hate mail such as this: "It's time to reflect on your act of sorrow. It's your one year anniversary on sentencing families of Canadian geese to death. Sleep well." On July 11, 2001, a postcard arrived:

Dear AnnMary Baisley,
In living memory of the Canadian Geese that you had assassinated two years ago.
May you never forget the peaceful, loving lives you destroyed.
*   A dedicated resident.*

. . .

Canada geese, *Branta canadensis* (and *Branta hutchinsii*), with their distinctive black heads and necks and white "chin strap" feathers, number perhaps 8 to 10 million in North America and are a collection of at least eleven subspecies ranging from the smallest, the cackling Canada goose (*Branta canadensis minima*), which weighs about three pounds and travels fast and far, to the largest, *Branta canadensis maxima*, or the giant Canada goose, which weighs ten to twenty pounds and migrates relatively short distances. They can live for twenty-four years, they mate for life, and typically begin breeding at age three. Adult pairs try to return to the same place each spring to nest. The female lays two to eight eggs, sitting on them for about twenty-five to twenty-eight days, until they hatch, while the male helps ward off predators, which range from Arctic foxes and gulls in the far North to raccoons and ravens in temperate zones.

One of the beautiful displays of nature in North America is a V-shaped formation of fifty or sixty Canada geese one thousand feet up in a crisp late-autumn sky, winging south at thirty miles an hour and calling attention to themselves with a honking cacophony as the sun sets in a reddening horizon. They head south along four principal routes, or flyways, along the Atlantic coast, the Mississippi Valley, the Rocky Mountain West, and the Pacific coast. They travel varying distances, but in general they go far enough south to find winter water that doesn't ice over and grass and grain fields that don't disappear under snow. On the Atlantic flyway, they congregate along the Labrador coast, Newfoundland, and Hudson and James bays, then head south to spend the winter as far north as central New York and as far south as North Carolina. They aggregate by the hundreds, even thousands, in fields to feed by day and then fly to a body of water to spend the night afloat, relatively safe from predators. If the winter turns harsh and their pond freezes over, they'll pick up and head south again until open water presents itself. In the spring, they reverse course, winging a thousand miles from, say, Maryland's Eastern Shore to the tundra at Ungava Bay, Quebec, to mate, molt, and nest on newly thawed terrain bursting with sun-warmed flora to sustain them and their newly hatched goslings.

The contrast couldn't be sharper between these migrating flocks, estimated at 4 million, and the geese that occupy the local landscape and seem to go nowhere very fast. For some people, these stay-put geese, estimated at more than 4 million, are just as majestic as the ones that migrate. From a distance, a flock of geese on a corporate lawn or a golf course fairway give man-made landscapes a more natural look. But *majestic* isn't a word that leaps to mind for many people who live close to local birds. To them the geese have lost their wild elegance. They have become web-footed vagrants. Some people call them "lawn carp."

Clashes over these resident geese may not have been the most important things on the minds of Americans as they entered the new millennium, but I found no end of places around the country in which people were fighting over what to do about growing numbers of them in their midst. The geese had become a kind of army of occupation on all sorts of grassy landscapes and bodies of water that people had created for their own enjoyment: public parks, lakes, beaches, athletic fields, ponds, and golf courses. They had moved into cemeteries, college campuses, hospital grounds, amusement parks, residential subdivisions, airports, and corporate parks.

Although they can be noisy and have been known to harass people and pets, geese have a much more notable trait: their inner workings. This trait was not only well known to our agrarian ancestors but was also turned into a metaphor for speed. General George Patton during the Second World War, for example, pleading for supplies to propel his Third Army through German defenses, supposedly said, "Now if Ike stops holding Monty's hand and gives me the supplies, I'll go through the Siegfried Line [Germany's border fortifications] like shit through a goose."

The digestive tract of a goose evolved to its present small and light-

weight form to make flying easier, but at the expense of digestive efficiency. Canada geese are herbivores almost exclusively. They feed mainly
on grasses and sedges in summer and on seeds, grains, berries, and other
higher-energy foods in fall and winter. Usually, less than 40 percent of
this food is digested while passing through their systems in thirty minutes to an hour. This process creates a lot of feces, which geese void
from their bowels in the form of wet droppings roughly five times an
hour. Progoose and antigoose people argue about fecal output. The age
and size of the bird, the time of year, and the availability of food are all
factors. One oft-quoted claim is that one goose can produce 1.5 pounds
(dry weight) of feces per day. That means one hundred geese would daily
produce 150 pounds of feces. This has been called a gross exaggeration.
Ask people who live or work around geese how much excrement geese
produce, however, and most say, "Too much!"

The evidence is readily available. A lot of people find these droppings just as objectionable as dog poop and more ubiquitous, messy,
and unhealthy. Local health officials worry that excess fecal coliform, or
intestinal bacteria, from geese threaten drinking-water supplies and potentially endangers swimmers. Goose feces runoff reduces water quality
in ponds and lakes, causing algal blooms, oxygen deprivation, and death
to fish and other organisms—a process called eutrophication. Other
people say the geese and their feces are an annoyance, not a threat to
public health.

The battle lines in the goose wars I looked into all tended to be
similarly drawn. On one side were goose partisans who didn't want to
see beautiful birds killed for any reason. Some of these people liked
having the birds around. When the geese first turned up, they were
the first large wild creatures many suburbanites and their children
had seen in their neighborhoods. Standing three feet tall, with wing-
spans sometimes exceeding five feet, the geese were docile enough to
be approached with bread and other food. Feeding them conditioned
the birds to stay around. Other goose partisans didn't want the birds

disturbed on principle. They thought wild creatures deserved the right to live out their lives and that people should oblige them. That obligation entailed protecting them from human abuses, including hunting. They argued that people had invaded the habitat of the geese with their subdivisions, malls, and sprawl, so people had a special obligation to live in harmony, or at the very least coexist, with the birds. On the other side were people who believed that the birds were messy nuisances and wanted their populations sharply reduced or eliminated by any means, including lethal removal.

Entrepreneurs, eyeing a dispute from which they might profit, jumped into the fray on both sides. To the antikilling factions they suggested ways to save the geese and avoid their messes. They offered to sell all sorts of contraptions and noisemakers to scare the geese away. They proffered trained border collies and handlers to chase the geese somewhere else. Experts were available to find nests and addle or oil eggs to stop them from hatching and thereby limit population growth without killing adult geese. Chemical repellents and goose birth control pills were touted. Landscapers offered to create terrain geese didn't like. Counselors gave seminars for residents on peaceful coexistence with geese and tolerance of their messes. Contractors could be hired to round up geese and remove them for processing into food for the needy. Federal agents offered up their removal services. National animal rights and animal protection groups against lethal removals offered advice and solicited donations. A few entrepreneurs even built machines like hockey-ice Zambonis to vacuum goose feces off grass.

For years, residents of Clarkstown, New York, a town across the Hudson River from Lake Carmel and only twenty-five miles north of New York City, watched the growth of a Canada goose flock in their midst with mixed feelings. As nuisance complaints about the geese grew, town officials decided to have several hundred birds rounded up and killed. The plan, announced in 1993, set off an uproar. Clarkstown had a sizable population of people who had grown up in New York and had moved there to live in suburbia and commute back to the city to work. Many of these people had views about nature in general and geese in particular that local officials said were neither practical nor informed. But these residents had connections and organizational skills to stir up a fuss about issues they were concerned about—and "gassing geese" became an instant concern. They organized, held meetings, and staged protests. One group began referring to the plan as a "goose Holocaust" and invited a real Holocaust survivor to speak against killing geese. Alec Baldwin, the actor, drew a big crowd to one meeting. Various speakers talked about the horrible effects goose killing had on the minds of young children, how border collies worked perfectly well to chase geese away, and how the problems with geese were the results of a conspiracy between hunters, who wanted more geese to kill, and state wildlife officials, who made money selling hunting licenses.

These goose partisans were few but noisy. A member of one group told me that he thought it was amazing what one person with a computer and e-mail could do. Add a website and you're a movement, he said. The Internet was a modern megaphone. He told me that activists in his group never amounted to more than a dozen people but could make it appear as though they were a large national organization, even a network of organizations. In the 1990s, nuisance geese were popping up all over the map, in towns from coast to coast, and these goose partisans were quick to jump into local disputes with advice on how to organize political and media pressure on local officials to save local birds.

In the 1990s, complaints about Canada geese were also flooding the offices of state wildlife agencies around the country. The geese seemed to be everywhere, usurping and despoiling space designed for people, and the costs of dealing with them were ballooning. New York City was spending $1.5 million a year to keep geese and other birds from degrading drinking water in its upstate reservoirs.

The battle of Clarkstown lasted three years. Then, in 1996 and 1997, town officials paid $6,500 to remove 452 geese. That amounted to only

$14.38 per bird—a bargain in comparison to what happened next. The goose partisans upped political pressure on town officials and got enough votes to stop the lethal roundups and instead hire Mary Felegy, president of Fair Game Goose Management, and her border collies to hound the remaining three hundred or so geese off town parks and ponds. The geese flee because the collies mimic their historic predators, foxes and wolves. Felegy was paid $36,000 a year. That's $120 per bird—eight times more than lethal removal and, in the opinion of the town supervisor, Charlie Holbrook, a waste of taxpayer money. At $14.38 per dead bird, the yield is goose breast meat at a relative bargain price of about $5 a pound. Harassed geese at a cost of $120 per bird yields nothing but more excrement somewhere else.

"The collie people have a great thing going," Gregory Chasko, a Connecticut wildlife official, told me at the time. "They chase the geese off the park in the morning and they fly to the golf course. Then they chase them off the golf course in the afternoon and they fly back to the park."

That happened, Felegy admitted to me. But the idea, she said, was for the harassed geese to eventually settle into "nonconflict" areas where people aren't bothered by them: on median strips of expressways, around shopping malls, or in more rural areas. Felegy said what mattered most was that federal permits to remove migratory birds or their eggs seemed to take forever, and she was available tomorrow.

Shooing geese somewhere else, of course, doesn't reduce the goose population. But this course of action, however costly, became the politically correct choice for local government and corporate officials who didn't want to be labeled "goose killers" by goose partisans. All sorts of border collie owners started goose-chasing businesses. One of them, Geese Police, went national.

In 2003, when I caught up with him, Charlie Holbrook, the Clarkstown supervisor, told me that he had heard from people all over the country who were either for or against the Clarkstown goose removal.

He said most people thought of goose problems as a local issue confined to their neighborhood, town, or region. Not true. Battles over Canada geese were happening nationwide.

"This is a big deal," he told me, only half-joking. "Heck, you could run for president on this issue."

. . .

Why did the geese stop migrating? Answers varied—some logical, some funny, all wrong. I remember dinner guests in Connecticut one weekend offering a comic explanation of how *migratis interruptus* might have played out: A spring flock in a tight V-formation is heading toward the tundra when its leader—an aging but innovative gander worn out from these 1,500-mile, back-and-forth biannual commutes—spots a new expanse of grass below and decides to check it out. This isn't one of their normal pit stops, his followers grumble. "He's losing it," one says, hinting at a coup d'état. Tired and hungry, however, they follow the old gander down, dropping out of the sky onto a rolling expanse of lawns and ponds that turns out to be a new golf course near Greenwich. Its fairway grass is freshly mowed and delicious. Its long, open sight lines make predators easy to spot. Its ponds offer convenient floating roosts. This is too good to be true! Why fly another thousand miles to the godforsaken barrens when everything we need is right here? Tundra schmundra! If hedge fund kings can live in Greenwich, so can we.

A serious explanation had to be more complicated. Canada geese, like many birds, have strong migratory instincts. So why would they stop doing what they are genetically programmed to do? Something major must have happened to trigger such a drastic change in behavior. The most common explanation that I heard from nonprofessionals was global warming, and this explanation turned up unquestioned in all sorts of news accounts of nuisance geese. In a 1992 story on global warming, for example, the *Wall Street Journal* reported: "Canada geese no longer feel the need to fly south for the Louisiana winter, when Chicago is warm enough to keep them happy." In 2009, the *Montgomery County Gazette* in Maryland published a story about local officials buying a border collie for $4,500 to chase some three hundred geese residing in a fifty-acre public park called Brookside Gardens. A spokesman for the garden said the geese stayed because of global warming. The reporter wrote: "As the North American climate has warmed and geese have ceased flying south for the winter, too many have invited themselves to stay year-round at Brookside Gardens and other county parks."

. . .

The correct answer is that today's geese did not stop migrating. They never migrated. Neither did their parents, grandparents, and great-grandparents. You'd have to go back at least a century to find ancestors of these geese that migrated. And you would have to go back much further to discover why they stopped.

The skies over Jamestown and Plymouth colonies were so filled with migrating birds in the spring and fall that they sometimes darkened the sky like a solar eclipse. Along the Atlantic coast, millions of ducks and geese moved through Cape Cod and Long Island Sound into the Chesapeake Bay and farther south. In the Midwest, millions more birds funneled down the Mississippi watershed to Arkansas and beyond.

Colonists made use of waterfowl for food. They stuffed mattresses and quilts with feathers and down. But early settlers were few and their firearms were relatively primitive, so their impact on waterfowl populations was minimal for more than a century. As immigrant populations swelled, however, markets for game birds grew. Firearms improved. Shotguns got smaller, lighter, and deadlier, improving a market gunner's efficiency.

By the early nineteenth century, waterfowl market gunners were embarked on an arms race to deliver more killing power to their targets.

They opted for bigger guns—guns so big that a man couldn't lift them. They had to be mounted on boats. The biggest of these, called punt guns, had barrels up to two inches in diameter. They held a pound of shot pellets and had to be strapped down so the boat could absorb the enormous recoil. Wildlife historian James Trefethen explained how they worked:

> These instruments of mass slaughter operated only at night. The gunner paddled silently to the edge of a feeding flock of [floating] birds, adjusted the position of the boat so the gun pointed at the thickest part, and pulled the lanyard as the birds began to take alarm. The resultant shot cut a swath of death up to eight feet wide and a hundred yards long. A hundred or more geese or ducks with a single shot was not unusual.

To help lure birds in and keep them around, the gunners would spread shelled corn across fields and shallow feeding marshes and hide in raft-like shooting platforms called sinkboxes that made them difficult to notice from the air and impossible to see from the water.

Perhaps the best tools at their disposal, however, were live decoys. In the nineteenth and early twentieth centuries, waterfowlers—including men wealthy enough to belong to shooting clubs—brought out, in addition to wooden decoys, dozens of live geese or ducks, some tethered and others trained, to bob in the marsh or strut in the cornfield and make noise, adding all-important authenticity to the ruse. The use of live decoys may have originated with shoemakers in Brockton, Massachusetts, in 1840. These men built a shoe-making shack on a pond, put up a blind nearby, and went about their cobbling inside until they heard the honking of migrating geese above. Then they dropped their awls and hammers, grabbed guns and calls, and slipped into the blind. If the geese came in to land, they got blasted. In those days, a single goose could be sold for an entire day's wage in the shoe trade.

As with any kind of wing shooting, birds were sometimes hit but not killed. Standard procedure was to dispatch them quickly with a second shot. Sometimes a bird was hit by only a few pellets—enough to bring it down but wound it only slightly. For these birds the shoemakers had an idea. They took the injured geese home, treated them, fed and watered them, and nursed them back to health. When the birds had recovered they were taken back to the blind, and tied to it with a string of leather.

Live decoys worked well, and word of their effectiveness spread quickly. Other hunting groups started their own captured flocks, tethering them or plucking flight feathers or amputating wingtips so the birds couldn't fly. Called tollers, because they honked to call in birds as a church bell calls parishioners, these birds were sometimes so well trained that they didn't have to be tethered or altered. Some started tolling on their own, spotting overhead birds before hunters did.

Raising wild geese and ducks to stock the decoy flocks of market shooters and hunting clubs became a lucrative sideline for farmers. Captive birds laid clutches of eggs that were bought and sold, hatched out, and raised for sale. "Wild" meat and eggs had a cachet at the time, and farmers, meat markets, and restaurants could sell them at a premium. Feathers could be sold as well. By the second half of the nineteenth century flocks of live decoys were common along the Atlantic coast and up and down the Mississippi watershed.

Over time, one of the favorite specimens for inclusion in live decoy flocks was an unusually large bird from the Upper Midwest and Great Plains—the giant Canada goose. Native to fifteen states and three provinces, this bird weighed several pounds more than average-sized geese, and that made it easier to see from the air. Hunters believed that adding the big birds to decoy flocks gave them an edge.

. . .

In the decades after the Civil War, waterfowl weren't the only birds under assault. All sorts of other game birds were being killed off for commercial sale and consumption. Nests were looted for eggs to eat or collect. Birds with beautiful plumage were decimated. Even songbirds were dispatched for meat and feathers. Stopping this carnage was a major triumph of the American conservation movement, but it took decades.

One of the most important victories took place in 1916. Because many states adamantly opposed enacting limits and enforcing them, various plans were circulated in the United States Congress to bring migrating birds under federal control on the grounds that they crossed state lines and international borders. But advocates of states' rights were loath to see any federal measures that would erode state sovereignty, and most of these efforts went nowhere.

In 1916, the United States and Great Britain (acting on behalf of Canada) ratified the Migratory Bird Treaty. Legislation implementing it was passed by the Senate and House and signed by President Woodrow Wilson in 1918. Two years later, a legal challenge failed when the Supreme Court affirmed 7–2 that treaties entered into by the federal government were the "supreme law of the land."

The other threat to ducks and geese was habitat destruction, and it took even more of a toll on waterfowl populations than market gunners. By the late 1920s, with the nation on the verge of the Great Depression, a series of droughts hit the Midwest and Great Plains, drying out the topsoil. Soil turned by the plow blew away. Potholes and marshes dried up. The grasses around them died. The subsequent dust storms hit the Oklahoma region particularly hard and had devastating effects up and down the Great Plains. The drought was an ecological disaster for wildlife in general and waterfowl in particular. Birds died of starvation and thirst or were picked off by predators as they searched for water.

In 1933, Franklin Delano Roosevelt became president, and as part of the New Deal to pull the nation out of the Great Depression he created the Civilian Conservation Corps, a government make-work program for the jobless that included building breeding and feeding refuges for waterfowl. In January 1934, Roosevelt appointed a three-man committee to recommend ways to pay for waterfowl restoration. On it was Aldo Leopold, of the U.S. Forest Service; Thomas Beck, editor of *Collier's* magazine; and Jay Norwood Darling, a political cartoonist for the *Des Moines Register* and a Republican. Darling's cartoons appeared in more than one hundred newspapers and had won him a Pulitzer Prize and the nickname "Ding." The cartoons regularly dinged Roosevelt, so his appointment surprised many, including Darling himself. Some saw his appointment as a way to get him off Roosevelt's back. But he was an ardent and knowledgeable conservationist, as well as a good speaker and writer. In any case, less than two months after the committee went to work, the director of the Bureau of Biological Survey, which was a precursor of the Fish and Wildlife Service, suddenly resigned, and Darling was asked to take his place. Two weeks after that, Roosevelt signed the Migratory Bird Hunting Stamp Act, under which waterfowl hunters paid one dollar for a federal stamp, the proceeds for use to acquire land for what became the 5.2-million-acre National Wildlife Refuge System. One goal was to create refuges along the continent's four major migratory flyways at intervals of about one hundred miles. With a pencil, Darling sketched on paper a pair of alighting mallards that became the design for the first duck stamp.

Darling turned out to be an energetic administrator. When he took over, the bureau had only twenty-four game wardens for the whole country. He hired more and dispatched them in strike forces to poaching hot spots, eventually using airplanes to spot lawbreakers. In 1935, he imposed the tightest hunting restrictions yet seen, banning the use of corn and other grains as bait, shutting the hunting season down to thirty days, cutting bag limits to ten ducks and four geese, outlawing shotguns that could hold more than three shots at a time, banning sinkboxes and offshore blinds, and fending off critics in Congress, whose constituents howled at the restrictions.

The most significant move that Darling made, by far, was to outlaw the use of live decoys. Writing in the *New York Times,* H. P. Sheldon, an official with the Bureau of Biological Survey, said Darling's new rules would make waterfowling more sporting: "The new regulations practically wipe out all the artificial aids which the fowler has used for so many seasons and restores more wholesome principles to the sport of shooting. The man who is successful this season will need to know more than how to handle a shotgun; he will need to know wind, weather and the habits of the birds. He will be a duck hunter rather than a duck shooter."

. . .

No one could foresee it at the time, but outlawing live decoy flocks was the first step in creating large populations of nuisance Canada geese. The regulations suddenly made ducks and geese in these flocks legally unusable for hunting. Enforcement was ramped up, and because decoy flocks were visible and obvious, continuing to use them made hunters vulnerable to arrest, and that gave them pause. Most replaced their live birds with wooden facsimiles. The result was that tens of thousands of live decoys became superfluous, including an estimated fifteen thousand geese along the Atlantic coast alone. The market for them collapsed.

Some hunting groups gave their birds away. Others sold them for pennies on the dollar. Suddenly live decoy birds were either free or a bargain, and people began to buy them up for other uses. Farmers took them to raise as barnyard fowl for meat, eggs, and feathers. Towns and wealthy landowners bought some to adorn their ponds or to join the odd peacock on the village square. More important, state fish and wildlife departments snapped them up as breeding flocks to stock local marshes and newly created waterfowl refuges in hopes of growing healthy populations to supplement imperiled migratory flocks. These restocking efforts went on for decades—well into the 1990s in some states.

Migrating birds have a little-understood internal compass—an instinctual homing ability tied, perhaps, to magnetic direction—to fly back to the place where they first learned to fly or where they nested as adults in previous years. Captive geese hadn't migrated in many generations, but wildlife managers hoped that once they were put out into local marshes and refuges they would eventually take up migration. That didn't happen. The problem was that the birds had been born and learned to fly locally and had nested locally. They were already "home," so to speak. They were at or nearby their birthplace and nesting location. Goslings learn habits from parents and other geese around them, and those birds had been conditioned to hang around and rely on their human handlers for food.

"After release, there was little biological incentive for the flocks to change their behavior," Jack Hope wrote in *Audubon* magazine. On their own, they could forage in farm fields and roost in open water in all but the coldest and snowiest weather. In the spring, they nested nearby.

. . .

On a blustery winter day in mid-January 1962, near Silver Lake in Rochester, Minnesota, a research biologist from the Illinois Natural History Survey named Harold C. Hanson brought the giant Canada goose back from the dead. That is to say, he discovered that *Branta canadensis maxima* was not, as widely believed for decades, extinct. In the somewhat circumscribed world of goose biology, this was sensational news— a kind of Jurassic Park moment, almost like stumbling upon a living, breathing specimen of *Tyrannosaurus rex*.

Hanson specialized in goose taxonomy. He was an expert in distinguishing the physical and behavioral characteristics important in classifying geese into species and subspecies. He was also a fisherman who made annual autumn trips to Minnesota in pursuit of walleyes and other denizens of the northern lakes. Driving home one autumn, Hanson made note of some geese in a Rochester city park. They seemed rather large. He made some inquiries and learned that some of these birds flew to southeastern Manitoba each spring to nest or molt, or both, and returned each autumn to Rochester, a distance of, perhaps, two hundred miles. That piqued his interest because he knew that short migration was a characteristic of the old giants.

The big natural advantage the giants had was a large body mass that allowed them to endure colder temperatures than smaller geese, and that meant they didn't have to migrate very far south in winter to warmer climes. Their size also meant that flying took more effort than it did for smaller birds. For this and perhaps other reasons, the giants didn't migrate to the tundra to nest and molt in the spring like smaller geese. Early explorers reported finding large geese nesting in trees and along the bluffs of the Missouri River hundreds of miles to the south of where other subspecies went to lay their eggs. They were big, were easy to find and kill, and had plenty of edible flesh. They became a favorite source of food and feathers for pioneer settlers, and the targets of market gunners and waterfowl sportsmen as well. They were all but killed out of their historic range at the beginning of the twentieth century. By the 1920s, they were extinct in the wild—or so it was believed.

Rochester's Silver Lake was to the north of the giants' historic winter range but was an ideal place to winter. The lake, only twenty acres in size, was created in 1936 by damming the south fork of the Zumbro River. Its water was used to cool the city's electrical generating plant and was returned to the lake warm enough to prevent the lake from freezing over in the winter. In other words, it was a man-made winter refuge. A large area around the lake was closed to hunting, and hundreds of lakeside acres of lawns provided plenty of food, as did a regular supplemental feeding program in winter. Vendors sold shelled corn to visitors to feed the big birds.

Hanson got permission from Minnesota wildlife officials to trap, weigh, and band a two-hundred-bird sample of the flock. And on the appointed day in mid-January, with the temperature hovering near zero, he and seven others from Minnesota and federal agencies did just that. When they first began catching, banding, and weighing the geese, the men thought their scales were faulty because the birds weighed far too much. So one member of the group was dispatched to a grocery store to buy a five-pound bag of sugar and a ten-pound bag of flour—which he placed on the store scales to confirm their weights. Back at the lake, the men weighed the sugar and flour and discovered that their scales were indeed accurate. They were weighing very large geese, some over twenty pounds. Returning home, Hanson read all the goose literature that he could find and concluded that the Rochester geese were indeed *Branta canadensis maxima*!

The Hanson discovery energized wildlife agents and researchers. Perhaps more giants existed, and now that they knew from Hanson what to look for, they began to comb the countryside for more specimens of *maximas* and quickly found them. "Hundreds of former nest-robbers and subsistence hunters, along with onetime market hunters, owned small, un-tallied flocks of the birds," wrote Jack Hope. Not only that. Some goose restoration programs had been using giants for years without knowing it. The state of Missouri, for example, had bought some geese from a local farmer in the early 1950s for breeding and stocking. To thwart most predators, they fastened galvanized washtubs on top of poles for the geese to nest in.

"They happened to be giants, but nobody connected the dots until Harold [a decade later] made his discovery," Dave Graber, a senior research biologist with the Missouri Department of Conservation, told me. As it turned out, farmers had a lot of giants in their flocks that the wildlife people weren't aware of. The U.S. Fish and Wildlife Service would later estimate that at the time of the Hanson discovery some sixty-three thousand *maximas* lived in the midwestern and plains states. The giants were hidden in plain sight.

State agencies rushed to propagate the big birds. Geese of all kinds were still so scarce that hunting them was prohibited across wide regions. Perhaps the giants could fill the void. In his 1965 book *The Giant Canada Goose,* Hanson noted that towns in Minnesota were starting flocks of giants on their lakes and was encouraged enough to pronounce the future of the giants "indeed bright"—a phrase a U.S. Fish and Wildlife Service waterfowl expert would later call "a gross understatement."

The size of the giants made them relatively lethargic. They didn't need to migrate very far. The captive breeding programs only reinforced those proclivities. They were raised on farms, fenced in, fed poultry mash, and wintered in buildings like chicken coops. Transferred to waterfowl refuges as goslings, they flourished. Wildlife agents congratulated themselves, oblivious to trouble ahead.

"Most of us took credit for and promoted the restoration of giant Canada geese," Ollie Torgerson, head of the Wildlife Division at the Missouri Department of Conservation, told me. "In Missouri, we got landowners to put up nesting tubs, moved geese around the state, had a formal goose restoration program and plan, traded geese to other states that wanted them, and so on. It was big time stuff."

The zealotry of restoration efforts was understandable. The government agents had been restoring wetlands and creating waterfowl refuges in which geese could flourish to the delight of hunters, and now they were helping to save a species from extinction—or so they thought. Ironically, they were building healthy goose populations in newly created refuges where the birds had never permanently existed or nested before.

While goose restoration efforts were going on, the American population was sprawling out across the suburban, exurban, and rural landscape, creating as they went an almost perfect ecological niche in which goose populations could explode. To accommodate these people, developers turned millions of acres of farmland and woods into lawns, ponds, golf courses, corporate parks, school campuses, soccer fields, playgrounds, and parks, all planted in what happened to be the favorite food of Canada geese: grass. Better still, because it was mowed regularly, this grass always had plenty of fresh, tender growth that was much more palatable than tough grown-up grass. These grassy landscapes had long sight lines—which made geese feel comfortable because they could more easily spot any predators that might be sneaking up on them. Most of the people who lived and worked in these places were more likely to feed geese than hunt them. The birds were embraced—at first—as novelties.

Complaints about nuisance geese, however, weren't unheard of. Jim Forbes, a retired federal agent who had dealt with problem wildlife issues in New York for decades, told me he'd heard that President Dwight D. Eisenhower was playing golf at a country club in Westchester County in suburban New York in the 1950s when he stepped into a tee box with his driver and almost fell down.

"It's said that Ike slipped on some goose doo-doo and turned to one of his aides and asked: 'Can't something be done about this?'" Forbes didn't know where the story came from. His point was that as early as the 1950s and into the 1980s, excess Canada geese in Westchester and Rockland counties north of New York City were rounded up and relocated. Lots of states in the East were eager to take them to establish their own colonies in order to bring back goose hunting. Except for Forbes and a few others, nobody was paying attention. But as people moved into the sprawl and resident bird populations grew, goose problems multiplied.

"I don't think anybody ever saw the resident-goose problem coming," Bob Trost, a federal wildlife biologist in Oregon, told *Audubon* magazine.

. . .

The first big dustup over resident geese played out in Minneapolis and St. Paul, the Twin Cities, a seven-county region that is a great place to be a goose. It is flat, low-lying terrain, with 949 lakes, three big rivers, and numerous marshes. Canada geese had not lived there for decades until 1955, when Minnesota wildlife officials began seeding the area with farm-raised birds. The effort went on for nineteen years.

By 1968, the Twin Cities had an estimated 480 birds, and they were popular. People took their children on walks to see and hear them, and took along some bread or shelled corn to feed them. State wildlife agents hoped to manage their populations with autumn hunting seasons. But as people sprawled beyond the downtowns of Minneapolis and St. Paul, waterfowl hunting was increasingly constricted because sprawl dwellers expressed concerns about hunting on marshes and lakes near their homes—a concern reinforced when shotgun pellets occasionally rained onto their roofs. Twin City predators weren't up to the management task either. Adult geese, because of their large size and aggressiveness, have few predators to begin with, although wolves, coyotes, bears, owls, and eagles have been known to take nesting adults. Few of these creatures existed in Twin Cities sprawl. Egg predators, including raccoons, foxes, crows, snakes, snapping turtles, and various raptors and gulls, were more numerous but not very effective. Parental geese are fierce nest defenders.

In any case, by 1974 the population of introduced geese and their offspring had grown to an estimated 1,500 birds. By 1982, the flock was put at more than 12,000, and complaints about them were on the rise. Local officials had been mulling the idea of catching and relocating troublesome birds, and Dr. James Cooper, a professor at the University of Minnesota, devised a plan to do just that. With help from the Minnesota Department of Natural Resources, 456 geese were captured during their 1982 summer molting season at Lake of the Isles and moved to Oklahoma. Early in the century, state agencies had developed the habit of swapping wild species they had plenty of—say deer and geese— for species they wanted, such as beavers and turkeys. The Twin Cities relocations attracted little attention at first, probably because most people who liked geese saw no problem in moving them to places where they might thrive. But opposition did appear in the form of people who were against moving the birds to places where they might be hunted. Of course they were already being hunted and thousands killed annually in the more remote parts of the Twin Cities region.

. . .

Across the nation as flocks grew, state wildlife agencies were on the front lines of the goose wars, fielding appeals for help from citizens to "do something now" about the messy birds, Ollie Torgerson told me. "I got personally involved because our regional Fish and Wildlife Service office would not issue kill permits." While state wildlife agents could deal with many species of nuisance wildlife, the 1916 Migratory Bird Treaty gave the federal government jurisdiction over migrating birds. Federal rules implementing the treaty directed the Department of the Interior to decide what forms of hunting and killing abided by the treaty's provisions. The secretary delegated the decision making to its subordinate agency, the U.S. Fish and Wildlife Service. That agency could issue permits to kill birds if, "under extraordinary conditions," they "become seriously injurious to agricultural or other interests." These were judgment calls and, as in the case of many bureaucracies, not easily made. The treaty that had saved geese and other birds from the ravages of market hunters was now saving birds that many people didn't want saved. Roundup permits seemed to be tangled in red tape, and the mere mention of the possibility of lethal control was enough to set off goose partisans and animal protection groups and their lawyers.

For state agencies, the incremental steps authorized by Fish and Wildlife were by the early 1990s clearly not working. Relocating birds was no longer a solution because nobody wanted them. Expanding the hunting seasons to target more resident geese reduced them in some places, but the very suburban sprawl landscapes on which problem geese had taken up residence were full of people opposed to hunting. Paul Schmidt, the Fish and Wildlife Service's assistant director for birds, told me that while the agency hadn't moved "as fast as we would have liked, there was no intended foot-dragging." One problem was that the agency's work on geese had been slowed by lawsuits filed by animal protection groups.

Back in the Twin Cities, meanwhile, it was clear that the annual relocations had slowed growth but were failing to reduce the goose population. By the mid-1990s, Dr. Cooper's program was relocating between 6,000 and 8,000 geese from the Twin Cities annually. In 1995, for example, 6,858 geese were captured and trucked out of state, and hunters killed another 15,000. But the overall goose population had grown to 24,000, complaints about them had soared, and other states wanted no more adult geese, only goslings. So Dr. Cooper devised a pilot program of lethal roundups, with goose breasts donated to local food pantries.

Geese partisans viewed lethal roundups as drastic measures and, perhaps, illegal—although why they differed from hunting, which was lethal and legal, wasn't made clear. In 1998, the Humane Society of the United States (HSUS), along with the Friends of Animals and Their Environment and the Minnesota Humane Society, filed a lawsuit against the U.S. Fish and Wildlife Service, claiming, among other things, that the roundups weren't necessary because the geese caused no "serious injury" as required in the implementing language of the 1916 treaty. That suit was tossed, but HSUS can quickly generate publicity aimed at swaying public opinion, while other groups or individuals focus on specific arguments that can slow down any course of action they oppose. In the Twin Cities, for example, one small group—essentially one woman from Oshkosh, Wisconsin—asserted in letters that goose numbers were exaggerated by people who wanted to remove them and that there was no scientific proof that the geese or their feces were harmful. She argued that geese feces runoff made lakes look polluted but that the fecal coliform in it had not been shown to be harmful to swimmers. For people who had watched gaggles of resident geese grow, seen the messes they made, and seen ponds and lakes cloud up from runoff, these arguments had the ring of a Groucho Marx line uttered when his wife finds him in bed with another woman: "Who you gonna believe, me or your lying eyes?"

In any case, in five years the lethal roundups reduced the Twin Cities resident goose population to fewer than nineteen thousand birds, a level that most residents could probably live with. Without culling and hunting, Dr. Cooper estimated that their numbers would have grown to three hundred thousand before the year 2000 and would have eventually reached a biological carrying capacity in the seven-county region of five hundred thousand geese.

The Twin Cities was fortunate to get a permit in 1995 for lethal roundups. Other cities and state wildlife agencies weren't so lucky. Federal permits were very difficult to get. That year, the Fish and Wildlife Service informed state officials that it was considering a plan to give states authority to issue kill permits between April 1 and August 31 each year, a period that included the molting season. The officials went home from the meeting thinking federal help was on the way. But it wasn't. Three years passed. Nothing happened. Frustrated by inaction, the umbrella group for state government fish and wildlife departments, the Association of Fish and Wildlife Agencies (AFWA), formed a Resident Canada Geese Working Group in 1998 with Ollie Torgerson as its chairman. The group's purpose was to agitate for speedy permission from Washington to destroy eggs and kill geese. In December of 1998, Torgerson warned the Feds that some AFWA members wanted to sue the federal government or to call on their friends on Capitol Hill to hold hearings and ask embarrassing questions. Torgerson said Missouri might issue kill permits unilaterally and challenge Fish and Wildlife to take legal action to stop them—a move that was sure to generate lots of publicity.

Finally, in 2002, after three years of public meetings, the Fish and Wildlife Service issued a Draft Environmental Impact Statement (DEIS) saying it favored, among other options, giving states authority to issue kill permits. The HSUS called it a plan for "mass killing" and said it would violate the language and spirit of the Migratory Bird Treaty. Animal protection groups argued that the term *resident geese* was a convenient fiction to deny those birds legal protections in the treaty.

It took the federal government more than a decade to change the rules, and during that time animal rights and animal protection groups fought Washington every step of the way. In November 2005, a Final Environmental Impact Statement was completed, and in August 2006, new rules went into effect allowing states broad latitude in permitting and conducting lethal culls. The statement said the goal was to reduce resident geese by up to a million birds nationwide and to stabilize resident populations at 3.68 million. To do that, the statement said, would require killing 636,000 adults or 1.3 million goslings, or destroying eggs in 787,000 nests annually over the next ten years—a daunting task that would require airports, military airfields, private landowners, public land managers, agricultural producers, state wildlife agencies, and hunters to mount massive efforts.

Goose partisans vowed to fight on to protect the birds. But by then fewer and fewer people believed they needed protection. Then, on January 15, 2009, US Airways Flight 1549 sucked geese into both its engines and had to abort its flight and land in the Hudson River. The Airbus A320 had taken off from New York's LaGuardia Airport ninety seconds before it reached an altitude of 2,700 feet and ran into a gaggle of geese, knocking out its engines. The plane was en route to Charlotte, North Carolina, with 155 passengers and crew. Captain Chesley B. Sullenberger brought the plane down on the Hudson and all were rescued, but a $60 million aircraft was destroyed.

Live television coverage of Flight 1549's Hudson River landing and the dramatic rescue of its passengers, repeated on CNN, MSNBC, and other cable channels around the clock, focused national attention on the dangers of aircraft-bird collisions. Two days later, the front page of the *New York Post* showed a flying Canada goose in gun sights behind a headline reading "PLUCK 'EM!" The subhead read, "Kill the geese before they down another NY jet."

At the time, most people weren't aware of the aircraft-bird collision problem. Federal figures showed that such collisions had quadrupled from 1,759 in 1990 to 7,666 in 2007. Most caused minor damage because the birds involved were relatively small. Collisions with geese were far more serious. In 1995, for example, Canada geese were ingested in two of four engines on an Air France Concorde departing JFK International, causing more than $7 million in damage. That same year, four Canada geese were sucked into the engines of an Air Force jet in Alaska, causing it to crash and killing all twenty-four people aboard.

In the days after the Flight 1549 collisions, the dangers posed by Canada geese around New York airports were widely reported. "The bottom line," Richard A. Dolbeer, a retired U.S. Department of Agriculture bird strike expert, told the *New York Times*, "is that they truly are the most hazardous species of bird that poses a threat to aviation."

Bryan Swift, New York State's ranking goose specialist, told me that the New York metropolitan area had an estimated twenty-five thousand resident geese—five times more than he believed to be a tolerable number. And, he added, "I think the [goose population] goal near any airport should be close to zero."

In June, New York mayor Michael Bloomberg announced that the city and airports had contracted with the U.S. Department of Agriculture's Wildlife Services to "remove and dispose of" up to two thousand Canada geese from as many as forty parks and other city-owned properties within five miles of LaGuardia and JFK airports.

"There are people who care very much about the geese. But in the end the safety of the public is No. 1 and that's what we're going to do." he said on his weekly radio show. "There is not a lot of cost involved in rounding up a couple of thousand geese and letting them go to sleep with nice dreams."

Predictably, animal rights bloggers expressed outrage. One typed: "Protests, contacting the media and/or videotaping this massacre so that the world can witness this atrocity need to take action—NOW. Shame on Mayor Bloomberg."

The mayor was reflecting public sentiment. Most Americans, including New Yorkers, could easily see themselves as passengers on Flight 1549 and imagine what its passengers had gone through. However eager many of them were to side with almost any creature distressed by people, most were pragmatic when the stakes were personal and life-threatening.

The popularity of Canada geese clearly took a nosedive. Calls for a "mass demonstration" in front of the headquarters of the Port Authority of New York and New Jersey, which ran the airports, drew only a few dozen people chanting, "How many geese did you gas today?"

Flight 1549 lent new urgency to a plan, drawn up earlier by federal and state agents, to cull 450,000 resident geese along the Atlantic flyway, with areas around airports getting priority. In 2009, Wildlife Services and city agencies found and oiled 1,739 eggs around New York airports and rounded up 1,235 geese at seventeen locations. A year later, another 1,676 geese were removed within an eight-mile range of La-Guardia and John F. Kennedy airports, including 368 from Brooklyn's Prospect Park, where people liked to feed them bread and doughnuts. They were euthanized in carbon dioxide gas chambers. The *Brooklyn Paper,* a neighborhood weekly and website, without the slightest irony called it "a horrifying crime that not only calls into question our abilities as stewards of the earth, but also our core values as a species."

The *New York Post*'s headline read, "Gassed Geese? Good." The HSUS called the culling "wrong and unacceptable." The *Huffington Post* said "Good Riddance." But perhaps the most telling comment came from a headline on the Allvoices website: "Where Is the Uproar?"

Chapter Seven

Gobblers

On a warm spring morning not long ago, I was sitting in the dark on the ground, my back up against the trunk of a small oak tree, and a 12-gauge shotgun resting on my right knee. Roy Rhodes sat one tree over, scratching a piece of artificial slate with a rosewood striker to create the soft purr of a wild turkey hen with sex on her mind. We were on the edge of a woodlot, facing out onto a pasture. Twenty feet in front of us in the open field, a plastic decoy hen on a stick bobbed up and down. We had walked half a mile in the morning darkness down a farm lane and path beside the woods, our flashlight beams leading the way. The only sounds were the shuffle of our boots and our breathing, until a bird in the distance let out with a "what cheer, cheer, cheer."

"That's the red bird," Roy whispered. He had spent enough time outdoors before dawn to know that the cardinal was the first bird to sing in the morning in this part of northern Arkansas. The tall, reed-thin son of a Mississippi sharecropper, Roy had won duck-calling and turkey-calling competitions as a boy. I'd met him the previous fall, and he'd offered to take me on what he called the best hunt left in American hunting. We were on a farm near Batesville. Its owner had invited Roy to "thin out" the wild turkeys on his land. He said they'd gotten so thick that they plucked seed corn out of the ground almost as fast as he could plant it. The turkeys were costing him money. We were dressed head to toe in hunter camouflage, including face masks pulled up over our noses like those of stagecoach bandits in old westerns. We sat in silence for what seemed like an eternity, listening for gobbles as dawn slowly broke. To our left in the distance, I heard a faint gobble. Roy nodded. In back of us, much closer, another tom gobbled. Roy answered with another gentle purr on his slate. More silence. I tried to stay still. Turkeys can spot the slightest movement, perceive danger, and sprint away, Roy told me. It's said they can hear a twig snap or a mouse squeak a mile away.

Turkey hunting in the spring is about sex and deceit. It is a game of sounds. Normally, males gobble and hens come running. Males are serial breeders. But each impregnated hen means that there's one less to breed. As interested hens thin out, the gobbler's sex drive propels him to look for more. Spring turkey hunters pretend they are hens, or competing toms, with their calls. Some hunters can imitate turkeys with their own vocal cords and mouths. Others use reeds, wooden boxes, and slates designed to mimic a range of more than two dozen yelps, clucks, cackles, and purrs turkeys use to communicate. The hunter's call has to sound convincing enough to overcome the gobbler's wariness.

We waited like statues. Roy purred on his slate, then he nodded ever so slightly to my left. Down the pasture fence line about one hundred yards I saw a black dot. It was moving our way. It was a turkey all right, but I couldn't tell what sex or size. As the bird moved to eighty yards, then sixty, Roy spotted a telltale beard—a clump of black bristles, perhaps eight inches long, hanging from its chest. It was a gobbler, and a big one.

We had agreed that Roy would take the first shot. But he had a problem. He had to move his shotgun's barrel from twelve o'clock, or straight ahead, to nine o'clock, the direction the bird was coming from. Turkey hunters know never to move when a turkey is looking. They must wait until the bird pecks the ground, looks away, or moves behind a bush or tree, or else the turkey will spot them and flee. This was a dicey moment. I could feel my heart pounding. As the bird moved in, Roy's eyes were glued to it. He inched his barrel over every time the bird's head went behind a fence post. Roy's purring must have been convincing, because suddenly the tom stopped, spread his tail feathers, fluffed his chest feathers, and began to strut in front of the decoy hen—but still slightly out of shooting range. The bird looked huge. Its wingtips were dragging on the ground. My nose itched.

Suddenly I spotted movement to my left. It was another turkey, coming into the pasture between the gobbler and the decoy. It was a hen, smaller and lighter in color. The hen took about five steps into the pasture, then turned and darted back into the woods. The gobbler tore off after her, abandoning interest in the decoy despite Roy's frantic purring. Roy could have sounded like the Julia Roberts of turkeys with his slate, but it was no use. The tom went after the real thing.

. . .

The history of North America's largest ground-nesting bird has been controlled by man for as long as the two species have existed together on the continent, and it is filled with human rapacity and stewardship, conservation and ignorance. Wild turkeys seemed to be everywhere, perhaps 10 million strong, when European settlers arrived. They were easy to find and kill for food and feathers, and their numbers were steadily reduced. By the early twentieth century they were facing extinction in isolated, remnant flocks. By 1920, conservationists estimated that as few as thirty thousand birds were left on the entire continent.

Early restoration attempts failed. Not until the 1950s did government wildlife agents develop successful techniques for repopulating regions where turkeys had been extirpated. After that, turkey propagators redoubled their efforts and succeeded in spreading the birds into their old haunts, and beyond. In their zeal, in fact, the agents and hunting groups spread the birds far beyond their historic ranges—into ten states, including Hawaii, where they hadn't lived since the last Ice Age, if at all. These efforts were hailed as a conservation triumph.

As the big birds multiplied, however, problems arose. Farmers were first to complain, accusing turkeys of eating their crops. Sprawl dwellers began to report that aggressive birds were menacing them, their pets, and their children. Environmentalists complained that in some places the turkeys were an invasive species damaging ecosystems meant for native animals and plants. The more turkeys, the more problems people had with them.

. . .

Meleagris gallopavo is a Galliform, an order of plump-bodied birds that includes chickens, quail, and grouse. It doesn't migrate. It feeds on the ground on plants and insects. It is most closely related to pheasants and guinea fowl. Five turkey subspecies are recognized in North America. Adult birds weigh ten to forty pounds, stand three to four feet tall, and have a wingspan of nearly six feet. They are fast flyers over short distances, but they use their wings, for the most part, to escape predators and to fly up to roosting spots in the tops of trees. They prefer to run, can trot twelve miles an hour, and can sprint at twenty-five miles per hour.

They mate in the spring, with a hen laying eight to twenty eggs, one a day, which she turns regularly in the nest and sits on to incubate for twenty-eight days. Newly hatched poults roost under their mother's wings for four or five weeks and stay with her until they reach adulthood in nine months. Their life span ranges from ten to fifteen years, if predators don't get them first. Lots of wild creatures eat eggs: skunks, snakes, crows, opossums, squirrels, raccoons, coyotes, ravens, dogs, and blue jays, to name some. These predators, along with hawks, owls, foxes, mink, cats, weasels, and eagles, catch and eat hatchlings. Only half of hatched poults live beyond three weeks.

Researchers say Indians in south-central Mexico domesticated turkeys around 800 B.C., and they have found evidence that domesticated birds existed around 200 B.C. in the southwestern United States. The birds were raised, initially, for their feathers. An adult turkey has more than 3,500 feathers, and they were used by Indians in ceremonies, for decoration, and to make robes and feather blankets. When the Spanish arrived in 1518, they reported finding both wild and domesticated turkeys in the villages of Mogollon, Anasazi, Hopi, and Pueblo cultures. In his 1540–42 expedition, Francisco Vásquez de Coronado reported finding turkeys in what is now Kansas, Oklahoma, Texas, and New Mexico. Montezuma, the Aztec emperor, gave Hernán Cortés six turkeys made of gold as a gift, fueling the conquistador's lust for more of the yellow metal.

It isn't clear who brought the first turkeys from the New World to Europe, but when wealthy aristocrats heard about the big birds, they wanted them in their gardens alongside pheasants from China and Persia, guinea fowl from Africa, and peacocks from India. Turkeys were misnamed and confused with peacocks and guinea hens for a long time.

The new birds were raised as food too, at first for European elites. They were meaty and, it turned out, easy to grow. By the 1530s, they were a common item in food markets, eventually selling for less than chickens. By 1573, turkeys had become a main course in English Christmas dinners. In the eighteenth century, it was common for employers to reward their workers with gift turkeys at Christmas, as Ebenezer Scrooge did to Bob Cratchit, his clerk, in Charles Dickens's *A Christmas Carol* (1843).

In New York, European settlers reported finding wild turkeys that were big, docile, and almost everywhere. And unlike migrating ducks and geese, wild turkeys were available to hunt year round. They were very easy to shoot, reported Thomas Morton, "because, the one being killed, the other sit fast nevertheless." Killing a dozen birds in a half-day outing was easy, and some, he reported, weighed forty-eight pounds and seemed almost too fat to fly.

The demise of the wild turkey followed a familiar pattern. Settlers killed them to eat, market hunters killed them to sell, and turkey habitat fell to the ax and plow. By 1672, according to the colonial author John Josselyn, "English and Indian hunters had 'now destroyed the breed, so that 'tis very rare to meet with a wild turkie in the woods.'" By 1851, Massachusetts had none, and by the end of the Civil War, they were gone from all of New England. Forest destruction in the Midwest erased turkey habitat, creating largely treeless farms that were terrible habitat for a tree-roosting bird (but prime habitat for the imported ringed-neck pheasant). Ohio's turkeys were gone by 1878, Michigan's by 1897. By 1920, wild turkeys had been extirpated from eighteen of the thirty-nine states of their ancestral range. Always the pessimist, conservationist William Hornaday, director of the New York Zoological Park, pronounced them goners. Fragmentary populations were known to exist in Maryland, West Virginia, Virginia, and the Carolinas, and in isolated swamps in the Deep South. A population of three thousand or so birds was situated in the ridge and valley region of central Pennsylvania in an area unsuited for either logging or farming.

The first restoration efforts began before 1900. They failed. Restorers gathered wild birds, hatched their eggs and raised the poults in pens, and released them as young adults into isolated public forests. Lacking survival skills, they died. For a long time conservationists had more enthusiasm than hope. They thought they could adjust their rearing and releasing techniques so that farm-raised birds released into the wild would thrive. The birds didn't cooperate. In one early effort, more than 330,000 pen-raised turkeys were released at nearly eight hundred different sites in thirty-six states. In all but forty sites, they failed. Why? Diseases were sometimes cited as factors. But essentially, farm-raised birds were too docile. They behaved like the domesticated turkeys they were.

Conservationists offered many explanations for this behavior. One was that breeding stocks of wild birds had been contaminated by the genes of domestic birds. Another was that penned hens couldn't teach their poults about predators, food sources, and survival tactics in the wild. The restorers tried gathering eggs in the wild and hatching them.

But the poults grew up docile. When farmed birds were released, one of two things happened: If they were released into deep forest, they perished. If they were released closer in, they often walked home, strutting down roads and roosting near the farm buildings where food handouts came from.

Another intriguing explanation of wild turkey docility was that birds in the wild weren't wild at all. Indians in some places, remember, essentially farmed the forest, creating habitat and food for the wild species they needed to survive. Certainly by regular burning of forest understory and meadows they allowed growth of young plants and grasses that turkeys liked to eat. Indian husbandry of nut trees such as oaks and hickory, not to mention fruit trees, helped. They had domesticated turkeys in southern Mexico at least 2,400 years before Europeans turned up, and they had spread maize agriculture—the farming of corn, squash, beans, pumpkins, and other crops—across parts of North America by between A.D. 800 and 1000. There is little reason to think that they couldn't have spread turkey domestication know-how as well. That could explain why European settlers found "wild" turkeys to be docile. The birds had essentially been trained to stick around by Indians using corn and other food. It is also possible that, after European epidemics decimated Indian populations, turkeys went feral. In any case, settlers found them to be relatively unafraid of people and easy to kill.

The contrast couldn't be sharper between those old birds and the ones eventually restored successfully in the mid–twentieth century. The restored birds were very wild—turkeys so skittish and fearful of man that they fled at the movement of a human eyeball. Why? Some turkey biologists believe that the wildest birds were the only ones left. Hunters had historically killed the turkeys that were easiest to kill—the biggest and slowest. The birds that survived were smaller, quicker, and more wary. Michael Gregonis, Connecticut's state wild turkey program biologist, told me, "As wild turkey populations declined, I believe that the survivors were birds that had very good survival instincts, and populations of these hardy birds continued to exist in isolated pockets in a small portion of their range. Over time these birds were trapped and relocated, and they maintained their wariness."

The idea of trapping and moving wild, fast turkeys instead of using tame farm-raised stock wasn't new, but catching turkeys in the wild wasn't easy. Indians had used traps built with poles and nets and funnel-like entrances baited with corn, but these were difficult to build and not big enough to catch many birds. Conservationists tried luring birds with corn under so-called drop nets and had some success, but the big breakthrough came in 1948, when Herb Dill, the manager of the Swan Lake National Wildlife Refuge in Missouri, and his assistant, Howard Thornsberry, developed a unique trap to catch Canada geese and mallard ducks in the wild. Their trap was the first "cannon net." Using war surplus gunpowder from howitzer shells, the men attached hand-fashioned rockets (think Fourth of July) to the leading edge of a light nylon-mesh net, hid this rig in a blind, waited for ducks or geese to land and swim in close, and fired the net up and over them. Cannon nets were first used successfully on wild turkeys in 1951 in Missouri and South Carolina. Lured within range with shelled corn, feeding birds were netted, tagged, tested, and moved to relocation sites within hours.

It worked. The transplanted wild birds adjusted to their new homes and survived as farm-raised birds had not. The U.S. Fish and Wildlife Service and state wildlife agents had found the key to successful re-stocking, and what had been a sputtering and frustratingly slow campaign to bring back wild turkeys shifted into overdrive using cannon nets. By 1959, the birds numbered an estimated five hundred thousand, but hardly any Americans besides lucky hunters and woodsmen had ever seen one.

By 1973, the wild turkey population had grown to 1.3 million. That year the National Wild Turkey Federation was organized as a 501(c)3 nonprofit, and it launched an aggressive restocking program of its own. By 1975, the turkey population had been spread to forty-three states.

In the next quarter century, turkey hunting was the fastest-growing gun sport in the country. By 2001, the population was up to perhaps 5.5 million, and some 2.6 million hunters were pursuing the big birds in spring and fall in every state but Alaska. The hunting was relatively difficult, but hunters found that the game they had to play to draw turkeys within target range was enormous fun.

"There's a mystique to it," James Earl Kennamer, a senior official with the National Wild Turkey Federation (NWTF), told me. "Watching a turkey strut and go through courtship rituals—that gets me up at 3:30 morning after morning during the season."

By 2009, there were an estimated 8 million birds, and in some places there were clearly too many, and they had changed their behavior. Instead of staying clear of people, they moved in on them.

Farm damage complaints mounted. In southern Maine, the birds were accused of eating the blueberry crop. In vineyards in California, Maryland, Virginia, Rhode Island, New York, and Connecticut, the big birds were said to be feasting on grapes destined for fine wines. In eastern Montana, ranchers complained of turkeys breaking into their hay bales in winter, spreading the hay to pick out seeds, and then spoiling it as cattle feed with their urine and feces. Nationwide, crop damage by all wildlife in 1998 was estimated at $4.5 billion, and in subsequent years an increasing amount of it was being blamed on wild turkeys.

In western Maryland, grape growers used dogs, shotguns, turkey distress calls, falcons, even high-volume radio to scare away flocks of turkeys. Paul Roberts, an owner of Deep Creek Cellars, told the *Baltimore Sun,* "I cannot guarantee it will work with easy-listening music . . . but Christian talk radio seems to drive every wild animal insane." A Christian broadcaster retorted: "They've got to be left-wing turkeys." The newspaper quoted a Washington County grape grower, Dawson Ahalt: "The state people say the turkeys aren't to blame, but I've seen turkeys eating my grapes with my own eyes." A friend's solution: "Try the oven at 400 degrees."

The Turkey Federation came to the bird's defense. In 2002 and 2003, it funded studies in three states using remote cameras in vineyards where damage was reported. The cameras, turned on by motion sensors, recorded results day and night—some 1,588 photographs in all. They showed that while wild turkeys appeared in 45 percent of the photos, they were caught eating grapes in only 7 percent of them. Higher percentages of deer, foxes, squirrels, and raccoons were photographed eating grapes. The camera study was repeated in New York, Virginia, and Connecticut in 2004, with similar results. Tom Hughes, a federation biologist, said the turkeys were actually helping the grape grower: "The cameras capture wild turkeys in the vineyards in all three states and many times they were actually feeding on insects harmful to grape crops."

In 2003, the federation funded Purdue University extension service agents to study crop damage on 529 farms in north-central Indiana. The agents set up video cameras with night vision scopes and attached transmitters to turkeys, raccoons, and deer to track their movements for two growing seasons. No damage by turkeys was recorded. Farmers saw the big birds in their fields during daylight hours and assumed they were eating their crops. Deer and raccoons, however, were photographed after dark with their mouths full of corn and soybeans. Those two animals caused 95 percent of the damage, and squirrels, groundhogs, and other species—but not turkeys—caused the rest. Turkeys, said Brian McGowan, a biologist involved in the study, were scapegoats.

"The turkeys are kind of guilty by association," he said. "They are large animals, and they are out there in the daytime, so the farmers see them and think they did the damage. It's like seeing teenagers on the corner and assuming they're up to no good."

Portraying proliferating populations of wild turkeys to be vineyard innocents—indeed helpmates—was a hard sell for California grape farmers. The vineyard growers could point to James Dickson's 1992 reference book, *The Wild Turkey: Biology and Management*, sponsored by the National Wild Turkey Federation itself, for evidence that turkeys ate not only acorns, insects, and all sorts of seeds, berries, and roots but ripe grapes as well. Indeed, the book calls the grape "a favorite fall food." The state legislature sided with the growers, authorizing depredation permits for wild turkeys in 2005. Both animal rights groups and hunting groups protested.

In Wisconsin, an insurgent wild turkey population had become a menace to ginseng farmers. The big birds had been killed out of the state by 1881, around the time farmers there first tried to cultivate ginseng as a cash crop. They were restocked in 1976, when no one thought they posed a threat to ginseng. But by 2004, the turkey population had grown to three hundred thousand, and the state's Wildlife Damage Abatement and Claims Program paid farmers $196,000 that year in turkey damage claims, most of it to ginseng farmers in Marathon County.

Wildlife biologists were surprised by how easily turkeys adapted to people. Connecticut's Gregonis said that as the birds expanded into suburban settings they became habituated to feeding near homes and lost their fear of people, sometimes becoming aggressive. Glen Cole, a retired New York State wildlife officer and turkey specialist, told me that during early transplants biologists had believed turkeys could thrive only in large tracts of isolated forests. But it turns out, he said, that "they do just great in small woodlots, farms, even villages and towns."

By century's end, flocks of turkeys were turning up in unexpected places from the backyards of Sonoma to the suburbs of Staten Island. People in the sprawl helped make them feel welcome. They put up bird feeders in hopes of attracting feathered friends the size of chickadees, only to be greeted one day by a twenty-pound bird with a five-foot wing-span. Later the big bird might return with two dozen of his buddies and lots of attitude. That's when the "do something" phone calls started.

"Aggressive turkeys" were reported attacking pedestrians in Norman, Oklahoma; Acton, Massachusetts; and Urbana, Illinois, and assaulting a tyke on a tricycle in Montgomery County, Pennsylvania. They were flying into windshields on the Maine Turnpike and on highways in Connecticut, and scratching and pecking at their reflections in the doors and fenders of shiny cars. In suburban Boston, a Danvers postal worker said he had started carrying a broom on his rounds to ward off turkeys. A woman in Peabody claimed turkeys had rushed at her when she went to get the morning paper. A Walpole grandmother said she had been assaulted while walking her grandchildren. In Brookline, town officials distributed a pamphlet on how to handle turkeys if they chased children, joggers, bicyclists, or cars: Establish dominance, carry an umbrella.

In 2008, in an increasingly frequent kind of encounter, Peggy Orenstein was walking her five-year-old daughter to a playground on the edge of Berkeley, California, when they were confronted by a flock of turkeys, each taller than her little girl. The birds didn't budge and seemed threatening. Mother and daughter changed course. In the *New York Times,* Ms. Orenstein wrote: "It's only a matter of time before the turkeys complete the circuit from novelty to nuisance. Until they become like the deer who ate $300 worth of landscaping. Or the geese who have turned jogging around a nearby lake into a trip through a sewer. Or worse: in October a raccoon slid open a screen door of a house across the street, jumped up on the bed where my neighbor was napping with her newborn son and bit her."

• • •

Turkeys stood accused of damaging crops and menacing people with growing frequency, but it was the federal government that accused the big birds of committing crimes against ecosystems where they didn't belong, namely national parks in states where they were not a native species. In 2004, Michael Tollefson, the superintendent of Yosemite National Park, decreed that any turkeys found in park boundaries would be shot on sight. By then, the National Park Service, California grape growers, and several local ecosystem preservation groups were locked in a bizarre battle with the National Wild Turkey Federation, the California Department of Fish and Game, and local turkey-hunting groups over whether the birds were an unwanted invasive species or welcome natives.

In early years of restoration, neither the Turkey Federation nor state wildlife agencies gave much thought to the question of whether wild turkeys were native or not. If local hunters wanted turkeys to hunt, propagators did their best to establish them. They trumpeted their successes wherever they occurred. "One of the most dramatic accomplishments of the turkey-restoration program was the establishment of huntable populations of Merriam's wild turkeys in nearly all of the Rocky Mountain and Pacific coastal states where wild turkeys had not occurred in the days of the Indians," wrote James Trefethen, author of *An American Crusade for Wildlife*.

The California story began to unfold in 1986, when turkeys were spotted on the edge of Yosemite National Park and in the vineyards of Sonoma County. Both park rangers and grape growers recoiled, the rangers fearing the kind of ecosystem damage that other non-native species had wrought, and the grape growers fearing crop damage. But the state's fish and game department and the National Wild Turkey Federation had aggressive plans to transplant and grow turkey populations statewide on behalf of the state's turkey hunters.

Arguments on both sides heated up when state game officials in 1992 proposed releasing three hundred turkeys at six sites on U.S. Forest Service land in the mountains of Northern California for hunters. The state's turkey population was estimated at one hundred thousand, but many of the birds were on private land off limits to hunters. The National Wild Turkey Federation, which backed the release, was at the time paying half the salary of the state's turkey biologist, an arrangement that helped the cash-strapped agency do its turkey work but opened it to conflict-of-interest charges. By then the turkeys had taken up residence in three national parks in the state—Yosemite, Point Reyes, and Sequoia. The then superintendent of Yosemite, David Mihalic, said, "We are all the more surprised at this proposal considering the massive and growing body of scientific evidence that shows nonnative species represent one of the greatest threats to native ecosystems."

State fish and game officials argued that there were no studies of damage and that no serious environmental problems were linked to turkeys. "This is a case of some zealots in the federal government trying to dictate to the state of California what they should and shouldn't do outside the parks," Charlie Ryan, a regional director for the Turkey Federation, told the *Los Angeles Times*. "This is not turning feral pigs loose in the Garden of Eden."

The turkey-stocking effort went ahead. In 1996, the California Native Plant Society and a group called Save Our Ranchlands and Forests sued the state to stop introduction of non-native species. The Turkey Federation set out to prove the birds were California natives. In 2003, it paid the Page Museum $37,000 to fund a study of fossil turkey bones found in the La Brea Tar Pits in downtown Los Angeles and compare them to the bones of contemporary turkeys. The museum, which houses the La Brea bones, hired Zbigniew Bochenski, a bird paleontologist (noted for his comparative study of crows) at the Polish Academy of Sciences in Krakow, to make the comparison, and Kenneth Campbell, curator of ornithology at the L.A. County Natural History Museum, to direct the study. The research team found that the fossil bones were similar to the modern bones—proof, in the federation's view, that turkeys were California natives. Others weren't convinced, mainly because between the last known fossil birds and the introduction of their modern counterparts there was a ten thousand–year period during which turkeys were not known to be present in the state. The National Park Service continued to classify them as a non-native species. Its policy for Yosemite and other national parks in the state held that wild turkeys, like spotted knapweed, yellow star-thistle, bull thistle, Himalayan blackberry, white-tailed ptarmigan, bullfrogs, and various species of introduced fish, were an invasive species to be eradicated if possible. In 2004, five turkeys and 1,600 bullfrogs were killed in Yosemite.

. . .

Across much of the country, complaints about wild turkeys grew. Some were justified but many were not. Defenders of the big birds such as the Turkey Federation and animal protection groups such as the Humane Society of the United States said most people-turkey conflicts could be avoided if people knew more about the birds and exercised a modicum of caution. Unlike white-tailed deer, wild turkeys don't get people killed or send them to the hospital. Unlike resident Canada geese, turkeys don't render parks and soccer fields unusable. But wild turkeys have had the same comeback history as deer and geese, and an even sharper trajectory, going from the edge of extinction in the 1920s to abundance a half century later. Then, just as quickly, they too went from novelties to nuisances. Here was one of the wiliest of wild creatures, one that would in the deep woods flee in an instant at the slightest movement by a hunter otherwise invisible in camouflage, suddenly turning up where people lived in the suburbs like an overgrown robin. How this happened has not been completely sorted out, but there is no reason to think that sprawl, with its food, edges, roosts, and unthreatening people, would be any more off limits to turkeys than it is to black bears.

Chapter Eight

Teddies

Some years ago I got a call from Wayne Pacelle, who was at the time a young vice president for the Humane Society of the United States. One of Pacelle's jobs in those days was to call up journalists and suggest story ideas about the ways people mistreated animals. He was persistent and he knew how to tweak a reporter's curiosity. Pacelle tried to shine a light on all sorts of human activities that in the view of his group involved the abuse of animals, including hunting. He was widely quoted as saying he would end both hunting and trapping if he could, but he told me that even in his brashest early days as an activist he didn't think a ban on hunting was achievable. A more practical goal, he said, was to curb the worst abuses of hunting and "to hold hunters to their own standards" of sportsmanship and fair chase.

Pacelle told me that the mythic portrayal of the canny woods-wise hunter tracking his prey in the wild was way off the mark when it came to most modern bear hunting, which he called "junk hunting" because of the techniques guides used to find bears for easy kills. Guides put out food—including, Pacelle stressed, jelly doughnuts—to lure bears in close. Or they used dogs to find bears and chase them up trees, where they were easy targets. These were "canned hunts," in which lodge operators often advertised that their clients—Pacelle called them "slobs"— were "guaranteed" shots at trophy bruins. This wasn't hunting at all, he said, it was killing, pure and simple, and it wasn't ethical. To someone like me—a former Michigan farm boy who grew up hunting wild birds, squirrels, rabbits, and deer without giving a thought to hunting fairness—the idea that hunting something as exotic as a bear could be done fairly or unfairly was intriguing. To find out more, I questioned fish and wildlife officials, bear-hunting guides, hunting-lodge owners in bear country, and bear-hunting critics. I learned that hunting bears over bait was legal in ten states and that hunting them with dogs was legal in nineteen states.

I focused on Maine, one of the top bear-hunting states. Before 1980, I was told, very little baiting had been done in the Pine Tree State. As bear populations grew, however, baiting became a mainstay of a small hunting and guiding industry catering to out-of-state hunters who would spend good money for a chance to kill a trophy black bear. Critics of the practice, including some former guides, charged that baiting helped one hundred or so hunting lodges and guiding services to maintain a North Woods monopoly because they rented seven thousand to twelve thousand bait sites, some miles apart, across millions of acres of Maine woods, effectively tying up huge chunks of bear habitat. In theory, individuals who hunted independent of the lodges and guides had a right to hunt wherever they wanted. In practice, they were encouraged to stay away. Some operators advertised "controlled access," meaning that hunters not under their control weren't allowed in. North Maine Woods Inc., a caretaker company that managed about 4 million acres belonging to families, investment funds, paper companies, conservation groups, and the state, rented out some three thousand bait sites a year at $46 per site for commercial hunting operations. For $30 a site, individual hunters or groups could rent three bait sites, but some local hunters said commercial operators tied up the best bear habitat and put out word that independents should stay away.

Baiting became routine. Guides typically put out food a month in advance of the bear-hunting season. For each bait station, they fill a five-gallon pail or a fifty-five-gallon barrel with all sorts of smelly, high-caloric food such as fresh or rotten meat, dog food, honey, molasses, bacon grease, oil of anise, and pastries. Some baiters use the heads and shucks of lobsters as "stink bait" to bring in bears from afar. Once bears find the bait, the container is refilled regularly to condition the animals to return for easy food. The bait stations are set up close enough to roads to allow quick access by foot or all-terrain vehicle (ATV). Guides erect tree stands or blinds above or near the bait stations. For hunters using bows and arrows, these stands need to be close—say twenty yards from the bait. Hunters using rifles can be stationed fifty yards away or more. A hunter typically books lodging and guides for two to five days. Hunts are usually conducted from afternoon until dark. The guide drives a hunter down logging roads to a bait-station blind. There the hunter sits motionless, making as little noise as possible, waiting. Bears typically come at dusk. One advantage of hunting over bait is that hunters can usually get a good look at their target. Doing so allows them to avoid shooting a sow with cubs or to otherwise be more selective in their kill. Arrows and bullets need to be placed accurately behind the bear's front shoulder—a five-inch-square patch leading to its vital organs dubbed the "boiler room." Even then, a wounded bear can run for miles before dying, requiring a sometimes long and grueling search down its blood trail.

"Hounding" bears takes specially trained dogs equipped with radio collars that allow their guide-handlers to know where each dog is at all times. The guide's first task is to find a relatively fresh bear scent trail. To do this, he drives a dog with an especially keen nose down roads in a pickup truck until it sniffs fresh bear scent and signals with a bark or a whine. Next, typically, four dogs are uncaged and set loose on the scent. Their handlers monitor the chase on their radios and by listening to the dogs yelp. They ride in trucks, trying to stay within earshot of the dogs. As the dogs close in on their prey, danger increases for both bear and dogs. If the dogs corner the bear before it can climb a tree, they could attack it and tear it apart; or the bear, in defending itself, could kill or wound the dogs. Once the bear is up a tree, the dogs change their barking patterns and the guides and hunter move in. On arrival, they look over the bear to decide whether it is a worthy trophy, and, if so, the hunter delivers the coup de grace.

In terms of how bait and dogs are used, what Pacelle had told me was more or less correct. To get a second opinion on whether these techniques were considered to be fair, I called Jim Posewitz, a hunter, noted fair-chase advocate, and author in Montana. He told me that one way to look at "fair chase" was the equivalent of a fair fight in a bar in which the outcome wasn't predetermined. One fighter couldn't pull out a switchblade and still call it a "fair fight." In "fair chase," the hunter sometimes kills his prey but often doesn't.

Posewitz told me that much of what had been called "hunting" in recent decades didn't fit his notions of fair chase. He didn't think it was fair, for example, for hunters of deer, elk, bears, and other large game animals to use mechanized forms of pursuit: that is, to chase their prey with trucks, Humvees, Range Rovers, ATVs, or snowmobiles. He didn't think it was very sporting to use electronic devices such as radios, range finders, sighting lasers, night vision goggles, trail cameras, or global positioning satellite systems to help find prey either. Posewitz said that using dogs was fair if done right, but modern electronics and mobility had taken much of the fairness out of it. Bear baiting, he said, was not a form of hunting—it was a form of killing, pure and simple. It was a rare occurrence in my experience to have an antihunter and an avid hunter on the same side of a wildlife issue, but Pacelle and Posewitz were in at least partial agreement.

Why was bear killing with bait or hounds allowed in the first place? Black bears are large, shy, perpetually hungry omnivores and predators, but as long as they keep their distance from people, conflicts are rare. What worried state wildlife managers was a potential increase in dangerous conflicts as bear populations grew and spread and people did the same. These managers couldn't control people other than to attempt to educate them on good behavior when bears were around. While animal protection groups urged fertility control, state game managers knew that finding bears and injecting them with fertility control chemicals was even more difficult with bruins than it was with deer. They believed they could control the growth in bear populations with the traditional model of allowing hunters to kill an agreed-upon number of bruins each year. How hunters did this was irrelevant to the ultimate goal.

For many Americans, bear killing itself was the problem. While killing animals for any reason was considered wrong by some people, killing bears evoked especially strong reactions in many more. The question was why, and the answer was easy: Lots of people did not think of bears as large, wild, potentially threatening animals at all. Bears were, first and foremost, the beloved companions of childhood. They were also the bears-as-people stars of screen fantasies and documentaries. For many people bears were like children, and luring them to their deaths with jelly doughnuts was repulsive.

The blurring of fantasy and reality was understandable in the case of bears because real bears weren't a presence in the lives of today's Americans, or their parents or grandparents either. Other fantasy creatures had real-life counterparts. The animals of rhymes, folktales, and cartoons—the Three Little Pigs, Bugs Bunny, the Three Blind Mice, Felix the Cat, and so on—were in the barnyard or around the farm. Real wild bears, on the other hand, had been gone for more than a century.

. . .

Historically, Indians hunted bears for their meat, fat, and fur, and they killed bears that threatened them or stole their food. European settlers were especially eager to remove bears from around their settlements because, like other large predators, notably wolves and cougars, perpetually hungry bruins were attracted to their crops, food stores, and livestock. These creatures were feared and demonized, and their extermination was encouraged by the payment of bounties. Colonial administrators in Maine, for example, first authorized bounties for dead bears in 1770, and the state continued the practice until 1957, when $15 was the going rate. Settlers not only killed bears, they destroyed bear habitat by cutting down forests and draining swamps across huge swaths of what had once been ideal bear country. By 1800, bears had been wiped out of New England except for the mountainous reaches of Maine, New Hampshire, and Vermont. By then, people were killing off wildlife and clearing land in Kentucky and the Ohio Valley for farms. Daniel and Rebecca Boone were among the first to traverse the Cumberland Gap into Kentucky to settle. During a single hunting season along the Big Sandy River, he reportedly killed 155 bears, and she helped him render their fat and sell their hides and meat.

Settlers like the Boones marched across the continent, and they were bad news for bears. For pioneers, the only good bear was a dead bear. Arkansas had thousands of bears—so many before the Civil War that it was nicknamed "the Bear State." By 1928, only about twenty-five were left. Even then, people wanted them dead, according to a report by the state's game and fish commission: "As a general rule the average person believes in killing a bear on sight, and, if one is not easily sighted, there is strong inclination to get the dogs and chase him down."

So it was that the North American black bear, a once-common species, was relegated by the mid–nineteenth century to remnant populations in isolated redoubts left to a few adventurers, hunters, trappers, and hermits. The larger grizzly or brown bear was confined to pockets in the Northwest, Canada, and Alaska. Polar bears were farther north, with the Inuits. The only real bears most people saw were in zoos and circuses.

Long before the modern era, however, bears had taken their unique place in European cultural mythology. Extirpated from most of Europe for centuries, they became the subjects of stories, folktales, and books, often portrayed as cute, even cuddly, and almost human. Later, in films and on television, they could be shown to behave like people. As real wild bears receded from memory, anthropomorphized bears took their places.

Among the earliest humanized bruins were the characters in "The Story of the Three Bears," published in 1837 by Robert Southey in England, where bears had been exterminated more than 1,300 years earlier. Here, three good, honest bears, wee, middle-sized, and huge, lived together in a house in the forest just like people. They cooked food, sat in chairs, and slept in beds. The original story, handed down orally, involved either a female fox or a malicious old woman. In Southey's version she is a woman—an unkempt, foul-mouthed vagrant who enters the bears' house while they are away. She eats their porridge, sits in their chairs, and tries out their beds. When the bears return and find her sleeping in the wee bear's bed, she awakens and, startled, flees out the bedroom window and is never seen again. The author speculates that she may have been arrested by a constable and jailed. By the turn of the century, the bad old woman had morphed into a young girl named Goldilocks and the three bears had become a warm and loving family of Papa, Mama, and Baby. They would do no harm to an innocent little girl, and they were so portrayed in an animated short film by Walt Disney in 1922.

Baloo, the sleepy but serious brown bear in Rudyard Kipling's 1894 tale *The Jungle Book,* teaches wolf pack cubs the Law of the Jungle—a code for living in the wilds of the Indian subcontinent. When a feral child named Mowgli turns up, Baloo becomes his mentor and advises the wolf pack to let the "man's cub" run with it. In the animated 1967 Disney film of the story, Baloo is transformed into a silly, lazy, fun-loving critter who champions a life of leisure living off the land—in sharp contrast to a real bear's constant, frantic quest for food.

The teddy bear was, essentially, America's first original toy, and it began its climb to fame on November 14, 1902, while President Theodore Roosevelt was hunting bears in the Mississippi Delta with a group of local big shots. Their guide, a legendary African American bear tracker and hunter named Holt Collier, and his pack of hounds caught up to an old 235-pound bruin, and he bugled for the president and others to come with their rifles. Before they arrived, however, the bear took a swipe at one of Collier's dogs, killing it. The guide, in turn, whacked the bear on the head with his rifle barrel, lassoed it, and tied it to an oak tree. Roosevelt arrived, looked at the bound and injured bear, and declined to shoot it, asking that someone else put it out of its misery. Three days later, the *Washington Post* published a political cartoon by Clifford Berryman portraying Roosevelt's refusal and depicting the bear as a cub—the first of many cartoons in which the bear got smaller and cuter. Rose Michtom, in Brooklyn, New York, was inspired by the cartoons to make two toy bears to celebrate the president's act. Her husband, Morris, put them in the window of their novelty store and quickly sold them. Morris then wrote the president, asking if they could market toy bears as "Teddy's Bear," and the president supposedly agreed. Sales took off. The Michtoms started the Ideal Novelty and Toy Company and made a fortune. Margarete Steiff, a seamstress in Giengen, Germany, was persuaded by her nephew to make a prototype stuffed bear out of mohair. In 1903, Steiff's company turned out 12,000 toy bears. In 1907, it made 974,000, and all sorts of copycats rushed into the teddy bear business. Suddenly a large and potentially dangerous animal, respected in the wild, had become a cuddly pillow toy.

Fantasy bears proliferated. A. A. Milne, the English writer, created in 1926 his classic children's book *Winnie-the-Pooh*, about a "bear of very little brain" who is nonetheless world-wise, especially in pursuit of honey. (Bears actually prefer the larvae in beehives to the honey.) Pooh was the teddy bear that belonged to Milne's son, Christopher Robin, in the book.

In 1932, Jimmy Kennedy added music to John W. Bratton's 1907 lyrics and produced a hit song called "The Teddy Bears' Picnic." In 1944, the U.S. Forest Service created a mascot named Smokey to help educate the public to the dangers of forest fires. Smokey wore a ranger hat and belt, carried a shovel, and pointed his finger from posters, saying, "Only You Can Prevent Forest Fires." In 1955, the grizzly bear was celebrated in outdoor writer Harold McCracken's book *The Beast That Walks Like Man: The Story of the Grizzly Bear.* In 1965, Walt Morey published *Gentle Ben*, a fantasy about a friendship between a young boy and a black bear. That led to a popular television series and several movies in which a trained bear played Ben. In 1974, a grizzly also named Ben became a star in the 1974 runaway movie success *Grizzly Adams,* about a trapper who discovers an orphaned cub, raises it, and becomes its best pal. The movie cost $140,000 to make and earned $65 million in theaters. It spawned a TV series in 1977. Using trained animals, the movie and TV show depicted bears that seemed to have thoughts and feelings.

With careful filming and editing, even untrained bears could act as if they were human. When nature photographers began to film bears in the wild—Disney's True-Life Adventure series offered *Bear Country* in 1953—some of the most memorable scenes were of bears engaged in human-like conduct. Bear cubs performed childlike antics. Adult bears stood erect like people and seemed to be compassionate—all thanks to careful camera and darkroom work. These films, along with lots of cartoon and puppet bears, later including Fozzie, one of the Muppets, helped generations of Americans grow up vaguely imagining that bears were like people. No other wild creature drew our affection more than the bear. Bambi may have been as well known, but children did not sleep with stuffed Bambis.

Few Americans had any contact with bears in the wild. One of the few places where ordinary people could see wild bears was in Yellowstone National Park. Since its founding in 1872, one of the park's top tourist attractions was watching bears feed at garbage dumps. Park rangers erected an amphitheater at the Otter Creek dump in the park, where five hundred visitors behind a chain-link fence could watch as many as fifty black bears (and an occasional grizzly) noshing while a ranger delivered a lecture on bear behavior. These bear shows were stopped in 1942, but bears had by this time learned to "beg" for food from tourists. For decades, admonitions against feeding them in Yellowstone and other national parks went largely unheeded because park bears rarely hurt people. In 1958, Yogi Bear made his first appearance on Hanna-Barbera Studios' TV cartoon series *The Huckleberry Hound Show*. Yogi personified the mischievous but benign park bear. His best friend, Boo Boo, a cub sporting a bow tie, had the role of keeping Yogi, despite himself, in the good graces of Ranger Smith. Incidents involving bears and people in the national parks ebbed and flowed over the years. Rangers periodically toughened rules against feeding bears—Yellowstone outlawed feeding and closed garbage dumps in 1970—but visitors paid little heed.

Wild bear populations outside parks were rarely seen, but they made a slow comeback in the last half of the twentieth century, thanks to the regrowth of their forest habitat and conservation efforts that included ending bounties and banning bear hunting in areas where they were scarce. Sightings and encounters grew as people sprawled into the forested countryside. In some areas, bears were turning up in people's backyards by the 1990s. And when that happened, many people were confused. Their eyes told them that here was a large animal rifling their garbage can. Their minds summoned up images of make-believe bears. For wildlife officials concerned about bear-people conflicts, the best outcome was for the resident to get a bear-proof garbage can, bring in pet food, take down bird feeders, and clean the grease out of their grills. The worst:

"Quick, get a jelly doughnut."

. . .

North American black bears (*Ursus americanus*) are much smaller than grizzlies and polar bears. They are omnivores and nocturnal for the most part. According to scientists, bears aren't true hibernators. They wake occasionally in their dens but do not eat or drink for five to seven months starting in late fall. They emerge in the spring hungry and spend most of their time over the next several months looking for food and eating it. They see as well as humans, hear better, and have a very keen sense of smell. About 95 percent of a black bear's diet is nuts, berries, fruits, roots, and flowers. Like beavers, they peel bark off trees to eat the cambium layer beneath. They eat insects, love the contents of anthills, and raid beehives. Fish, birds, and other mammals are targets of opportunity. Black bears prefer beechnuts and acorns but will eat anything, including fellow bears, if the opportunity presents itself.

The average adult male weighs 250 pounds but can reach 600 or more. Females weigh 160 pounds on average. On their hind legs, black bears can stand four and a half feet to six feet tall. Males become sexually mature at four to six years of age, females at age two to five. Females breed every other year and have litters of two or three rat-sized cubs but may not breed if available food is limited. Cubs stay with their mother and den with her during their first winter, then emerge the following spring as yearlings and are shooed off to find their own territory. Yearlings can travel dozens or even hundreds of miles to find a place to live without competing bears. If they happen into the domain of a territorial adult male, they may be killed. Like other territorial species, bears spread out as their populations grow. How much space a single bear needs depends on how much food is around. An adult male usually needs several square miles of exclusive territory but will roam far beyond to find food. Black bears avoid people, but where people—unthinkingly or on purpose—put out food, bears will eat it, learn to associate the smell of humans with food, and lose their wariness of them—much faster than many people learn to be wary of bears.

By 2002, the World Wildlife Fund reported that black bears had rebounded to an estimated population of between 735,000 and 941,000. Licensed bear hunting was allowed in twenty-seven states, but bear hunting was on the decline. Bear hunters had long been a small minority of hunters: only about 370,000 people bought bear hunting licenses in the United States (compared with more than 10 million deer hunters).[19] As old hunters died off, few young people took up the bear hunt.

In addition to promoting the successful 1996 ballot initiative banning "cruel" traps in Massachusetts, the Humane Society of the United States helped fund successful ballot initiatives banning bear baiting, hunting bears with dogs, and using traps on them in Colorado in 1992 and Oregon in 1994. Both states contained relatively large numbers of young, antihunting adults who voted for the bans. In 1996, HSUS supported a similar initiative in Washington, which passed, and in Idaho and Michigan, which failed.

In 2004, Wayne Pacelle, promoted to president of HSUS that year, announced that the organization's next targets against unfair bear hunting would be Maine and Alaska, the two most prominent "North Woods" states, where bears and hunters were abundant and where businesses offering hunting guides, lodging, and other services catered to sportsmen nationwide. In both states, hunting was a significant contributor to the economy, and some people thought that Pacelle could never succeed. But he knew that in both states cities and suburbs had gained substantial numbers of new, relatively young residents who didn't hunt themselves and tended to be against hunting and trapping. Meanwhile, rural areas, where the hunting economy and sentiment were strong,

---

19. About forty thousand black bears were legally killed annually in the twenty-seven states and nine Canadian provinces where hunting them was allowed. Another forty thousand bears were believed to be killed by poachers every year for the Asian bear-parts market. In the Far East and in North America, some Asians paid handsomely for gallbladders and bile, which they consumed as "medicine." Bear paws made into soup were prized virility enhancers. Idaho, Maine, New Hampshire, New York, Vermont, Virginia, and Wyoming allowed the sale of bear parts from legally hunted bears.

were losing population. Demographers portrayed Maine as split in two: the poor north, losing jobs, population, and economic vitality; and the affluent and growing south. The southern parts of the state attracted newcomers from Boston and beyond, often young people who wanted to be closer to nature and the rural life—but not too close. Voters in the south outnumbered northern Maine voters 2 to 1.

To campaign for the initiative, HSUS joined Maine Citizens for Fair Bear Hunting and Hunters for Fair Bear Hunting, groups that included some former hunters, trappers, and guides. They were supported by two other national groups, the Fund for Animals and the American Society for the Prevention of Cruelty to Animals. Aligned against the ban was a coalition of hunting interests called Maine's Fish and Wildlife Conservation Council, which also included bear hunters, trappers, and guides. They were aided by three national hunting groups: the U.S. Sportsmen's Alliance, the Ballot Issues Coalition, and Safari Club International.

The state government agency that regulates bear hunting, the Department of Inland Fisheries and Wildlife, sided with the hunters and trappers it regulated. Its officials used the now-familiar argument that to allow uninformed voters to decide wildlife management techniques was to sanction "ballot box biology" over professional expertise.

"The end of the bait hunt in Maine is the end of bear management in Maine," said Randy Cross, one of the state's bear biologists. "This [baiting] is the only feasible way that we can kill the bears we need to stabilize the population." He said that keeping the black bear population relatively stable required hunters to kill 3,500 to 4,000 bruins annually; otherwise the population would explode with potentially dangerous consequences. Nobody knew, of course, how many bears could be killed if bait and dogs were prohibited, but state officials had statistics on how many bears were killed with them. In 2003, 92 percent of the 3,951 bear killings by hunters involved the use of bait or dogs. Even so, only one in four hunters bagged a bear. Without using bait and dogs, said Ken Elowe, Maine's chief wildlife biologist, the hunting success rate would plummet to around 6 percent, and cause most out-of-state hunters to go elsewhere to hunt. Without these hunters, Maine's bear population (estimated at twenty-three thousand) could grow 50 percent in five years, to thirty-five thousand, "a level much higher than Maine's citizens want or will tolerate," he said.

Supporters of the ban on baiting and dogs argued that a bear population explosion was not inevitable. They cited the case of Colorado, where baiting, hounding, and spring hunting had been outlawed in 1992. Colorado's bear population did grow, complaints about miscreant bears mounted, and wildlife agents had to be called in to kill more nuisance bears. To compensate, however, the state doubled the length of the bear-hunting season and, as a result, sold twice as many licenses as before the ban. The hunters, in turn, killed twice as many bears. In all, Coloradans judged the new rules a success, even though by 2011 wildlife agents were having to kill record numbers of nuisance bears.

Jennifer Vashon, Maine's chief bear biologist, said the Colorado example wouldn't work in Maine because of differences in terrain. Colorado had high mountains with lots of wide-open landscape. Hunters with binoculars could see bears moving on the ground and that made stalking them easier. Much of Maine's bear habitat, by contrast, was densely forested, with thickets and cedar swamps. Seeing and stalking bears on this terrain was almost impossible, so killing enough bruins annually to keep their population stable would not be possible.

Only about three hundred nuisance-bear complaints were received by Maine wardens annually, and many of those were multiple sightings of the same bear. Many people phoned in a mere sighting of a bear, even though its presence near people—possibly just moving through—wasn't threatening in itself. Offensive or threatening bears were hunted down by game wardens using dogs, then tranquilized, ear-tagged, moved sixty miles or more, and released. Repeat offenders were killed, and this, officials stressed, was likely to increase as bear populations grew. Since bears would inevitably die, they argued, wasn't it better for the state to license hunters to kill them than to use tax dollars to pay someone else to kill them?

The issue of fairness was at the heart of the Maine initiative, and to many Maine voters the practice of putting out jelly doughnuts to lure bears to their deaths didn't seem fair. However, Maine had a lot of hunters, trappers, and fishermen who did a lot of things that people not engaged in these activities might consider unfair. In his weekly column, one outdoor writer asked: Was putting out decoys and using calls to lure in ducks and turkeys fair? What about planting clover or using sexual attractants to bring in deer? Was treeing raccoons with hounds different from treeing bears? Was baiting, trapping, and then boiling alive a Maine lobster fair? All were common practices. What was the difference between putting out food for bears and baiting a hook with a worm to get fish to bite?

When I called Wayne Pacelle a few weeks before the 2004 elections, he seemed confident of winning in both Maine and Alaska. Early polls suggested that 70 percent of Mainers opposed bear baiting and trapping, and a series of last-minute TV ads would, hopefully, cement a victory. "We have some devastating footage of bears in traps, and we are aiming it straight for people's hearts," he told me.

On November 2, 2004, Maine Question 2, called "An Act Prohibiting Certain Bear Hunting Practices"—that is, making it a crime to hunt bears with bait, traps, or dogs, except to protect property and public safety or conduct research—went down to defeat, even though its supporters outspent opponents $2.2 million to $1.7 million. Commentators said economic self-interest trumped concerns over bear-hunting fairness. But the vote was 53 percent against and 47 percent for, meaning that what Pacelle had said was right: Sentiment against "junk hunting" was on the rise. Alaska's ballot measure, called "Prohibiting Bear Baiting or Feeding," also failed, 57 percent to 43 percent. That vote, too, was evidence of the growing power of urban and suburban populations in the state.

Meanwhile, many of the same people who thought feeding bears to hunt them was unfair continued to ignore warnings that their own behavior around bears was unsafe. Superintendents of the nation's national parks continually issued warnings about bears, as they had for decades. For many years, visitors to Yosemite National Park had been required to sign an entry form acknowledging that they had been informed of bear danger, but that seemed to do little good. People put out food for bears or unthinkingly left food in their locked cars, which the bears regularly broke into. In 2002, after a spike in "human-bear" incidents in Yosemite National Park, Superintendent David A. Mihalic said, "Bears kill people. That is my fear. Part of our challenge is to get people to understand these bears are powerful wild animals."

Tim Treadwell certainly didn't understand. In the annals of tragic anthropomorphism involving bears, what happened to Timothy Treadwell in 2003 ranked near the top of any list. Born Tim Dexter in 1957, he grew up in Ronkonkoma, on New York's Long Island, where the only bears were stuffed. A college dropout, he moved to California, got odd jobs, professed to be an aspiring actor—changing his surname to Treadwell—and became a serious alcoholic and drug addict. After a nearly fatal cocaine-heroin overdose, Treadwell went to Katmai National Park in Alaska in 1989 with a friend to watch bears.

Coincidentally that year, the Bambi of bear movies, *The Bear*, came out. Trained bears played heavily edited roles, and humans supplied various bear sound effects. In the story, a wounded male grizzly meets and befriends an abandoned cub and, instead of eating it, bonds with it, while hunters and their dogs give chase. At one point, the big bear confronts a cowering hunter he could easily kill but doesn't. The bear, seemingly affected by his hunter's whimpering, turns and leaves. The big bear then saves the cub from a cougar, and they embrace and settle into a cave for winter. The film critic for *Parenting* magazine called it "one of the most perfect films imaginable for parents to see with their children." Pauline Kael, in the *New Yorker*, called it fake nature, adding, "It's saying that we shouldn't kill bears because they're so much like us—after it fakes the evidence that they are."

Treadwell's Alaska trip was a revelation to him. He saw the natural world as benign—unlike the civilization he had experienced, which was nasty. He became a self-proclaimed eco-warrior. For the next thirteen summers, with his teddy bear in hand, he ventured back to Katmai on Alaska's southern coast to camp near the world's largest terrestrial carnivore—a subspecies of the grizzly (*Ursus arctos middendorffi*) called the Alaskan brown bear or Kodiak bear. These bears normally weigh 800 to 1,200 pounds but can reach 1,700 pounds and can stand eleven feet tall on their hind legs.

Treadwell claimed to be "protecting" the bears from poachers. Park superintendent Deb Liggett called his actions "misguided" and "dangerous." By hanging around with the bears, he was conditioning them not to be wary of humans. "If Timothy models unsafe behavior, that ultimately puts bears and other visitors at risk," Liggett told the *Anchorage Daily News.*

Treadwell filmed himself getting very close—within touching distance—to the bears. He called them his "friends." He told his camera he "loved" them. He gave them names: Mr. Chocolate, Sgt. Brown, Booble, Ed, Cupcake, Rowdy. He wrote a book in 1997 entitled *Among Grizzlies: Living with Wild Bears in Alaska* and drew national attention by appearing on *The Late Show with David Letterman* in 2001 to promote it. He said he felt safer around the bears than he did running in New York's Central Park. He made public appearances as an environmental activist, talking to schoolchildren. He helped found Grizzly People, a fund-raising group to protect bears and their habitat.

In 2003, Treadwell, then forty-six years old, and his girlfriend, Amie Huguenard, thirty-seven, were back camping out with the bears. Toward the end of this, his thirteenth visit, on the evening of October 5, the pair was attacked by one or two bears believed to be newcomers around the camp. Both people died. A six-minute audio recording of the deaths, found in a video camera that was turned on inside their tent, confirmed that Treadwell and Huguenard had been eaten alive. The audiotape, never made public but played by investigators and others, recorded the screams and shouts of two human beings experiencing slow, agonizing deaths. Rangers later carried out four garbage bags of half-eaten body parts that had been strewn around the scene. They killed two bears, a large male and an adolescent, and found body parts of Treadwell and Huguenard in their stomachs. Werner Herzog, the filmmaker, produced a one-hour-and-forty-minute documentary, *Grizzly Man,* about the episode, using Treadwell's footage, recordings, and interviews. Herzog, after viewing hours of Treadwell's bear video, which included the large male, said, "Tim may have seen all sorts of things in this bear's eyes, but all I can see is indifferent hunger."

. . .

Black bears, in contrast to Treadwell's grizzlies, are not only much smaller but also not ferocious. Lynn Rogers, a wildlife biologist who has spent a lifetime studying black bears up close in the wild, calls them timid, docile, and motivated by fear and food. He has campaigned to de-demonize them.

But black bears do attack and kill people, and in many cases the people are at fault. Between 1900 and 2009, they killed sixty-three people in fifty-nine attacks—most of those (86 percent) in the last forty years, according to a recent study. Whoever was at fault, state wildlife managers had a responsibility to mitigate conflicts between people and wild animals, including bears, and this task was becoming increasingly difficult as the populations of both expanded into each other's habitat.

By 2010, North American black bears had made significant population gains, numbering anywhere from 800,000 to more than 1 million—

depending on who was estimating. They had moved aggressively into their old haunts, now occupied by both second-growth forests and human sprawl. In the Northeast, New Hampshire and Vermont each had populations of 5,000 or so bears, and New York's population was put at 6,000 to 7,000; both populations were growing and spreading. Connecticut had about 500 and Massachusetts had around 3,500—the most in two centuries, Jim Cardoza, the state's bear specialist, told me. Virginia's mountainous west had a population of 4,000 to 6,000. People-bear conflicts grew apace.

New Jersey is illustrative. The state banned bear hunting in 1971, when a remnant population of no more than one hundred animals lived in the hilly forests in the northwest, far away from human populations concentrated in the New York–Newark metropolitan region in the central-eastern part of the state. During the next three decades some two hundred thousand acres of farmland reverted to forest, and people sprawled out into it. Developers created sprawl for people, of course, but bears liked it too. Between 1995 and 2000, the territory New Jersey's bears occupied nearly doubled. Bears turned up in several southern counties. The big enticement was easy food. In 2002, the state outlawed bear feeding, but enforcement was minimal, and all sorts of institutions, ranging from fast-food restaurants to nursing homes, were putting out food waste in garbage cans and Dumpsters without thinking about bears. By 2003, bears had been sighted in all twenty-one New Jersey counties, and the state authorized a six-day hunt beginning on December 8, 2003, in the five northwestern counties. Hunters, using neither bait nor dogs, killed 328 bears. Televised demonstrators, the sight of dead bears, and attendant publicity appeared to galvanize anti-hunting groups, who warned state politicians that if the hunt continued they would pay a price at the ballot box. The 2004 bear hunt was called off. *New York Times* columnist Peter Applebome called New Jersey "the epicenter of anti-hunting absolutism." Another six-day hunt was approved for December of 2005. The New Jersey Supreme Court dismissed a last-minute legal attempt to block it. HSUS denounced the hunt and launched a new initiative called "Wildlife Abuse Campaign: Ending the Killing of Animals for Trophies and Fun." Hunters killed 297 bears.

As the Democratic candidate for governor that fall, Jon Corzine committed himself to nonlethal bear management, and after his election he ruled out future hunts. Bear complaints grew and spread. In May of 2006, a 225-pound black bear wandered into downtown Trenton, the state capital, and was captured and killed. By 2009, New Jersey, the nation's most densely populated state, had 8.7 million people and perhaps 3,500 bears commingling over an area of 7,417 square miles, but nobody had been killed or seriously injured by a bear. This was reason enough not to reinstate bear hunting, the governor said. Bear-hunting proponents argued that lethal attacks were only a matter of time without bear hunting, and they campaigned to help defeat Corzine in November of 2009. The new governor, Chris Christie, reinstated bear hunting in 2010. In six days in December, hunters killed 591 bears.

. . .

The Florida black bear, *Ursus americanus floridanus,* is arguably smaller and has a flatter head than other black bears. An estimated 11,500 of these bears once roamed southern Georgia, Alabama, and Mississippi and thrived throughout Florida until heavy logging wiped out much of their forested habitat. By 1974, only a few hundred were left in Florida, and the state restricted the hunting of them to two national forests and two sparsely populated counties. They were subsequently declared a threatened species, and in 1994 bear hunting was outlawed. Environmentalists sought to declare the bear an endangered subspecies, but in 1998 the federal government declined to do so, estimating its population at 3,000 and rebounding.

The Ocala National Forest, a 637.5-square-mile federal preserve in central Florida, held the state's largest black bear population, 730 to

1,100 bruins. The forest is surrounded by fast-growing retirement communities and is only forty miles to the north of Orlando, a city of 2 million that sprawls over four counties. Because young bears, especially yearling males, are expelled by their parents from the territory in which they were raised, they are very likely to wander outside the national forest onto roads and highways and into areas populated by people, most of whom have moved in from out of state.

On a trip to the region, I arranged to meet Tom Shupe, a forty-seven-year-old biologist with the Florida Fish and Wildlife Commission who was responsible for dealing with bear-people conflicts in what was called the central Florida "hot zone." Shupe told me that in the eighteen years he had been on the job he had seen an influx of people who were increasingly nature-illiterate. They knew little about the flora and fauna back home and even less about it in Florida. Mention bears to them, he said, and they're more likely to bring up the entertainers in bear suits at nearby Disney World than the real thing.

Shupe drove me to see a new underpass for bears (and other wildlife) built beneath a highway on the northern edge of Orlando. Being hit and killed by motor vehicles was the biggest danger to bears in Florida, by far. Since 1990, roadkill bear numbers had more than tripled to 143 in 2005, spiking at 171 in 2007 and 169 in 2010. Florida had taken the lead in building dozens of wildlife underpasses and overpasses, most along Interstate 75, to help protect bears and the endangered Florida panther.

Off the roadways, reports of sightings or encounters with bears, but not necessarily conflicts, had soared from just 90 in 1995 to 3,275 in 2009. Many of those were in central Florida and involved bears rifling garbage cans or turning up in people's yards. Shupe emphasized during my visit that, just as in New Jersey, bears had never killed or seriously harmed anyone in Florida.[20] However, as an officer responsible for the safety

---

20. Relatively speaking, bears were a minor wildlife worry in a state with a burgeoning population of 1.5 million alligators and mounting gator attacks on pets and people.

of both bears and people in the region, Shupe said he was increasingly worried.

Because Orlando is laced with sloughs and swamps, bears could make their way into the heart of the city with relative ease. By way of illustration, we visited a motel on the north side of town managed by immigrants from India. Not long before, the Indians, who had never seen a bear, had become horrified to discover a large black creature in their motel Dumpster. They called 911, and the operator alerted the police and Shupe. With the help of police and a team of wildlife agents, Shupe used a large box trap to catch the bear, a 240-pound male. They loaded the bruin into a truck, drove it into the Ocala Forest, and released it.

Revisiting the Dumpster, Shupe walked me around the back to a chain-link fence. Before the bear had turned up, the fence had been pried apart by some homeless men. Behind the fence was a slope where the men sometimes slept. The slope descended to a watery slough. The bear had apparently wandered into the slough and followed its nose uphill to the Dumpster. Shupe had told the Indians to keep their motel Dumpster closed. The Indians told him that the homeless men who Dumpster-dived (presumably not at the same time as the bear) opened it regularly. In any case, no other bears turned up.

Inadvertent bear feeding was one problem Shupe had to deal with. The other was people who fed bears deliberately, ignoring the dangers. Newcomers to Orlando's gated subdivisions full of McMansions on multiacre lots tended to assume that the money they put into their new homes guaranteed a certain amount of order and protection. Community gates and guards, however, did nothing to keep away bears and other creatures. Wildlife was lured up into backyards by the smell of food in garbage cans, compost heaps, grills, pet dishes, and bird feeders.

Alligators killed three people in Florida in May 2005. Since 1948, they had killed seventeen people.

Many residents ignored admonitions about not leaving food outside. For Shupe, this was a far more insidious problem.

"Oh, isn't he cute. Let's toss him a cookie. Get the camera."

Shupe spit out the words and shook his head. Feeding bears is illegal in Florida. People who did it were often so excited that they lost all sense that they were feeding a large, wild creature, or that the cute hundred-pound yearling that showed up last year might soon return as a three-hundred-pound adult. The progression, Shupe said, usually went like this: A cookie or doughnut is tossed in the backyard for the bear; the bear turns up and is photographed. The next time, the bear ambles around the yard and finds the bird feeder or the dog's dish. The people get a little anxious but keep photographing "their bear" and perhaps start a bear album to show their friends. Sooner or later, the bear tries to get in the back door to enter the house. At this point, said Shupe, people panic. They call 911. Their possessiveness evaporates.

"We interrogate these people later. They'll admit to illegal feeding. I've had some people bring out three or four photo albums of *their* bear," Shupe told me. "Before they get scared, they say it's *their* bear. When they call us, it's 'What are you going to do about *your* bear?'"

By this time, whoever's bear it is, it is too late, and it is the bear that pays the price. To hold off the inevitable day when a Florida black bear kills someone, Shupe and his fellow officials follow a strict set of procedures, as do their counterparts in many other states. If the animal is judged to be too aggressive, it's killed on the spot. Otherwise, it is tranquilized, tagged, and relocated, either back to the Ocala National Forest or farther away. In recent years, Shupe and other wildlife agents were relocating fifty to one hundred bears annually. Relocation doesn't always work. If a bear has learned to associate the human scent with food, it is likely to turn up in some other backyard. If that happens a third time, the bear is executed. The number of Florida nuisance bears euthanized with a bullet to the head grew from zero in 2000 to twenty-two in

2006 to thirty-five in 2009. It doesn't matter whether people toss a bear a cookie in an act of compassion or leave their garbage out by mistake, it is the bear that pays the ultimate price.

. . .

As black bear populations continue to grow and spread across the land-scape, their conflicts with people grow too. Both bears and people will have to be managed to minimize those conflicts and the potential dangers they entail. Habituating bears to associate with people in order to gain access to the food that people supply, either deliberately or inadvertently, will make things worse. Educating people to take down bird feeders, clean their outdoor grills, keep pet food indoors, lock their garbage receptacles, and keep their Dumpsters shut works only to the extent that people take heed. Laws against wildlife feeding, along with tough enforcement, would help minimize conflicts and dangers, but all sorts of laws regulating people's actions related to pets and wildlife go unenforced. It will probably take a series of tragedies in which bears kill or injure people for people to change their behavior or for authorities to forcefully mandate such changes.

As for the bears, negative conditioning—that is, doing things to make bruins associate people with danger, disturbance, or discomfort—can make them steer clear of people. Managing bear numbers by hunting and killing them can work, but only up to a point. As we have seen, bear hunters are dwindling as popular sentiment against bear hunting has grown. Also, hunting bears in places where bear-people conflicts are likely to grow—that is, in the sprawl—is problematic. Killing problem bears will, therefore, continue to be the work of government agents paid for by taxpayers.

In our minds, we have always given animals human traits. We romanticize and sentimentalize them as members of the animal kingdom to which we belong. Children grow up surrounded by images of wild animals presented as furry or feathery little people like them. We learn from our pets how some animals live and then mistakenly project that knowledge onto wild creatures living a much different reality. In the past, however, people had enough direct experience in the natural world to sort sentiment from reality. Not so today. Today's denatured adults often continue to see bears and other wild animals the way they did as children without the corrective lens of direct experience.

PART THREE

DENATURED LIFE

The growth of conflicts between people and wildlife is the result, as we have seen, of a proliferation of wild animals and birds across a landscape where forests have made major comebacks; the sprawl of people across that landscape; and changes in people's relationships with the natural world they inhabit.

People have embraced pets and wild creatures as never before, and they believe strongly in protecting the natural environment. At the same time, they have distanced themselves from the landscape they inhabit and traverse, and in doing so they have come to treat and mistreat the environment and its natural inhabitants in mindless ways, either unintentionally or with the best of intentions. In some cases, they justify their actions on the grounds that they are doing good, or at least not doing harm. In other cases, they are only vaguely aware of what they are doing. Either way, their ancestors would more than likely have found some of the things they do to be bizarre, if not incredible.

Take, for example, running over creatures with motor vehicles. The idea that roads would be smooth enough, vehicles fast enough, and wildlife abundant enough to create today's carnage on our roadways would have been unthinkable not long ago. Now not only is it thinkable, it has a name, roadkill, that has become the subject of endless jokes, and it is widely thought to be an unavoidable cost of modern mobility.

People spend billions of dollars annually to buy seeds to feed wild birds. My Depression-era grandparents would certainly be shaking their heads at such a waste of hard-earned money. They, of course, would have had no idea how much disposable income their relatively flush grandchildren would have to spend on such non-necessities as birdseed. But perhaps what they would find most unbelievable is that their descendants would be so disconnected from nature that the number one way they interacted with wildlife would be by feeding wild birds.

My parsimonious grandparents back on the farm would no doubt have ridiculed people who think of their pets as surrogate children and lavish tens of billions of dollars annually on them for human-grade food, birthday parties, organic snacks, dietary supplements, cemetery plots, stress pills, breath deodorants, and hip replacement surgery. On the other hand, they could easily understand befriending a stray cat with a little food, since such acts of kindness have been going on for as long as cats and people have existed together. They would also have heard arguments over whether strays were a scourge on the landscape best eradicated or helpless victims deserving of care. More difficult for them to understand would be the latest cat care movement: helping stray cats to remain stray cats by catching and neutering them, then putting them back where they were caught in the quixotic belief that their burgeoning populations will eventually abate.

What stands out about roadkill, feeding birds, and saving stray cats is how huge, expensive, and commonplace they have become and how many people take them for granted—as if these phenomena had been going on for generations. They haven't. As we shall see, they are the products of the modern era, and the history of how they grew coincides with our estrangement from the natural world.

Chapter Nine

Doers to Viewers

Americans had three hundred years of subduing and exploiting the landscape to create a path to plenty before the American frontier came to an end and the era of industrialization began to demolish the Jeffersonian ideal of families on the land. The manufacturing revolution that took off in the 1880s would put more people to work in factories than in fields. Big farms got bigger. Small farms became obsolete; rural labor, superfluous. Hands-on farm families still made up 38 percent of the American population in 1900, but they shrank to just 1 percent in the course of the next century as people traded dawn-to-dusk toil and dirty fingernails for a modern world of unprecedented affluence and convenience—and detachment from the land.

Much of the natural landscape went from something exploited for fur, feathers, food, lumber, and minerals to something exploited for scenery and recreation. In the nineteenth century, what was left of untamed land came to be seen as unspoiled beauty worth saving, enjoying, and even paying to visit. In the twentieth century, Americans became fascinated by distant wilderness and the wild creatures that inhabited it, and writers found an eager market among members of a growing urban middle class for realistic stories about animals in the wild. The writers, among them Jack London, Ernest Thompson Seton, Charles D. Roberts, and William J. Long, crafted bestsellers that they maintained were largely faithful to the natural world. But for the sake of narrative drive and sales, they took certain liberties: A crafty fox leads a pack of hounds into the path of an oncoming train; a porcupine rolls down a hill for fun; a bird breaks a leg and fashions its own splint; a wolf kills a caribou with a single bite through its chest into its heart. These writers imbued wild creatures with humanlike talents. They wrote stories about animal heroes and told them from the animal's point of view, describing its experiences and even its thoughts.

To John Burroughs, they were "sham naturalists," and in the March 1903 issue of the *Atlantic Monthly,* this self-taught naturalist, writer, and friend of the conservationist president Theodore Roosevelt called them on it. These writers were out to make a buck at the expense of scientific reality, he wrote. Four years later, in a magazine interview, President Roosevelt called them "nature fakers." He saw in nature ruthless competition, instinct, and survival of the fittest. "If the child mind is fed with stories that are false to nature," he said, "the children will go to the haunts of the animal only to meet with disappointment . . . disbelief, and the death of interest." Nevertheless, as people removed themselves from direct contact with wild animals, the genre of anthropomorphism grew.

In addition to books, one late-nineteenth-century substitute for real nature was film. Beginning with the invention of the motion picture camera in the 1880s, the camera supplied views of nature that could be staged and cropped to produce salable celluloid products. "Poised at the intersection of art, science, and entertainment, natural history film would transform American perceptions of and interactions with wildlife over the course of the twentieth century," wrote Gregg Mitman in *Reel Nature: America's Romance with Wildlife on Film.*

Some filmmakers, to deliver entertainment that was commercially successful, resorted to shortcuts. Some of them staged scenes using zoo animals to depict scenes in the wild. Colonel William N. Selig reenacted Theodore Roosevelt's 1910 expedition to Africa in a Chicago studio. Others condensed hours of film and edited sequences to show wild animals acting like people. In this way, the humanized creatures in filmed nature increasingly supplanted the instinctive and competitive ones in a nature that was indifferent and amoral. Wrote Mitman: "Just as Burroughs cautioned writers against taking undue license with the facts of nature for literary effect, so too the naturalist-photographer in developing a faithful picture walked a thin line between capturing the authentic drama and beauty of nature and artificially fabricating drama to create a box-office sensation."

In the 1920s, filmmakers promoting conservation not only gave wild animals names but also portrayed them as adorable pets. In William Finley's 1929 movie-lecture, *Camera Hunting on the Continental Divide,* about an expedition to Glacier National Park and the Rocky Mountains, the filmmakers befriended moose, elk, bears, marmots, and bighorn sheep. A grouse was tame enough to pet, as were Emma the mule deer and Chippie the chipmunk. This film and others did wonders to promote conservation, and in them man played the role of both despoiler and savior.

Soon, however, films took to portraying man as the natural world's enemy. In *Bambi,* Walt Disney's 1942 animated classic, no humans appear, but the destructiveness of humans is powerfully portrayed in man's dogs chasing the young deer, the forest carelessly set ablaze, and, of course, the shooting of Bambi's mother—evoking a young child's worst nightmare, losing a parent.[21]

"It has become perhaps the single most successful and enduring statement in American popular culture against hunting," wrote Ralph H. Lutts. "It was targeted at children in their most impressionable, formative years. The memory of the incident remains with them even into adulthood." *Bambi* cost $1 million more than it earned during its first

---

21. In 2005, Sir Paul McCartney, the former Beatle, said he had become an antihunting animal rights advocate because of the movie: "If you think of Bambi, its mum gets killed by a hunter, and I think that made me grow up thinking hunting isn't cool," he said in an interview.

run, but it was rereleased each subsequent decade, made lots of money—$267.5 million by 2010—and distressed each new generation of children with the prospect of parental loss.

Because animation was expensive, the Walt Disney studio turned after the Second World War to True-Life Adventures, a series purporting to depict nature unspoiled by man. The people who actually took their cameras into the wild were admonished not to show any evidence of man or his work in their footage. The first, *Seal Island,* won an Academy Award.

"While Disney's True-Life Adventures revealed the purity of nature through a wide-angle lens, they simultaneously purified nature through anthropomorphic conventions that introduced familiar portraits of animal life," wrote Mitman. Female seals arrive to the tune of "Here Comes the Bride." *Variety* magazine joked that Disney was turning the audience into "peeping tom naturalists." Violence was muted to present "a sentimental version of animals in the wild that sanctified the universal 'natural' family as a cornerstone of the American way of life," wrote Mitman. Footage of baby seals being trampled to death by bulls on Seal Island was edited out.

Disney claimed True-Life Adventures were unstaged and true to nature even though they were full of anthropomorphisms. Bosley Crowther, the *New York Times* film critic in 1954, called *Beaver Valley* a "synthetic reconstruction of nature . . . passed off as real." For example, the filmmakers used cages and glass barriers to show a coyote and a beaver close to each other—a rare occurrence in the wild.

Zoo Parade made its debut on NBC on May 28, 1950. Its host was Marlin Perkins, director of the Lincoln Park Zoo in Chicago. The show, broadcast live on Sunday afternoons, was a runaway hit—and was widely seen as wholesome entertainment for children and parents alike. Perkins made his creatures part of the family. In apparent contradiction to the traditional Christian notion of human dominion over animals, his Easter Sunday program preached that animals and humans were

loved equally by God. Animals and children shared a bond of inno-
cence and were part of a family under threat from larger forces. Mitman
wrote: "In sheltering young, be they animal or human, from nuclear
annihilation, the threat of communism, and the more insidious side of
commercial culture, Americans in the 1950s upheld the nuclear family as
a safe haven." Television offered up role models in such family situation
comedies as *Father Knows Best, Ozzie and Harriet, Leave It to Beaver,*
and *The Donna Reed Show.*

· · ·

Today, it is difficult to imagine a lifestyle devoid of the conveniences and
comforts we take for granted. It is easier to find people worried about
what modern amenities are doing to separate people from nature. One
of those early worriers was John D. Rockefeller Jr. (1874–1960). He came
of age during the industrial revolution and grew concerned that people
were being separated from the natural world because of it.

"My grandfather grew up amid all this change, watching the agricultural ideal give way before the industrial maelstrom," wrote Ann
Rockefeller Roberts in *Mr. Rockefeller's Roads: The Untold Story of Acadia's
Carriage Roads and Their Creator.* By the 1920s, people traveled in trains
and automobiles "at rates of speed that insulated them from the sounds
and smells of the earth," she wrote. Nature was seeping from their lives.
"By then, most Americans lived in houses that protected them from the
vagaries of the weather but also removed them from nature's own cycles
and rhythms. Remarkable and welcomed labor-saving devices such as
the electric washing machine and dryer, indoor plumbing, and running
water increasingly kept everyone inside and separated from the earth. In
fact, nearly every invention born of modern technology served to insu-
late people more and more from the land."

It is also difficult today to imagine how harsh farm life was. The
Rockefellers and other well-heeled Americans may have had access to

all those comforting and labor-saving devices of the early twentieth century, but most of them had not arrived in rural America.

In Iowa during the Depression, for example, Mildred Armstrong Kalish grew up on a farm that had no electricity, no running water, no central heating, and no money. One of four children raised by a single mother, Kalish experienced the kind of hands-on rural life that all but disappeared in the postwar years. In her wonderful 2007 book, *Little Heathens,* Kalish notes that kids were an important source of farm labor. Among their chores was gathering kindling for the kitchen stove, pulling weeds, picking vegetables, shocking sheaves of oats and corn, putting up hay, and killing farm animals.

> Getting a chicken ready for the supper table was another of those jobs that we kids could do. . . . From the age of about eight, all of us kids, boys and girls alike, knew how to snatch a chicken by both legs . . . and quickly dispatch the frantic fowl with a hand ax. We had several methods, but the preferred one was to grasp the legs and the wing tips in the left hand, lay the head of the chicken on the chopping block, stroke the top and the back of the head gently a couple of times, and then deal the fatal blow with the ax. . . . Once the head is chopped off, you release the chicken, allowing it to flop wildly about the barnyard until it stops of its own accord. And now you know the origin of the expression "running around like a chicken with its head cut off."

That was just the first step. The dead bird then had to be doused in scalding water and stripped of its smelly feathers. Next its underhairs were singed off with the flame of a lit newspaper. That left a naked corpse ready for eviscerating. From a hole cut into the bird's rear end, the kids pulled out innards, setting aside the liver, gizzard, and heart. At that point the chicken resembled the whole birds sold in today's markets.

Rabbits? Kalish was an eight-year-old expert at dispatching bunnies with a sharp whack to the back of their necks—and skinning them:

On our farm there really was only one way to do it and even us little kids knew how. While someone holds the animal by the head, you take a hefty folding knife and run the sharp blade in a circle just at the base of the neck. Now, with both hands, firmly grip the fur at the shoulders and pull the skin down the body. Presto! The skin turns inside out and all you have to do is cut the skin at the back feet.

While Kalish and her siblings were spared from watching an adult kill a pig by whacking it on the head with a sledgehammer, they were later presented with the hog's head to clean, using toothbrushes and baking soda, as the first step in making head cheese.

Kalish noted that modern conveniences weren't entirely absent from the region. For example, she remembered that perhaps four homes in the little village of Garrison, three miles away, had indoor flush toilets. Everybody else had outhouses. This being the 1930s, toilet paper was an unknown commodity. In her family, you tore a page out of the Montgomery Ward or Sears Roebuck catalog, crumpled and recrumpled until it got relatively soft. Men in many families, she wrote, used corncobs.

. . .

When I read Kalish's book, I couldn't help thinking back to rural Michigan in the 1950s. It was amazing how little had changed—at least for us. Two decades had passed. The Second World War had come and gone, and Americans were beginning to climb into an era of unprecedented affluence—that is, except our family and others like us.

The farmhouse my family moved into in 1951, when I was eight years old, had electric lightbulbs dangling from wires in the ceiling, no running water, and no central heating. It was situated on sixty acres, most of them covered in young trees and brush, on a gravel road in the central part of the state.

Every drop of water we used for drinking, making coffee, cooking, washing our faces and hands in a tiny washbowl, washing dishes in a small basin, and taking baths in a galvanized tub (usually once a week whether we needed it or not) had to be hand-pumped and carried in buckets from a well across the road—a distance of fifty yards. I got a lot of experience carrying water, priming the stubborn pump, carrying boiling water to it in the winter to thaw it out before it could be primed, carrying water over ice and through snow. None of it was fun. But doing it taught me not to waste water and to think ahead about the season and weather and what would be required to fetch water. It also taught me to forever treasure clean, instantly available running water, which we got a year later. A water heater and an indoor flush toilet had to wait.

Our outhouse sat on the side of a hill just beyond our garden, about thirty yards from the house. As the joke goes, in the winter it was thirty yards too far and in the summer it was thirty yards too near.

The smell of human and livestock waste was part of farm life. On a good, hot summer day when the wind was right, we smelled manure from our neighbor's farm down the road. These everyday smells have gone missing from the lives of most Americans, as have the smells of horse and pig manure that filled the air of big cities when horses were the chief mode of transportation and pigs ate the garbage. Manure smells have become so alien that second-home buyers are sometimes startled when it wafts into their new country abodes from a nearby dairy farm or pigsty. They expected a kind of quiet landscaped outdoor museum in which their views never changed and the smells were all pleasant. The concept of a working landscape didn't occur to them.

"It amazes me how naive urban folks are when it relates to farming," Mark Knudsen, director of planning in Ottawa County, Michigan, told a local newspaper. The county was a bucolic landscape, 38 percent farmland, abutting Lake Michigan in the southwest corner of the state, that had attracted city dwellers. To help educate these people before they moved in, his agency published in 2003 a two-page brochure with the warning, "If you are thinking about moving to the country, you may want to consider this . . ." and a scratch 'n' sniff sample of what manure smells like. The brochure noted that over two hundred years of farm productivity had helped create the Midwest's designation of "Breadbasket of the World," adding, "Ironically, it is those individuals who purchase their dream home in the country that are the most vocal advocates of preserving farmland, but the most likely to complain about a farmer's hours of operation, as well as pesticide, fertilizer, and manure application."

We never made head cheese on our farm, but we did kill, clean, and eat birds and animals, both domestic and wild. When we needed meat, we loaded a pig or a cow into the back of the truck and took it to a slaughterhouse, where it was dispatched out of sight and mind and came back as various cuts wrapped in butcher paper and frozen. However, my teachers evidently thought watching cows and pigs die was an essential part of the education of ten-year-olds, because our class trip in the spring of 1953 was to nearby Chesaning, home of the Peet Packing Company, a year-round slaughterhouse that produced "Farmer Peet's Tasty Meats."

We began our tour watching squealing hogs herded into a killing room, where they were stunned and hoisted upside-down with a chain onto an overhead conveyor line. Then a man with a long knife slit their throats, sending blood gushing out onto the floors and all over the walls, workers, and their boots and coats. Viscera and feces spilled out when the hog bellies were slit. As we continued through the plant, the rooms cooled off. The hogs were cut in half, lengthwise, with band saws, then dismembered into various cuts for wrapping and shipping to meat markets. The smells and sights got more pleasant toward the end of the tour as we watched bologna being ground, mixed with spices, and extruded into large casings. At the end, a man in a white coat thanked us for visiting Farmer Peet's and gave us each a couple of hot dogs as souvenirs, but after our exposure to the realities of meat production, I didn't see anyone eating them on the bus ride home. Did any of my classmates become vegetarians? I don't know. I doubt it. More than half of them were farm kids. They already knew that the production of food required harvesting and that in the case of animal protein, harvesting meant killing. The cows on our farm had names, so when we sent one to be slaughtered and it came back in frozen parts, it still had a name. "Is this Rosey?" I remember asking Mom, peering into her pot of beef stew.

. . .

Zoo Parade was canceled in 1957. But by 1963, Marlin Perkins was back on the air and traveling to exotic places, filming the wild animals he found and broadcasting on a new show called *Mutual of Omaha's Wild Kingdom*. Enormously popular, *Wild Kingdom* took the audience on adventures in which Perkins and his ruggedly handsome sidekick Jim Fowler interacted with creatures in the wild and taught lessons of wildlife conservation. Some programs portrayed animals in apparently pristine environments with no people in them—more evidence that without man's interference all was well.

. . .

In the 1970s, a new generation of Americans launched a back-to-the-land movement—young adults, mainly, estranged from mainstream life and things money could buy, some antiwar, some prodrugs, most seeking an alternative to modern life. Upward of a million people, many of them young idealists, dropped out of society and formed communes or created homesteads and farmsteads with their own labor, trying to attain self-sufficiency and celebrating the virtues of simple living. There was one big problem: They didn't know how to do it, and thumbing through the *Whole Earth Catalog* was not an altogether satisfactory substitute for the hands-on know-how painstakingly acquired by their ancestors.

In her 2004 book *Back from the Land*, Eleanor Agnew tells about her experiences in this movement and realities that were unforeseen: the relentless toil to survive and the harshness of the natural world. She writes: "We discovered nature's darker underbelly. . . . Sunsets and new calves were beautiful, but to the uninitiated, natural processes, agrarian activities, and survival in the wilderness had many downsides. The natural world could be intimidating; farming could be daunting. How many of us had ever watched the blood spurt from a slaughtered animal before, watched the light fade from its eyes—by our own hand, no less."

In contrast to Mildred Kalish in the 1930s, and me in the 1950s, very few people moving back to the land in the 1970s had ever seen an animal killed for food or had done the killing themselves. "You can imagine how upsetting it was to slaughter chickens, turkeys, rabbits, or the annual pig. I abhorred it," Agnew writes. "But the purpose of raising animals was to eat them. That was what self-sufficiency was all about. It had to be done. Like most other back-to-the-land people, however, I hadn't been born into a farm family and had already been irreversibly socialized to feel repelled at the sight and smell of the blood, guts, and feathers that flew far and wide when a squawking chicken or turkey was slaughtered."

It is obvious that people would eat a lot less meat if they had to hunt, kill, skin or pluck, eviscerate, disassemble, and cook whatever animal or bird or fish they wanted to consume. These tasks are work, and many people would find them unpleasant. The modern protein industry made it much easier and cheaper to get battered, ready-to-eat chicken parts from the freezer section of a food store and pop them into a microwave or toaster oven. Even serious cooks buy raw chickens, whole or in parts, with feathers, heads, and feet removed, usually packaged in a plastic tray, resting on a little paper diaper, and sealed in a clear plastic wrap. Those birds have come a long way from the chicken coop.

Likewise, growing and harvesting crops is dirty, sweaty labor. The people who supply farmers' markets know this. Those in the vanguard of the "locavore" and "slow food" movements are learning all about farm toil too. It is physical exercise that other people pay thousands of dollars to replicate in clean, air-conditioned health clubs. For many people the disconnect from farm food is all but complete. They consume industrially prepared, inexpensive, sugar-filled, high-caloric, processed meals so far removed from the farm that, as Michael Pollan wrote, their grandmothers wouldn't recognize it as food.

Whatever their motivation, the 1970s back-to-the-landers learned a great deal about what subsistence required and how to work a landscape. This was knowledge few people then or later had a chance to gain because all sorts of improvements were built into their lifestyles that they took for granted.

Take central heating and air-conditioning. Few people gave a second thought to indoor air that was uniformly warm or cool and kept that way by a thermostat around the clock. Americans lived and worked in air produced by heaters and coolers and fans year round—even when the temperature of the air outdoors was comfortable and could be accessed by opening a window. Air temperature, one of the great variables of nature, had been tamed inside, and that was where people spent most of their time.

"We don't like exposure to nature," said Margaret J. King, director of Cultural Studies & Analysis, a consumer research think tank in Philadelphia. "We have evolved . . . to have as little to do with Nature as possible."

• • •

In the decades after the Second World War, the spaces that Americans occupied both indoors and outdoors were transformed. Natural landscapes were replaced by man-made landscapes designed for people with money to spend.

The first fantasy environments were department stores, state fairs, arcades, and amusement parks. Movie palaces arrived before the Second World War. Soon, shopping malls appeared. Suburbia transformed America in ways that made suburbanites nostalgic for the small-town and rural America of their youth or of their parents' generation. Walt Disney capitalized on the idea that people generally retained fond memories of the past. With Disneyland, opened in 1955 in Anaheim, California, Disney created a theme park that gave adults an idealized version of the community of their childhood—one that contrasted sharply with the Southern California sprawl around it. A quarter century earlier, Sinclair Lewis in his book *Main Street* had "excoriated the conventionality that Walt now idealized," observed the *LA Weekly*. For the nostalgic parents' children, Disney offered a safe venue to experience fantasy worlds that kids watched weekly on television.

. . .

The divide between people who experienced the natural world hands-on and those who experienced it indirectly did not occur suddenly and was not distinctly generational. It widened, however, as baby boomers came of age. In a 1993 speech to state wildlife agency officials at Lake Placid in Adirondack Park, Governor Mario Cuomo of New York talked about "an expanding fault line" between the two:

> This rift has many causes. The conservation community has roots in rural, agricultural America. The environmental community—born in the late '60s and early '70s—is largely an urban movement. The conservation community learned about the out-of-doors out in the woods. In many cases, learning for the environmentalists has come from more abstract sources usually found indoors—books and other media.
>
> Separate languages have developed. Hunters talk about habitat; environmentalists, ecosystems.
>
> Here in the Adirondacks and elsewhere in the state, that rift has been aggravated by the willingness of some people to push to extremes,

to demonize the views of the others until the gulf between them seems too great to cross. These differences are worsening, I believe, in part from the separation of a growing segment of our citizens from the land. As we become an increasingly urban and suburban society, we have lost our sense of nature and of our ties to it. Television and video games, suburban lawns and swimming pools, foster in youth an understanding of the world that is different from those who grew up checking out what was under rocks in streams.

This misunderstanding shows itself in the annual cacophony over legislative proposals that once brought sportsmen and women together with environmentalists. It shows itself in the lack of understanding that game sports [hunting] are not only important pastimes, but that they are also appropriate tools for managing wildlife populations. And it shows itself in the breakup of the constituency for wildlife habitat protection.

. . .

The 76 million baby boomers born between 1946 and 1964 were a demographic bulge likened to a pig inside a python. Many of them would come of age in front of the television set, eating a TV dinner. Machinery, technology, and commerce allowed most boomers to work indoors. Outdoors was where they *played*, and because there were so many of them, boomers set participation records in all sorts of outdoor recreation. They plunged into gardening with a passion. They manicured their lawns with a sense of duty. They played on golf courses, ball fields, and tennis courts. They were runners and physical fitness buffs who plied roadsides and treadmills. They took up biking, hiking, camping, and boating. Gradually, however, as their lives became busier, they became more spectators than participants.

In his 2005 book, *Last Child in the Woods: Saving Our Children from Nature-Deficit Disorder*, Richard Louv wrote: "In the space of a century, the American experience of nature has gone from direct utilitarianism to romantic attachment to electronic detachment." Postwar baby boomers, he wrote, "may constitute the last generation of Americans to share an intimate, familial attachment to the land and water. Many of us now in our forties or older knew farmland or forests at the suburban rim and had farm-family relatives."

What that meant was that early boomers were the last generation to be able to appreciate a nature presentation on film for what it was and not confuse it with the real world. They knew the difference from experience as subsequent generations could not. As a preboomer, I certainly did. We farm kids of the late 1940s and 1950s put down our Porky Pig comic books and went out to slop the hogs. We watched Bugs Bunny on TV and then watched Dad shoot a rabbit and Mom skin and cook it for dinner. I watched Daffy Duck cartoons and also accompanied my uncle into the swamp come autumn to shoot green-headed mallards I dubbed "Daffy ducks."

In subsequent decades, the proliferation of cable television channels created vast new markets for films about nature and wildlife, and the availability of digital video cameras allowed almost anyone the opportunity to fill airtime. Filmmakers created products portraying the natural world that were just as fake and staged as their early counterparts, only instead of harmony, natural balance, and animal family togetherness, they presented what came to be known as "Fang TV" and "Nature Porn." In these productions, animals were constantly killing and devouring each other, or copulating. No wonder that when children had a chance to travel to Africa and see real lions on the landscape they were not impressed. The big cats hardly seemed to move at all. They dozed. They didn't kill anything or have sex. They were boring. In recent years, new technology, including digital high-definition cinematography, has allowed a new generation of nature filmmakers for the British Broadcasting Company and the Discovery Channel to produce beautiful new series such as *Blue Planet* and *Planet Earth*. Others, including *Life* and

Winged Migration, have stood out, but clunkers abound: *Chased by Sea Monsters* and *Ocean's Deadliest.* In 2010, National Geographic Television broadcast a seven-hour series called *Great Migrations* containing some spectacular footage larded with what the *New York Times* TV critic called "a maximum of anthropomorphizing drama: the watchful eyes of concerned parents, the tender wisdom of mothers, albatrosses 'renewing their vows,' the zebra father and son who have 'thrown in their lot together.'" It was clear to the critic that nature films were still back in 1950s sentimentality.

· · ·

By 2011, Americans had become so immersed in the virtual reality brought to them on electronic screens and earphones that the real world had become something of a distraction, at times a perilous one. Drivers, diverted by their cell phones, had become dangerous enough for several states to outlaw talking and texting behind the wheel. Pedestrians were so preoccupied with chattering, listening to voice-mail, checking e-mail, and tweeting that they bumped into other people and stumbled into things. Teenagers spent more time harnessed to video and audio delivery systems than they spent sleeping or in school.

These electronic tools and toys revolutionized the flow of digitized pictures, words, and sounds to people by delivering them practically anywhere and anytime. They worked fast enough to encourage shortcuts. People could call up almost any feature or creature in nature and learn about it, which was good. On the other hand, they allowed purveyors and users to chop images, language, and the written word into bits and pieces, dispensing with backgrounds, introductions, and narrative. In the process, some social scientists asserted, they were turning people into scatterbrains.

Unlike the old desktop computer, the wired telephone, the living room television set, and the neighborhood movie house, portable digital gadgets were able to draw users into a virtual world instantly, more completely, and for longer periods than previous generations could imagine. They could summon up various reproductions of reality, often in real time, but not reality itself. They made reality easier to ignore.

. . .

Not all Americans, of course, prefer to have the natural world delivered to them on a digital screen. Lots of people spend time outdoors hiking, camping, kayaking, mountain biking, and hunting, and they take pleasure in nature. However, their time is often limited, and trips must be organized with itineraries that preclude serendipitous adventures. Visits to national parks, for example, are often organized to do as many things as quickly as possible. Some people come to collect experiences more than to experience nature. Some are physical fitness buffs preoccupied with putting themselves through tests and fulfilling personal achievement goals. I was reminded by a friend not long ago of a Jim Harrison novella set in Michigan's Upper Peninsula. The narrator, a local, woodswise character named Brown Dog, meets a college kid from Ann Arbor named Brad, who has come to study northern Indian cultures. When they meet again, Brad has just ridden his bike thirty miles in less than two hours to the Hurricane River and back. Brown Dog asks Brad if he happened to see the moose that had been hanging around the river.

"I see nothing but road," Brad replies. Then Brad jumps in the bay and swims three miles to Lonesome Point and back. Says Brown Dog, "I didn't bother asking him if he had seen any fish."

Chapter Ten

Roadkill

Brewster Bartlett was one of forty New England science teachers chosen to attend a three-week seminar at Simmons College in Boston in the summer of 1992 devoted to teaching the use of e-mail and introducing it to their students. In those days e-mail was still a novel way of communicating, and using it was something of an ordeal involving complex commands and long address strings. The seminar was sponsored by the National Science Foundation's EnviroNet teacher enhancement program. The teachers were asked to design a project for their classrooms that would involve monitoring some aspect of the environment and using e-mail to send results for tabulation. They decided to monitor lichens.

Bartlett knew a few things about lichens, the branching fungi that grow on trees and rocks and incorporate algae into their systems to perform photosynthesis and produce nutrients for them. He knew that lichens grow very slowly—far slower than grass. He knew that some people find lichens fascinating. He knew that his ninth-grade science students were not among them. While it was true that the vigor of lichens was related to air quality and that consequently measuring their growth rates across New England might produce some useful data, Bartlett thought it would be more interesting to the teachers than to his students at Pinkerton Academy in Derry, New Hampshire. Even he thought lichens were boring. What else could students monitor to hold their interest? Driving to Pinkerton one morning that fall, Bartlett noticed a lump beside the road. As he passed, he saw it was a dead skunk—an identification his nose quickly confirmed. His first thought, as he tells it, was of the song "Dead Skunk (in the Middle of the Road)," written in 1972 by Loudon Wainwright III. His second thought was:

"Omigod! That's it!"

Roadkill!

Dead animals and birds littered America's roads and highways in the 1990s and have been littering them ever since. Anybody who drives a car can see that. Many drivers have had the experience of flattening a squirrel or an opossum, hitting a bird, or crunching into a deer. But was anyone keeping track?

Bartlett phoned the New Hampshire Department of Fisheries and Wildlife and was told that his state, like others, had neither the manpower nor the money to monitor roadkill other than large mammals such as deer, bears, and moose, and that even those data were spotty. Collisions with smaller creatures—little crumps under tires or dings on the grill—got no more than a quick expression of remorse from a driver. Here was a significant aspect of modern wildlife management: critter control by family car. Yet nobody, it seemed, had bothered to assess the carnage.

Bartlett had been a teacher long enough to know that student interest in nature had waned as attention spans shortened and as video games, computers, and other digital gizmos captured their interest. He also knew from experience that bored students could have a sardonic edge. Later that fall, the EnviroNet teachers met again and Bartlett proposed his roadkill idea. Some teachers still liked lichens better, but twenty-five of them signed up their classes to tabulate roadkill. Some of their students considered the exercise to be too gross and opted out. Those interested and willing began the count in the spring of 1993. For six weeks the students monitored sections of New England roads they traveled to and from school on buses and, in some cases, on foot. They counted and identified as best they could every dead animal they passed. They counted the corpses of chipmunks, beavers, coyotes, muskrats, rabbits, raccoons, skunks, frogs, foxes, cats, birds, salamanders, snakes, squirrels, deer, bats, and many others. Early on, they found that some critters were so flattened by multiple tires that they were impossible to identify, so these were dubbed URPs, for Unidentified Road Pizzas.

That first spring's tally came to 1,923 identifiable creatures: 82 percent mammals, 15 percent birds, and 3 percent reptiles and amphibians. Since this count was the first known effort to tabulate the slaughter, it made news. Other teachers and students heard about it and joined the project. Bartlett got the nickname "Dr. Splatt." In 1994, classes in forty-five schools signed up. In the spring of 2002, I visited Windermere Elementary School in Ellington, Connecticut, a leafy exurb of Hartford, where twenty-five fifth graders in Steve Rogers's classroom were participating in the count. In nine weeks they had tallied 190 creatures, including 10 skunks, 35 gray squirrels, 22 birds, 8 rabbits, and 56 URPs. I talked with another teacher, Robert Buyea, in Bethany, Connecticut, fifty miles to the southwest. During the same period, his fourth graders counted 266 dead animals, including 45 opossums, 10 deer, and 2 coyotes. Students I interviewed said the project was just weird enough to be interesting. They said it "freaked out" their parents—a positive outcome in their minds. It certainly got talked about. As the project's website, http:// roadkill.edutel.com, put it: "Monitoring roadkill brings excitement and stimulating conversation to all. The unmotivated student becomes extremely interested in a gruesome subject. Students soon realize that there are many animals killed or injured by motor vehicles."

How many nationally was anybody's guess. The toll varied greatly with geography, time of year, time of day or night, even phases of the moon. Dr. Splatt's students each spring covered such a minuscule portion of the nation's road grid that their findings gave only a hint of a huge national toll.

Henry David Thoreau wrote about the effects of a wagon wheel running over a turtle in the mid–nineteenth century, but most people gave little thought to roadkill until late in the twentieth century. Indeed, the term *road ecology* wasn't coined until 1994. By then, collisions of motor vehicles and wild animals and birds were killing untold numbers of wild creatures and hundreds of people every year.

How did this happen? Many Americans profess such fealty to wild creatures that they treat them as pets. They argue endlessly with one another about how to look after them. They file lawsuits and stage demonstrations on their behalf. They give hundreds of millions of dollars to save and protect them. How is it, then, that many of these same Americans now routinely slaughter supposedly treasured wild animals and birds with their motor vehicles? The short answer is more wildlife, more roads, more driving, more speed, and more people who pay less heed to what's around them and think that hitting these creatures often can't be avoided.

. . .

For the first 4,500 years of road building and road use, overland commerce went no faster than a donkey or camel could walk, and nothing traveled faster than a horse. That was still the case when Thomas Jefferson became the third president of the United States in 1801. The best road at the time ran 175 miles from Boston to New York, and a light horse-drawn stagecoach carrying only passengers, baggage, and mail took three days to make the trip. By 1861, when Abraham Lincoln was sworn in as president, railroads were moving freight and people at twenty-five miles per hour, their locomotives outfitted with cowcatchers, or pilots, which were V-shaped metal grills used to sweep objects, including animals, off the tracks without derailing the train. Most Americans traveled little. Transport was limited and expensive. Just to go from where you were into the nearest city was an event.

Cars began running over animals as soon as the first ones were invented in nineteenth-century Europe. By 1900, more than four hundred companies in the United States, most tiny and many one- or two-man operations, were building automobiles, mainly by hand. The founders of the conservation movement couldn't have imagined how this machine would alter the landscape. When Theodore Roosevelt became president in 1901, automobiles were few, roads were slow-going, and suburbs were tiny bastions of the cosseted elite. Fast was thirty miles an hour. The odd chicken may have been at risk, but not much else. Populations of wild birds and animals were at or near their historic lows. White-tailed deer, as we have seen, had gone from more than 25 million to fewer than 500,000. (In 2012, by some estimates, drivers alone killed more than three times that many.) When Henry Ford's Model-Ts were produced in 1908, seeing a wild creature of any size was a rare event. Hitting one or running over one was news, or cause for conversation.

The first lobbyists for good roads were late nineteenth-century bicyclists. They were joined by farmers who wanted to get crops to market and an army concerned with wartime logistics and national defense. As a young army officer, Dwight D. Eisenhower promoted trucking to move supplies and later, as president, built the interstate highway system.

The interstates and beltways around cities became the conduits of sprawl and transformed the way Americans lived. They were the arteries of a circulatory road system that stretched 5 million miles across North America, and they allowed people to go farther and faster than ever before. Driving speeds of fifty-five to seventy miles per hour became the new "normal."

"Humans have spread an enormous net over the land. As the largest human artifact on earth, this vast, nearly five million mile road network used by a quarter billion vehicles permeates virtually every corner of North America," wrote Richard T. T. Forman in the preface to *Road Ecology,* a 2003 book he and thirteen other scholars wrote on the subject. "The network is both an engineering marvel and an economic success story. Indeed, it provides unprecedented human mobility, greatly facilitates the movement of goods, and stretches the boundary of social interactions. In effect, roads and vehicles are at the core of today's economy and society."

Melvin Webber, another author, described this net as "an efficient personal and commercial network connecting everywhere to everywhere." Growth in the size, quality, maintenance, and use of this network is astonishing to contemplate. In the decades after the Second World War, millions of miles of roads were built, hardened, or widened. By 2003, the U.S. road network was 3,997,456 miles long, and roughly two-thirds of it was surfaced either with asphalt (95 percent) or with concrete (5 percent).

Most roads and highways were maintained better than most other parts of our civil infrastructure. They were kept clear of snow and ice in winter with plows, salt, and sand, and kept from being flooded in summer by culverts, ditches, and other drainage structures that swept water away from their surfaces.

The designers and engineers of this network gave little if any thought to the effects of its hard surfaces on nature—except, perhaps, their positive effects in cutting down on dust. At the beginning of the twentieth century, most wild animal and bird populations were small, and the conservation movement was in its infancy. But campaigns to bring wildlife populations back began to show results after the Second World War, and, as it turned out, the population rebounds coincided with the explosion of driving.

In 2007, Americans were driving 254.4 million motor vehicles 3 trillion miles—double the number just a decade earlier. Nine out of ten people traveled by car, more concerned about traffic jams and gridlock than ruts and washouts.

Although drivers could see dead animals beside the roads they drove, few of them in my experience were aware of the extent to which hard-surface roads, local or long distance, were wildlife magnets. Forman reported that perhaps 15 million acres of road surface and 12 million acres of roadside cover the United States, for a total of 27 million acres—excluding 2.8 million acres of parking lots. These surfaces, especially asphalt, absorb heat during the day. Crickets, grasshoppers, and other insects, at home in grassy mowed roadsides, crawl onto the warm surfaces and stay active at night. So do slugs and worms on wet nights. Asphalt warms cold-blooded reptiles and amphibians too. Insect-eating animals such as skunks and foxes come onto the roadway to eat. Small mammals such as mice and voles appear, and they attract owls and other avian predators. Once they're run over, other protein eaters, including vultures and coyotes, come along to eat them. Deer, moose, and other ungulates eat freshly mowed roadside grass in summer. Some birds and animals eat salt spread in winter. Birds flock in to eat bugs and swallow gullet stones. Other birds such as gulls and crows land to feast on leftover fries casually tossed out car windows. In the spring, skunks come out of hibernation and hungrily head for food sources in backyards and along roads. Squirrels and raccoons get out and about. Snakes and frogs wake up and begin moving. Turtles lumber across asphalt on seasonal migrations.

Highways with wide and frequently mowed aprons and medians allow both drivers and animals greater visibility, but the higher speeds vehicles travel on them reduce safety for both, especially at night. In the past, some misguided maintenance departments, in the name of highway beautification, planted flowering bushes close to highways. They both cut visibility and attracted wildlife. Some of them planted sunflowers and vetch—gourmet food that attracts seed eaters. Brewster Bartlett's student tabulators found, however, that roadkill numbers were consistently higher on local roads than on most highways, and they believed the reasons were obvious: These roads were narrower, and the roadsides were usually lined with trees, ditches, brush, and weeds that served as both hiding places and travel corridors for wildlife. Bartlett thought a more important reason was that drivers regularly ignored speed limits on local roads. For drivers coming off a seventy-mile-per-hour highway, a thirty-mile-per-hour side road feels very slow, and drivers routinely exceed the speed limit, especially on familiar roads near home.

. . .

In the 1970s, as deer densities climbed, a new acronym slipped into the language through auto body repair shops and state wildlife agencies: *DVC*s. It stood for "deer-vehicle collisions," but most people weren't aware of it unless they had a friend or relative for whom a DVC was up close and personal, or they heard a roadkill joke like the one I heard not long ago on *A Prairie Home Companion*'s annual joke show:

"Why did the chicken cross the road?"

"To show the deer how it's done."

Few states collected DVC data, and most did it haphazardly. Local or state police dispatched to the scene of a car crash would note a deer's involvement if they saw one. But those reports rarely made it into state accident statistics. By the 1990s, deer-vehicle collisions were getting a lot of attention because growing numbers of people were being seriously injured or killed in the crashes, and repair costs to damaged vehicles were skyrocketing.

The first serious national estimate I found came from researchers at the Jack H. Berryman Institute at Utah State University in Logan. Michael R. Conover, one of its directors, and four graduate students in 1992 surveyed thirty-five state agencies, massaged and extrapolated the data they collected, and reported their findings in the *Wildlife Society Bulletin* in 1995. Those estimates were shocking: more than 1 million DVCs annually. Strikingly, the researchers also believed that half of all these crashes weren't reported to authorities.

More than 90 percent of the deer died, and their deaths weren't pleasant. Here is how Johan T. du Toit, of the Berryman Institute, put it: "There are few more dramatic manifestations of human-wildlife conflict than squealing brakes, a sickening crunch, flying gravel, and then silence except for the weakly spasmodic scrabbling of a semi-pulverized deer as it lies dying on the side of a highway."

People died too. Indeed, the million-plus crashes resulted in more than two hundred human fatalities a year, on average, and another twenty-nine thousand people injured enough to require hospitalization. While the number of fatalities was tiny in comparison with the forty thousand people who died each year on the nation's highways, it exceeded the annual number of people killed in all commercial airline, train, and bus crashes—combined. But few insurance companies were paying attention because the highly profitable auto policies they sold covered crashes involving wildlife under "comprehensive" damage, a grab bag of things that might happen—a car is stolen, a window is broken, or the car is damaged by a flood, a fire, hail, wind, or a bird or animal. When I asked Conover for an update in 2012, he said three thousand to four thousand DVCs daily was a safe estimate. He had raised his estimate of vehicle damage to $1.5 billion—$1 billion for reported crashes and $500 million for those unreported. He stressed that accurate data were still not easy to find, but he thought the human fatality rate was probably far higher than two hundred annually. The problem was that deer weren't identified as the cause in many crashes because people lost control of their cars and rolled over or hit something else, such as a car in the oncoming lane. "In these cases, the person [driver] is dead so authorities cannot ask the victim why he veered into the other lane," Conover said. "Hence, the fatality is attributed to a head-on collision rather than a DVC."

At first, states and counties used public money to hire contractors to pick up dead deer and other animals as a public service. South Dakota taxpayers spent $380,000 a year to hire people to remove dead animals twice a week from roughly 75 percent of the state's highways. Brett McDonnell, a private contractor in Buffalo, New York, was paid $115 for each dead deer he picked up in surrounding Erie County. "For every dead animal you see beside the road, there's ten more you can't see in the weeds," he told me. Wayne Langman patrolled 850 miles of roads around Terre Haute, Indiana, in 2002, picking up deer and other road-kill for the state highway department at a cost of about $42,000 a year in salary and expenses, including $9.40 per trip to the landfill. "We joke around here that the only deer predator left is a Chevy pickup."

Some people eat roadkill deer, although the impact of collisions spoils much of the meat. In an experiment a few years back, the work crew at Tamarack Preserve, a shooting and hunting club near Millbrook, New York, picked up five fresh deer killed by vehicles and butchered them to see how much meat they could extract. In all of the animals, the impact of the collision had bruised and bloodied so much muscle that what ed-ible protein remained wasn't worth the effort to get it, Tim Bontecou, a Tamarack member, told me. Others say the tenderloins near the spine are often undamaged and salvageable. They collect the bruised meat too, to feed their dogs.

When moose or elk are hit by vehicles, they die from the crash or are so injured that they are shot. Parts of these animals that can be salvaged become edible protein in some areas—sometimes hundreds of pounds of good meat. Since it is illegal to sell the meat of wild animals, it must be either consumed by the person who killed it or given away. In Mon-tana, for example, big animals end up in food banks, where volunteers butcher them. In other states and in many counties, sheriffs or police maintain lists of phone numbers of people who want roadkill—usually deer—to eat. When called to a collision, they assess the condition of the dead animal, and if they judge parts of it okay to eat, they call the next person on their list to come and get it. In 2010, during the great recession, a few states passed laws making it easier for people to salvage roadkill deer and other animals. Essentially, however, what America did with virtually all of the million-plus deer killed by motor vehicles is throw them away. That's a lot of wasted protein.[22] But it is minuscule in comparison to the three hundred billion pounds of food Americans waste through spoilage, damage, and other factors each year.

. . .

By the late 1980s and early 1990s, some state highway departments moved beyond simply putting up deer-crossing signs to addressing what could otherwise be done to save more creatures from becoming roadkill. However, Richard Forman found that people in other countries were far more concerned and active in finding solutions than were Americans. He noted that in western Europe, particularly England, citizens disturbed by massive numbers of frogs and toads squashed by tires during seasonal amphibian migration periods launched a "Toads on Roads" campaign to build tunnels under roads for safe passage. In the 1980s, Germany, Switzerland, and the Netherlands pioneered the use of fences, signs, wildlife underpasses, and bridges to create "landscape connectors." Hunters in France were so disturbed by road-upgrading projects that they pressured the government to build more than 150 "game bridges" over the improved roadways so wildlife could cross safely. Canada took action to mitigate moose-car and bear-car crashes in the Canadian Rockies. The government built twenty-four underpasses and overpasses with corridor fencing along a twenty-two-mile stretch of the four-lane highway

---

22. An average wild white-tailed deer yields about sixty pounds of boned meat. Let's say half is edible. At a conservative estimate of a million roadkill deer a year, we are wasting upward of 30 million pounds of venison annually. That's roughly 120 million meals. In 2009, I checked venison prices on the Internet and found that they were around $6 per pound for ground meat, $13 for roast, $22 for chops and medallions, and $30 for tenderloin. (This was farm-raised venison, which is legal to sell.) If we put an arbitrary value on boneless deer meat of $9 to $12 a pound, the value of the discarded meat is between $270 million and $360 million a year.

that cuts through Banff National Park in Alberta and claimed to have reduced animal-vehicle crashes by 80 percent. Electronic monitors recorded thousands of elk, moose, deer, wolves, mountain sheep, cougars, and bears—both black and grizzlies—safely passing over and under the highway.

Perhaps the most notable effort in the United States was made in Florida in the 1980s and '90s when the state built twenty-three underpasses and thirteen bridges along Interstate 75 to reduce highway deaths of Florida black bears and panthers. Nationally, interest in highway mitigation schemes for wildlife grew, but money and efforts to create them lagged.

One problem, Forman concluded, was that Americans thought of the places they lived as landscapes that had been degraded by their presence. That is to say, once people moved into the sprawl, they considered it to be damaged habitat, no longer natural and thus less worthy of protection. Europeans, on the other hand, viewed the places they lived as natural ecosystems that required intensive human management, however heavily populated. Living spaces in Europe were thought of as "in a sense, human-created nature or natural systems." In North America, in contrast, the primary policy goal was the protection of nature that was as pristine as possible—meaning the largely peopleless nature over the horizon, up north or out west.

The Wildlife Society, a national association of professional wildlife managers, organized a symposium in 2000 on the effects of modern highway systems on wildlife, mainly roadkill and habitat fragmentation, and reported that highway impacts were "greater than [at] any other period in history." In 2002, Bill Ruediger, a wildlife biologist for the U.S. Forest Service and one of the leading experts on roadkill, told me, "People are wildly underestimating the numbers. They are far, far higher now than most people think." Just how high, nobody knew exactly.

Merritt Clifton, the editor of a publication called *Animal People,* roughly extrapolated Bartlett's 1993 counts to roadways nationwide and guessed that motor vehicles were probably killing at least 41 million squirrels, 26 million cats, 22 million rats, 19 million opossums, 15 million raccoons, 6 million dogs, and 350,000 deer annually. Around that time, animal protection charities such as the Animal Protection Institute and Defenders of Wildlife began to say that motor vehicles were hitting or running over more than a million birds and animals every day on the nation's streets, roads, and highways. These groups had no research to back up this number. It was designed to shock people to pay attention and perhaps give a donation. They stopped using the 1 million figure for three reasons: It was a guess; doing something about the carnage was complicated, expensive, and more the realm of highway departments than animal protection charities; and it detracted from a more passionate goal of some of these organizations, which was to outlaw hunting.

In 1997, the Fund for Animals (since merged with the Humane Society of the United States) asserted that hunters killed 134 million creatures annually. This, the group asserted, was an enormous and needless toll that should be ended by the abolition of hunting in America. It didn't take long for someone to point out that at a million creatures a day, drivers—many of them against hunting—were killing 365 million animals a year, nearly three times as many as hunters. For their part, hunters could argue that they made use of the creatures they killed, while roadkill was virtually all wasted despite Roadkill Café humor: "From your grill to ours."

. . .

Hitting a creature with a motor vehicle is usually an act of inadvertence. It is not something people do for sport or pleasure. Just the opposite: People try to avoid it, sometimes veering dangerously to miss the creature in the headlights. Hitting a small creature makes most drivers feel a brief pang of guilt while driving on. Some people exercise caution, especially at dusk, to avoid larger animals. They are alert on roads where they have hit animals in the past. But most people in my experience tend to feel that roadkill is not something they can do much about. It is a price of transportation, like gasoline and maintenance. It is not something people consider to be a form of wildlife management, although it certainly is.

In contrast to roadkill, some things Americans do to the natural world are considered to be positive—such as putting out birdseed.

Chapter Eleven

Feathered Friends

Peter Kilham was sprawled on his living room couch on a spring afternoon in 1968, staring blankly into middle space in what a Sherlock Holmes story would call a "brown study." Suddenly, he bolted upright, leapt to his feet, peered intently out the picture window for a few seconds, and then, according to his wife, disappeared into his basement workshop.

Kilham was one of six children. His father, Walter Kilham, was a noted architect in Boston. One of his brothers, Lawrence Kilham, was a Harvard-trained physician and a research ornithologist specializing in the behavior of woodpeckers. Peter was an engineer and inventor, a jack-of-all-trades who idolized Leonardo da Vinci. During the Second World War, he designed a gun sight for the navy. Later, he built a line of efficient wood-burning stoves and developed metal-bending machines for manufacturing plants. Around 1960, he and Alan Bemis started a record company to capture and preserve the sounds of New England, from steamboats and steam trains, to birds chirping in the morning, to Yankee dialects, old stories, and humor, all of which were disappearing fast. They helped launch a famous series of comedy records called "Bert and I," in which humorist Mike Dodge told old Maine stories in Down East dialects.

On that afternoon in 1968 in the workshop of his home in Barrington, Rhode Island, Peter found a section of plastic tubing left over from a project he had been working on for a professor at the Rhode Island School of Design. With it, he fashioned an ingenious new feeder for wild birds—one that would not only propel bird feeding's popularity but also help turn a budding pastime into the paramount way Americans interacted with wildlife.

The feeder was made of clear tubular Lucite, 2½ inches in diameter and 16 inches long, with six quarter-sized holes along its length for birds to poke their beaks in to feed, orange cardboard baffles to keep seeds from falling out of the holes, and a wooden dowel under each hole for birds to perch on while eating. It was capped on both ends and topped with a wire for easy hanging.

With his wife, Dorothy, doing the paperwork and marketing, Kilham began making and selling his feeder, which he named the A6-F, under the brand of Droll Yankees, the name of his recording company. Sales of the A6-F soared, quickly eclipsing all sorts of bird feeders already on the market. Other feeders ranged from simple platforms and baskets that held seeds to the relatively hi-tech Flight Deck Windowsill—a Masonite tray that clipped to windowsills and held seeds, water, even peanut butter. The Flight Deck was invented in 1952 by Gil Dunn, a World War II aircraft maintenance man who founded a feeder company called Duncraft.

People had been feeding and watering wild birds for centuries. Henry David Thoreau tossed out corn and bread crumbs for birds to eat at Walden Pond in 1845. Housewives who baked and sliced their own bread did the same. But the A6-F would fundamentally change bird feeding. It was easy to use, easy to hang close to a window or anywhere in the yard, and more squirrel-resistant than its predecessors, and viewers could easily see both the seeds in it and the birds perched on it. Of all its attributes, however, none was as important as timing: The A6-F came along just in time for the baby boomer generation and its offspring.

By 1968, the youngest boomers were four years old, the oldest twenty-two and beginning to start families of their own. More of them lived in suburbs than anywhere else, and many suburban tracts of ranch-style houses gave residents the feeling of being close to nature—certainly much closer than living in a crowded city. These houses were one story and featured large picture windows and sliding glass doors that allowed residents to watch nature from inside, Gregg Mitman wrote in *Reel Nature*:

> Just as a [Disney] True-Life Adventure established the audience as a spectator of nature, so the windows and sliding glass doors of the ranch-style home, which opened onto the same levels as the surrounding tame and pastoral landscape, facilitated intimacy with nature through observation rather than active participation. These glass walls, like the television screen, nevertheless marked a clear boundary between the world of humans and that of nature.

The bird feeder brought nature, in the form of wild birds, close to that boundary. Bird feeding's popularity took off in the 1980s and boomed in the 1990s, in part because it was an easy, convenient, and inexpensive hobby. Unlike serious birders, who took trips to see and photograph new, interesting, and rare species, bird feeders didn't need study or special knowledge. Indeed, 87 percent of Americans could identify no more than twenty of some eight hundred bird species that turn up regularly in North America, according to a 2003 report by the U.S. Fish and Wildlife Service. People who fed birds could forgo binoculars, and birding clubs, and predawn treks through some godforsaken swamp in hopes of glimpsing or hearing the tweet of the rare purple-breasted hadada.

For those who preferred to watch nature through plate glass or lying down, the A6-F was a godsend. All you had to do was fill it, hang it, and become a couch potato bird watcher. This was important because as boomers aged they spent more time working than playing, and more time in their homes, offices, and cars than in the outdoors. Their children were distancing themselves from the natural world too. Advocates

saw bird feeding not just as a hobby but as a way for Americans to re-
connect to nature. In the space of a few decades, a pastime that began
with a few bread crumbs tossed out in winter had grown into a hobby
in which more than 50 million Americans spent almost $3.5 billion an-
nually on hundreds of thousands of tons of seed. This was a remarkable
turnaround from the days less than a century before, when Americans
were preoccupied not with feeding wild birds but with feeding on them.

. . .

European settlers caught and killed birds of all sizes for meat, eggs, and
feathers, but pressure on bird populations was not great. As immigrant
populations swelled, however, so did demand for wild birds, which, like
minerals, trees, fertile soil, and other natural resources, were thought to
be inexhaustible.

People who today enjoy watching birds come to their feeders or poke
for worms in their yards might not be aware that their nineteenth- and
early twentieth-century ancestors ate robins and other small birds; that
pigeons were netted by the tens of millions and shipped to food purveyors; that eggs of almost any species of wild bird were looted from nests
for food; that whooping cranes, ibises, egrets, pelicans, terns, plovers,
swans, and even hummingbirds were caught and killed for their feathers;
and that ducks and geese, as we have seen, succumbed to cannon-sized
shotguns. Market hunters lured birds with shelled corn, then dropped
nets on them. Pigeoners baited areas near roosts and nesting areas and
captured the birds in drop nets. They tied live pigeons to the tops of
little stands called stools—"stool pigeons"—to lure others to their nets.
The pigeons were killed, iced down, and shipped by rail to New York
and other cities. In 1875, pigeon netters in Michigan shipped 2 million
pounds of young birds (squabs) and 2.4 million older birds to American
and European cities, James Trefethen reported. In 1878, the last great
nesting colony of passenger pigeons was discovered near Petoskey, near

Lake Michigan. Netters, some 2,500 strong, descended on it and within a few weeks were reported to have killed more than a billion birds.

"Of all the meat-shooters, the market-gunners who prey on wild fowl and ground game birds for the big-city markets are the most deadly to wildlife," wrote William T. Hornaday in 1913. As director of the New York Zoological Park (now the Wildlife Conservation Society, known locally as the Bronx Zoo), Hornaday was an ardent crusader for wildlife protection. "Enough geese, ducks, quail, ruffed grouse, prairie chickens, heath hens and wild pigeons have been butchered by gunners and net-ters for 'the market' to have stocked the whole world," he wrote. Muse-ums, zoological parks, and learning institutions were not without blame themselves. They sanctioned the killing of tens of thousands of wild and exotic birds for research and display. Not until Carl Zeiss developed prism binoculars in the 1930s, making sight identification of birds on the wing possible, did killing in the name of science abate.

Ornithologists at the turn of the century were outraged that people killed and ate small birds. In the preface to his 1912 book *Our Vanish-ing Wildlife,* Hornaday scolded poor southerners: "The great increase in the slaughter of song birds for food [in the South] . . . has become an unbearable scourge to our migratory birds—the very birds on which farmers north and south depend for protection from the insect hordes, the very birds that are most near and dear to the people of the North."

Eating crow (boiled), like a humble pie of animal innards, may have been distasteful, but eating small birds was a treat, and commonplace. In many parts of the world, people still relish them. For some people, eating a robin might have all the appeal of dining on the family dog. Robins may seem too small to eat, but they aren't much smaller than doves, woodcock, squab, and quail—all gourmet edibles today.

Feathered hats and boas became highly fashionable in the nineteenth century, and the suppliers of feathers, called plume hunters, made big profits killing exotic shorebirds to sell their plumes to milliners. Con-servationists thought this trade was unconscionable and vowed to shut it down. Their efforts began with a public campaign for bird protection laws, kicked off in an 1884 speech by ornithologist William Brewster, curator of birds for the Museum of Comparative Zoology at Harvard, to the American Ornithologists Union. George Bird Grinnell, the editor of *Forest and Stream* weekly, announced in 1886 the formation of a society named in honor of John James Audubon. Men who joined were required to pledge not to kill or capture any wild bird they didn't eat. Woman members had to promise not to use feathers for decorative purposes. The campaign worked—up to a point. Many states adopted bird protection laws, but they were full of loopholes. Theodore Roosevelt, a bird lover who had learned taxidermy as a boy, was an enthusiastic supporter of the campaign. He thought killing birds for hats and feather boas should be a federal crime. Elected governor of New York in 1898, Roosevelt signed the Hallock Bird Protection Bill into law, making it illegal in New York to kill and sell nongame birds for commercial purposes. The idea was to shut down the so-called Milliners Mile of hatmakers in New York City. Plume hunters in the South, however, continued to ravage rookeries to sell to these establishments. In 1900, in his second annual address to the state legislature, Roosevelt gave what was perhaps the first bird rights speech. Calling for their protection and for the protection of their forest habitat, he said in part:

> The State should not permit within its limits factories to make bird skins or bird feathers into articles of ornament on wearing apparel. Ordinary birds, and especially song birds, should be rigidly protected. Game birds should never be shot to a greater extent than will offset the natural rate of increase.

That same year, Roosevelt's good friend Frank Chapman, head of ornithology at the American Museum of Natural History, gave a speech in New York aimed at shaming women out of wearing feathers. The *New York Times* headlined the speech: "PLEADING FOR THE BIRDS.

Women Startled at the Audubon Society's Annual Meeting." Chapman described the slaughter of rare birds in grisly detail, the *Times* reported: "The women who listened to the talk . . . yesterday afternoon, went home vowing that never again would they wear anything but the feathers of the [domesticated] ostrich on their hats."

The market for bird feathers, however, was global. Rare birds from distant parts of the planet flooded into feather markets not only in New York but also in London. At the London Millinery Feather Market's quarterly sale in August of 1912, the feathered skins of 1,600 hummingbirds, bound for bonnets, sold for two cents each. The New York Zoological Society, in a gesture, bought them to get them off the market.

Later as president, Roosevelt would create the nation's first wildlife refuges—Pelican Island in Florida and Breton Island in Louisiana—to save birds from plume hunters. In the years that followed, the Migratory Bird Treaty of 1916 and three subsequent bilateral treaties approved by the U.S. Senate gave the federal government responsibility for protecting 836 species of birds that flew across international boundaries in North America, but neither federal nor state laws did much to save birds. Some species, as we have seen, had already been killed to extinction, and that possibility loomed for many more. The last known great auk, a penguinlike bird, was killed on the coast of Iceland in 1840. The last known Labrador duck was shot in Long Island Sound in 1872. The last passenger pigeon died in the Cincinnati Zoological Garden on September 1, 1914. The heath hen was killed out of all its range by 1850 everywhere but Martha's Vineyard, where it slowly succumbed to predation, fires, habitat loss, and a diminished gene pool. The last one was seen alive on March 11, 1932.

Conservationists felt a sense of urgency. Slowly, over the first half of the twentieth century, federal and state governments strengthened enforcement and initiated wild bird and habitat restoration projects (they emphasized bringing back game birds, but these projects helped other birds as well). By midcentury, state fish and game agencies were beginning to embrace the relatively new sciences of wildlife management and conservation biology. During this same period, however, an entirely new threat to wild bird populations began to loom: pollution. During and after the Second World War, America changed in profound ways. Factories and utilities belched smoke and chemicals into the air or discharged them into rivers and lakes as never before. Farmers plied their fields with chemical fertilizers, pesticides, and herbicides in unprecedented quantities. One of these was a chemical first synthesized in 1873, but its insect-killing properties weren't discovered until 1939, when a Swiss chemist, Paul Hermann Müller, synthesized his own batches and noticed how effectively they poisoned insects. After the war this chemical, dichlorodiphenyltrichloroethane, was put to use in agriculture, and its application skyrocketed. Müller was awarded the Nobel Prize in Physiology or Medicine in 1948.

The chemical's acronym, DDT, had become a household name—especially in farm households—long before a naturalist for the U.S. Fish and Wildlife Service, Rachel Carson, called attention to its poisonous effects on birds in her 1962 book *Silent Spring*. DDT was banned in the United States in 1972, two years after the first Earth Day. By then environmentalism had become a serious movement and cleaning up air and water polluted by man's chemicals and waste a national quest.

· · ·

Farmers had the keenest interest in birds, which they viewed as either harmful or helpful. Chicken-stealing hawks and other raptors were killed on sight, as were crows and other species they deemed harmful to livestock, orchards, and field crops. Helpful birds were insect eaters. Conservationists had long preached that birds were far more valuable keeping down insect damage than they were as a meal or on a hat.

Before the twentieth century, books about wild birds were largely confined to how to hunt and prepare them for dinner. Although birding, or bird-watching, went back to eighteenth-century England, interest in birds for aesthetic rather than culinary reasons was minimal. Bird identification and study was confined to a few scientists and eccentrics and didn't draw much interest in America until well into the twentieth century. One of the first birding guidebooks was Frank Chapman's *Handbook of Birds of Eastern North America,* published in 1895, but it was technical and difficult for nonscientists to use. Roger Tory Peterson's *Field Guide to Birds of North America* was easy to use but didn't arrive until thirty-nine years later. Books on befriending wild birds were also rare. One of the first was Gilbert H. Trafton's *Methods of Attracting Birds,* published in 1910. Putting up birdhouses and birdbaths, planting bird-friendly shrubbery and trees, and feeding birds in winter, he wrote, would both help the birds and keep them around in summer eating insects, and on hand for watching. *How to Make Friends with Birds,* by Niel Morrow Ladd, came out in 1916 and *Wild Bird Guests: How to Entertain Them,* by Ernest Harold Baynes, was published in 1915. Seed mixes developed by the poultry industry could be used to feed wild birds, he wrote. Hemp (marijuana) was highly recommended. Like the others, Edward Howe Forbush, in *Food, Feeding, and Drinking Appliances and Nesting Material to Attract Birds,* published in 1918, talked about feeding wild birds in winter. Feeding birds year round was largely unheard of.

The first market for packaged birdseed was racing pigeons and caged indoor birds such as canaries and parrots. Knauf & Tesch (K&T, later Kaytee), a general store for dairy farmers in Chilton, Wisconsin, began selling bags of dried peas for racing pigeons in the late nineteenth century, and in the 1920s the store marketed pigeon food nationally. Wagner Bros. Seed Company, founded in New York in 1894 to sell feed for chickens and horses, packaged seeds for caged canaries and parrots, but the idea of buying seed to feed wild outdoor birds went nowhere during the Depression and world wars. After the Second World War, both K&T and Wagner introduced bags of mixed seed to grocery stores. In

1948, Wagner came out with Winter Life in five-pound bags. Because 90 percent of its sales occurred in winter months, the company realized that to expand the market it had to persuade people to feed birds year round. In 1956, Wagner marketed a brand called Four Seasons, but sales of it and other brands were sluggish for the next two decades.

When the U.S. Fish and Wildlife Service conducted its first national survey of outdoor sports participation in 1955, it confined its research to sportsmen, mainly 20.8 million fishermen and 11.8 million hunters. Its 1970 survey, in contrast, reported that 128 million Americans participated in hunting, fishing, bird-watching, wildlife photography, and nature walking. Surveying nonconsumptive outdoor activities—that is, activities in which animals, birds, and fish were not killed—was an important shift. "The significance was in the inclusion of groups that no one thought to mention fifteen years earlier," wrote Dian Olson Belanger and Adrian Kinnane in *Managing American Wildlife*, a 2002 history of the International Association of Fish and Wildlife Agencies (IAFWA), a lobbying group for state wildlife agencies. These nonconsumptive users could no longer be ignored. By the 1980 survey, the total number of participants had grown to 181 million. Hunters and fishermen numbered just under 60 million, while nonconsumptive outdoor "participants" had grown to more than 121 million, and of those, nearly 116 million were classified as residential—meaning they included people who put out seeds for birds.

In the 1980s, the manufacture, packaging, and selling of seed, feeders, and other supplies for people who fed wild birds became one of the nation's fastest-growing industries. Birdseed moved onto the shelves of national chains of grocery, home improvement, hardware, discount, and drugstores. In 1981, Wild Birds Unlimited, a franchise dedicated solely to bird-feeding equipment and supplies, opened in Indianapolis and quickly spread across the nation. In 1985, Wild Bird Centers of America joined the specialty competition.

The packagers of birdseed sold bags containing pure unmixed seeds, such as black sunflower, but the real money was in selling seed mixtures. Bulk seeds were commodities with fairly inelastic prices. That is to say, one company couldn't sell black sunflower for three times more than another company sold it for. Seed mixtures, on the other hand, could be used to differentiate a brand. Mixtures could be blended to be economical and sold in large bags as all-in-one feed for a variety of birds. Or they could blended with seeds known to attract desirable species such as cardinals and then could be priced at a premium. As birdseed companies grew and competition increased, branded blends proliferated. Soon there were special blends for many bird species, for regions of the country, and for seasons of the year.

By this time, state and federal agencies involved in wildlife issues were publishing all sorts of advice about public interactions with wild birds and animals, including hunting, fishing, and wildlife viewing and photographing. As bird feeding grew as a popular outdoor activity, it was natural for the agencies to offer advice on it too. Several states published bird-feeding pamphlets on the subject. Florida, for one, recommended not using seed mixtures because they often contained seeds birds didn't like and were thus wasted. It recommended buying seeds such as sunflower, nyjer, or safflower in bulk and filling each feeder with just one kind of seed. This was an indirect way of cautioning buyers to beware of seed packagers who were diluting their mixtures with cheap "junk seeds"—for example, oats, wheat, sawgrass, and red milo—that ended up on the ground. Some seed sellers emphasized in advertisements that they didn't use cheap filler seeds or otherwise adulterate their blends. The U.S. Fish and Wildlife Service, in its own pamphlet, also advised against using blends. Seed sellers took these recommendations as an affront. The Florida pamphlet so offended one major seed company chief that he demanded that state officials recall it. He was refused. Outraged, he organized fellow seed company owners into the Wild Bird Feeding Institute (WBFI), a trade group. The institute's professed agenda was to promote the virtues of feeding wild birds. Its immediate goal, however, was to pressure state and federal wildlife agencies into keeping their hands off the bird-feeding business. To warn other states against doing what Florida had done, the institute launched a lobbying campaign in Washington aimed at preventing use of federal funds by state agencies for nongame projects such as bird-feeding advice.

The trade group also began lobbying against excise taxes like those paid by hunters and fishermen on the gear they bought. Those taxes were imposed by the passage of the Pittman-Robertson Act of 1937 (for hunters) and the Dingell-Johnson Act of 1950 (for fishermen). They were, in effect, user fees, and they brought in hundreds of millions of dollars annually to fund wildlife habitat restoration programs for game fish, birds, and wild animals. But hunting and fishing were on the decline, state wildlife agencies were increasingly cash-strapped, and non-consumptive outdoor industries, especially bird feeding, were making tons of money but not contributing. So it became logical for wildlife agencies and environmental groups to envision a similar tax on purchases of outdoor equipment and supplies by people who didn't hunt and fish, including bird-watchers and bird feeders. Legislation to get such a tax, however, went nowhere because the big equipment and supply corporations—including birdseed suppliers—had the lobbying clout to thwart it in Congress.

In 1994, the International Association of Fish and Wildlife Agencies tried to get the tax with a campaign called Teaming with Wildlife. Nearly every major environmental, hunting, fishing, and outdoor recreation group signed on. All sorts of outdoor equipment makers, and even some birdseed sellers—more than three thousand organizations and businesses in all—joined the effort, including binocular makers Swarovski Optik and Carl Zeiss Optics, fishing equipment giant Bass Pro Shops, and American AGCO Trading Company, a big birdseed seller in Minnesota. Once again, however, the effort was stalled when the Wild Bird Feeding Institute and the Outdoor Recreation Coalition, a trade group representing the camping equipment industry, came out against it. Then, one day in 1996, it died altogether. A presidential election campaign was under way. The Republicans, as usual, portrayed the Democrats as tax-and-spend liberals. President Bill Clinton's interior secretary, Bruce Babbitt, at one point called Teaming with Wildlife an interesting idea. Bob Dole, the Republican candidate, accused him of stooping so low as to advocate a tax on birdseed. Campaign crowds hooted, and Clinton reminded Babbitt that they were in an election year. Teaming with Wildlife was dead, and the companies that profited from sales of nonconsumptive outdoor recreation supplies, including birdseed, would continue to benefit from conservation programs that were paid for by hunters and fishermen.

By 2006, bird feeding had become a huge industry. In a report that year, the U.S. Fish and Wildlife Service said 56 million Americans sixteen years old and older fed wild birds as a hobby and spent nearly $3.5 billion annually on birdseed and another $801 million a year on feeders, nest boxes, birdbaths, and other equipment. More adults fed wild birds than the 30 million who fished and the 12 million who hunted combined. While participation in other forms of outdoor recreation—including birding and wildlife watching, wildlife photography, hiking, backpacking, wilderness camping, hunting, and fishing—were static or in decline, putting out food for wild birds continued to grow as a pastime. To further encourage growth, the bird-feeding industry coached customers that costly products were better at attracting desirable birds. Kaytee's website, for example, said:

> If you are just beginning to feed Song Birds, it is best to start by resisting the temptation to purchase the least expensive food and feeders available. It is advisable that you purchase a premium mix that contains a high percentage of quality seeds like Black Oil Sunflower and Millet. This high concentration of Sunflower and Millet will bring Song Birds to your backyard faster and with less waste than less costly mixes.

In addition, birdseed sellers lifted a page from the pet products industry. Just as pets morphed into family members deserving of premium foods and toys, wild birds were portrayed as "backyard guests" and "outdoor pets" worthy of feeding pricey mixes. On websites, the mixes were advertised as being environmentally, nutritionally, and even socially correct.

Red River Commodities, a large specialty grain and seed company in Fargo, North Dakota, for example, marketed in 2008 a premium brand called Valley Splendor Boutique Collection—four seed blends with what it called a "classy look and gourmet appeal." The blends, named Afinchionado, Beak Bistro, Berry Necessities, and Nutcracker Tweet, were marketed, not as bird food, but as "wild bird cuisine." Beak Bistro's advertising evoked a no-worries world in which "a man and a woman sit in a small bistro along the carefree streets of Italy," drinking wine and nibbling food. (Bistros, of course, are French. Italy has trattorias.) "Beak Bistro takes you into a dream world of romance, relaxation, and lightheartedness that creates an emotional attachment that will last a lifetime."

Bird feeding had become such a popular pastime that all sorts of people started magazines, radio programs, newspaper columns, Internet sites, and blogs to join the party and cash in on it. Virtually all of these people, along with the sellers of birdseed and bird-feeding equipment, promoted backyard bird feeding as a win-win activity for both birds and people. For people, they said, watching birds feed reduced stress, lowered high blood pressure, helped children do better in school, gave comfort to recovering patients and shut-ins, and, most important, reconnected people young and old to nature.

"From their purely esthetical value in millions of backyards, to their usefulness in building inquiry skills among classroom students, to their applications in peer-reviewed, quantitative, environmental monitoring, bird feeders present extraordinary connections between our human culture and the natural world," John W. Fitzpatrick, director of the Cornell Laboratory of Ornithology, told me in a letter. The lab promotes feeding and lists seed and equipment sellers among its corporate sponsors.

Cornell and other promoters called feeding a largely benign activity in terms of its effects on birds and the environment. Some advertisers of seed and feeders portrayed feeding as being helpful to birds, and surveys showed that most people who fed birds genuinely believed that they were helping them. Promoters were understandably defensive about assertions that feeding wasn't necessary, did little good, and was, in some cases, harmful to some birds.

Feeding wild birds is, in essence, a form of wildlife management— some say *use*—in which participants manipulate the natural world to create outcomes they want—in this case, using food to lure birds into viewing range. Depending on whose figures you believe, feeders put anywhere from 500,000 to 1.2 million tons of seed annually into the environment. This is food that wouldn't otherwise be there. Feeding advocates argue that it could be considered a replacement for the natural food sources lost to developers and sprawl.

Ornithologists and wildlife biologists I talked to said that putting all that seed out isn't helpful most of the time because wild birds don't need supplemental feeding, although feeding might on occasion—say in the dead of winter—help the small subset of birds attracted to feeders. In Minnesota, for example, only about 40 of the state's 240 bird species visited feeders, and those were among the most common birds. "Birds in decline don't come to feeders," and they are the species that need conservation help most, Carrol Henderson, a wild bird expert and author, and supervisor of the Nongame Wildlife Program of Minnesota's Department of Natural Resources, told me.

Bird feeders are wildlife aggregation devices. The food in them makes up a sizable portion of the smorgasbord people consciously or unwittingly put out and maintain in the form of lawns, gardens, garbage cans, mulch bins, and Dumpsters. Putting out birdseed is akin to hunters' practice of putting out salt licks and apples to attract deer, or buckets of pastries to lure in black bears (although the purpose of feeding birds is not to kill them, of course). Besides squirrels and chipmunks, birdseed attracts opossums, skunks, raccoons, foxes, and bears. And of course the birds who visit feeders attract bird predators. For hawks and house cats, feeders are fast-food outlets.

People-wildlife mitigation has become a growth industry, and operators of nuisance wildlife control companies say the bird feeders can take part of the credit. "I hate to sound cynical, but people who feed birds are our best customers," Alan Huot, who operates Nuisance Wildlife Services in Simsbury, Connecticut, told me. "They don't think much about all the unwanted animals they are attracting." Those animals can take up residence in attics, in chimneys, and under porches. They are usually more alarming or annoying than dangerous, but electrical wires can be chewed and shorted, and houses can mysteriously burn down.

"The first thing I tell people with nuisance animal problems is that they have to remove these artificial food sources," said Bob Noonan, editor of *Trapper's Post* and former editor of *WCT* (Wildlife Control Technology), a trade magazine for the nuisance wildlife control industry. Some people take down their feeders and reinforce their garbage cans—especially after the first bear turns up. Some don't.

The bird-feeding industry, on the other hand, encourages the opposite in its efforts to sell more products that attract more wildlife. Many birdseed companies were bought out by gardening and lawn care companies in recent years to create publicly traded outdoor product empires. They pushed aggressively into sales of equipment and plants to create backyard habitats instead of boring lawns. They encouraged home owners to buy and install natural-looking ponds, plant special shrubs and trees, and make other landscaping improvements that add more food, hiding places, and edges. Along with conservation groups such as the National Wildlife Federation, the industry joined in promotions to create and certify backyard habitats as a way of reconnecting children to nature—an admirable quest. Attracting butterflies, frogs, and songbirds was the goal. Attracting skunks and opossums was not, but they often showed up too, and the local nuisance wildlife control operator was more than happy to show up next.

Wildlife biologists know that aggregating wildlife with food in concentrations not found in the wild increases the potential of spreading diseases. One well-known example, as we have seen, is the spread of bovine tuberculosis in deer. Mucus from an infected deer is left on a food pile, and a healthy deer feeds and picks it up. Likewise, an infected bird poking its head and beak into the hole of a tubular feeder can leave its disease for the next customers. Bird droppings under feeders can contain bacteria and parasites that infect ground-feeding birds. Cleaning feeders regularly—say once or twice a month in a mild solution of bleach and water—stymies feeder disease. Some people do this religiously. Most don't.

"It rarely happens, and that's not going to change," Jason Rogers, a teacher and wildlife biologist in Calgary, Alberta, wrote in *Birdchat,* an Internet chat room.

> What regularly happens is this: wild birds become food stressed in winter and, thus, become more prone to infection; the sickest birds become the most frequent visitors to the place where food can be obtained most easily (i.e. birdfeeders); and pathogens are transmitted to healthy birds at feeders via the secretions and excretions of sick birds.
>
> Does this happen in nature? Let's put it this way: when was the last time you found a natural food source that caused a flock of birds to occupy the same four-foot-square patch of ground several times a day for a week?

Diseases spread by bird feeders aren't the chief cause of backyard bird mortality. A 1992 study by Erica Dunn in conjunction with the

Cornell lab found that the most important cause of backyard bird deaths was window collisions (51 percent), followed by predation by cats (36 percent) and then disease (11 percent). Feeders weren't directly implicated, but in aggregating birds closer to windows and within the grasp of cats, their role was implied. But how important are feeders in the overall health of bird populations? Not very, said Dr. Dunn in her 1999 book, *Birds at Your Feeder*. She argued that "bird feeding is not having a broad-scale negative impact on bird populations" and that "bird feeding does not cause mortality to rise above natural levels." In an e-mail to me, Cornell's Fitzpatrick added: "Bottom line: there is not a shred of solid evidence, for any species in my knowledge, that bird feeders have a negative effect on native bird populations."

Put another way, birds die because of feeders, but their overall effect on avian populations is minimal. Feeding defenders pointed out that half of all birds die in any year anyway, making numbers of feeder-caused deaths tiny in comparison. Defenders of hunting and trapping could, of course, say the same thing—but would likely be jeered for doing so. "We could make the same argument," said Noonan. "We remove surplus animals that are going to die over the winter." So could advocates of letting house cats and strays run around loose to prey on birds, as we shall see.

Bird feeders assert that of all man's interactions with the natural landscape and its wild inhabitants, surely feeding birds ranks as one of the most benign, and very low on any list of pursuits with negative consequences. Still, feeding wild birds is a form of nature management, although a lot of people who do it do not recognize their hobby as a form of nature manipulation. Many cannot conceive that they may be doing something that's not beneficial to either birds or their environment, and some become almost aggressively sanctimonious at the suggestion that what they do is the least bit harmful.

On one thing, most bird feeders, birders, ornithologists, wildlife biologists, bird conservation groups, and government wildlife agencies wholeheartedly agree: Cats kill birds by the hundreds of millions, or billions, annually. Pet cats and stray cats are a paramount source of preventable avian mortality.

But as we shall see in the next chapter, there is one group that adamantly disagrees: cat lovers. Interestingly, cat lovers make some of the same arguments as bird feeders make, mainly that human manipulation of the environment, from habitat destruction to pollution, causes far more harm to birds and other creatures than do cats. And as species partisans go, cat lovers and protectors are far more self-righteous in defense of their feline friends than any other group. Theirs is an ideology rooted in casual observation of Fluffy playing with a ball of string in the living room, not outside at night. They say, "Oh, I know Fluffy. When I put her out at night, she won't go ten feet from the door. She's afraid of her own shadow. She wouldn't hurt a flea."

Chapter Twelve

Feral Felines

Kaye Draper lived in a modest house in the town of Cassopolis in south-western Michigan in 1947 with her cat—one of just 4 million house cats people kept as pets in the years after the Second World War. In those days the biggest drawback to keeping a cat, especially if you wanted to keep it indoors, was its foul-smelling urine—a trait stemming from its evolution as a wild creature in the water-short environment of the North African desert. Cats urinate infrequently to preserve body moisture. Their urine concentrates into one of the animal kingdom's most noxious odors—an ammonia-like smell that in those days tested the tolerance of home owners and visitors.

Keeping cats outdoors was considered the best policy in earlier eras, when most Americans lived on farms and cats could sleep in the barn, up in the hayloft, and stay warm. People who wanted to keep cats indoors, at least part of the time, had to train them to urinate and defecate outdoors or to provide a box indoors in which they could do their business. People placed these indoor boxes on porches, in back rooms, or in bathrooms (for those with indoor plumbing) and filled them with newspapers, sand, sawdust, wood shavings, or ashes. The boxes had to be cleaned often to keep down the smell.

Kaye Draper kept a litter box on her porch. At first she filled it with ashes, but her cat tracked ash soot into the house. She tried sand next, but in the cold, damp air of Michigan winters sand froze, making it incapable of absorbing urine. One frigid January day in 1947, she asked her neighbor, a young navy veteran named Edward Lowe, for some sawdust. Lowe had come home from the war in 1945 and gone to work for his father, who ran a company selling industrial absorbents, mainly sawdust, to factories and garages to sop up spilled grease, oil, and other chemicals. Sawdust is a good absorbent, with one drawback: It is flammable. Lowe's father had been experimenting with a fireproof alternative—a kiln-dried granulated clay called fuller's earth.[23] As it happened, Ed Lowe had a bag of fuller's earth in the trunk of his car and suggested that Draper try some. When Lowe caught up with Draper a few days later, she asked for more. She said the clay was wonderfully absorbent of both urine and its smell, and, being heavier than sand and ashes, didn't track up the house.

Lowe, thinking other cat owners might buy it, filled ten brown paper bags with five pounds of clay each, wrote "Kitty Litter"—a name, he said, that just came to him—on the side of each bag, took them to a local pet store, and suggested selling them for 65¢ a bag, or 13¢ a pound. The store's owner all but hooted him out the door. Sand was selling for a penny a pound at the time. Why would anyone pay so much for clay? "So give it away," Lowe is reported to have told him. Soon the store's customers were returning, asking for "Kitty Litter" by name and paying a premium price to get it.

Over the next decade, Lowe crossed the country in a 1943 Chevrolet Coupe promoting Kitty Litter at pet shows. He tried for a decade to persuade supermarkets to stock Kitty Litter. When some finally did in 1957, his product got far more public exposure than it did in pet stores, and sales took off. Lowe's Inc. products, Kitty Litter and Tidy Cat, dominated an emerging market, but competitors soon produced

---

23. The clay got its name from garment workers called "fullers" in medieval England, who used it with water to sop up lanolin, grease, and human oils from woolen garments. Once dried, the clay was shaken and brushed off the garments, which were then fluffed up or "fulled" by the workers.

products named Go Cat Go and Kitty Diggins. In the 1970s, Clorox launched the first national advertising campaign for a litter box product called Litter Green, made of alfalfa pellets. Kitty Litter was falling behind. "We were still selling plain dirt in a bag," Lowe told the *Wall Street Journal*. "I was just an old country boy bumbling along."

Lowe decided he needed to make some changes, and to make them he hired some "button-down-collar guys," including a marketing research specialist named David Tooker. Lowe's clay mix absorbed urine and partially masked its smell. Americans, however, had become increasingly odor-phobic. The air in their homes was becoming filtered and cooled, and advertisers were urging people to mask odors with underarm sprays and bathroom aerosols. The hint of a foul smell was portrayed in ads as a social stigma. Lowe and Tooker realized that a deodorant might greatly improve Kitty Litter, and, as it turned out, Monsanto, the chemical company, had a new product called Malodor-counteractant. Lowe bought the rights to use it, and Tooker marketed this new Kitty Litter, now a combination of baked clay mixed with green-colored deodorant flecks, as the Cadillac of cat box fillers.

Kitty Litter and its competitors changed cat keeping in major ways. In the 1960s and '70s, cats became pets of convenience. They were easier than dogs to maintain. They didn't have to be walked. Although they frequently scratched, they usually didn't bite. And, at long last, they didn't stink up the house. Cat popularity soared. From just 4 million in 1947, the pet cat population grew to 47 million by 1984. In 1985, cats passed dogs as America's favorite pets. By 1990 the cat population stood at 58 million, and by 2011 Americans kept 86.4 million cats (and 78.2 million dogs). Spending on cats grew apace, with owners paying out, on average, $930 a year on each of their cats for visits to veterinarians, food and snack "treats," litter, toys, shampoo, and other supplies.

One reason for the increased spending was that pet owners increasingly thought of their pets as four-legged people with human feelings. People had always engaged in this kind of anthropomorphism, of course, but the growing pet products industry saw the market expansion possibilities in encouraging this proclivity. Veterinarians also encouraged it as a way of promoting pet care and curbing abuse. By the 1990s, the industry and animal protection charities were persuading people to think of their pets as "companion animals," "members of the family," and "surrogate children." The phrase "pet owners" gave way to "companion animal guardians," a wording that implied legal and other obligations. The more dogs and cats were humanized in the minds of their owners, the more human concerns—about fashions and fads, health, luxury, the environment, mental well-being—could be projected onto them.

Concern over "junk food" for people, for example, led to all sorts of designer pet food products advertised as healthy, organic, and "human grade." People snacked, so why not snacks and treats to make pets feel happy? If pets got fat, a host of low-calorie and pet diet products were available, including weight loss pills. Like children, pets needed lots of toys. A pet's bad breath, like a human's, could be eliminated by oral care products. Like people, pets needed vitamins and "medications," including natural cures, homeopathic remedies, and holistic treatments, not to mention pills to reduce tension, soothe separation anxiety, or prevent travel stress.

The American Pet Products Manufacturers Association (APPMA, now APPA), the industry trade group, held its annual trade show in Chicago in 2002, and I attended. The group's research forecast that spending on pets that year would be $29.5 billion—more than people would spend that year on toys for children ($25 billion) or candy ($23.8 billion). It would exceed $50 billion in 2012. Back then, I was struck by the displays of pet products that mimicked trendy products for people. *Natural* was a word peppering human products then—food, shampoos, pills. I met Susan Weiss, from Naples, Florida, who told me about her efforts six years earlier to market "Ark Naturals," a line of pet dental supplies, "wellness products," and dietary supplement treatments such as glucosamine for treating dog and cat joint problems. When she first took her samples around to pet stores, nobody was interested.

"I could have been selling real estate on Mars," she told me. Pet store operators thought of her products as gimmicks. They didn't understand the potential appeal of dietary supplements because they focused on the pets instead of on how pet owners thought. Where did people who understood dietary supplements shop? Health food stores, of course. So Weiss began visiting them. Their operators "got it" instantly. People who believed in dietary supplements for themselves could easily see that their pets might need them too. Soon displays of Ark Naturals for Pets were popping up in health food stores.

"These products aren't really about pets," Weiss told me. "These products are about human behavior."

The April 2005 issue of *Pet Product News* carried an article about people who sought to "spoil" their cats: "Cat lifestyle products are growing in popularity as more cat owners go the way of the dog and begin to seek out products that spoil their kitties and help define themselves as cat owners." Such items included high-end food and water bowls, fancy litter boxes, stylish cat-carrying bags, cat clothing and cologne, designer scratching posts, upscale cat day care, cat birthday party caterers, and gift registries.[24]

It wasn't always this way. When the majority of Americans lived on farms and had dogs and cats around, the animals were domesticated— they were trained more or less to behave in ways their owners desired— but they also had the freedom to act more or less as their genetic makeup dictated. Cats had real jobs policing corncribs and other crop storage places for rats, mice, and other food-stealing vermin. They could practice

24. In 2006, Americans spent $9.6 billion on the health of their pets—with visits to the vet the single highest expense. Pets now had MRIs (magnetic resonance imaging), CAT (computed axial tomography) scans, dialysis, hip replacements, chemotherapy, and kidney transplants.

stealth. Dogs worked as guards, barking at intruders. They herded sheep and cows, hunted rabbits and pheasants, and retrieved waterfowl. There was plenty of room to run and prowl, to burn off energy. But modern pets were increasingly confined to backyards and indoors, unable to do what they were designed to do. When they chased things or chewed and scratched furniture, they were said to be having behavior problems. They didn't act the way their owners wanted them to.

In the old days, owners who no longer wanted their dogs or cats, or who had too many, either gave them away or, especially in rural areas, simply killed them. Old pets were "put to sleep." Sick pets were "put out of their misery." Superfluous cat litters were often drowned. "Dog pounds" were run for the most part by local governments (and located in many cases near town dumps) and were primarily in the business of housing stray animals—that is, dogs running around loose. Relatively little attention was paid to stray cats. Stray dogs were considered to be menaces; they might scare working horses or bite people; dogs spread rabies and sometimes formed marauding packs that killed livestock and threatened people. These animals were killed within hours after being caught—unless they were claimed by their owners or identified by a collar or tag. After the Second World War, stray dogs strained sheltering facilities and some unclaimed dogs and cats were turned over to government and university labs for biomedical research. Animal protection groups fought to end the practice.

The phrase "pet overpopulation" began to creep into the vocabulary in the 1960s, just as the pet boom was taking off. In those days, sterilizing pets wasn't in vogue—indeed, some people considered the procedures harmful to the animals. So lots of pets were producing lots of offspring. Kittens and puppies could be had for little or no money. In the 1960s and '70s, pets were showing up at animal shelters not because they had become lost or become strays but because they were unwanted. Perhaps their owners had had second thoughts about the doggie in the window or the cute kitty down the street, or else the animals didn't behave as their owners had expected. Animal shelters proliferated, promising to find new homes for unwanted pets.

In reality, new homes couldn't be found for abandoned pets all that often. People who came to shelters to adopt a dog or cat didn't want one with the very behavior troubles that got it to the shelter in the first place. Shelters had neither the money nor the capacity to keep animals for long. More and more they were turning into execution chambers, but most people didn't know it, or overlooked it.

It took until 1993 for concerned veterinarians, researchers, humane societies, and pet-breeding groups to get together to address the overpopulation of dogs and cats. They set up the National Council on Pet Population Study and Policy to gather data. In 1994, they compiled a list of 5,042 shelters housing more than one hundred dogs and cats a year each and asked them to supply data over the next four years. Fewer than one in four responded, some, it was suggested, because they didn't want the amount of killing they were doing to be known for fear that donations would drop. Those who did respond reported that, in all, 63.6 percent of the dogs and cats they sheltered were eventually euthanized. Broken down, that was 56.4 percent of dogs, and 71 percent of cats. *Euthanasia,* translated from the Greek, means "good death," and it was carried out in most shelters by the injection of sodium pentobarbital, a barbiturate anesthetic that causes unconsciousness and death and, in 2001, reportedly cost $2.88 per animal in materials and labor. In some states, shelters and nuisance wildlife control operators are allowed to use gas chambers filled with carbon monoxide, carbon dioxide, or nitrogen.

The study provoked widespread outrage. People who had been led to believe that their unwanted pet might find a new home realized they were very likely condemning it to death. In response, shelters scrambled to reclaim their images as "shelters" and not death camps. Some of them began to distinguish themselves by advertising that they no longer killed animals, period. They contrasted themselves from those public tax-supported shelters that were required by law to accept all unwanted pets. These included the sick, mean, or old, and most of those animals ended up dead. The new "no-kill" operations, some private and some public, assured people that they would find new homes for all the animals they took in. People who brought pets to them could be confident that Mittens would not die. To further soothe their conscience, they could make a generous contribution to the shelter to assist its humane work. For a while, "no-kill" shelters became magnets for money from a public deceived. In 1997, Roger Caras, president of the American Society for the Prevention of Cruelty to Animals, said that while an end to killing was a worthy aspiration, no-kill shelters were "more hoax than fact." What many of them did, he said, was accept only adoptable animals and turn away all others. What other shelters did was to advertise themselves as no-kill but quietly dispatch animals no one would adopt. "No-kill" in either case was a ruse that allowed many shelters to skim off the most adoptable pets, compile favorable statistics, and use them to reap more contributions.

Another alternative to a public shelter death sentence was pet abandonment. For people who no longer wanted their dogs, couldn't give them away, and didn't want to take them to a shelter, there was the alternative of dog dumping. This, however, was an ordeal. If your intent was keeping the animal alive, you had to drop it off far from home, so it wouldn't find its way back, and hope someone would take it in before someone else called the animal control officer for a ride to the dog pound. Cats, on the other hand, were easy to dump. Some people acquired cats and cared for them with the same diligence they would an offspring. Others thought of cats as ornaments, acquired on impulse, like a pair of shoes or a kilim couch pillow. Cats could just as easily be discarded as last year's toy or an unfashionable coat. Still, they were living creatures, a truth that first-time cat owners sometimes hadn't really considered (many parents gave their children "starter pets" such as fish, hermit crabs, or hamsters to teach the rudiments of caring for a living creature). Sometimes new cat owners got more or less than they bar-

gained for: animals with diseases, other afflictions, or behavioral problems. Sometimes pet cats scratched their owners or peed on the rug.
Sometimes they simply became inconvenient or untimely, as when a
student ended his summer job and headed for college, or a sailor on a
land base shipped out, or a family moved or broke up. Many cat owners, of course, would endeavor to find good homes for their pets. But
many abandoned them, even though that meant they were condemning
them to the hazards of homelessness, disease, trauma, malnutrition, and
death.

Dogs were taken much more seriously than cats in both law and
practice. The ways people reacted to stray dogs and cats differed too.
Dogs were treated with caution. They were larger than cats, more un-
predictable, and sometimes aggressive. Home owners were much more
willing to toss out some food for a wandering cat than for a stray dog.
At workplaces, stray cats were routinely fed by employees. Behind restaurants and malls, on the grounds of colleges and hospitals, cats aggregated around Dumpsters that offered steady meals. Cats gathered
at places where food was served to them by "cat ladies" who thought of
themselves as compassionate caretakers. Laws or company rules against
feeding cats were largely ignored because they were rarely enforced.
What was the harm in extending a handout to a poor, hungry kitty cat?
Ironically, the very compassion extended to strays by their caretakers
made it easier for other people to throw away their cats.

So it was that more and more cats were abandoned by their owners
and left to make it on their own with whatever help they could find from
people around them. These strays, however, presented problems. Like
dogs, they could spread rabies and other diseases and infections to both
people and other animals. This raised legal liability concerns for businesses, landlords, campuses, and other institutions. Some people didn't
want cats around shrieking and fighting at night, or digging, urinating,
and defecating in their gardens and yards. Burgeoning populations of
unwanted stray and feral cats had to be dealt with, and companies and

property owners turned increasingly to municipal animal control or to nuisance wildlife control companies to come in and trap and remove the cats. Cat removal wasn't something a lot of professionals liked to get involved with. The trouble wasn't cats, some told me, it was "cat people."

To see what they meant, I tagged along with Frank Spiecker, a wiry thirty-five-year-old who ran Harbor Wildlife Control (now Garden State Pest Management Inc.) in northern New Jersey and did a lot of cat jobs all over New Jersey and New York's Staten Island. I asked him to show me places where he had trapped cats. We drove by strip malls, fast-food joints, gas stations, and the clutter of an aging suburb to a garden apartment complex in the town of Old Bridge, the site of his first cat job. We passed rows of semidetached two-story rental units about the length of a football field, to the back edge of the property. A rickety wooden fence separated the apartments from a hillside and val-ley beyond. "This used to be all cleared land," he said, motioning to the valley. "Now it's woods."

Indeed, the woods came right up to the back fence and extended across the valley as far as the eye could see. The fence was porous, and inside it sat Dumpsters where residents put their garbage. Signs asked residents to keep the lids on the Dumpsters shut. But those signs were often not obeyed, and the Dumpsters became restaurants for flies, ants, and roaches, as well as for opossums, raccoons, and cats that lived in the woods or in holes and hiding places among the apartment buildings. These animals were nocturnal and did their Dumpster diving at night, sometimes noisily enough to draw complaints. But the wild animals were rarely seen. Tenants did see cats around the complex, and some put food out for them. Signs placed around the complex imploring residents not to feed the cats were easily ignored. Enforcement was nil. Other residents neither cared for the cats nor liked them around. They com-plained to management, saying they felt threatened and worried about being bitten or scratched. Just as when bats moved in, or squirrels, management was legally liable to remove potentially harmful or dangerous creatures. Frank Spiecker was hired to remove the cats.

Removing raccoons from chimneys and squirrels from attics is fairly straightforward work. Spiecker usually set up a cage trap near the spot where the animal went in and out and baited it. When his Garden State Pest Management pickup turned up to remove these intruders, he was usually greeted warmly by residents. Removing the odd backyard skunk made him a hero. Trapping stray cats, which accounted for about 40 percent of his work in those days, was a different story. When Spiecker arrived to trap cats, his welcome did not extend beyond the apartment manager and, perhaps, a few complainers. Many residents considered him to be a hired killer. The cat lovers, he told me, were often very emotional. Cat partisans had threatened him with bodily harm. They had pushed and jostled him, screamed at him and spit on him. His truck had been jumped on and pounded on with fists, his traps run over by cars. The cats he caught in traps were sometimes freed by residents before he arrived to pick them up.

"The screamers I can handle," he told me. "It's the quiet ones you have to watch."

Spiecker drove me next to a well-maintained 1,200-unit garden apartment complex of neat winding drives and sidewalks and small patches of lawn. Two years before, management there had become worried after a woman living in the complex told them she had been walking her small dog one evening when a wild and aggressive cat attacked the beloved pooch. There were no witnesses, but the management, fearing a lawsuit, hired Spiecker to trap and remove the cats for $50 apiece. During the next six months, he trapped 370 cats and delivered them to the Old Bridge Township Animal Shelter. There, Barbara Lee Brucker, a woman with twenty-one years' experience in shelter work, charged $15 apiece to accept them. New Jersey state law required that municipal shelters hold animals for seven days. During that time she contacted the owners of those cats with ID collars or tags. Some people came to collect their cats, some didn't. Brucker judged about 100 of the 370 cats to be potentially adoptable—that is, they weren't too feral and thus might revert to being pets again. She found homes for some of them. The others were judged to be too wild or too sick to keep. They were given lethal injections of sodium pentobarbital and their carcasses were stored in the shelter's freezer. When the freezer was full, Brucker telephoned the Abbey Glen Pet Memorial Park in Lafayette, New Jersey.

Abbey Glen offered a full line of pet funerals, interments, cremations, and grief counseling. The last time I checked, Abbey Glen would pick up your dead cat for $100 and cremate it for $210 (if it weighed five to ten pounds), urn included. Cat caskets cost $295 plus a 7 percent sales tax. Burial plots on site went for $485, granite headstones cost $280, and bronze cost $820. The cost of gravesite maintenance was $45 a year or could be arranged in perpetuity for $963, state sales tax included. Abbey Glen also offered cut-rate services for shelter cats. After Brucker's call, it dispatched a truck, picked up the frozen cat carcasses, weighed them, and cremated them at a bulk rate of 35¢ a pound.

Julie K. Levy, a veterinarian at the University of Florida who has studied feral cats extensively, reported in 2003 that evidence suggested that "approximately 2.5 to 3 million cats" were euthanized annually at animal shelters. Many of these, she asserted, were adoptable but were killed within a few days because there was not enough space to house them. Since feral cats were generally the least adoptable, they were understandably killed in disproportionately high numbers.

Nobody knows how many feral cats exist at any one time. The lowest estimate is about 30 million, but researchers generally agree that the number ranges somewhere between 60 million and 100 million. Dr. Levy said the feral population "is suspected to approach that of pet cats." In 2011, the APPA estimated that there were 86.4 million owned cats. Thus the total cat population, both pet and feral, could be somewhere between 146 million and 186 million. Any number above 165 million means that there were more cats in America at any one time than cattle (96.7 million), pigs (59.1 million), sheep (5.7 million), and goats (2.9 million) combined.

By 2003, it was estimated that between 82 percent and 91 percent of all pet cats had been sterilized (after producing a litter of kittens, in some cases). Feral cats, unless sterilized before being abandoned, were likely to be fertile. Thus they produced more offspring. Dr. Levy estimated that they produced 80 percent of the kittens born each year in the United States and were "the most important source of cat overpopulation."

Like people with pet cats, many of those who fed feral cats around their house, the neighborhood, or the community became attached to and protective of these animals. Over the years, feral cats were seen as victims—animals that had once purred before the hearth, now suddenly tossed out into a cold and cruel world. But as their numbers kept growing, roundups and death sentences became more common because communities concerned about cat overpopulation seemed to have no choice. What to do?

One way to reduce the killing of unwanted cats was to reform and expand animal shelters, create programs within them to treat sick or injured inmates to make them more adoptable, and encourage more adoptions. Several animal protection charities supported these programs. Maddie's Fund, endowed in 2001 with $300 million by a California computer software magnate, funded veterinary schools to teach shelter medicine and campaigned to create a "no-kill nation" by 2015. Best Friends Animal Society, which receives donations of up to $45 million a year, ran the nation's largest no-kill pet sanctuary (some 1,700 animals, on average) in Kanab, Utah, and started a "No More Homeless Pets" campaign to lower euthanasia rates in shelters. But these and other similar campaigns were aimed at adoptable animals, and most feral cats were deemed too wild to be adopted.

For people who wanted to keep feral cats out of shelters and the likelihood of death, an apparently miraculous solution presented itself in the early 1990s. It was called TNR, which stood for "trap, neuter, release" or "trap, neuter, return." Advocates proposed catching the cats, sterilizing them, and then setting them free again, preferably where they were caught or nearby. The cats would live out their lives without producing more kittens. They would become part of a "managed colony" given food and water by volunteers. The cats would eventually die and the population would go down—a humane solution to a terrible problem, or so it seemed.

Ellen Perry Berkeley, a writer who became an advocate of the TNR method, reported that the technique had gotten its start in Europe in the 1950s. In 1990, Berkeley wrote in *Cat Fancy* magazine that she had found active neuter-and-release proponents in at least six states, some of whom had been "at it for 20 years." One woman told her, "There's an army of people out there neutering feral cats." That is to say, they were arranging for qualified veterinarians to sterilize them. Among those people, Berkeley wrote, were Louise Holton and Becky Robinson, who were caring for fifty-six cats that lived in an alley in the Adams-Morgan neighborhood in Washington, D.C. The women claimed that sterilization efforts had stopped new kittens from being born, thus stabilizing the population of the cat colony. When this was reported, Robinson and Holton were, writes Berkeley, "deluged by requests for help." In 1991, as a result, the two women started a national feral cat network called Alley Cat Allies. In 2001, the group sponsored National Feral Cat Day, now an annual event.

In the 1990s, Berkeley wrote, TNR "took off." By 2004, Alley Cat Allies (ACA) claimed to have seventy-five thousand supporters and a budget approaching $4 million a year. In 2010, it received $5.2 million in donations. Trap-Neuter-Return had become a "movement," Berkeley wrote. As word spread, the numbers of cat lovers who embraced TNR grew rapidly. Advocates organized regional and national networks to spread the TNR story. They pleaded with local officials to stop roundups altogether and adopt TNR in laws as the official method for feral cat control, citing testimonials from elsewhere that TNR "worked." There were plenty of veterinarians to back them up. Three out of four vets treat pets only, mainly dogs and cats. Some of them have been at the forefront of efforts to lower cat overpopulation. By 2010, according to Alley Cat Allies, more than 360 feral cat protection groups were registered as 501(c)(3) charities and were proclaiming TNR to be the *only* humane solution to cat overpopulation. Donors contributed tens of millions of dollars annually to their cause. ACA adopted the rallying cry "Feralpower!"

As the movement grew, TNR activists, using political advocacy software, websites, and blogs, became adept at responding quickly and in large numbers with e-mails and letters when lethal removals of feral cats were proposed in local communities. They alerted attorneys, some eager to do pro bono animal protection work. These activists sometimes offered money, volunteers, and discounted veterinary services as enticements for local governments to adopt their nonlethal methods. For cash-strapped communities, solving a cat problem without having to pay for it was a powerful incentive. If enticements failed, activists provided local groups with how-to help with organizing protests, getting media attention, and writing press releases and letters to editors—even providing sample texts to copy. They supplied easy-to-understand "Truth Cards" asserting why TNR works and why "catch and kill" doesn't. For example:

> Trap-Neuter-Return does work. No more kittens. The population stabilizes and their lives are improved. The behaviors and stresses associated with mating, such as yowling or fighting, stop. The cats are vaccinated before being returned to their outdoor home. Not only does Trap-Neuter-Return make good sense, it is also a responsible, humane method of care for outdoor cats.

TNR gained momentum nationwide, with each new supposed success story used to convince other communities that TNR success could be theirs too. Success meant that cats in a TNR colony were spared almost certain death in shelters, and that was the "right" way for "progressive communities" to act.

Mayors, city managers, and councilpeople in large metropolitan regions had gained experience over the years in facing both species partisans and their opponents. They had also grown accustomed to outside pressure groups weighing in to advocate their particular solution to problems with deer, geese, beavers, cats, and other species. Smaller and more isolated communities, however, often found themselves caught unaware when these outsiders got wind of a local situation that wasn't being solved their way. That was what happened in the tiny town of Randolph (population 209 at the time) in the southwestern corner of Iowa in the spring of 2008.

Vance Trively, the mayor of Randolph, told me that some residents, himself included, had gotten fed up with the growing number of cats, maybe 150 or more, running around town. Some strays had taken up more or less permanent residence in his storage shed, and some people who lived near it were feeding them. Trively, seventy years old at the time and still active in the livestock transport business, said he and Randolph's five councilpersons discussed the cat problem at the council's February meeting. After that meeting, as was usual, Trively sent out a "Mayor's Newsletter" to residents. This one read in part:

I have had several of our residents call about the increasing numbers of wild cats in town. This problem along with the dogs on the loose, was brought up at our last council meeting. It was decided to get our citizens to help with this problem by putting a $5.00 bounty payment for the catching and delivering live to me, any loose cat or dog caught in town. I want to stress to our pet owners, have a collar on your pet. If I can identify the pet by the collar, I will return it to its owner. The owner will be charged the cost of the $5.00 bounty that the city paid the person who caught it. Those cats and dogs without ID will be taken to the vet in Sidney for disposal.

Randolph is situated forty-nine miles southeast of Omaha, deep in the American agricultural heartland, and its officials were not keeping up with the latest dogmatics of big, national cat protection groups. They certainly did not foresee the consequences of using the words *bounty* and *cat* in the same sentence. Word spread fast.

When Alley Cat Allies, headquartered in Bethesda, Maryland, got the news, it immediately e-mailed an action alert to supporters. Mayor Trively said 726 e-mails and letters arrived in short order, some nasty and threatening, some from foreign countries. In a March 12 press release, ACA's Becky Robinson called the bounty "absolutely barbaric and ludicrous," adding, "Providing a financial incentive to have an animal spayed or neutered is a great idea. But in our civilized society, the notion of offering cash to produce a cat for slaughter is completely unacceptable." Robinson telephoned David Schmitt, the Iowa state veterinarian, and asked him to investigate whether the mayor was guilty of "animal neglect" under state law. Schmitt sent a cease-and-desist order to the mayor and alerted the local sheriff. That evening, when the mayor and five councilpersons gathered at the storefront that served as City Hall, representatives of six cat protection groups, lots of media, and a handful of local residents turned up. The mayor was handed a letter from Alley Cat Allies that said, in part, "The world is watching, and we are here to help you make the right . . . decision." It wasn't difficult, on top of all the other letters, to see that statement as a threat and to believe that the assembled cat groups were out to confront the town in front of the TV cameras. The mayor told me later that he felt like a deer caught in headlights. Had the council imposed a "catch fee" instead of a "bounty," nobody would have paid attention, he told a local radio station. In any case, the council voted to end the bounty and agreed to allow the cat groups to set up a trap-neuter-return project even though few if any people in Randolph understood what TNR was. The cat care groups met with the mayor to explain how TNR would work. As an incentive to win support for it, they offered free spaying or neutering of both feral cats and pet cats in Randolph. In this planned first phase, twenty-nine cats were trapped, or collected, and neutered at a cost of $6,000 (about $207 per cat). Then a problem arose: The mayor refused to return the fixed cats to the exact spots, including his shed, where they had been trapped—as TNR orthodoxy demanded. Five of the six TNR groups involved, including Alley Cat Allies, quit, and the project fell apart.

. . .

There are two very big problems with trap-neuter-return, critics assert: First, as a solution to reducing the overall feral cat population in the United States, it is a mirage; second, it allows these invasive predators access to plunder ecosystems of native wild birds and animals.

"It's all the rage across the United States," wrote Ted Williams in *Audubon* magazine in 2009. "And it doesn't work."

Even if all of Randolph's strays had been caught and neutered, and even if such success were replicated in one thousand Randolphs, even ten thousand or one hundred thousand, TNR still wouldn't make a dent in a feral cat population of 60 to 100 million. Such volunteer efforts are tiny in an ocean of need. TNR, say critics, is a quixotic quest, its ultimate goal possible in theory but impossible in reality. This quest allows TNR supporters to feel good and to believe that they are headed in the right direction and that with more donations, vets, and effort they will succeed in stabilizing and reducing feral populations.

The preeminent organization of veterinarians, the American Veterinary Medical Association (AVMA), however, takes the position that success isn't possible. In a statement first adopted in 2004, the AVMA says it "neither endorses nor opposes appropriately managed cat colony programs." Why not endorse? Because TNR-managed cats amount to "an insignificant percentage of the total number of un-owned free-roaming and feral cats," and therefore any population reductions resulting are "insignificant." The organization did not expressly oppose "properly managed" TNR colonies for the simple reason that its core members are pet veterinarians, many of whom specialize in cat medicine exclusively and are among the most vociferous defenders of TNR programs.

Critics, including one who set up a website called TNRrealitycheck .com, say that after decades of TNR projects in which more feral cats are neutered each year, the total number of sterilized cats probably adds up to less than 1 percent of all the ferals out there at any one time. It isn't difficult to understand why. Veterinarians do the neutering. There are forty-six thousand veterinarians who confine their practices to treating dogs and cats (and the odd reptile, bird, ferret, rabbit, or other pet). If every pet vet volunteered or was paid to spay and neuter one hundred feral cats a year, they could sterilize 4.6 million animals. If every pet vet spayed or neutered one feral cat per day for a year, the annual total would be 16,790,000 sterile cats. But even that many is small in relation to the estimated 60 to 100 million ferals out there.

In 2010, Best Friends trumpeted a study asserting that, in theory, it would be cheaper to trap-neuter-return all feral cats in America than to kill them. Sponsored by PetSmart Charities, an arm of the pet store chain, the study put the cost of trapping and killing 87 million ferals at $15.74 billion. Performing TNR, however, would cost only $14 billion, it asserted, and that could be cut to less than $7 billion using volunteer vets and community workers.

"The study appears to be one whose design was determined by the conclusion desired," said Dr. David A. Jessup, the senior wildlife veterinarian with the California Department of Fish and Game. Dr. Brent Martin, a vet in Toledo, Ohio, noted that euthanasia costs could likewise be cut in half if the cats weren't sheltered, fed, and tested before being killed. Another vet, Dr. Jack W. Zimmerly, markets two sizes of carbon monoxide euthanasia chambers, ranging from $6,500 for a small one to $20,000 for both. They can euthanize forty cats an hour at an operating cost of 11¢ per cat, he said.

To succeed, TNR volunteers have to trap all the cats in any area. This is very difficult. Cats not caught continue to reproduce, and it doesn't take many fertile females, at two litters a year and four to five kittens per litter, even if half the newborns die, to increase the population—thus thwarting TNR's ultimate objective. To succeed, TNR caregivers must also keep new unsterilized strays from joining the colony. Yet the food they put out attracts more cats (and wild animals), and the presence of a colony that is cared for invites people to dump their unwanted cats into it. TNR advocates say this doesn't happen because feral cats are territorial and keep these outsiders out, while catching and killing them creates a vacuum so that new cats move in. The same "vacuum effect" is argued by defenders of deer, geese, beavers, and other species, but nuisance wildlife controllers say it doesn't happen in the short or medium term—meaning years go by before new animals begin to trickle in.

"I got the same line from every TNR outfit I consulted," wrote Williams. "It's rubbish." Stop feeding them and the cats will go elsewhere to eat, he wrote.

TNR practitioners argue that as "community cats," ferals are just as healthy as owned pets. One of the "Truth Cards" that Alley Cat Allies offers donors to help them argue the case asserts, "Feral cats can have the same lifespan as pet cats. And they are just as healthy, too. The incidence of disease in feral cats is just as low as in pet cats. They live healthy, natural lives on their own, content in their outdoor home."

In their fund-raising materials and on websites, TNR advocate groups almost always portray feral cats as clean, well-groomed, and healthy specimens, frequently being snuggled by a caregiver. But critics paint a different picture, and these include some of the nation's most prominent animal protection groups. PETA (People for the Ethical Treatment of Animals), for example, calls TNR cruel to the cats, and the Humane Society of the United States once called the practice "subsidized abandonment." (HSUS reversed itself in 2006, saying it was better to have ferals managed than unmanaged. Others told me, however, that cat lovers are such important sources of donations that animal protection charities can't afford to alienate them with positions and policies they oppose.)

The feral cat help groups that came to Randolph's aid fought over whether the "R" in TNR stood for "release" or "return," but critics say the R means that the cats are "reabandoned" to become parasite ridden, scrawny, and sick. Whether subjected to TNR or not, the veterinary association said, strays suffer: "Unfortunately, most of these cats will suffer premature mortality from disease, starvation and trauma. Their suffering is of sufficient magnitude that it constitutes a national tragedy of epidemic proportions." In other words, the do-gooders save feral cats, neuter them, and return them in more or less supervised colonies to live what are often short and miserable lives.

TNR partisans primarily concern themselves with the welfare of stray cats, a narrowly focused issue, ignoring or discounting the environmental impact of a fast-multiplying, non-native, midsized predator proliferating across native ecosystems and killing birds and small animals. According to the AVMA, however, "These free-roaming abandoned and feral cats also represent a significant factor in the mortality of hundreds of millions of birds, small mammals, reptiles, amphibians, and fish." One reason Dr. Jessup, the top California vet, faulted the Best Friends study was that it didn't factor in the cost of the environmental damage caused by cat feces, the health risks and costs of disease transmission, or the millions of wild birds and animals that feral cats kill. "Wild animals are not only killed by cats but are also maimed, mauled, dismembered, ripped apart, and gutted while still alive, and if they survive the encounter, they often die of sepsis [blood infection] because of the virulent nature of the oral flora [mouth bacteria] of cats," Jessup wrote.

The International Union for Conservation of Nature includes cats in a list of the one hundred worst invasive species on the planet. The American Bird Conservancy said it believes free-roaming cats, in which it includes ferals and pet cats allowed to spend time outdoors, kill 500 million birds in the United States a year, and some estimates for bird kills in North America go up to a billion annually.

Pamela Jo Hatley, an attorney who has researched feral cats in Florida for the U.S. Fish and Wildlife Service and fought TNR programs in court, likened cat predation on wild birds to the overuse of pesticides described in Rachel Carson's *Silent Spring.* Ted Williams in *Audubon* magazine put it this way: "With something like 150 million free-ranging house cats wreaking havoc on our wildlife, the last thing we need is Americans sustaining them in the wild." He added: "TNR is a symptom of the gross ecological illiteracy that blights this nation. It's cruel to cats and dangerous to people and wildlife."

Ignorance of wildlife environments is not confined to ordinary people. As a group, veterinarians are largely uninformed about wildlife ecosystems and their management, yet because they practice animal medicine many people assume they know how animals interact in the natural world.

Because they are "doctors," like physicians who treat people, vets are trusted to offer guidance about domesticated animals and wildlife alike. Veterinarians are trained to do the former but are almost universally unqualified to do the latter.

The twenty-eight accredited veterinary medicine schools in the United States turn out about 2,500 graduates annually (about 70 percent of them women), and most graduates become private practitioners treating pets because that's where the money is. According to the AVMA, three out of four vets in private practice treated dogs, cats, and other pets. (Sixteen percent treated livestock, and 6 percent worked exclusively with horses.) In 2008, fewer than 400 out of 59,700 practicing vets (according to the Bureau of Labor Statistics) worked with wildlife, mainly in zoos and aquariums.

The care of domestic animals and the management of wildlife ecosystems are two very different worlds. Col. Paul L. Barrows (Ret.) is one of the few people who knows both. He is a veterinarian with a doctorate in wildlife diseases. Formerly the chief of the U.S. Army Veterinary Corps and the Pentagon's veterinary affairs director, he worked to outlaw feeding stray cats at military installations and established programs to trap and euthanize strays. He told me that veterinarians who support TNR had "gotten out of their lane" because most of them have little or no education and understanding of wildlife ecosystems and the effect that overpopulations of animals, including cats, have on them.

"Veterinary education focuses nearly exclusively on domestic pets and livestock and the anatomical, physiological, pathological, medical and surgical aspects associated with their 'states of health,'" he wrote. "People think that if an issue is animal-related, the veterinarian must either be an expert, or at least well-versed, on it. Not so! Veterinarians are well trained in their rather narrow focus on animal health, mainly domestic, and that's about it."

Some vet schools offer a wildlife option or wildlife elective courses, but these mainly focus on wildlife rehabilitation—treating and healing hurt creatures—or dealing with captive wildlife in zoos, circuses, and aquariums. Barrows explained: "Detailed instruction on life histories, ecological relationships, habitat requirements, and so on, of free-ranging wildlife is not part of a veterinary education. . . . The science of wildlife management is a complicated and academically challenging profession in its own right. Pre-veterinary and veterinary students, by and large, have no formal academic background in this area. Their understanding of ecological principles is generally poor. Quite frankly, other than the fact that both professional arenas involve animals, practitioners of each have little to no knowledge of the other's professional areas."

A tiny minority of veterinarians specializes in issues involving wild animals, and most are among the three hundred members of the American Association of Wildlife Veterinarians, which in 1996 called for the elimination of feral cat colonies on public lands and their discouragement on private property. Colin M. Gillin, the association's president, told me this:

> Very few veterinarians know anything beyond the Discovery Channel about wildlife medicine, wildlife disease, life histories, ecology, or habitat involving free-ranging wildlife or, for that matter, individual wild animals. It is not part of the standard veterinary education. Even with schools that have wildlife medicine signature programs like Tufts, the basics of wildlife ecology, biology, and conservation are not taught. One would have had to acquire that education through pre-veterinary education such as a BS or MS degree in Wildlife Conservation or Fisheries and Wildlife. Very few veterinarians have that education track and even many of the state agency wildlife vets have not gone that route.

This lack of knowledge about wildlife has legal ramifications. In speeches and articles, Dr. Barrows, Dr. Jessup, and others have warned vets that their participation in TNR programs is in potential violation of the Federal Endangered Species Act and the Migratory Bird Treaty. In 2003, the Pennsylvania Game Commission noted that it was illegal to release house cats into the wild and that therefore TNR programs that rerelease them are also illegal. Enforcement of these and other statutes and ordinances is very weak and something of a political hot potato. TNR promoters campaign to overturn such laws and to pass new ones expressly endorsing trap-neuter-return programs. They also call studies of cat predation on wildlife biased or unscientific and argue that the damage caused by cats is minor in comparison to habitat destruction by man. Alley Cat Allies, for example, says conservation groups use "flawed data and faulty logic. Research shows that human activities are by far the number one threat to birds and wildlife all over the world." It argues that anti-TNR arguments are "naïve and uninformed" and that "progressive communities" embrace TNR, whereas conservation groups "want to turn back the clock" and kill cats. Dr. Jessup's retort: "From a wildlife agency perspective, the release of non-native predators is just as illegal as poisoning or poaching wildlife or bulldozing their habitat."

Cat people do not take kindly to such assertions. After his 1993 study estimated that cats kill about 8 million birds in rural Wisconsin annually, Professor Stanley Temple, who had never killed a cat, got a message on his telephone answering machine calling him a "cat-murdering bastard," followed by a death threat. At an American Ornithologists' Union roundtable in 2008, several scientists raised their hands when asked if they'd gotten death threats. (Save-the-deer and save-the-geese people can be vociferous but they do not, in my experience, make death threats.) When her National Geographic Society documentary film on cat predation, *The Secret Life of Cats,* came out in 1998, producer-director Allison Argo received death threats, she told me. (Alley Cat Allies called the film "inaccurate, incomplete and dangerous" and urged supporters to "demand" that its distribution be withdrawn immediately.)

A long list of professional wildlife support groups, including the Wildlife Society and the Association of Fish and Wildlife Agencies, condemn cat abandonment and TNR support programs. The International Union for Conservation of Nature says cats are responsible for the extinction of at least thirty-three bird species.

. . .

Questions regarding the value or inutility of the domestic cat, and problems connected with limiting its more or less unwelcome outdoor activities, are causing much dissension. The discussion has reached an acute stage. Medical men, game protectors and bird lovers call on legislators to enact restrictive laws. Then ardent cat lovers rouse themselves for combat. In the excitement of partisanship many loose and ill-considered statements are made, some recently published assertions for and against the cat, freely bandied about, have absolutely no foundation in fact.

That statement was made in 1916 by Edward Howe Forbush, the state ornithologist of Massachusetts, in the preface to a 112-page treatise published as Economic Bulletin No. 2 of the State Board of Agriculture and entitled *The Domestic Cat: Bird Killer, Mouser and Destroyer of Wild Life; Means of Utilizing and Controlling It.* Today the situation is reversed: Legislators and local leaders are under pressure from rich and powerful feral cat advocacy groups to expressly protect ferals as "community cats" and pass laws against removing or harming them.

In 1910, the feral cat population in New York's Central Park was judged to be so out of control that a professional sniper was hired to kill them in the name of protecting birds. In six months, the sharpshooter killed 161 cats and was praised for his performance in the July-August issue of *Bird-Lore* magazine.

In 1913, in *Our Vanishing Wild Life,* William Hornaday called the domestic cat "probably the greatest four-legged scourge of bird life" but admitted that thousands of people who had never seen a hunting cat in action wouldn't believe him. A cat invasion of his zoo park had all but exterminated the chipmunks, rabbits, robins, quail, thrushes, and squirrels that lived there, he said. The park decided to get rid of the cats. "We killed every cat that was found hunting in the park. . . . We eliminated that pest," and, he reported, the wildlife slowly came back.

In Australia, feral cats are considered to be a significant threat to that continent's unique marsupial wildlife. In 2004, the National Heritage Trust and the government of New South Wales, which includes Sydney, issued an eight-page how-to pamphlet on shooting feral cats, a technique deemed "labor intensive" but useful. It recommended head or chest shots using small-bore rifles such as .22-caliber or .243, with telescopic sights and hollow-point ammunition. (The American Veterinary Medical Association lists shooting as a humane method of eradication in some cases.)

In the United States two years later, by way of contrast, Jim Stevenson, the founder of the Galveston Ornithological Society, used a .22-caliber rifle to shoot a cat he had seen stalking piping plovers, an endangered shorebird, on a beach under a bridge over the San Luis Pass in Texas. This cat was in violation of local laws banning cats from beaches and requiring that they wear ID tags. Stevenson, however, was arrested and indicted on a felony charge of animal cruelty, punishable by two years in prison. At his trial, prosecutors had to prove that the cat was one of several strays that a nearby bridge toll collector regularly fed and, therefore "owned." Killing "owned" animals was a crime. The case drew national attention, with people and groups divided over whether Stevenson was a hero or a criminal. "It reflects the attitudes of people in the United States—there are cat lovers and others who love biodiversity, including birds," he told the *New York Times* after the jury deadlocked and the judge declared a mistrial.

. . .

Cats hunt mainly with their ears. They can hear sounds at pitches higher than can be heard by people or even dogs. With some twenty muscles in their external ears, they can swivel their ears independently of one another and home in on the sound of potential prey. According to Dennis C. Turner, a zoologist at the University of Zurich, and Patrick Bateson, an animal behaviorist at Cambridge University, once they hear prey, they stalk it and then, in the case of birds and small mammals such as rabbits, ambush it. If a chipmunk disappears into a hole, cats will not dig after it but will wait silently for it to emerge and then snatch it. Cats usually kill their prey by biting it on the back of the neck and severing its spinal cord. Cats hunt and kill for food when they are hungry and for practice when they are not.

In my experience, people and organizations with vested economic interests in not having cats around find ways to remove them quietly without calling attention to their activities or alerting cat protection groups. Duck-hunting groups have shown that trapping predators in areas where ducks lay and hatch their eggs, such as the Prairie Pothole region of the Dakotas and Canada, greatly increases the hatching success rates and survivability of young ducklings. At European shooting estates, Georgia quail plantations, Dakota pheasant ranches, and hunting preserves and clubs nationwide, hundreds of millions of dollars are at stake. To keep hunting first-rate, their habitat and game managers employ vigorous predator control programs—mainly trapping—to increase the survival rate of the birds they propagate.

The managers of more than eighty plantations in the Red Hills of Georgia and Florida control predators on behalf of bobwhite quail, and in killing cats, opossums, weasels, and other predators they help protect many other wild species. The Red Hills consist of 515.6 square miles and are home to some of the last remnant longleaf pine and wiregrass forests in the nation—forests officially listed as among the nation's criticially endangered ecosystems. They are a refuge of biodiversity, with more than one hundred bird species, including endangered red-cockaded woodpeckers and rare Bachman's sparrows, brown-headed nuthatches, and Henslow's sparrows, plus the threatened gopher tortoise and rare Florida pine snake.

In 1931, Herbert L. Stoddard published a landmark treatise on the management of quail entitled *The Bobwhite Quail: Its Habits, Preserva-*

tion and Increase. The book was the product of a five-year study he conducted for the U.S. Bureau of Biological Survey in the Red Hills.

The region was a prime wintering destination for northerners in the days before air-conditioning made central and south Florida comfortably habitable. Stoddard discovered that when these northerners went home in the spring they sometimes left their cats behind.

"Cats are the most serious enemies of the bobwhite quail here," he reported. "House cats roam the fields during the night time, catching quail of all ages. Although only one chick may be caught by [a cat's leap] into a full-winged covey, all chicks during their earlier days are at the mercy of cats that discover them." Stoddard said cat kills were easy to identify because cats usually bit off quail wings and left them at the scene.

Stoddard discovered that because of their keen hearing cats employ a special hunting technique unmatched by other predators. Bobwhites build nests on the ground and deposit eggs in them. Unlike other quail predators, such as opossums, armadillos, and raccoons, cats rarely destroy and eat quail eggs. Instead, the cats wait until they hear baby chicks pecking out of their shells to hatch and come running to devour them at first cheep.

Epilogue

The extraordinary changes to the American landscape that I have described here—the destruction and regrowth of forests, the slaughter and comeback of wildlife, and the spread of people into suburban, exurban, and rural sprawl—happened very quickly in historical terms.

In the first three hundred years following the 1492 landing of Columbus, Europeans and Indians established a vast network to exploit wild animals for their furs and hides, but settlers established little more than toeholds on the eastern edge of the continent. The nineteenth century saw waves of settlers push westward and immigrants from Europe pour in, and these people made speedy work of the destruction of forests and wildlife, culminating in a rampage of devastation so egregious and worrisome that it spawned a backlash: the conservation movement. By 1880, great expanses of forest had been reduced to levels not seen before or since, but trees were already making a comeback. In the early twentieth century, conservationists moved to end commercial hunting, create refuges and preserves, and enforce wildlife protection laws. By the 1950s, forests had recolonized huge swaths of the eastern landscape, and wildlife rehabilitation programs were well under way. In the 1960s and 1970s, the environmental movement turned national attention to stopping man-made chemical pollution of air, water, and land. All the while, cheap gasoline was fueling the spread of urbanites out of cities and into expanding sprawl. By 1970, more Americans lived in the sprawl than in cities or on farms. By 2000, for the first time, the majority of Americans were sprawl dwellers.

Early conservationists hadn't envisioned sprawl. When the first state and federal wildlife agencies were created in the late nineteenth and early twentieth centuries, sprawl didn't exist, and populations of most wild species were at such low ebbs that wildlife managers saw their task primarily as one of getting more animals and birds back on the land. Over the next several decades this involved finding or creating habitat in rural areas where reintroduced populations might survive and thrive. Efforts concentrated on species attractive to sport hunters such as deer, waterfowl, and wild turkeys, but habitat restoration helped many other species as well. By reintroducing long-gone beavers, for example, they brought back rodent engineers to create new wetlands habitat for all sorts of birds and animals, and they made trappers happy too. In the decades after the Second World War, the efforts of government wildlife agencies and private conservation groups were paying off. Depending on place and time, people were seeing wild animals and birds their parents and grandparents had rarely, if ever, seen. Nuisance wildlife problems were few, mainly rural, and could for the most part be resolved by family, friends, or neighbors.

The first suburbs were extensions of cities, and off the wildlife manager's radar screen. As they spread outward in the 1970s and 1980s, they were widely condemned as wasteful, inefficient, and a blight on the landscape. Both conservationists and environmentalists saw them as the enemy of the natural landscape, one that fragmented and destroyed habitat, reduced species diversity, and harmed or endangered all sorts of wild creatures. How human encroachment hurts wildlife has been the subject of so many books, articles, websites, and slide shows that it has been common knowledge for decades. This knowledge isn't wrong, but it is only half the story and, as such, a misconception.

Wildlife researchers and practitioners in the growing business of nuisance wildlife control have long known what sprawl dwellers eventually found out: Many wild creatures, such as coyotes and wild turkeys, adjust to life among benign and protective sprawl dwellers. Some animals, such as deer, not only adapt, but proliferate in far greater numbers than they would in the wild. And why not? Access is easy because their habitat has become more or less continuous. The doughnut of farms that used to stand between forests and cities is gone in many places. Trees and thick brush often blanket the land right up to the edge of town. Many cities themselves have created greenbelts; they are laced with brushy corridors, along rail lines, for example, and have woodsy preserves and parks. Suburbs are covered with trees and bushes and are full of places to hide and reproduce.

This was a new arrangement for man, beast, and tree. Rather suddenly, in just a few decades, we have seen an integration of forests, wild animals and birds, and people on a scale and in numbers that are unique. Few people were prepared for its consequences. While wildlife managers concentrated on maintaining healthy wild populations, animal protection organizations focused on saving creatures from human harm. Neither group was prepared for overabundance or for managing people's interactions with wild populations.

In 2002, the *Journal of Biogeography* published a paper entitled "Wildlife Dynamics in the Changing New England Landscape," by David Foster and Glenn Motzkin, Harvard Forest associates, and Debra Bernardos and James Cardoza, state wildlife biologists. The authors noted that maturing forests, growing populations of large wild animals and birds (deer, bear, fisher, turkey, moose, eagles, herons, vultures, coyotes, to name some), and expansion of human sprawl made conflicts inevitable because the natural carrying capacity of the landscape for wild populations was expanding while people's tolerance of those populations was "ironically declining." People didn't want too many critters around but didn't want them controlled either. Unless attitudes changed, conflicts would mount, the authors wrote, adding, "This is a formidable task for a suburbanized human population that is generally poorly informed about nature and wildlife dynamics and is largely opposed to the most ready means of wildlife regulation: hunting and trapping."

The idea of wildlife overabundance is difficult for many people to accept. We have been trying to nurture wild populations back to health and protect them from human despoliation for so long that it is hard to believe we have too many of them or that people might need protection from them. Generations of Americans have grown up with the narrative of environmental loss trapped in their minds like an unrelenting memory loop. Everywhere they looked, it seemed, man was destroying some part of the natural landscape. The need for protection was reinforced by all sorts of government agencies and private groups campaigning to save wilderness or rain forests from human abuse, or to save grizzlies, wolves, and other species threatened by people. It was far easier to raise money to save a creature threatened by man than one threatened by another creature or a disease, and saviors proliferated and specialized. Some groups formed to save whales, while others sought to protect swamps. All required money. To raise it, nonprofits competed for charitable contributions, often by stressing impending crisis or doom for their particular creature, landscape, or concern. A Rainforest Alliance solicitation, for example, read, "By this time tomorrow, nearly 100 species of wildlife will tumble into extinction." The narrative of loss spilled out of virtually every envelope and e-mail containing an appeal for funds, and there are thousands of environmental and animal protection charities tugging at the heartstrings. To look at a desktop full of these appeals, or to scan websites dedicated to similar fund-raising efforts, is to come away convinced that the world is doomed.

It may well be. Make no mistake: All sorts of worthy battles are being fought to save the landscape and its wild inhabitants from the relentless growth of the human population; the natural resources it devours; the air, land, and water it befouls; and the climate it changes. The global environment has been seriously degraded in recent decades by increased human consumption of food, fresh water, timber, fiber, and fuel.

Biodiversity is shrinking. There are plenty of imperiled species to go around. The International Union for Conservation of Nature listed, as of 2010, more than 18,300 species of animals, insects, and plants known to be threatened. As of 2012, the U.S. Fish and Wildlife Service had 593 animals and 794 plants on its endangered species list. Lots more species will be added to those lists in the coming years unless human consumption is reduced to sustainable levels and habitats are protected—unlikely achievements on a planet adding more than ten thousand new people an hour. *Sustainability,* a word reportedly first used in the 1970s to describe an outcome of good stewardship, means in this context using wild animals, birds, trees, and plants only to the point of not harming the ability of future generations to make use of them too. An obvious example of failure in this regard is fisheries. We could make use of the ocean's bounty sustainably, that is by harvesting only enough cod or bluefin tuna to ensure that their populations rebounded so there would be a lot of fish to harvest next year. For these and many other species, however, the opposite has happened.

· · ·

This book is not about environmental loss or dire straits. It is about too much of a good thing in the United States. The new nature wars are being fought over riches unimaginable to people in many places around the globe where poverty and resource depletion are the norm. In our little corner of the planet, the losses have been eclipsed for a moment by a regrowth of forests and an overabundance of some wild species. Our battles over critters and trees are mainly about how to deal with excess, and while they are being fought we tolerate enormous cost and waste—because we can afford to. Collisions between motor vehicles and wildlife cost society, by one estimate, $6 billion to $12 billion annually. Americans would not pay that price, let alone throw away the salvageable meat and hides of 1 or 2 million dead deer, moose, and other creatures, if we were poor. We wouldn't allow proliferating beaver populations to wreak havoc on our roads, rails, fields, utilities, water supplies, and sewer systems if we couldn't afford repairs. We wouldn't allow deer, turkeys, and geese to damage and degrade our crops, yards, and prime human habitat such as playing fields and parks if we couldn't pay to replant and clean up the mess. We wouldn't be spending $50 billion a year on our pets and $5 billion to feed wild birds—outlays that actually increased during our recent economic downturn—if we had to spend those dollars on essentials.

Our affluence has even helped advance the cause of animal rights: that is, the notion that sentient, nonhuman creatures have a right to life and legal protection against discrimination or abuse, as do humans disadvantaged because of their ethnicity, sex, or handicaps. The idea that man should not harm or kill other living beings isn't new, of course. It has been part of the belief systems of Buddhists and Jains, among other religious and cultural groups, for centuries. After France freed black slaves and gave them rights, the philosopher Jeremy Bentham in 1789 famously wrote that perhaps one day "the rest of the animal creation may acquire those rights." This thought stayed on the cultural fringe until recent decades. After all, America rose to greatness by exploiting natural resources, many of them living beings.

The phrase "Animal Liberation" first appeared in the media in 1973 in the *New York Review of Books* in a headline of a review by Peter Singer, the Australian philosopher, of *Animals, Men, and Morals,* a collection of essays on the treatment of animals. Singer's own book on the subject, *Animal Liberation,* in 1975, focused attention on the suffering of animals subjected to experiments in research laboratories and abuse inflicted upon livestock on modern factory farms. His book and the writings of others raised our collective consciousness about the mistreatment of all animals, including pets and wildlife, and they helped fuel the growth of animal rights, animal protection, and animal welfare advocates. Often confused, these groups adhere to positions along a continuum from essentially treating animals the same as people to allowing use of animals for human needs. Animal rights groups such as PETA are against humans killing animals or using them for human benefit in any way, including for food, clothing, labor, or fun. Animal protection advocates, such as HSUS, don't object to responsible use of animals for legitimate human needs as long as they aren't abused in the process. They consider many factory farming practices, hunting, and trapping to be forms of abuse. These two groups support people who come to the defense of individual animals or species, and they, along with Singer, believe that wildlife should be left alone unless a population of one species is harming itself or others, in which cases fertility reduction might be called for—if it could be made to work.

Animal welfare advocates, such as the AVMA, specifically reject animal rights philosophy and believe in responsible care for and use of animals, including wildlife, for human purposes. That care includes humane euthanasia when necessary. Conservationists generally agree with the veterinary group and emphasize that making use of wild animals and birds for meat, fur, feathers, and sport necessitates managing wildlife and its habitat not only for useful wild creatures but for the health of the ecosystem as a whole.

Michael Hutchins, executive director of the Wildlife Society, an international group of wildlife managers, researchers, and conservationists, worries that compassion for individual animals and species partisanship relieves people of their obligation to be good stewards of their ecosystems. The notion that, left alone by man, wild creatures will live out their lives in peace and harmony with one another is misguided, he says. Nature's inhumanity can exceed man's, Hutchins argues. Wolves have been known, for example, to literally tear apart piece by piece a weak but alive adult moose. A man with an accurate high-powered rifle can dispatch a moose far more quickly and humanely.

"It would be wonderful if we could all get along," Hutchins wrote, "but it is time to recognize that some ideas are superior to others because they clearly result in the 'greatest good.' As a conservationist, I reject animal rights philosophy. This unrealistic and highly reductionist view, which focuses exclusively on individual sentient animals, is not a good foundation for the future of life on our planet and does not recognize the interrelationships that exist among various species in functioning ecosystems."

. . .

In the course of researching and writing this book, I came across countless ideas for resolving human-wildlife conflicts. Some are imaginary, like fertility control chemicals in salt licks. Some are totally unrealistic, such as moving people out of wildlife habitats or, in effect, segregating man and beast. Others are sensible, like encouraging people not to feed wild creatures and imposing fines or other penalties on those who do. A few, are, in my view, elegant.

Take deer. It's clear that a lot more of them have to die, especially Bambi's mom and other females, in order to lower their populations in areas where they cause damage. Yet by 2010 it was also clear to many researchers that the white-tailed deer overpopulation problem, in many places, especially in the sprawl, was not going to be resolved by sport hunting. Not long ago, Terry Messmer, a wildlife damage specialist at Utah State's Berryman Institute, told me, "What we know definitely is that white-tailed deer populations are exploding, and we don't have enough hunters [in many places] to reduce these populations. This sets up a major train wreck for deer-human conflicts if we don't come up with another alternative."

The problem is that hunters kill roughly 6 million whitetails each fall and that other predators, including cougars, wolves, bears, coyotes, and motor vehicles, might kill another 6 million. Other causes of death, such as diseases, take their toll. But with fertility control impractical, far more deer across the nation would need to die, the bulk of them females, simply to stop the population from growing. The practical question is: How? Suggestions include some form of guns for hire, a throwback to market-hunting days, or a British-style system of paying stalkers to periodically thin out the herds.

Gary Alt, who led a valiant but unsuccessful whitetail reduction effort as Pennsylvania's state deer manager, suggested a few years ago that a return to market hunting may be the only way to reduce deer herds in that state's big forests in order to restore habitat devastated by decades of overpopulation. The state's organized hunters would have none of it.

In recent years, hunters have become new saviors in some suburbs, and the popularity of hiring professionals to cull deer and paying them with tax dollars has grown. The Wildlife Services Division of the U.S. Department of Agriculture, private companies, and nonprofits such as White Buffalo Inc. all field teams of sharpshooters. Some are efficient and almost invisible to residents—but they are expensive and sometimes have waiting lists. In most cases, culled deer are butchered and the venison is donated to a food pantry, or they are thrown away.

Bryon Shissler has a better idea. Shissler, of National Resource Consultants, Inc., advised Lower Makefield Township in Bucks County, Pennsylvania, to hire a sharpshooting company. In addition, he recommended that the sharpshooters train carefully selected recreational hunters in the community—typically policemen, firemen, and others—in sharpshooting techniques over two years. These "urban deer managers," perhaps a team of five carefully screened people and fifteen assistants and backups, would then carry on the program at far less cost to taxpayers. Periodic culling would gradually reduce deer densities, lower deer-vehicle collisions, lessen landscape and crop damage, and decrease Lyme disease to levels acceptable to most, if not all, residents. Enough deer would remain for those who like having them around, and dead deer—here's the key—would be put to use locally. That is, to help recoup sharpshooting costs, Shissler suggests selling the venison at local farmers' markets. That would appeal to locavores who might eschew industrially farmed meat and would not like to kill deer themselves. They might like to buy and eat a local, renewable resource grown without antibiotics, chemicals, feedlots, or cages. Call it locavore market hunting. As author Steven Rinella put it in a 2007 *New York Times* op ed article, wild venison is "free-range, grass-fed, organic, locally produced, locally harvested, sustainable, native, low-stress, low-impact, humanely slaughtered meat."

It seems like a good solution, but it probably won't happen anytime soon. Selling wild game, including venison, is illegal. Outlawing commercial hunting was a foundation of the conservation movement's wildlife comeback successes, and most fish and game departments remain wedded to the idea. Bringing back market hunting in any form is apostasy to them. State game agencies and the legislatures that fund them have traditionally sided with hunting groups and often insist that hunters be allowed in before they will issue a permit for a cull by sharpshooters. Deer farmers would object. An estimated 20 percent of the 7,800 deer farms in America raise venison for commercial sale to markets and restaurants. Venison sales and consumption are so small in the United States that the Department of Agriculture doesn't keep track of them. Still, the growing popularity of venison has deer farmers anticipating substantial market growth. There's even foreign policy to consider. Most of the venison that restaurants sell is imported from 3,500 deer farms in New Zealand. Its representatives in Washington would complain. Animal rights people would no doubt raise the specter that culled deer might not be safe to eat because of disease or other factors. The U.S. Department of Agriculture would insist on butchering and testing at approved and inspected abattoirs, which would raise costs. Still, it is a worthy idea, and it could be done.

Sometimes a jolt of reality breaks the gridlock. The downing of US Airways Flight 1549 by geese in 2009 did more in just ninety seconds than a decade's work by the federal government tried to do—over the objections of save-the-geese groups—to reduce burgeoning populations of resident Canada geese. This was a moment of clarity. Suddenly Americans could visualize a threat to their personal safety, and just as suddenly the goose partisans melted away. As a journalist, I had been in contact with some of these people for years. They were eager for public attention. After Flight 1549, they stopped answering my e-mails and returning my phone calls.

Similar dangers of death and serious injury from collisions of motor vehicles with deer and other large animals have made many people more aware and cautious, yet most people feel helpless to do anything about the never-ending carnage of wild animals and birds, large and small, on our roads and highways. The roadkill counts by schoolchildren, organized by Brewster Bartlett, called attention to the issue. Insurance companies put out annual alerts and offer advice on avoiding large animals. State highway departments have for years put up deer-crossing signage, and a few have built wildlife overpasses and underpasses. But roadkill is a subject, aside from jokes about it, that people have preferred to ignore.

Since the phrase *road ecology* was coined less than a decade ago, however, the relationship between roads and the natural environment has become an academic and research subject—a subdiscipline of ecology that has involved everything from studying the effects of road noise on bird nesting patterns to establishing roadkill-mapping websites on which anyone with a GPS-enabled cell phone can report and pinpoint the location of a dead roadside animal. This information is used to pinpoint roadkill hot spots. In 2010, a diverse group of academics, transportation professionals, citizens, and nonprofit researchers published *Safe Passages: Highways, Wildlife, and Habitat Connectivity,* a collection of papers on dealing with roadways and wildlife. That year, the Western Transportation Institute at Montana State University sponsored a contest with a $40,000 prize to design a critter-friendly highway overpass that would encourage wild animals large and small to safely cross an interstate near Vail, Colorado. Two of the contestants submitted lavish

designs that would probably cost $10 million to $12 million to build—
something unlikely to happen in an era of tight government budgets.

Reducing the damage beavers do as their populations grow isn't easy
or cheap either. Trappers, the main predators of beavers in most places,
have become a threatened species, their numbers dwindling by the year.
Antifur activists have convinced many people that wearing fur means
cruelly killing animals, not making use of a renewable resource.

In some places, such as the arid West, beavers are still welcomed as
creatures that contain valuable water and help keep underground water
tables high. In most other places beavers have worn out their welcome
and become a costly nuisance.

The story of the nutria runs parallel to the beaver's, but with a very
different trajectory. After the South American rodents became scarce
in the wild, people in Argentina began to farm them. Nutria farming
was spread to North America, Europe, and Asia in the late nineteenth
and early twentieth centuries by promoters who sold expensive breeding
stock and promised would-be growers big money selling fur, meat, and
live animals for weed control. When instant riches didn't materialize
due to fur market vagaries, some farmers quit and freed their nutria into
the wild. Others escaped. Escaped nutria from a Louisiana farm in the
1930s proliferated in Gulf Coast wetlands. From a Maryland farm in
the 1940s, they invaded Chesapeake Bay. Their populations eventually
expanded into at least sixteen states.

Trappers helped keep nutria populations in check when fur demand
was high, but populations in the wild continued to grow and expand. In
the 1980s, international fur prices collapsed for several reasons: overpro-
duction of farmed furs in Europe, shifts in fashion to leather and plastic
fleece, and animal rights demonstrators. Theatrical protests by groups
such as PETA, in which activists raided retail furriers and dumped
paint on women wearing fur coats, garnered much media attention and
helped make wearing fur politically incorrect.

Most nutria trapping stopped, and before long the pesky rodent gained notoriety as one of the most damaging invasive species in North America (feral cats and wild pigs are among others). Nutria eat farm crops, including corn, rice, and sugarcane, and damage complaints from farmers rose sharply. More important, nutria destroy vital coastal wetlands, the complex ecosystem that supports all sorts of aquatic plants and animals and protect people from the vagaries of the Gulf of Mexico. They dig out and eat the roots of swamp vegetation that hold soils in place, causing erosion, sedimentation, and seawater intrusion. Swamps between land and sea disappear. U.S. Department of Agriculture agents blame nutria and rising sea levels for the destruction of nearly fifty thousand acres of Chesapeake area wetlands. In Louisiana and other coastal states, nutria dig burrows into earthen flood control levees. In 2002, in an effort to get trappers back into the swamps, Louisiana began paying trappers a $4 bounty on them, raising it to $5 in 2006.

In 2009, the Barataria-Terrebonne Estuary Foundation, in Thibodaux, Louisiana, awarded a grant to Cree McCree, a New Orleans designer who founded Righteous Fur, to make, promote, and sell fur fashions made out of nutria. In the fall of 2010, after three fashion shows in New Orleans, she and twenty other designers held a fashion show in an art gallery in New York City, a bastion of antifur sentiment. The event was covered by the *New York Times*.

"Nutria-Palooza: Is Their Pest Your Clean Conscience?" read the *Times* headline. The article under it hailed nutria as "guilt free" fur. Micha Michelle Melancon, one of the designers, said that "unlike other soft and furry animals, nutria is being rebranded as a socially acceptable and environmentally friendly alternative way to wear fur."

How did making fashion items out of fur skinned off an aquatic rodent become socially acceptable? For starters, Hurricane Katrina in 2005 and the BP oil spill in 2010 sensitized many Americans outside the Gulf Coast to the value of coastal wetlands and the importance of saving them from storms, oil spills, or an invasive species out of control. To some people, using traps to control nutria populations, and making and wearing clothing and fashion accessories out of nutria fur, became not only tolerable but also environmentally correct. Suddenly, the double long-spring No. 2 leg-hold trap, the Conibear A220-2 body gripper, and the choke-hold snare were friends of the ecosystem. Since the dead animals were mostly dumped in landfills and going to waste, said Ms. McCree, "why not make something beautiful out of them."

Control of another invasive species, the house cat gone feral, isn't working. Wildlife biologists, bird conservation groups, and others have become more vocal in recent years about feral cat predation on native wildlife, but their voices continue to be all but drowned out by loud and well-financed feral cat protection groups wedded to the ideology of TNR—trapping, neutering, and returning the cats to where they were found. Among species partisans, feral cat defenders generate the most noise by far. Advocates of TNR are often so enthusiastic and eager to promote their cause that they have been likened to members of a cult who perceive critics as the enemies and believe their quest is so worthy that any tactics that save cats' lives are justified, including intimidating people, shouting down opponents, and threatening decision makers. Although a bounty on nutria is acceptable to many people, putting a bounty on feral cats, as happened in Randolph, Iowa, can trigger a firestorm of indignation and threats. Defenders of deer and Canada geese acknowledge that lethal removal is sometimes necessary. Feral cat defenders almost never do.

In late 2010, the agriculture extension service of the University of Nebraska at Lincoln published a circular entitled *Feral Cats and Their Management*, reviewing the threats ferals posed, particularly to birds. It recommended a common control strategy used on other troublesome species, called integrated pest management (IPM), to reduce feral cat impacts to tolerable levels. IPM includes nonlethal methods such as habitat modification, repellents, and fertility control, but the circular recommended against TNR, saying that while it might reduce some feral populations, large-scale reductions were anecdotal, and evidence of colonies eliminated with TNR didn't exist. The lethal IPM methods recommended included live-trapping and euthanizing, kill-trapping—and shooting, a method approved by the American Veterinary Medical Association. The Nebraska circular's language was almost the same as what the AVMA uses in its euthanasia guidelines, but its recommendations raised a national ruckus. Feral cat advocates denounced them while bird defenders praised them. Alley Cat Allies called the circular "barbaric and utterly disturbing." And Best Friends Animal Society, another TNR advocacy group, called it "biased" and "thinly veiled advocacy" for cat killing. The American Bird Conservancy, the bird protection group, on the other hand, called it a "must-read."

The impact of feral and free-roaming cats on wildlife and natural ecosystems alarms wildlife biologists. However, they have been unable to generate much concern in comparison to the national attention lavished on cats. As *Audubon* columnist Ted Williams pointed out, "The political power of wildlife advocates is dwarfed by that of the feral cat lobby."

Coyotes have made a remarkable adjustment to life among people, in small part, it seems, by snacking on their pet cats. From their native range in the High Plains and southwestern deserts, these wily canines now roam from the northern tip of Alaska to the Panama Canal and across the continent to all but northern Quebec and the Canadian Arctic. Thousands of them live in Los Angeles. Stanley D. Gehrt estimates the coyote population in greater Chicago at more than two thousand. Between 2000 and 2006, Gehrt, an associate professor at Ohio State University, and a research team captured 253 coyotes in Chicago and put radio collars on 175 to monitor their habits day and night, watching how they have learned to live among people without fear and how they have been encouraged to do so by people who feed them.

"It's not just us encroaching on their territory, they're encroaching on us," Gehrt told the *New York Times* after coyotes attacked two young girls in Rye, New York, in June 2010. "They find a bounty of food, they have a lack of predators, there's no hunting and trapping. Once they crash that threshold into that urbanized landscape, they find that the living is pretty good." There's enough brush behind the average family garage to hide a mother coyote raising her pups—even, said Gehrt, near the Chicago Loop.

Coyote attacks on pets and children are still rare, but they are growing. Coyote partisans seem to be increasing as well. After one attacked a twenty-pound terrier in Wheaton, Illinois, in 2010, and Rob Erickson, operator of On Target Animal Damage Control, was called in to trap coyotes, including the perpetrator, word spread fast and protests poured in from hundreds of coyote supporters nationwide. Erickson quickly discovered that two women had been putting out dog food for the coyotes. He trapped two animals and shot two more.[25] Then the death threats started. If he didn't stop, one caller told his answering message, "we'll kill you." Another caller threatened to burn down his house. Members of the city council who had voted to remove coyotes received mailed threats from outside the state. Since it is an illegal terrorist act to use the U.S. Postal Service to make threats, the FBI launched an investigation.

When I last checked with Deputy Police Chief Tom Meloni, in Wheaton, the coyote war had quieted down a bit, but the FBI's investigation was "ongoing." In late 2010, Wheaton officials adopted a seventeen-page coyote management plan that included a campaign to teach people how to haze coyotes by shouting, using air horns, banging pans, and throwing rocks or golf balls at them to reinstill their fear of humans. The town also increased fines for illegal feeding to $950 from $100 and warned that people who fed the animals would be tracked down and arrested. The plan said that as a last resort "full control techniques will

---

25. The coyotes had sarcoptic mange so severe that they were in the latter stages of a long, grueling death, Erickson told me. Mange occurs when mites burrow into the animal's skin and lay eggs, causing itching which they scratch, leading to infection, sores, loss of hair, and death.

likely be required"—meaning lethal methods. Many states, meanwhile, have approved hunting coyotes year round in efforts to control burgeoning populations of the animal.

Coyotes have gotten closer to people a lot faster than people have gotten reconnected to nature and the working landscape their grandparents knew. Those reconnections, however, are happening.

Brian Donahue and his community farming colleagues in Weston, Massachusetts, for example, had been turning out locavores for decades before the word was invented. In 1970, Donahue's mentor, Bill McElwain, started Green Power Farm on town-owned land to grow vegetables and interest students in farming. By then even the students' boomer parents were estranged from the land. In his 1999 book *Reclaiming the Commons: Community Farms and Forests in a New England Town,* Donahue wrote: "Once upon a time suburban families at least mowed their lawns, trimmed the shrubbery, and planted young trees around the house; today even that work is largely hired out to pros. The residents in these nonplaces typically move every decade, if not twice. Such transient people tend to form only temporary ties to neighbors and nature, cultural and ecological slipknots."

In 1980, their project incorporated as a nonprofit called Land's Sake and began to hire local middle and high school students to plant, tend, harvest, and sell crops at its farm stand. In addition, the children made and sold maple syrup and cider and tended sheep. "It is good for children to learn that it is possible to treat animals with affection and respect and still kill and eat them," Donahue told me. In 1981, when Land's Sake started thinning Weston's 1,700-acre town forest and selling firewood, letters from outraged residents poured in. It was one thing to tap maple trees for syrup, but cutting them down with a chain saw and selling them to burn? Donahue, who also teaches environmental studies at Brandeis University, took objecting residents for walks in the woods, explaining how thinning a forest, like thinning a garden, helped its overall health. Soon Land's Sake was cutting and selling fifty cords of firewood annually. In 1989, a local student named John Potter came home from the Yale School of Forestry and devised a long-range plan for Weston's forest that involved cutting and harvesting timber from ten acres of trees annually to mimic natural disturbances such as fires and hurricanes that help forests regenerate. That wood would be sold as lumber. The plan was difficult to implement because processing and selling lumber locally was not easy in an affluent suburb without a sawmill. But Land's Sake continues to harvest firewood, and occasionally some lumber as well.

Land's Sake invites students and their parents into the woods each winter for a volunteer day to explain forest management and watch a professional with a chain saw kill a tree. When I caught up with Donahue a few years ago, he had taken an environmental science class of Weston High School seniors to watch a tree being felled. Only one member of that class, he said, had seen a tree cut down before.

In 1984, William E. Geist wrote a column in the *New York Times* about opposition to the opening of a new Korean grocery store selling fruits and vegetables outdoors at the corner of Park Avenue and Seventy-fifth Street in a very wealthy zip code. One of the people who took offense was a matron who lived in a multi-million-dollar apartment near the store.

"Do the residents of Park Avenue want to look out the window at vegetables? They most certainly do not," she told Geist.

Refrigerated barges and railroad cars in the nineteenth century brought us the first cheap food over long distances. The creation of the interstate highway system after the Second World War allowed trucks burning inexpensive gasoline to supply large quantities of perishable food quickly and cheaply from anywhere to supermarkets, where housewives found convenience, attractive packaging, and fruits and vegetables that were out of season locally. This distribution system was a marvel of efficiency and scale that put local farmers out of business and ushered in the era of the tasteless tomato, the preprocessed food, and the microwave meal.

How times have changed. The movement away from industrial food and toward fresh food grown locally is spreading. It may still be small in comparison to the consumption of cheap, government-subsidized calories and the health and obesity problems that are a result, but it has raised the consciousness of millions of Americans to what good food is and how to get it, cook it, and eat it. The organic foods movement has sprouted national chains such as Whole Foods. Even Walmart has gone partly organic.

Local farmers' markets have doubled in the last decade to more than 6,200 and, in the process, have introduced millions of people to fresh, locally grown vegetables, fruit, meat, eggs, and dairy products. People from cities and suburbs have flocked to the countryside to take up small-plot agriculture, organic farming, the raising of specialty livestock like heritage breeds, and the production of artisanal foods such as cheese, sausage, and jams. They have taken over previously unused roofs, vacant lots, and other spaces to create "city slicker farms." Urban chicken coops, illegal in some places, produce local eggs and pluck-it-yourself poultry. City beekeepers have put hives in places where they were previously outlawed. In 2010, the *Wall Street Journal* reported a rise in "urban share-cropping," in which would-be farmers grow crops in other people's yards and share the harvest with them. Office and company gardens have become the new watercoolers. Local butchers and meat purveyors not only deliver cuts of beef, pork, and lamb but teach pricey courses—often sold out months in advance—on how to dismember livestock yourself. Fleisher's Meats, in Kingston, New York, run by Joshua and Jessica Applestone, offers butchering classes that run from five days to eight weeks and cost $2,000 to $10,000. A proliferation of cooking classes and shows on cable television has opened up a forgotten world of food preparation to millions of Americans. Some of them are corny and hackneyed, but others have gotten adults back into the kitchen and helped make cooking fashionable for a new generation.

The surge in popularity of farm-raised "wild game" on restaurant menus has caused some postboomers, who once considered hunting to be an anathema, to head for the woods in search of real wild game for their home tables. In his 2006 bestseller *The Omnivore's Dilemma: A Natural History of Four Meals,* Michael Pollan, a middle-aged baby boomer from Long Island, decides to go hunting to get meat for a meal made up entirely of foods he has gathered in the wild. He has never hunted or fired a gun before. His friend, Angelo, invites Pollan and Jean-Pierre, a chef at Alice Waters's famous restaurant, Chez Panisse, in Berkeley, California, to a thousand-acre property in northern Sonoma County owned by another friend, to hunt pigs.

"Angelo hunts deer and turkey and duck, too, but for a number of reasons I felt more comfortable going for wild pig," Pollan writes. Wild pigs are non-native, feral, destructive pests that now number 4 to 5 million in the United States and are spreading fast. As such, they give Pollan an environmental rationale to help overcome his qualms about hunting—qualms that quickly fade.

"Walking with a loaded rifle in an unfamiliar forest bristling with the signs of your prey is thrilling," he admits. "It embarrasses me to write that, but it is true." The hunt unexpectedly enlivens his senses and heightens his mental acuity. After killing his prey, he says: "I enjoyed shooting a pig a whole lot more than I ever thought I should have." In the process, he has done the Sonoma ecosystem a small favor and is rewarded with fresh, tasty meat.

The good foods movement is part of a slow but growing realignment of attitudes about food and nature. It is reconnecting people to their food and the working landscape and showing new generations not only where their food comes from but how to grow and prepare it. It is a movement that aggregates a diverse collective that includes chefs, would-be chefs, new farmers, foodies, locavores, hunters, and people who disapprove of industrial farming, to name a few. Some of these people believe that making use of plentiful wild creatures around them isn't such a bad idea, especially if doing so helps the ecosystem around them.

Making use of locally grown food is an easy sell in comparison to convincing sprawl dwellers to cut down and use nearby trees. When wood production and consumption peaked in 1906, America's forests had been so reduced that President Theodore Roosevelt warned the nation that it was running out of trees and called for urgent conservation measures to head off a looming timber famine. His forestry chief, Gifford Pinchot, was a wise-use advocate who wanted to continue tree harvesting in remaining forests but to impose controls to avoid the devastation wrought by logging in the past. John Muir, the famed naturalist, wanted the nation's remaining wild places, most of them in the West, preserved as they were, undisturbed by man. Fights over preservation and wise use have gone on ever since, and although they are often portrayed as either-or battles, the choices are not so well defined. Forests come in all shapes, sizes, and ages.

The Wilderness Act of 1964 presented this definition: *"A wilderness, in contrast with those areas where man and his own works dominate the landscape, is hereby recognized as an area where the earth and community of life are untrammeled by man, where man himself is a visitor who does not remain."* In the 1970s and 1980s, environmentalists attacked the clearcutting techniques loggers used in government-owned forests in the Pacific Northwest. They focused on old-growth stands of trees within them, invoking the plight of the northern spotted owl, an endangered species and local resident. Federal lawmakers moved to curtail logging in owl habitat by declaring large areas of national forests to be official wilderness. By the 1990s, clear-cutting in national forests had been reduced by 90 percent, but environmental groups wanted more protection. They broadened their attention to national forests in general, campaigning with some success to make some of their 190 million acres off limits to logging and road building. These highly publicized efforts raised the environmental consciousness of many Americans as Earth Day had in 1970. Many people turned against tree cutting in general, their predilections reinforced in the same period by horror stories and pictures of the destruction of the Amazon rain forest. For many people, tree cutting of any kind was bad.

While the idea of protecting a wild area of old-growth forests may be just as appealing as saving that old oak in the backyard, saving all trees presents problems. Trees are renewable natural resources. They grow back. We cut them and use them to make all sorts of wood products, and most are neither in some wilderness nor in our backyards. They occupy part of the working landscape of private and public lands where resources are grown and harvested for our use. Nationally, 56 percent of our forests are privately owned. In the eastern third of the country, 75 percent are in private hands.

In 2002, the Harvard Forest published a study entitled *The Illusion of Preservation: A Global Environmental Argument for the Local Production of Natural Resources*. The study noted that while Americans may imagine that preserving trees domestically is helping nature, they continue to be voracious consumers of wood products that come from somewhere— often from fragile forests in poor countries where regulation is lax or easily corrupted. The result is "greater global environmental degradation." To curtail this means using more local trees. Massachusetts, for example, is a wonderful place to grow trees; so good, in fact, that the state is more than 60 percent forest covered and the state's trees hold more wood than they have in two hundred years. Yet less than 2 percent of the wood products its citizens consume comes from within. Residents of the Bay State, like Americans as a whole, use 2.5 times more wood and paper than do Europeans; since 1970, new American houses have gotten 48 percent larger but families have gotten 16 percent smaller. With intensive management, careful logging, and strict monitoring, in combination with lowered consumption and increased recycling, the paper asserted, Massachusetts could get 50 percent of its wood products from its own forests on a sustainable basis.

So why not do it? Because of "attitudes that scorn timber management," the researchers asserted. In fact, the "ideology of preservation" is so strong that "a majority of people believes that logging is worse than non-management." Many landowners don't need income from harvesting trees. They place a higher value on them for wildlife habitat, recreation, privacy, views, and, perhaps, a misplaced feeling of virtue for doing their bit to help the planet. According to the authors:

> As long as the global consequences of consumption are ignored, widespread protectionism is heralded, and logging is abhorred (especially in one's backyard), efforts to reduce wood consumption or to encourage sound management in areas of low ecological impact will be fruitless. Such efforts will only succeed if they are coupled with a fundamental change in attitude that reconciles the ideology of preservation with the reality that using wood means cutting trees—somewhere.

In 2005, a team of Harvard Forest researchers published *Wildlands and Woodlands,* a study that called for a "vision" for managing the forests of Massachusetts over thirty years to achieve several goals at once, including both protecting them and using them to produce more wood products. The state was currently losing about forty acres of open space daily to development, and the primary goal, they said, was to keep 50 percent of the state forested—forever. To achieve this, the largest areas of forest, some 2.25 million acres, most on private land, would be organized into "managed woodland" and used for a variety of purposes, including sustainable timber production; the maintenance of home owner views and other aesthetic values; outdoor recreation, including hunting, fishing, hiking, and camping; and environmental protection. A relatively small portion, about 250,000 acres, would be set aside as "wildland reserves," essentially unmanaged and undisturbed by human hands. These reserves, most of them on public land and many already shielded from development, would protect old-growth forests and water supplies, serve as a venue for scientific research to promote natural processes and biodiversity, and "afford special educational, recreational, aesthetic and spiritual benefits" that come from keeping them essentially wild.

In 2010, the Harvard Forest researchers expanded their *Wildlands and Woodlands* concept to all New England states— Connecticut, Rhode Island, Massachusetts, Vermont, New Hampshire, and Maine—which comprise the nation's most heavily forested region, with 33 million of its 42 million acres (79 percent) covered in trees. "Today there is more forest cover between Long Island Sound and the Canadian border than at any time in the past two centuries," the report said. This remarkable regrowth offers a rare second chance to save the region from a new wave of deforestation more ominous than the "soft deforestation" of the past: "The hard deforestation today, often involving the land's development to asphalt, concrete, and steel, is much more difficult to reverse than the historical clearing of land for farms and pasture."

The report said that for the first time in two hundred years "forest cover is declining in every New England state." It proposed a fifty-year goal of keeping 70 percent of the landscape in forests, "permanently free from development," including wildlands containing some 53,000 acres of old-growth trees and woodlands that would be used for recreation and timbering. According to the report:

> The 33 million acres of trees, waters, and wetlands that blanket New England provide areas for recreation, hunting, and other traditional uses; wood and other forest products; clean and abundant water; a continental-scale habitat corridor; and a globally important source of renewable energy and carbon storage—key factors in slowing the rate of climate change. It is an expansive landscape worthy of a vision commensurate in its ambition and reach.

Remember my battle with the feral grapes in the meadow on Mount Desert Island in Maine? I saw those grapes as non-native intruders in a northern spruce forest and tried to pull, root, and chop them out. In the course of researching this book, I changed my mind about those entangled vines. I learned how precious meadows are and how much work it takes to keep trees from invading and destroying them. Without the grapes, the forest would have grabbed that meadow in no time. Realizing this, I defected to the side of the grapes. They are growing back and spreading again, and I am cheering them on.

Forty years ago, many Americans believed that without human interference forests grew to maturity and stayed that way as so-called climax forests. What people who study forests today will tell you is that the one constant applicable to forests is change. Forests grow so slowly that their changes can be overlooked—the regrowth of eastern forests being a prime example. Natural assaults on them may not happen for a century, but eventually a fire, tornado, flood, or some other disturbance will sweep through and alter them, often in major ways.

Likewise, some people believe that wild animals and birds live in a natural balance if left undisturbed by the destructive interventions of man. Wildlife biologists know that wild populations are subject to frequent changes depending on food supplies, diseases, and other factors and that one or more species can proliferate to the disadvantage of others, especially in areas where people and their trappings are on the scene.

The old ideas were largely illusory, but they helped bolster arguments for protecting the natural landscape that our forebears exploited and sullied. The best thing to do was leave nature alone. Getting man out of nature became a kind of default mode for some environmental activists. Opting out of management and stewardship roles was less damaging than opting in and mucking things up some more. This default mode now seems ironic and hypocritical. Americans already occupy much of the natural landscape, however estranged from it they have become in their romance with the digital world. They are actively managing the nature around them in ways they barely recognize or think about—with their gardens, lawns, landscapes, mulch bins, garbage cans, bird feeders, pets, cars, and species partisanship, to name a few examples. Even officially designated "wilderness" or the Harvard Forest's envisioned "wildlands" require human oversight.

The optimistic implication of the Harvard Forest reports for managing forests is that people today can do things better than their forebears did. People can learn lessons from past mistakes and correct them and can learn new ways of thinking about issues and dealing with them. The reports discuss ideas for local stewardship as they affect the global environment and local ecosystems, and they imply that people have an obligation to put those ideas into practice. Not doing so would amount to setting our responsibilities aside. To do that in many parts of the country would amount to abdicating management of our forests to white-tailed deer.

Helping modern Americans understand and accept the need for human oversight isn't an easy task. It involves reconnecting people to their ecosystems again—getting Americans outdoors and reengaged with the land and the natural world in ways that, to put it bluntly, get dirt under their fingernails, blood on their hands, and even a wood splinter or two in their kneecaps or butts. It requires helping kids discover nature and learn from it on their own, letting them wade barefooted in streams and turn over rocks. It means getting up in the morning darkness now and then, walking into a forest, sitting under a tree, listening to the sounds, and watching nature's day begin.

ACKNOWLEDGMENTS

Four people read the first draft of this manuscript and offered invaluable suggestions: Ward Just and Joseph Lelyveld, my friends; Robert Lescher, my agent; and Frances FitzGerald, my wife. Frances read subsequent revisions, and did enough encouraging and hand-holding to blunt the effects of her sharp pencil.

The idea for this book began to take shape in the 1980s when after many years of living in Asia I came home. While away I had visited my parents in Michigan over the years but paid little attention to the landscape where I grew up. Now, with time to explore old haunts and talk to old friends, I began to see and hear about enormous change. Pheasants had all but vanished. Deer were everywhere. Land I had plowed and hunted as a boy was covered by young forest.

In the 1990s, I began to write stories for the *Wall Street Journal* about hunting and trapping and the rise of animal protection groups that wanted to end both. In the spring of 1999, I went to Jordan, Montana, to spend time with John Graham, one of the last full-time professional trappers in the country. Graham, then thirty-seven, trapped, snared, and shot coyotes, bobcats, and other predators in Garfield County, a patch of Montana's eastern badlands almost the size of Connecticut. What he did benefited not only the sheep ranchers who paid a livestock head tax for his services but also the wild populations of elk, antelope, deer, grouse, and pheasants. Graham was regarded as a skilled range manager locally, but animal rights advocates called him cruel, even a murderer. What is crueler, he asked me, a snare choking a coyote to death or a coyote's jaws choking a lamb to death?

Graham was a remnant practitioner of one of the tough, gritty jobs that tamed and built America. Trappers, like hunters, lumberjacks, cowboys, soldiers, fishermen, and others, practiced what my front page editor at the *Wall Street Journal*, Ken Wells, called the manly arts. A product of Louisiana bayous, Wells grew up practicing the swamp craft that entailed many of these skills. In the nineteenth century, authors such as Zane Grey and Owen Wister turned these men into mythic heroes. Movies added to their legends. Prime-time television aired forty westerns a week in 1959, and Walt Disney's Davy Crockett became—said my story for the *Wall Street Journal*—"a rifle-toting, varmint-shooting, straight-talking role model for an entire generation of boys." In subsequent decades, however, these characters were demonized by new generations who accused them of exploiting natural resources, despoiling the environment, and inflicting pain and death on innocent wild creatures. Many of the accusations were true and, in the view of environmentalists, had to be stopped. One solution was, simply, to leave nature alone. The trouble was that people had been working the land for millennia to survive and accumulate personal and national wealth. People were integral fixtures in nature, even as they sprawled across a landscape they no longer worked and found wild animals and birds proliferating in their midst.

As people-wildlife conflicts mounted, Paul Steiger, the *Journal*'s editor, encouraged me to mine this rich vein, as did Dan Hertzberg, Mike Miller, and other *Journal* editors. I am grateful to them all, and to Seth Lipsky, Robert Keatley, and Peter Kann who invited me to write for a wonderful newspaper, and to Norman Pearlstine and Glynn Mapes who afforded me enormous latitude to do so.

My forestry education began in the summer of 1960 studying silviculture at the Michigan College of Mining and Technology on a

National Science Foundation (NSF) scholarship, thanks to the Russians. With the October 1957 launch of *Sputnik,* the Soviet Union had beat us into space. Washington panicked, and the NSF began showering high school students, including me, with scholarship money to interest them in careers in science and, in theory, to help redress the balance. I failed my nation, diverting into journalism. But that summer and the next, with another grant to study geology and paleontology at Montana State in Bozeman, cemented my interest in science and nature.

In recent years, David Foster, the director of the Harvard Forest, and Douglas MacCleery, a senior analyst with the U.S. Forest Service, patiently taught me the history of American forests, and caught and corrected numerous mistakes in my early chapters. Brian Donahue, an environmental historian at Brandeis University, was, likewise, an important educator and reader. William Cronon, an environmental historian at the University of Wisconsin, offered pivotal advice on essential reading and put me in touch with the invaluable Gregg Mitman.

I also thank Brian Hall, David Kitteridge, Richard Widmann, Rachel Riemann, Don LaFountain, Bob Noonan, Gordon Batcheller, Wayne Pacelle, Michael Conover, Terry Messmer, Richard E. McCabe, Bryon Shissler, Jan Dizard, Karl Jacoby, Mike Markarian, Tom O'Shea, Ollie Torgerson, Bryan Swift, Dave Graber, Paul Schmidt, William H. Clay, Col. Paul Barrows (ret), Linda Winter, Shelly Kotter, Barbara Williamson, Brewster Bartlett, Richard T. T. Forman, Dan McNichol, William C. Ruediger, Robert O. Paxton, and Dr. Harry Sears.

Others who have read parts of this manuscript include George Peckham, Des FitzGerald, Albert Francke, Tim Bontecou, John Heilferty, Renee Vollen, Eugene Shapiro, and Linda Charkassky.

On feral cats and numerous environmental and wildlife issues, I am grateful to Ted Williams, outdoorsman and gifted columnist for *Audubon* magazine. Tom Parr, curator of the North American Trap Collectors Museum in Galloway, Ohio, helped me flesh out the story of Frank Conibear and the trap he invented. Katharine Bailey gave me the marvelous book *Little Heathens* by Mildred Armstrong Kalish. Kelly and Brenda Anderson alerted me to Nigel Williams's book *From Wimbledon to Waco*. John McConnell reminded me of Brown Dog's encounter with Brad in Jim Harrison's *The Woman Lit by Fireflies*.

Luke Dempsey liked the subject enough to sign me up to write about it for Crown Jenna Ciongoli became my editor and, to my delight, shepherded the manuscript through the editing and production processes with great enthusiasm, expertise, and grace Crown also blessed me with a keen-eyed and meticulous copyeditor, Elisabeth Magnus. I am sure I omitted other readers and helpers, and I ask them to forgive me.

NOTES

INTRODUCTION

xii   **Gray wolves, declared extinct:** "Rare Gray Wolf Appears in Mass.," *USA Today,* March 4, 2008.

xiii   **a young 140-pound male was hit:** Mosi Secret, "Claims of Mountain Lion Roaming in Connecticut Drew Groans . . . Until Saturday": *New York Times,* June 12, 2011.

xiii   **an estimated 3,500 bears:** Peter J. Howe, "Making House Calls to Count State's Bears," *Boston Globe,* February 22, 2008.

xiii   **home to perhaps four thousand bruins:** New Jersey Department of Environmental Conservation website, FAQs, 2009.

xiii   **Connecticut bears:** Benjamin Curtin, "Bears More Plentiful, and Sociable, with Spring Weather," *Lakeville Journal,* May 6, 2010, http://state.nj.us/dep/fgw/bearpolicy10_faq.htm.

xiii   **state's moose population:** Maine Department of Inland Fisheries and Wildlife, 2010 estimate, "Moose Hunting Information," www.maine.gov/ifw/licenses_permits/lotteries/moose/index.htm.

xiii   **Massachusetts has nearly one thousand:** Massachusetts Division of Fisheries and Wildlife, 2007 estimate, "Moose in Massachusetts," MassWildlife, www.mass.gov/dfwele/dfw/wildlife/living/living_with_moose.htm.

xiii   **more than one hundred now roam:** Connecticut Department of Energy and Environmental Protection, 2010 estimate, "DEP Says CT Moose Population Growing," April 30, 2010, www.ct.gov/dep/cwp/view.asp?A=3847&Q=459608.

xiii   **female moose was spotted:** Debra West, "A Massachusetts Moose, Munching Through Mahopac," *New York Times,* December 25, 2005.

xiv   **nearly six hundred birds and animals:** U.S. Fish and Wildlife Service, February 2012, www.ecos.fws.gov/tess_public/pub/boxScore.jsp.

xvii   **"Ever since . . . narrative of loss":** Jan E. Dizard, *Going Wild: Hunting, Animal Rights, and the Contested Meaning of Nature* (Amherst: University of Massachusetts Press, 1999), p. 185.

xvii   **"sham naturalists":** Ralph H. Lutts, *The Nature Fakers: Wildlife, Science and Sentiment* (Charlottesville: University Press of Virginia, 1990), p. 42.

xvii **celluloid substitutes for nature:** Gregg Mitman, *Reel Nature: America's Romance with Wildlife on Film* (Cambridge, MA: Harvard University Press, 1999), p. 6.

xviii **sugar-coated educational films:** Mitman, *Reel Nature,* p. 3.

xix **"single species obsessives":** Paul Theroux, "Living with Geese," *Smithsonian* magazine, December 2006.

xx **coyote sightings in Wheaton:** Rob Erickson, interview, 2010.

xxi **Critter Control Inc.;** Kevin Clark, a Michigan all-state high school wrestler turned chimney sweep, started Critter Control in 1982 in a Detroit suburb after getting numerous requests to remove raccoons and other wild creatures from chimneys. He began franchising in 1987, and by 2009 the company's 132 franchises generated more than $43 million in sales.

xxiv **90 percent of their time indoors:** Environmental Protection Agency, "Indoor Air Quality," in *2008 Report on the Environment* (Washington, DC: Center for Environmental Assessment, 2008), http://cfpub.epa.gov/eroe/index.cfm?fuseaction=list.listBySubTopic&ch=46&s=343.

PART ONE: FOREST PEOPLE

2 **two-thirds of America's forests:** Brad W. Smith et al., *Forest Resources of the United States, 2007* (Washington, DC: U.S. Forest Service, 2007), table 3.

2 **"Simple, . . . the habitat is back":** Gordon Batcheller, interview, 2002.

2 **a vast regreening:** In "An Explosion of Green," an April 1995 article in the *Atlantic Monthly,* Bill McKibben called popular attention to eastern reforestation, writing that if you looked from space at North America with time-lapse glimpses over the last two centuries you'd see "a patch of green spreading like mold across bread, and spreading fast." He went on: "This unintentional and mostly unnoticed renewal of the rural and mountainous East—not the spotted owl, not the salvation of Alaska's pristine ranges—represents the great environmental story of the United States, and in some ways of the whole world. Here, where 'suburb' and 'megalopolis' were added to the world's vocabulary, an explosion of green is under way, one that could offer hope to much of the rest of the planet."

3 **collapse of the Mayan civilization:** David Foster, interview, 2002.

3 **nearly half to more than two-thirds of the landscape was reforested:** Douglas W. MacCleery, *American Forests: A History of Resiliency and Recovery* (Durham, NC: Forest History Society, 2002), p. 5.

3 **people didn't believe it:** Douglas W. MacCleery, *What on Earth Have We Done to Our Forests? A Brief Overview on the Condition and Trends of U.S. Forests* (Washington, DC: U.S. Forest Service, 1992).

3 **"surprising new analysis":** Elisabeth Rosenthal, "Study Finds New Growth in Forests," *New York Times,* November 13, 2006.

CHAPTER ONE: THE SPRUCE ILLUSION

8 **"History of this Parcel . . .":** Brown Farm deed, tract #190, William Otis Sawtelle Collections and Research Center, Acadia National Park.

8 **grapes were a remnant:** Prohibition-era table grapes, a Concord cousin.

10   **Indians first arrived:** David Sanger and Harald E. L. Prins, *An Island in Time: Three Thousand Years of Cultural Exchange on Mount Desert Island* (Bar Harbor, ME: Robert Abbe Museum, 1989).

11   **they did manage them:** Anthropologists estimate that the island resources could sustain a population of perhaps forty people, or three or four extended families, year round, and a community of about four hundred for about five weeks of camping annually. Excavations at Fernald Point in 1976–77 led David Sanger, a professor of anthropology at the University of Maine, to conclude that groups of twenty-five to fifty people had lived there seasonally during the thirteen centuries between A.D. 1 and 1300. They dug clams, gathered lobsters and mussels, and killed porpoises, seals, and an occasional whale. They cut trees for fires and building materials and built birch-bark canoes. They hunted bears, moose, deer, otters, beavers, and foxes and built portage trails across island lowlands. They created and maintained Fernald Point as a meadow, perhaps to distance their encampments from the forest and its creatures, including mosquitoes and blackflies, or from their enemies; to serve as lookout vantage points; and to grow grasses for weaving and berries for eating. The current owners of the Fernald Point meadow hire a commercial mower to keep the forest from swallowing it up.

11   **cod fishermen:** Samuel Eliot Morison, *The Story of Mount Desert Island* (Boston: Little, Brown, 1960).

12   **leaving brush to . . . catch fire:** Tom St. Germain and Jay Saunders, *Trails of History: The Story of Mount Desert Island's Paths from Norumbega to Acadia* (Bar Harbor, ME: Parkman Publications, 1993), p. 21: "Loggers raced each other to exhaust the supply of timber. In this mad rush they did everything they could to deplete the island's resources before their competition did the same."

12   **forest was gone:** Morison, *Story of Mount Desert Island*, p. 33.

12   **"Except in one or two inaccessible valleys . . .":** Clara Barnes Martin, *Mount Desert on the Coast of Maine* (Portland, ME: Loring, Short and Harmon, 1871).

12   **Hudson River school:** John Wilmerding, *The Artist's Mount Desert: American Painters on the Maine Coast* (Princeton: Princeton University Press, 1994).

13   **paintings inspired "rusticators":** Pamela J. Belanger, *Inventing Acadia: Artists and Tourists at Mount Desert* (Rockland, ME: Farnsworth Art Museum, 1999).

13   **there weren't enough farmhands:** Jaylene Roths, *A History of Mount Desert Island Agriculture* (Mount Desert, ME: Mount Desert Island Historical Society, 2005).

14   **carriage roads:** Ann Rockefeller Roberts, *Mr. Rockefeller's Roads: The Untold Story of Acadia's Carriage Roads and Their Creator* (Camden, ME: Down East Books, 1990).

14   **"The whole Island has been 'manhandled . . .'":** Charles W. Eliot II, *The Future of Mount Desert Island* (Bar Harbor, ME: Bar Harbor Village Improvement Association, 1928), p. 17.

15   **"Like many other outwardly satisfying ideas . . .":** Philip W. Conkling, *Islands in Time: A Natural and Human History of the Islands of Maine* (Camden, ME: Down East Books, 1981), p. xv.

16   "Today, it's worse. . . . I live in a hole in the woods": George Peckham, interview, 2005.

17   less than 10 percent: Gordon Longsworth, GIS Laboratory, College of the Atlantic, Bar Harbor, ME, e-mail, 2008.

CHAPTER TWO: AN EPIDEMIC OF TREES

20   fraught with difficulty and peril: Edward Johnson, *Johnson's Wonder-Working
Providence* (1654; repr., New York: Barnes and Noble, 1910), pp. 110–13.

20   Musketaquid: Brian Donahue, *The Great Meadow: Farmers and the Land in Colonial Concord* (New Haven: Yale University Press, 2004), p. 76.

22   Indian populations varied in time and place: Gordon G. Whitney and William C. Davis, "Thoreau and the Forest History of Concord, Massachusetts,"
Journal of Forest History 30 (April 1986): 70–81. "Most evidence suggests that
fires were important agents of change locally along the more densely populated
coastal sections of southern New England. Not surprisingly, fires do not appear
to have been nearly as common in the cooler, moister, more sparsely populated
upland areas of southern New England."

23   "widowed land": Francis Jennings, *The Invasion of America: Indians, Colonialism, and the Cant of Conquest* (Chapel Hill: University of North Carolina Press,
1975), p. 86.

23   "For the entirety . . . the interior remained blank": William Cronon, *Changes
in the Land: Indians, Colonists, and the Ecology of New England* (New York: Hill
and Wang, 1983), p. 19.

23   too much of it to measure: Michael Williams, *Americans and Their Forests: A
Historical Geography* (Cambridge: Cambridge University Press, 1989), p. 4.

24   federal government commissioned studies: Charles Sprague Sargent, the
director of the Arnold Arboretum at Harvard College, produced a 612-page
study, *Report on the Forests of North America (Exclusive of Mexico)* (Washington,
DC: Government Printing Office, 1884), as an amendment to the 1880 Federal
Census. But by then settlers and loggers had been cutting down trees for more
than 250 years.

25   on average, 93 percent forest covered: Royal S. Kellogg, *The Timber Supply of
the United States,* Circular 166 (Washington, DC: U.S. Forest Service, 1909),
p. 3. Kellogg asserted that in 1630 New York and Pennsylvania were 91 percent
forest covered. Maine was 92 percent, Connecticut 95 percent, Delaware 90
percent, Maryland 92 percent, Massachusetts 92 percent, New Hampshire 95
percent, New Jersey 91 percent, Rhode Island 97 percent, Vermont 94 percent,
and West Virginia 95 percent. The five states on the southern Atlantic coast—
Virginia, North Carolina, South Carolina, Georgia, and Florida—were, on
average, 93 percent forested.

25   girdling: A cleared acre of land might be occupied by the leafless skeletons of
one hundred to two hundred girdled trees of various sizes and in varying states
of decay. Branches fell off first. The trunk eventually tumbled and was burned.
Trees were also cut down with axes, left to dry out over years, then burned.
Ashes fertilized vegetation on which livestock foraged and subsequent crops,
planted around the tree stumps.

26   **fuel for heating and cooking:** Cutting and splitting cordwood to burn wasn't easy, but wood was there for the taking. A cord of wood is a stack four feet wide, eight feet long, and four feet high. An average colonial settler burned 4.5 cords of fuel wood per year. A family of four consumed 18 cords for heating and cooking. For fencing, a strong man could split logs into fifty to one hundred fence rails a day. Erecting a fence around a five-acre field required one thousand rails and ten to twenty man-days of labor.

26   **masts for sailing ships:** Robert Albion, *Forests and Sea Power: The Timber Problem of the Royal Navy, 1652–1862* (Cambridge, MA: Harvard University Press), 1926.

27   **Erie Canal:** Bruce Catton, *Michigan: A History* (New York: W. W. Norton, 1976), pp. 82, 97.

28   **built with Michigan trees:** Donald I. Dickmann and Larry A. Leefers, *The Forests of Michigan* (Ann Arbor: University of Michigan Press, 2003), p. 121.

28   **railroads consumed whole forests:** MacCleery, *American Forests*, p. 19.

28   **wood supplied 90 percent of the nation's energy:** MacCleery, *What on Earth*, p. 1.

29   **timber barons were rapacious:** Dickmann and Leefers, *Forests of Michigan*, p. 100.

29   **"Wood was virtually the only fuel . . .":** MacCleery, *What on Earth*, p. 3.

30   **"lands nobody wants":** It took decades for vegetation to make a comeback on these wounded lands, first weeds, then small woody plants and tree seedlings—a combination of natural regrowth and major tree-planting programs. Eventually, a young forest grew full of food that attracted wildlife, including a creature that had historically flourished in the mixed forests of the South: the white-tailed deer.

30   **"drawing on the surplus":** Williams, *Americans and Their Forests*, p. 430.

31   **"We are cutting our forests . . .":** Kellogg, *Timber Supply*, p. 23.

31   **"It was an alarming prospect . . .":** Michael Williams, *Deforesting the Earth: From Prehistory to Global Crisis* (Chicago: University of Chicago Press, 2006), p. 382.

32   **planetary popped zit:** The Volcanic Explosivity Index (VEI), similar to the Richter scale for earthquakes, weighs volcano blasts, the volumes of solids and gases they burp, how far up they go, and their overall explosive power, on a scale of 1 to 8, with each number ten times bigger than the last. There haven't been any 8s in human history, but Tambora was a 7. Krakatoa was a 6, or ten times less powerful; Mount Saint Helens, a 5; and Iceland's Eyjafjallajokull volcano in 2011, perhaps a 2 to 4.

34   **"The summer of 1816 . . .":** Henry Stommel and Elizabeth Stommel, *Volcano Weather: The Story of 1816, the Year without a Summer* (Newport, RI: Seven Seas Press, 1983).

34   **"climatically marginal for many crops":** M. Williams, *Americans and Their Forests*, p. 470.

36   **"retrogressive . . . sinful to contemplate":** Ibid., p. 468.

36   **more than just economic value:** George B. Emerson, *Report on the Trees and*

Shrubs Growing Naturally in the Forests of Massachusetts (Springfield, MA: Botanical Survey, 1923).

37   **conservation movement:** George Perkins Marsh, *Man and Nature; or, Physical Geography as Modified by Human Action* (1864; repr., Seattle: University of Washington Press, 2003).

38   **"For Muir . . . God's own temple":** William Cronon, *Uncommon Ground: Rethinking the Human Place in Nature* (New York: W. W. Norton, 1996), p. 72.

40   **"tree epidemic":** Nigel Williams, *From Wimbledon to Waco* (London: Faber and Faber, 1995), pp. 151–54.

41   **"In town meetings . . . folks often refer to the primeval forests":** Cynthia Hochswender, "Our Ever-Changing Landscape," *Lakeville Journal,* December 2007, p. 3.

42   **"post-agricultural hardwood forest":** Michael Pollan, *Second Nature: A Gardener's Education* (New York: Grove/Atlantic, 1991), p. 46.

CHAPTER THREE: SPRAWL

46   **"In 1970, for the first time in the history of the world":** Kenneth T. Jackson, *Crabgrass Frontier: The Suburbanization of the United States* (New York: Oxford University Press, 1985), p. 283.

47   **"the geography of nowhere":** James Howard Kunstler, *The Geography of Nowhere: The Rise and Decline of America's Man-Made Landscape* (New York: Simon & Schuster, 1993).

47   **Chicago's great fire:** William Cronon, *Nature's Metropolis: Chicago and the Great West* (New York: W. W. Norton, 1991), p. 348.

48   **"By 1947, you have millions of husbands and wives and children . . .":** Kenneth T. Jackson, speaking in "How the Suburbs Changed America," segment 9 of *The First Measured Century,* PBS, 2000, transcript, www.pbs.org/fmc/segments/progseg9.htm.

48   **Developers took over:** During the war, airplane manufacturers honed assembly-line techniques to turn out a plane every five minutes. Developers copied them after the war, turning out 2 million new single-family houses a year—which were cheaper to buy than to rent. In 1947, families began moving into Levittown, a new suburb built on a potato-farm land near Hicksville, Long Island, that would eventually contain 17,447 houses—Cape Cods with four rooms and a bath costing $6,990 and larger ranch styles costing $7,990. An ex-GI could own one for $56 a month.

49   **bored to tears:** "Little Boxes," a 1962 song by Malvina Reynolds about ticky-tacky lookalike suburban houses, was made famous by Pete Seeger.

49   **demographers had their eye on a countertrend:** Obituary for Calvin L. Beale, *New York Times,* September 4, 2008.

49   **sprawling out:** Kenneth M. Johnson, *The Rural Rebound,* Reports on America (Washington, DC: Population Reference Bureau, August 1999).

50   **"We're living in the age of the great dispersal":** David Brooks, "Our Sprawling, Supersize Utopia," *New York Times Magazine,* April 4, 2004.

51   **a nation of forest dwellers?:** The eastern forest, old and new, stretches from

the Atlantic to the Great Plains. At my request, William Lanoux, a GIS (geographic information system) expert at the University of Minnesota, drew a rough line around it, zigzagging to exclude nonforested farmland in the Midwest, and, using 2000 Census data, found that nearly 187 million people, or 66 percent of the U.S. population, lived within the line. By 2010, that number had grown to nearly 204 million.

51   **It obviously isn't officially defined forest:** The U.S. Forest Service defines a forest as acreage preserved as forest or under timber management as forest. This acreage must be allowed to regenerate as forest without human disturbance. It can be private or public land at least an acre in size and 120 feet wide, with tree cover of at least 10 percent but usually a lot more. That 10 percent might seem small, but it encompasses land on which forests have been cut down and readied for replanting. People don't live in these forests, but plenty of them live nearby. Estimates of their numbers vary. A 2005 study at the University of Wisconsin found that 38.5 percent of all American houses were in an area called the Wildland-Urban Interface: that is, situated on the edge of designated forests or other wild (undeveloped) land. In Connecticut, 72 percent of the land fit the interface definition. Rachel Riemann, a U.S. Department of Agriculture research forester-geographer with the U.S. Forest Service Northern Research Station in Troy, New York, found that in several heavily populated eastern states 63 percent of the population lived under or near tree cover—enough trees so that these areas would qualify as USDA-defined forest if people weren't living in them.

52   **"If you looked down . . . what you'd see was stockbrokers":** John C. Gordon, e-mail, June 6, 2008.

PART TWO: WILD BEASTS

54   **so-called pot hunters:** Karl Jacoby, *Crimes Against Nature: Squatters, Poachers, Thieves, and the Hidden History of American Conservation* (Berkeley: University of California Press, 2001), p. 64.

54   **Market hunters killed anything:** Frank Graham Jr., *Man's Dominion: The Story of Conservation in America* (New York: M. Evans, 1971).

56   **model of wildlife conservation:** Valerius Geist, "Triumph of the Commons: The North American Model of Wildlife Conservation as Means of Creating Wealth and Protecting Public Health While Generating Biodiversity," *Wild Lands Advocate* 12, no. 6 (2006): 5-11.

57   **Dumpsters that became cafeterias:** Kathleen M. White, "50 Years Bin There, Done That," *Waste Age* magazine, March 1, 2004.

CHAPTER FOUR: THE FIFTY-POUND RODENT

60   **"Many experts believe that the cost of beaver damage . . .":** U.S. Department of Agriculture, Wildlife Services Division, "USDA Wildlife Services Protects Property," 2004, www.scribd.com/doc/1697513/USDA-property.

62   **"Funny, . . . Then they need me":** Don LaFountain, interview, 2002.

63   **largest rodent in North America:** B. W. Baker and E. P. Hill, *Wild Mammals*

of North America: Biology, Management and Conservation, 2nd ed. (Baltimore: Johns Hopkins University Press, 2003), pp. 288–310.

65 **Indians made use of fur-bearing mammals:** Shepard Krech III, *The Ecological Indian: Myth and History* (New York: W. W. Norton, 1999), p. 79.

66 **bountiful furs the Indians possessed:** Paul Chrisler Phillips notes that at first Europe's royal rulers didn't know or care much about New World furs. Germany, the Netherlands, and Italy got furs they needed from Russia and eastern Europe. Spain's New World focus was on gold and other riches. France and England were searching without success for northern gold and a water passage to the East Indies. European rulers "were slow to realize that with an empire in the New World, they could open a market for their country's produce and satisfy their people's demand for furs." Paul Chrisler Phillips, *The Fur Trade* (Norman: University of Oklahoma Press, 1961), p. 14.

67 **fur of excellent quality:** Russell Shorto, *The Island at the Center of the World* (New York: Doubleday, 2004), pp. 32–33.

67 **raid at Wessagusset:** Nathaniel Philbrick, *Mayflower: A Story of Courage, Community, and War* (New York: Penguin Group, 2006), pp. 147–53.

67 **"Without the fur trade . . . the name of the ship would have faded into oblivion":** Nick Bunker, *Making Haste from Babylon: The Mayflower Pilgrims and Their World* (New York: Alfred A. Knopf, 2010), p. 233.

68 **Manhattan Island:** The headquarters of the Dutch West India Company was established on the southeastern tip of Manhattan at New Amsterdam. One hundred and forty miles to the north, at the conjunction of the Hudson and Mohawk rivers, Fort Orange became the center of the fur trade. As Shorto put it: "From far out of the uncharted west, Indians came down the Mohawk Valley with their heavy loads of pelts; traders bought them, stored them at the fort, then shipped them downriver to Manhattan" (Shorto, *Island at the Center,* pp. 75–76). There the pelts were stored in company warehouses and then shipped to Holland.

68 **the letter:** Shorto, *Island at the Center,* pp. 55–56.

70 **"the struggle for dominion in America":** Phillips, *The Fur Trade,* p. xix.

70 **primary use was to make felt for hats:** Beaver underhairs are serrated with tiny interlocking barbs that are easily matted into felt. Hatters who used cheaper fur, such as rabbit, to make felt had to perform a step called carroting in order to make the short hairs stick together. This involved brushing the pelts with a warm solution of mercurous nitrate, which hatters usually kept bubbling away in a pot in their poorly ventilated shops. The resulting poisonous mercury fumes were breathed in by the hatters and attacked their body organs, including the brain and nervous system. Symptoms include trembling, slurred speech, memory loss, anxiety, and depression. Hatters' muttering and dementia led to the phrase "mad as a hatter," from which the character of the Mad Hatter was drawn in 1865 in Lewis Carroll's *Alice in Wonderland.* The trembling also became known as St. Vitus' dance, after a ritual performed before a statue of the Sicilian saint, and, later, "the Danbury Shakes," after afflicted hatters centered in Danbury, Connecticut. Customers who bought these cheaper hats would

absorb residual mercury while wearing them and sometimes exhibit the mad hatter syndrome themselves—all the more reason to buy a beaver felt hat.

71   **saying in parting:** Richard M. Ketchum, "The Spirit of '54," *American Heritage,* August/September 2002.

72   **confirming the abundance of beavers:** Stephen E. Ambrose, *Undaunted Courage: Meriwether Lewis, Thomas Jefferson, and the Opening of the American West* (New York: Simon & Schuster, 1996), p. 218. John Jacob Astor was already there. Astor arrived in New York from London in 1783, intent on fur trading. By then, however, beavers had become scarce in the East, so Astor went west, establishing a trading post on the Pacific coast. By 1795, Astor had a fleet of twelve ships carrying furs to Europe and the Far East and bringing back manufactured goods and tea. In 1808, he established the American Fur Company to compete head on with the Hudson's Bay Company, and in 1811 he established Fort Astoria at the mouth of the Columbia River on the Oregon coast.

72   **isolated Northern Rockies:** Eric Jay Dolin, *Fur, Fortune, and Empire: The Epic History of the Fur Trade in America* (New York: W. W. Norton, 2010). This was the time of the fabled "mountain men," essentially white poachers brave or hungry enough to trespass on Indian lands in the Rocky Mountain West, where beavers were still plentiful. Astor bought several fur companies founded by mountain men and eventually created a virtual monopoly of the fur trade in the United States. His monopoly was strengthened in 1816, when Congress passed a law prohibiting foreigners from the trade in the United States. In 1834, Astor abruptly sold his fur business and used the money to buy land in New York City. It was not a minute too soon—but probably a couple of years too late for Astor to extract maximum profits.

73   **the Canadian outback:** Canada owed its very existence as a nation to competition for beaver fur. Indeed, finished beaver pelts served as Canada's first currency. Nowhere else in the world have beavers been more honored. A beaver was depicted on the first coat of arms in North America for what is now Nova Scotia. Four beavers adorned the coat of arms adopted by the Hudson's Bay Company in 1678. The beaver was featured on Canada's first postage stamp and on six subsequent stamp issues. And on March 24, 1975, in what Canadians said was the highest honor ever bestowed on a rodent, Queen Elizabeth II proclaimed the beaver to be the "Symbol of the Sovereignty of the Dominion of Canada."

74   **released thirty-four Canadian beavers into the Adirondacks:** John F. Organ et al., "A Case Study in the Sustained Use of Wildlife: The Management of Beaver in the Northeastern United States," in *Enhancing Sustainability: Resources for Our Future,* eds. H. A. van der Linde and M. H. Danskin, SUI Technical Series 1 (Cambridge: International Union for Conservation of Nature, 1998), p. 126.

74   **spilled into western Massachusetts:** Organ et al., "Case Study."

76   **"Management of beaver":** Ibid., p. 131.

77   **three-fourths of their $1.5 billion:** James P. Sterba, "Leave It to Beaver: As Forest Reclaims East, It's Man vs. Beast—with Trappers' Hands Tied," *Wall Street Journal,* May 21, 2002.

77 **fewer than one hundred sixty thousand trappers**: U.S. Fish and Wildlife Agencies, "Ownership and Use of Traps by Trappers in the United States in 2004," 2005.

77 **compared with 35 million fisherman**: H. Dale Hall, *1996 National Survey of Fishing, Hunting, and Wildlife-Associated Recreation* (Washington, DC: U.S. Fish and Wildlife Service, 1996), p. 6.

77 **Massachusetts beaver population was estimated at twenty-four thousand**: Massachusetts Department of Fish and Game, 1996 estimate, "Managing Beaver."

79 **"Voters shouldn't . . . fix what isn't broken"**: *Boston Globe,* editorial, October 21, 1996.

79 **"Emotion ruled over science . . ."**: Fen Montalgne, "Outdoors: State Wildlife-Management Goes Public as Voters Ban Certain Traps as Cruel," *Wall Street Journal,* February 7, 1997.

80 **"The majority of the voting public was . . . very misinformed"**: Evan Osnos, "Beaver Laws Trap Towns," *Chicago Tribune,* August 6, 2001.

80 **Frank Ralph Conibear**: Eric Collier, "Revolutionary New Trap," *Outdoor Life,* September-October 1957.

81 **"outstanding creativity in . . . more humane animal traps"**: In a study published in the *Journal of Wildlife Diseases* in 1995, wildlife researchers with the Alberta Research Council wrote that "a humane killing trap is a device that has the potential, at a 95% confidence level, to render ≥70% of target animals irreversibly unconscious in ≤ 3 min." A Conibear 330 trap, modified to make it more powerful, they said, fit that definition. Gilbert Proulx et al., "A Humane Killing Trap for Lynx *(Felix lynx):* The Conibear 330 with Clamping Bars," *Journal of Wildlife Diseases* 31, no. 1 (1995): 57-61.

81 **the Conibear had been lumped**: In 1946, someone in Juan Peron's military thought Argentina needed a fur industry and transplanted twenty-five pairs of beavers from Canada to Tierra del Fuego. By 1966, there were 2,500 beavers on the island; by 2008, they numbered 100,000 on both the Argentina and Chile sides of the island and were causing more forest damage, said one ecologist, than anything else in the last ten thousand years. Argentina wanted to trap out the rodents and export their fur to Europe, but Europe refused to buy because Argentina trappers at the time used leg-hold traps declared to be inhumane. So Argentina spent $50,000 to buy 1,100 traps the European Union defined as humane: Conibear 330s.

81 **"the most humane and effective device . . ."**: Marc Folco, "Trapping Opponents Have Made a Mess of Things in Massachusetts," *New Bedford Standard-Times,* April 13, 1999.

81 **"The 'cruel' Conibears . . ."**: Ted Williams, "Management by Majority," *Audubon* magazine, June 1999.

82 **"Beavers Driving Ipswich Batty"**: Coco McCabe, "Beavers Driving Ipswich Batty: Roads, Backyards, Trails Being Flooded," *Boston Globe,* August 30, 2001.

83 **growing expense for taxpayers**: For example, North Carolina spent $349,000 on beaver damage control in 2007, and the federal government spent $235,000 in the state. In Columbia, South Carolina, beavers had so clogged the city's

waterways, drainage ditches, and sewer systems that the city in 2009 signed a $1 million contract to clear them out.

CHAPTER FIVE: THE ELEGANT UNGULATE

86   **ten largest armed forces . . . combined:** According to the International Institute for Strategic Studies report *The Military Balance 2011* (New York: Taylor and Francis, 2011), the nations with the largest active duty armed forces were China (2,285,000), United States (1,564,000), India (1,325,000), North Korea (1,190,000), Russia (1,213,000), South Korea (655,000), Pakistan (617,000), Iran (523,000), Turkey (511,000), and Vietnam (482,000).

86   **"the most widely-distributed . . .":** Lowell K. Halls, Richard E. McCabe, and Lawrence R. Jahn, *White-Tailed Deer: Ecology and Management* (Washington, DC: Wildlife Management Institute, 1984), p. vi.

86   **$12 billion into the economy:** H. Dale Hall, *2006 National Survey of Fishing, Hunting, and Wildlife-Associated Recreation* (Washington, DC: U.S. Fish and Wildlife Service, 2007), http://wsfrprograms.fws.gov/Subpages/National Survey/nat_survey2006_final.pdf.

87   **lure amorous bucks:** Aldo Leopold, *A Sand County Almanac, with Essays on Conservation from Round River* (1949; repr., New York: Oxford University Press, 1966), p. 214. Way back in 1949, Leopold railed against the growing hunting supplies industry: "Then came the gadgeteer, otherwise known as the sport-goods dealer. He has draped the American outdoorsman with an infinity of contraptions, all offered as aids to self-reliance, hardihood, woodcraft, or marksmanship, but too often functioning as substitutes for them. Gadgets fill pockets, they dangle from neck and belt. . . . The sportsman has no leaders to tell him what is wrong. The sporting press no longer represents sport; it has turned billboard for the gadgeteer."

87   **their populations were growing unchecked:** William J. McShea, H. Brian Underwood, and John H. Rappole, *The Science of Overabundance: Deer Ecology and Population Management* (Washington, DC: Smithsonian Institution Press, 1997). Overabundance was defined by forty-two wildlife biologists and deer specialists in four contexts: (1) when it threatens human life or livelihood; (2) when it depresses densities of favored species (songbirds, for example); (3) when it is too populous for its own good; (4) when its numbers cause ecosystem dysfunction.

87   **Deer damage to farm crops:** Paul D. Curtis and Kristi L. Sullivan, *White-Tailed Deer,* Wildlife Damage Management Fact Sheet Series (Ithaca, NY: Cornell University Wildlife Publications, 2006).

88   **collisions of deer and motor vehicles:** Michael Conover, Berryman Institute, Utah State University, e-mail, August 6, 2006.

88   **"Forgive us . . .":** "When Cute Deer Go Bad," editorial, *New York Times,* March 20, 2005.

89   **"deer nirvana. It's one big edge":** William McShea, quoted in Anne Broache, "Oh Deer!," *Smithsonian* magazine, October 2005.

90   **off limits to hunting:** In the heavily populated eastern third of the state, roughly inside Interstate 495, these restrictions put 80 percent of the land off limits. In

the central third of the state, 50 percent of the area is restricted. In the western third, the least densely populated, 40 percent of the land is off limits. In addition, nearly half of the state's 351 municipalities impose prohibitions and restrictions on the discharge of firearms, hunting with firearms, or hunting with bows and arrows.

91 **deer are ruminants:** Halls, McCabe, and Jahn, *White-Tailed Deer.*

92 **the top predator:** Halls, McCabe, and Jahn, *White-Tailed Deer,* 27–34. Richard E. and Thomas R. McCabe reported that "undoubtedly, venison was the most widely available and reliable source of protein" and that perhaps 25 percent of the protein Indians ate was venison. From midden excavation reports, they estimated that members of some tribes probably ate, on average, 9.5 deer per capita annually, and that adults needed 3.5 hides for clothing and more for trading. They postulated that Indians were probably responsible for 30 to 50 percent of whitetail mortality—more than all other predators combined. They estimated that 14.2 to 32.8 million whitetails would be required to sustain the annual Indian harvest.

92 **deerskins and slaves:** Krech, *Ecological Indian,* p. 156.

93 **"Trains that ran on the labyrinth of tracks . . .":** Halls, McCabe, and Jahn, *White-Tailed Deer,* p. 66.

95 **North American model:** Geist, "Triumph of the Commons."

96 **fair play and fair chase:** These restraints were routinely abandoned by sport hunters who joined others in the slaughter and waste of the great herds of buffalo and elk in the West, and in the hunting, killing, and leaving to waste of all sorts of other creatures. Often these hunters "killed for count," a phrase that meant shooting as many birds and animals as they could. Sometimes they left their kills to rot or be scavenged, taking back nothing more than a set of trophy antlers, a head to mount on the wall, or a bearskin.

97 **"The poor, as well as the men of moderate means . . .":** Jacoby, *Crimes Against Nature.*

98 **poachers fought back:** John F. Reiger, *American Sportsmen and the Origins of Conservation* (Corvallis: Oregon State University Press, 2001), p. 93.

98 **Restocking became the proactive phase:** J. Scott McDonald and Karl V. Miller, *A History of White-Tailed Deer Restocking in the United States, 1878 to 2004* (Athens, GA: Quality Deer Management Association and D. B. Warnell School of Forest Resources, 2004). Deer had been wiped out of Vermont by 1865.

98 **"too many deer":** Bob Frye, *Deer Wars: Science, Tradition, and the Battle over Managing Whitetails in Pennsylvania* (1967; repr., University Park: Pennsylvania State University Press, 2006).

99 **Michigan's whitetail saga:** Eugene T. Peterson, "The History of Wildlife Conservation in Michigan, 1859–1921," Ph.D. diss., University of Michigan, 1952, p. 57.

101 **"deer problem":** Michigan Department of Natural Resources, "White-Tailed Deer (*Odocoileus virginianus*)," 2007, www.michigan.gov/dnr/0,4570,7-153-10370_12145_12205-56904--,00.html.

102 **deer population crashed:** Michigan Department of Natural Resources, "White-Tailed Deer."

103   **"putting garbage in the woods":** By the 1980s, Michigan hunters were putting out more than 3 million bushels of carrots, sugar beets, apples, potatoes,
pumpkins, and corn to lure deer into their hunting territories and keep them
there during the hunting season. Private hunting clubs bought food by the ton
from farmers to stock hundreds of feeding stations. Bait piles by the thousands
dotted the northeastern counties of Lower Michigan—an area dubbed "the
country club" because of its proliferation of privately owned and members-only
hunting clubs. Supplemental feeding worked. The deer population grew, reaching an all-time peak in 1989 of an estimated 2 million animals. By 1991, some
13.1 million bushels of food were put out to bait deer. Four out of ten hunters
used it. Doing so made killing deer easy. Appeals of fair chase advocates fell on
deaf ears.

104   **one hundred deer per square mile:** "Should Hired Guns Thin Local Deer
Herds?" *Detroit News,* January 1, 2006.

105   **"The cachet of the trip north . . .":** "Too Many Deer Here," *Detroit Free Press,*
January 15, 2006.

105   **model had broken down:** State deer managers were supposed to balance the
demands of hunters for more deer with the needs of keeping deer herds and
their habitats healthy. But what "healthy habitat" meant was an open question. Hunters were sportsmen, not environmentalists. They hunted in the same
places their fathers and grandfathers hunted, and if those places looked different or if deer were damaging that habitat, they didn't notice. In Pennsylvania,
for decades, organized deer hunters denied whitetail overpopulation. In 1999,
Gary Alt took over the state game commission's deer management program
and immediately criticized it as environmental "malpractice" and "the biggest
mistake in the history of wildlife management," with deer causing "immeasur-
able environmental and ecological damage." He quit in frustration in 2004.
In 2005, a case study by wildlife and forest experts for Audubon Pennsylvania
and the Pennsylvania Habitat Alliance—groups critical of deer management
in the state—concluded that "the history of deer-human interaction in the last
two centuries is one of overexploitation through unregulated hunting, followed
by 100 years of overprotection, population increase, and consequent habitat
destruction resulting from over-browsing by growing deer herds." Roger Earl
Latham et al., *Managing White-Tailed Deer in Forest Habitat from an Ecosystem
Perspective: Pennsylvania Case Study* (Harrisburg: Audubon Pennsylvania and
Pennsylvania Habitat Alliance, 2005).

106   **"they stepped into the vortex of conflicting values . . .":** Dizard, *Going Wild,*
p. 25.

106   **"they were not about to sit passively by . . .":** Ibid., p. 11.

106   **"It looked like the Serengeti Plain . . .":** David Kittredge, interview, 2002.

108   **hunters killed 576 deer:** Dizard, *Going Wild,* p. 168.

108   **"Two weeks ago I lost 576 of my closest friends there":** Ibid., p. 160.

109   **"bristling with arrows . . .":** James P. Sterba, "Even a Real Genius Notes That
Bambi Is a Relevant Factor," *Wall Street Journal,* October 12, 1989.

110   **"I like them. . . .":** Ibid.

110   **"I find it appalling . . . the Rambo mentality":** Ibid.

111   **deer reduction program, a success:** Animal rights advocates had long argued that culling of deer, geese, beavers, feral cats, and other overabundant species created a vacuum that was filled quickly from outside. However, in a 2008 study Anthony J. DeNicola and Scott Williams reported that after sharpshooters culled deer populations over three to seven years in Iowa City, Iowa, Princeton, New Jersey, and Solon, Ohio, "we found no indication that there was any significant level of immigration of deer into the communities from outside areas" after several years ("Sharpshooting Suburban White-Tailed Deer Reduces Deer-Vehicle Collisions," *Human-Wildlife Conflicts* 2 [2008]: 28–33). Wait long enough, of course, and deer and other wildlife will infiltrate, but not nearly as quickly as animal protection people suggested.

112   **found deer guts splattered:** Maria Newman, "Protesters Against Princeton's Deer Hunt Turn Increasingly Nasty," *New York Times,* March 5, 2002.

112   **"safe and effective":** Mayor Phyllis Marchand, letter to the editor, *New York Times,* March 10, 2002.

112   **hilarious satire:** Jay F. Kirkpatrick and John W. Turner, "Urban Deer Contraception: The Seven Stages of Grief," *Wildlife Society Bulletin* 25, no. 2 (1997): 515–19.

115   **Lower Makefield Township:** Lower Makefield's 18.3 square miles includes a publicly owned three-hundred-acre nature preserve called Five Mile Woods, where manager John Heilferty fenced off three ten-meter enclosures so deer couldn't browse in them. The results were dramatic. Ground vegetation quickly rebounded. In 2004, a partial aerial survey of the preserve and adjacent lands suggested a deer population of fifty-four per square mile.

115   **increasingly troubling mix:** Bryon P. Shissler, interview, 2007.

115   **Shissler submitted his report:** Bryon P. Shissler, *Deer Management Plan for Lower Makefield Twp.* (Fort Hill, PA: Natural Resource Consultants, 2007).

116   **"not acceptable":** Pete Stainthorpe, minutes of the meeting of the Lower Makefield Board of Supervisors, April 7, 2010.

CHAPTER SIX: LAWN CARP

118   **hired to round up the Canada geese:** Annmarie Baisley, Kathy Doherty, and Tom Maglaras, interviews, 2002.

120   **"It's time to reflect. . . . Sleep well":** letters to Baisley received July 11 and 27, 2001.

121   **at least eleven subspecies:** T. B. Mowbray et al., *Canada Goose: Branta canadensis,* Birds of North America 682 (Philadelphia: Birds of North America, 2002), p. 6.

122   **"Now . . . I'll go through the Siegfried Line . . . like shit through a goose":** Carlos D'Este, *Patton: A Genius for War* (New York: HarperCollins, 1995), p. 658.

123   **a gross exaggeration:** Dr. Bruce A. Manny, a biologist with the U.S. Geological Survey, told me in a 2009 e-mail that his research concluded that an average Canada goose drops 5.49 ounces of wet feces daily, which is only 1.15 ounces when dried.

124   **addle or oil eggs:** If eggs are taken from a nest, the female simply lays another

clutch. So eggs have to be rendered unhatchable and left in the nests by killing fetuses inside by shaking, puncturing, or painting them with oil—in essence, goose abortions.

125   **border collies**: Mary Felegy, interview, 2002. In Orangetown, New York, another bedroom community just south of Clarkstown, officials hired Felegy for $12,000 a year to loose her border collies into a forty-acre park and chase the geese there away. The municipal golf course, less than half a mile away, paid her another $12,000 to harass geese off fairways.

126   **"The collie people . . ."**: Gregory Chasko, interview, 2002.

127   **"This is a big deal . . ."**: Charlie Holbrook, interview, 2002.

127   **"Canada geese no longer feel the need . . ."**: Robert Johnson, "Warmer Weather Has Florida Roaches Moving to Chicago—Plants and Animals Are Finding New and Congenial Climes, Beware the Brown Reclus," *Wall Street Journal*, June 23, 1992.

128   **geese stayed because of global warming**: Amber Parches, "Parks Department Hiring Slump Doesn't Apply to Dogs," *Montgomery County Gazette*, November 11, 2009.

128   **Colonists made use of waterfowl**: Thomas Morton, *New English Canaan* (Amsterdam, Netherlands, 1637).

129   **"These instruments of mass slaughter . . ."**: James B. Trefethen, *An American Crusade for Wildlife* (New York: Winchester Press, 1975), p. 60.

129   **use of live decoys**: Trefethen, *American Crusade*, p. 61.

131   **Stopping this carnage**: Trefethen, *American Crusade*, p. 156.

131   **efforts went nowhere**: Bird conservationists got what they wanted through congressional sleight of hand: a 1913 rider called the Weeks-McLean Migratory Bird Act was slipped into an agriculture funding bill that President William Howard Taft signed into law in the face of arguments that it amounted to an unconstitutional violation of states' rights. Even the conservationists thought that these arguments had merit and that a court challenge was inevitable. The danger was that the Supreme Court would rule it to be an unconstitutional federal power grab, thereby dooming efforts to save migratory birds. To head off such a decision, they decided to introduce a resolution into the U.S. Senate authorizing the Department of State to negotiate a treaty with Great Britain (acting on behalf of Canada) to protect North American migratory birds. They would argue that under the Tenth Amendment, the so-called states' rights amendment, international treaties trumped states' rights. The senator chosen to table the resolution was one of the chamber's most distinguished internationalists, Elihu Root of New York. Root had been secretary of war under William McKinley and secretary of state under Theodore Roosevelt, and in 1912, for a work on international cooperation, he had been awarded the Nobel Peace Prize.

131   **"supreme law of the land"**: In theory, the Migratory Bird Treaty, the federal regulations enforcing it, and the Supreme Court decision upholding it ended the commercial and noncommercial killing of migratory birds once and for all, except for authorized sport hunting. In fact, the killers became outlaws.

132   **outlaw the use of live decoys**: Migratory Bird Treaty Regulations, Service and Regulatory Announcements, Regulation 3, August 1935.

133 "The new regulations practically wipe out all the artificial aids . . .": H. P. Sheldon, *New York Times*, September 15, 1935.

134 "After release . . . little biological incentive": Jack Hope, "The Geese That Came In from the Wild," *Audubon* magazine, March-April 2000.

135 Hanson got permission: Harold C. Hanson, *The Giant Canada Goose* (1965; repr., Carbondale: Southern Illinois University Press, 1997), p. xxi.

136 "Hundreds of former nest-robbers": Hope, "Geese That Came In."

136 "They happened to be giants . . .": Dave Graber, interview, 2009.

137 "Most of us . . . big time stuff": Ollie Torgerson, e-mail, May 17, 2007.

138 "It's said that Ike slipped on some goose doo-doo . . .": Jim Forbes, interview, 2002.

138 excess Canada geese: Some of them, especially adults, turned around and flew back "home." For geese, home is where they learned to fly. The most successful relocations involved goslings. They were moved to their new homes before they learned to fly.

138 "I don't think anybody ever saw the resident-goose problem . . .": Hope, "Geese That Came In."

139 Twin Cities relocations: Brian L. Leuth, Minnesota Department of Natural Resources, e-mail, November 24, 2009. In 1993, the People for the Ethical Treatment of Animals (PETA) filed a lawsuit charging that the relocations resulted in the geese being "harassed, cruelly manhandled, separated parents from goslings, and forcibly translocated. The goslings, unprotected by adults, will be easy prey for predators." All this, PETA asserted, violated state laws. To document the mishandling, PETA dispatched a veterinarian to where geese were being loaded into trailers for relocation. There she was not only welcomed but asked to demonstrate for the workers the correct way to handle a goose. According to Leuth, who was there, the PETA vet declined, saying that she had never handled a goose before. The lawsuit was ultimately dismissed.

140 "I got personally involved . . .": Ollie Torgerson, e-mail, May 17, 2007.

141 "as fast . . . no intended foot-dragging": Paul Schmidt, interview, May 7, 2007.

142 fewer than nineteen thousand birds: In 2006, nobody wanted Twin Cities goslings anymore, so they were killed along with adults. But because goslings don't have enough breast meat for people, they were sent to the Wildlife Service Center, a research facility in Forest Lake, and fed to red wolves and other carnivores under study there. After Dr. Cooper retired, his students took over the roundup program, setting up a company called Canada Goose Management Inc., run by Tom Keefe. In 2008, he reported, 879 adult geese and 1,873 goslings were trapped at 106 sites in the seven-county region. Workers also found 135 nests and destroyed 655 eggs. Hunters in an early fall hunting season for resident geese killed an estimated ten thousand to fifteen thousand birds, and about the same number of residents and migrants were killed during the regular fall season. These programs have for many years stabilized the Twin Cities resident goose population at an estimated sixteen thousand to nineteen thousand birds.

143 DEIS: Ron W. Kokel and Jon Andrew, *Draft Environmental Impact Statement: Resident Canada Goose Management* (Washington, DC: U.S. Fish and Wildlife Service, 2002).

143   **reduce resident geese by up to a million birds:** Matt Hogan, "Migratory Bird Hunting and Permits; Regulations for Managing Resident Canada Goose Populations; Final Rule," *Federal Register* 71, no. 154 (August 10, 2006).

144   **"PLUCK 'EM":** *New York Post,* January 17, 2009.

144   **"most hazardous species of bird":** Simon Akam, "For Culprits in Miracle on Hudson, the Flip Side of Glory," *New York Times,* October 2, 2009.

144   **"remove and dispose of":** Chris Dolmetsch, "NYC to Remove Canada Geese near LaGuardia and Kennedy Airports," Bloomberg News, June 11, 2009.

144   **"There are people who care . . . letting them go to sleep with nice dreams":** "Bloomberg to Canadian Geese: 'Nice Dreams,'" *New York Post,* June 12, 2009.

145   **"How many geese did you gas today?":** Rachel Cernansky, "Dozens Protest Killing of Geese near Airports," *New York Times,* June 16, 2009.

145   **"a horrifying crime . . .":** "Fed Geese Slaughter Was Wrong," editorial, *Brooklyn Paper,* July 14, 2010.

145   **"Gassed Geese? Good":** *New York Post,* July 18, 2010.

145   **"wrong and unacceptable":** Humane Society of the United States, "Canada Geese Round Ups," June 4, 2010, www.humanesociety.org/animals/geese/qa/goose_roundup_faq.html.

145   **"Good Riddance":** Dan Collins, "Good Riddance to Canada Geese," *Huffington Post,* July 15, 2010.

145   **"Where Is the Uproar?":** Karl Gotthardt, "Geese Culled in U.S., Beaten and Gased: Where Is the Uproar?" Allvoices, July 14, 2010, www.allvoices.com/contributed-news/6309398-geese-called-in-us-beaten-and-gased-where-is-the-uproar.

CHAPTER SEVEN: GOBBLERS

148   **facing extinction:** Trefethen, *American Crusade,* p. 252.

149   **a Galliform:** James G. Dickson, ed., *The Wild Turkey: Biology and Management* (Mechanicsburg, PA: Stackpole Books, 1992).

149   **Indians . . . domesticated turkeys:** Andrew F. Smith, *The Turkey: An American Story* (Chicago: University of Illinois Press, 2006), pp. 8–11.

150   **six turkeys made of gold:** Smith, *Turkey,* p. 10.

150   **gift turkeys at Christmas:** Smith, *Turkey,* p. 38.

150   **easy to shoot:** Morton, *New English Canaan,* p. 193.

151   **"English and Indian hunters had 'now destroyed the breed'":** Trefethen, *American Crusade,* p. 32.

151   **Hornaday . . . pronounced them goners:** Trefethen, *American Crusade,* p. 252.

151   **first restoration efforts . . . failed:** Dickson, *Wild Turkey,* p. 11.

152   **smaller, quicker, and more wary:** Michael Gregonis, e-mail, January 8, 2009.

153   **Conservationists tried luring birds . . . and had some success:** Restoration efforts got a financial boost in 1937 when President Roosevelt signed into law the Pittman-Robertson Act, extending an excise tax on sporting firearms and ammunition and designating that the proceeds go to wildlife recovery and habitat restoration programs in which states put in 25 percent—money they got from the sale of hunting licenses.

153   **first "cannon net":** Jeanne M. Harold, "From Air Boats to Rain Gauges," *Fish*

and Wildlife News, National Wildlife Refuge System Centennial special edition, spring 2003, p. 23.

154 "There's a mystique to it . . .": James Earl Kennamer, interview, 2001.

154 crop damage by all wildlife in 1998: Michael R. Conover, *Resolving Human-Wildlife Conflicts: The Science of Wildlife Damage Management* (Boca Raton: Lewis Publishers, 2002), p. 108.

154 "I cannot guarantee it will work . . . seems to drive every wild animal insane": Tom Pelton, "Wild Turkeys' Rebound Irritates Some," *Baltimore Sun,* November 25, 2004.

155 turkeys were actually helping the grape grower: National Wild Turkey Federation, press release, quoted in Nadine Lymn, "Talking Turkey as Thanksgiving Approaches," Ecological Society of America blog, EcoTone, November 23, 2010.

155 "The turkeys are kind of guilty by association . . .": Pelton, "Wild Turkeys' Rebound."

156 the grape "a favorite fall food": Dickson, *Wild Turkey,* p. 75.

156 a threat to ginseng: Jeff Starck, "Gobblers Gain Ground in Wisconsin," *Wausau Daily Herald,* April 9, 2006.

156 "they do just great . . .": Glen Cole, interview, 2001.

157 "It's only a matter of time . . . from novelty to nuisance": Peggy Orenstein, "Nature, Nuisance or Worse?," *New York Times,* December 5, 2008.

157 any turkeys found . . . would be shot on sight: Rone Tempest, "Wild Turkey Killings in Yosemite Ruffle Feathers," *Los Angeles Times,* November 24, 2005.

159 "We are all the more surprised . . . threats to native ecosystems": Steve Hymon, "Park Agencies Squabble over Wild Turkeys," *Los Angeles Times,* May 4, 2002.

159 "This is a case of some zealots . . .": Hymon, "Park Agencies Squabble."

159 La Brea Tar Pits: Stephanie Chavez, "Turkey Hunters Seek Birds' Roots," *Los Angeles Times,* November 16, 2003.

159 proof . . . turkeys were California natives: National Wild Turkey Federation, press release, January 22, 2007.

160 five turkeys and 1,600 bullfrogs: Tempest, "Wild Turkey Killings." There were partisan groups for virtually every species in California, no matter how lowly or invasive. For example, non-native bullfrogs became established in Yosemite National Park because a Save-the-Bullfrog group bought them from Chinese food vendors in San Francisco and "liberated" them.

CHAPTER EIGHT: TEDDIES

161 "to hold hunters to their own standards": Wayne Pacelle, interview, 2004.

161 "junk hunting": Ibid.

164 "fair chase": Jim Posewitz, interview, 2004, and e-mail, May 5, 2009.

166 "As a general rule . . . killing a bear on sight": Jon Gambrel, "Arkansas Reclaims Its Status as the Bear State," Associated Press, April 24, 2009.

167 Roosevelt was hunting bears: Douglas Brinkley, *The Wilderness Warrior: Theodore Roosevelt and the Crusade for America* (New York: HarperCollins, 2009), pp. 438–41.

169   **Yellowstone National Park:** Mitman, *Reel Nature,* p. 90.

173   **"The end of the bait hunt . . . is the end of bear management":** Randy Cross, quoted in Misty Edgecomb, "Maine-Campaign Launched to Change Bear Hunt," *Bangor Daily News,* April 23, 2003.

174   **"a level much higher than Maine's citizens want or will tolerate":** James P. Sterba, "Loaded for Bear: Is It Sporting to Lure Prey with Pastries? In Two Big Hunting States, Banning Bait Is on Ballot; Maine Fears Bruin Boom," *Wall Street Journal,* October 28, 2004.

174   **Colorado example wouldn't work:** Jennifer Vashon, Maine Department of Inland Fisheries and Wildlife, June 21, 2004.

175   **"We have some devastating footage of bears in traps . . .":** Wayne Pacelle, interview, 2004.

175   **economic self-interest:** Guides and outfitters in northern Maine took out fishermen and hunters of moose and deer but counted on out-of-state bear hunters for most of their income—in 2004 they expected to receive two-thirds of their earnings from bear hunters. Hunters paid $1,100 to $1,600, on average, for up to a week's worth of lodging, meals, and hunting. Maine law required out-of-state hunters to hire a licensed Maine guide. State officials, including the governor, said a ban on hunting with bait would cost the state $62.4 million in annual income and seven hundred jobs.

176   **"Bears kill people . . .":** Dean E. Murphy, "More Encounters Between Bears and Humans at Yosemite," *New York Times,* December 22, 2002.

176   **"one of the most perfect films imaginable . . .":** Michael Dare, review of *The Bear,* also in *Santa Monica News,* 1989, www.dareland.com/smnews .htm#The%20Bear.

177   **fake nature:** Pauline Kael, review of *The Bear, New Yorker,* November 13, 1989.

177   **Alaskan brown bear:** Grizzly (or brown) bears were estimated at 200,000 worldwide: 120,000 in Russia, 30,000 in Alaska, 25,000 in Canada. A population of 1,000 to 1,200 grizzlies was making enough of a comeback in the Lower 48—actually in the Northwest—to keep ranchers and backpackers on their toes.

177   **"If Timothy models unsafe behavior . . .":** Rachel d'Oro, "Bear Expert and Companion Killed in Bear Attack at Alaska Park," Associated Press, October 7, 2003.

178   **"Tim may have seen . . . but all I can see is indifferent hunger":** Werner Herzog, *Grizzly Man,* 2008.

179   **People-bear conflicts grew apace:** A 2008 study by the Wildlife Conservation Society found that twelve bears tracked around Lake Tahoe over ten years weighed 30 percent more than bears in the wild because they ate abundant garbage but that all died younger because motor vehicles ran into them. Cubs were especially vulnerable to such crashes. "Because of an abundant food source—namely garbage—bears are being drawn in from backcountry areas into urbanized landscapes where they meet their demise," wrote the researchers. Jon P. Beckmann and Carl W. Lackey, "Carnivores, Urban Landscapes, and Longitudinal Studies: A Case History of Black Bears," *Human-Wildlife Conflicts* 2 (Fall 2008): 168–74.

179 **"anti-hunting absolutism"**: Peter Applebome, "Beasts Rearing Up on Two Legs," *New York Times,* May 18, 2005. Unlike Maine's dense conifer forests, New Jersey's forests are mainly mixed hardwoods with relatively open understories (deer helped keep them open in many areas) affording better visibility and longer sight lines. Thus, hunting with bait and dogs was considered to be unnecessary.

183 **"Oh, isn't he cute . . ,"**: Tom Shupe, interview, 2006.

183 **"They'll admit to illegal feeding . . ."**: Tom Shupe, interview, 2006.

CHAPTER NINE: DOERS TO VIEWERS

190 **"sham naturalists"**: Lutts, *Nature Fakers,* p. 42.

190 **"nature fakers"**: Ibid., p. 129.

190 **"If the child mind is fed with stories . . ."**: Mitman, *Reel Nature,* p. 12.

190 **"Poised at the intersection of art, science . . ."**: Mitman, *Reel Nature,* p. 6.

191 **"Just as Burroughs cautioned writers"**: *Reel Nature,* p. 12.

191 **This film and others did wonders to promote conservation**: Conservationists saw hunting with a camera as the worthy pursuit of scientific discovery, but often the resulting footage, however realistic, was slow-moving and boring. Hollywood wanted action it could exploit, not authenticity. It got such successes as *Among the Cannibal Isles of the South Pacific* (1918), in which a petite American woman turns up amid headhunters and people eaters. In *Simba,* a 1928 hit, Martin and Osa Johnson retreat to Africa to live among elephants, lions, and other beasts for four years. The film got the endorsement of the American Museum of Natural History for authenticity. But it also contained enough canned thrills and comic fare to appeal to a wider public, and the Johnsons gained celebrity with films in which elephants had names and African natives, stripped of their culture and dignity, became props for racist sight gags and were portrayed as lazy and inferior.

191 **"It has become perhaps . . ."**: Ralph H. Lutts, "The Trouble with Bambi: Walt Disney's *Bambi* and the American Vision of Nature," *Forest and Conservation History* 36 (1992): 160–171.

193 **"In sheltering young"**: *Reel Nature,* p. 141.

193 **"My grandfather grew up . . ."**: Roberts, *Mr. Rockefeller's Roads,* p. 5.

194 **"Getting a chicken ready . . ."**: Mildred Armstrong Kalish, *Little Heathens: Hard Times and High Spirits on an Iowa Farm During the Great Depression* (New York: Bantam, 2007), p. 112.

194 **dispatching bunnies**: Kalish, *Little Heathens,* p. 137.

196 **manure that filled the air of big cities**: Blamed for a cholera outbreak in 1849, pigs were in 1860 banished below Manhattan's Eighty-sixth Street. Eventually, New York became a pig-free zone. Horses stayed, pulling carriages and producing fifteen to thirty pounds of manure daily each. That manure was ferried to farms in Brooklyn, Queens, and beyond and was used to fertilize fields of vegetables, hay, and other crops.

196 **"It amazes me how naive urban folks are . . ."**: John Seewer, "Tempers Rise When Cultures Collide," Associated Press, October 18, 2003.

196 **"If you are thinking about moving to the country . . ."**: *If You Are Thinking*

about Moving to the Country, You May Want to Consider This (West Olive, MI: Ottawa County Planning Department, June 2003).

197   **Peet Packing Company:** Farmer Peet's owed its later fame in large part to ace pitcher Denny McLain, who went 31-6 in 1968 and helped the Detroit Tigers win the World Series. In 1997, McLain was sentenced to eight years in prison for looting the Peet employee pension fund.

199   **"We discovered nature's darker underbelly . . .":** Eleanor Agnew, *Back from the Land: How Young Americans Went to Nature in the 1970s, and Why They Came Back* (Chicago: Ivan R. Dee, 2004), p. 89.

199   **"You can imagine how upsetting . . .":** Ibid., p. 105.

200   **"We don't like exposure to nature . . .":** Bruce A. Seruton, "The 'Disney Effect' on Bears," *New Jersey Herald,* October 10, 2007.

200   **first fantasy environments:** Mark Gottdiener, *The Theming of America: American Dreams, Media Fantasies, and Themed Environments* (Boulder, CO: Westview Press, 2001), p. 5.

201   **"This rift has many causes . . .":** Gov. Mario M. Cuomo, speech, Lake Placid, Adirondack Park, 1993.

202   **"In the space of a century . . . to electronic detachment":** Richard Louv, *Last Child in the Woods: Saving Our Children from Nature-Deficit Disorder* (Chapel Hill, NC: Algonquin Books, 2005), p. 16.

204   **"a maximum of anthropomorphizing drama":** Mike Hale, "It's Beauty-and-the-Beast Time Again," *New York Times,* November 5, 2010.

205   **"I see nothing but road":** Jim Harrison, *The Woman Lit by Fireflies* (New York: Grove Press, 1990), p. 27.

CHAPTER TEN: ROADKILL

207   **"Omigod! That's it!":** Brewster Bartlett, interview, 2008.

210   **lobbyists for good roads:** Dan McNichol, *The Roads That Built America: The Incredible Story of the U.S. Interstate System* (New York: Sterling, 2006).

210   **"Humans have spread an enormous net . . .":** Richard T. T. Forman et al., *Road Ecology: Science and Solutions* (Washington, DC: Island Press, 2003), p. xiii.

211   **"an efficient personal and commercial network . . .":** Forman, *Road Ecology,* p. 27.

211   **U.S. road network was 3,997,456 miles long:** Forman, *Road Ecology,* p. 43.

212   **salt spread in winter:** New Hampshire pioneered the use of road salt to melt snow and ice in 1938.

212   **gourmet food that attracts seed eaters:** A woody shrub from Asia called thorny *Elaeagnus* was planted for years along medians in Virginia to reduce headlight glare. It produces a juicy red berry in early spring when flocks of an elegant songbird called the cedar waxwing are migrating north. The birds swoop in for berries and are hit by cars going seventy miles an hour. In 2001, researchers from the College of William and Mary collected more than 1,600 dead birds along two stretches of highway—more than 350 of them from one site in a single day.

213   **roadkill joke:** *A Prairie Home Companion,* "Joke Show," February 7, 2007.

213   **Berryman Institute:** Founded in 1990 to study the new but fast-growing field of

human-wildlife conflicts and ways of resolving them, the institute was funded by the U.S. Department of Agriculture's Wildlife Services Division and was named after a Utah man who devoted his career to state and federal wildlife agencies.

213 **estimates were shocking:** Michael R. Conover et al., "Review of Human Injuries, Illnesses, and Economic Losses Caused by Wildlife in the United States," *Wildlife Society Bulletin* 23, no. 3 (1995): 407–14.

214 **"There are few more dramatic manifestations . . .":** Johan T. du Toit, "Standardizing the Data on Wildlife-Vehicle Collisions," *Human-Wildlife Conflicts* 2, no. 1 (2008): 5–8.

214 **"dying on the side of the highway":** In densely populated states with relatively few hunters and large segments of the landscape off limits to most hunting, motor vehicles by mid-decade had approached or passed hunters as the number one cause of deer mortality. In 2005 in Connecticut, for example, hunters killed 12,663 deer. Reported deer-vehicle collisions killed 2,667 deer. But a two-year study by the state's Department of Environmental Protection found that for every vehicle-killed deer that was reported to the Wildlife Division, perhaps five more went unreported. If so, roadkill deer in 2005 could have numbered 16,002—or 3,339 more deer than hunters killed that year.

214 **People died too:** Conover et al., "Review of Human Injuries."

214 **few insurance companies were paying attention:** One company, the Erie Insurance Group, of Erie, Pennsylvania, was alert enough to see the trend through the normal noise of claims. Erie insured 1.8 million auto owners in eleven northeastern and midwestern states—in the heart of the white-tailed deer's historic range—and watched DVC claims double in seven years. In 1995, it paid out $21.6 million to settle 15,114 claims. In 2001, it paid $49.7 million in 26,735 claims. Karen Rugare, an Erie spokesperson, told me that deer claims were growing 15 to 20 percent a year, much faster than the 4 to 6 percent growth in earnings from new insurance sales—a worrisome trend for any insurer.

214 **update in 2012:** Michael Conover, e-mail, February 15, 2012.

215 **"We joke . . . that the only deer predator left is a Chevy pickup":** As roadkill pickup expenses grew, states began to balk at paying them. In 2001, Wisconsin, which had over ninety thousand DVCs—more than any other state—ended a $575,000-a-year roadkill removal budget. New Jersey's Department of Transportation ended pickups in 2006, saving $1 million annually. In 2002, Ohio set up four 12-by-12-foot bins for making deer compost. "It's like a slow cooker," said a Ohio state garage manager. "It smells like pork chops." Composting caught on fast. Montana started doing it in 2003 after grizzly bears began turning up to feast on roadkill discarded by roadsides and dead livestock on the range. "Cooking piles" were built on asphalt pads with layers of watered wood chips and carcasses. By 2009, New York State had set up forty-two cooking piles for twenty-five thousand deer annually. Dead raccoons, opossums, coyotes, groundhogs, and other roadkill went in too. Jean Bonhotal, of the Cornell Waste Management Institute, told me it took carcasses a year to decompose into usable compost.

215 **impact of collisions spoils much of the meat:** Tim Bontecou interview, 2010.

215   **When moose or elk are hit:** Dr. Marcel Huijser, an engineer with the Western Transportation Institute at Montana State University in Bozeman, told me in 2009 that while every DVC cost society $6,617 ($2,622 for repairs, $2,702 for treatment of human injuries, $1,002 for human fatalities, $125 for towing and law enforcement investigation), the cost of hitting an elk was $17,483 and the cost for a moose was $30,760. Hitting a 150-pound deer might result in a crumpled fender and a broken windshield, or even a totaled car. But hitting a 1,000-pound moose is like being run over by an eighteen-wheeler and is often fatal to the driver. Maine, with a moose population estimated at 29,000, averages 800 moose-vehicle crashes a year. New Hampshire's moose herd, estimated at 6,000 and counting, resulted in 198 collisions in 2007.

216   **people in other countries:** Richard Forman, interview, 2010.

217   **"underestimating the numbers":** Bill Ruediger, interview, 2002.

CHAPTER ELEVEN: FEATHERED FRIENDS

220   **he bolted upright:** Betsey Colwell, president of Droll Yankees, e-mail, December 5, 2002.

221   **bread crumbs for birds:** Cronon, *Nature's Metropolis,* pp. 376–77. The demise of home bread crumbs began in 1871 in Minneapolis, when a French invention called the "middlings purifier" was installed in a flour mill to process the hard spring wheat grown on the northern plains. Before then, rollers had cracked the tough wheat kernel, darkening the flour, and the germ oil inside had turned the flour rancid. But the purifier simply blew off the kernels and germ, leaving pure white flour. Associated with wealth, white flour and white bread—although robbed of nutritional value—became hits. Wonder Bread, white, sliced and soft-crusted, was born in 1921. It and its ilk were cheap, convenient, and modern, contributing to the decline in home bread making and the inevitable bread crumbs.

222   **"Just as a [Disney] True-Life Adventure . . .":** Mitman, *Reel Nature,* p. 126.

223   **"stool pigeons":** Trefethen, *American Crusade,* pp. 63–64.

224   **"Of all the meat-shooters . . .":** William T. Hornaday, *Our Vanishing Wild Life: Its Extermination and Preservation* (New York: New York Zoological Society, 1913), pp. 63–64.

224   **"The great increase in the slaughter of song birds . . .":** Hornaday, *Our Vanishing Wild Life,* p. x.

225   **first bird rights speech:** Brinkley, *Wilderness Warrior,* p. 358.

225   **"PLEADING FOR THE BIRDS":** *New York Times,* June 3, 1900.

226   **feathered skins of 1,600 hummingbirds . . . for bonnets:** Hornaday, *Our Vanishing Wild Life,* p. 116.

228   **packaged seeds for caged canaries and parrots:** By 2008, Americans kept 16 million caged birds ranging from finches and canaries to large parrots and macaws. Globally, the capture, smuggling, and sale of exotic birds threatened and endangered many species.

229   **Surveying nonconsumptive outdoor activities:** Dian Olson Belanger and Adrian Kinnane, *Managing American Wildlife: A History of the International As-*

sociation of Fish and Wildlife Agencies (Rockville, MD: Montrose Press, 2002), p. 99.

230 **adulterate their blends:** Cole's Wild Bird Products, "Bird Seed Myths," 2007, www.coleswildbird.com/facts-and-fiction.php: "The most common way for companies to add 'vitamins' to their product is to simply coat it with mineral oil and add crushed rock. Current regulations allow a manufacturer to list the nutritional components of mineral oil (iron, zinc) and crushed rock (Vitamin A, calcium carbonate) separately, which can make the birdseed ingredients look more impressive than they really are. Adding mineral oil also makes it look shiny and helps to hide dirt and dust, and of course, the crushed rock adds weight to the final product."

232 **Clinton reminded Babbitt:** Bruce Babbitt, interview, 2010.

232 **bird feeding had become a huge industry:** Hall, *2006 National Survey,* pp. 36–37.

232 **"If you are just beginning to feed Song Birds . . .":** "Wild Birds: Backyard Enthusiast: Beginner," 2008, Kaytee, www.kaytee.com/wild-birds/backyard-enthusiast/beginner.htm.

233 **"wild bird cuisine":** Red River Commodities, "Boutique Collection," www.valleysplendor.com/Boutique.aspx.

233 **"From their purely esthetical value . . .":** John W. Fitzpatrick, letter, December 27, 2002.

234 **"Birds in decline don't come to feeders":** Carrol Henderson, interview, 2010.

235 **"I hate to sound cynical, but . . .":** Alan Huot, interview, 2002.

235 **"The first thing I tell people . . .":** Bob Noonan, interview, 2002.

236 **an infected bird . . . can leave its disease for the next customers:** The western house finch was released from pet shops on Long Island in the 1940s. House finch conjunctivitis, caused by a bacterium, *Mycoplasma gallisepticum,* was first spotted in the East in the winter of 1993. It causes the birds' eyes to get encrusted and swell shut, and then most die of starvation or predation. Visiting feeders, infected finches spread the disease. Feeding defenders say the epidemic would have spread even without feeders because the population lacked genetic diversity, which probably increased its vulnerability. In any case, house finch populations dropped an estimated 60 percent in the East because of it.

236 **"It rarely happens . . .":** Jason Rogers, e-mail, November 11, 2005.

237 **"bird feeding is not having a broad-scale negative impact":** Erica H. Dunn and Diane L. Tessaglia-Hymes, *Birds at Your Feeder: A Guide to Feeding Habitats, Behavior, Distribution and Abundance* (1999; repr., New York: W. W. Norton, 2001), p. 15.

237 **"Bottom line: there is not a shred of solid evidence . . .":** John W. Fitzpatrick, e-mail, January 13, 2003.

237 **half of all birds die in any year anyway:** The U.S. Fish and Wildlife Service estimates that a spring U.S. bird population of some 10 billion grows by fall to perhaps 20 billion. If half die, that's up to 10 billion deaths. Of those, deaths caused by people and their infrastructure are variously estimated: window strikes, 97 million to 976 million; communications towers, 40 million to 50

million; roadkill, 60 million; power transmission lines, 174 million; pesticides, 72 million. Feeder deaths weren't estimated. But if the 60 million adults who feed birds are responsible for 10 deaths, for a total of 600 million dead birds, using the high mortality estimates, people and their infrastructures (including feeders) might cause 19 percent of all bird deaths annually. U.S. Fish and Wildlife Service, "Migratory Bird Mortality," January 2002, www.fws.gov/birds/mortality-fact-sheet.pdf.

237   **"We could make the same argument . . .":** Bob Noonan, interview, 2002.

CHAPTER TWELVE: FERAL FELINES

239   **an ammonia-like smell:** Office for Science and Society, McGill University, "Why Does Cat Urine Smell So Bad and What Can I Do About It?" 2003, http://oss.mcgill.ca/yasked/caturine.pdf.

239   **keep down the smell:** George Plitt, a 1932 agriculture graduate of the State University of New York, is credited with creating the first commercial cat box filler made of wood ashes and bagged and sold as Kleen Kitty.

240   **young navy veteran:** "Edward Lowe, Creator of Kitty Litter, Succumbs in Sarasota After Surgery for Cerebral Hemorrhage," *Allentown Morning Call,* October 7, 1995.

240   **"Kitty Litter":** Andrew Kantor, "Non-Tech High Tech Litters the Landscape," *USA Today,* December 10, 2004.

240   **promoting Kitty Litter at pet shows:** Lowe volunteered to clean cat boxes. But instead of scooping out sand or sawdust coated with urine and feces, he would dismissively dump out all its contents and refill it with Kitty Litter. At pet stores, he would take out a whisky shot glass, fill it partway with Kitty Litter, and add water. While he delivered his sales pitch, the water vanished into the clay. Lowe left a shot glass and a small bag of Kitty Litter with each store so the owner could perform the stunt for customers.

241   **"We were still selling plain dirt in a bag":** Med Cox, "When Kitty Needs to Go Freshen Up, Technology Is Ready—Cat Litter, Once Mere Sand, Has Entered a New Era of Laboratories and Hype," *Wall Street Journal,* February 15, 1984.

241   **In 1985, cats passed dogs:** Linda Williams, "One Industry That Certainly Isn't in Danger of Going to the Dogs Is the One That Caters to the Needs of Cats," *Los Angeles Times,* November 28, 1988.

241   **Americans kept 86.4 million cats:** American Pet Products Manufacturers Association, *2010–11 APPMA National Pet Owners Survey* (Greenwich, CT: APPMA, 2011).

243   **"I could have been selling real estate on Mars":** Susan Weiss, interview, 2002.

243   **"Cat lifestyle products . . .":** Scott and Ann Springer, "Cat Owners Seek Out High-End Products," *Pet Product News,* April 2005.

245   **they didn't want the amount of killing they were doing to be known:** National Council on Pet Population Study and Policy, "The Shelter Statistics Survey, 1994-97," www.petpopulation.org/statsurvey.html.

246   **"more hoax than fact":** Maria L. LaGanga, "A Painful Debate for Animal Lovers," *Los Angeles Times,* August 27, 1997.

249   **he trapped 370 cats:** During the same six months in the apartment complex,

some six hundred opossums, raccoons, and skunks were caught in Spiecker's traps. He trucked them to isolated areas and released them.

250   **euthanized annually at animal shelters:** Julie K. Levy and P. Cynda Crawford, "Humane Strategies for Controlling Feral Cat Populations," *JAVMA* 225, no. 9 (2004): 1357.

250   **Nobody knows how many feral cats exist:** Levy and Crawford, "Humane Strategies," p. 1355.

252   **Ellen Perry Berkeley . . . an advocate of the TNR method:** Ellen Perry Berkeley, *TNR: Past, Present and Future: A History of the Trap-Neuter-Return Movement* (Washington, DC: Alley Cat Allies, 2004). TNR gained attention in the 1960s when a former British model, Celia Hammond, began garnering publicity for it, Berkeley wrote. By the early 1980s, Hammond had observed "many hundreds of neutered colonies" with stable populations "without any detrimental effect whatsoever" to their surroundings.

252   **had become a "movement":** Berkeley, *TNR*, p. 1.

253   **more than 360 feral cat protection groups:** Alley Cat Allies spokesperson, e-mail, February 29, 2012, www.alleycat.org.

254   **some residents . . . had gotten fed up:** Vance Trively, interview, August 20, 2010.

254   **"I have had several of our residents call . . .":** *Mayor's Newsletter,* February 2008.

255   **Word spread fast:** David Earlywine, e-mail, September 10, 2010. Earlywine, a resident, had earlier set up the Randolph Community Network, a website on which people could voice their opinions. When he got the mayor's newsletter, he read it and tore it up, thinking the bounty was a dumb idea. A few days later he fished the letter out of the trash, taped it back together, and scanned it onto the website for comment. Suddenly, the website lit up with thousands of hits, and e-mails poured in. "There were some pretty upset people out there," he told me.

255   **"absolutely barbaric and ludicrous":** Alley Cat Allies, "Alley Cat Allies Expresses Outrage at Iowa Town's 'Bounty' on Outdoor Cats," press release, March 12, 2008, http://world-wire.com/news/0803120001.html.

255   **"animal neglect":** Becky Robinson, president, Alley Cat Allies, letter to Dr. David Schmitt, Iowa state veterinarian, March 13, 2008.

255   **"The world is watching . . .":** Alley Cat Allies, "Alley Cat Allies Welcomes Decision by Iowa Town to Repeal 'Bounty' on Cats," press release, March 14, 2008.

256   **Then a problem arose:** Use of the word *bounty* had focused a national spotlight on Randolph, creating a rare moment—as in the aftermath of a hurricane, an earthquake, or a tsunami—when donors respond generously. Each of the groups involved in the Randolph Rescue Project—Feline Friendz of Omaha, the Raccoon Valley Animal Shelter in Des Moines, Hearts United for Animals in Auburn, Nebraska, and Best Friends from Utah—solicited donations on their websites to help Randolph's cats. The spotlight created a unique chance to showcase TNR by setting up and carrying out a model TNR effort for other towns to emulate, thus spreading the philosophy. Or so they thought. On April 4, the first twenty-nine cats either trapped or turned in by their owners

had been examined, vaccinated, spayed or neutered, implanted with microchip IDs, and returned to Randolph. "That's when the shit hit the fan," Joseph Pundzak, of Raccoon Valley, told me. Mayor Trively didn't want the cats back around his shed. A shouting match erupted. "He was so stubborn," said Larry Shackman, of Feline Friendz. "It was an ugly situation," Laurie Cook, of Feline Friendz, told me. She said her group's workers felt betrayed. They quit. Shelly Kotter, of Best Friends, sided with the mayor, saying that in some cases, relocation should be considered. Kotter accused the others of "demonizing the town," and "totally alienating town officials." She said they were more interested in making the mayor look bad than in helping the cats. "Limiting themselves to such stringent rules may not always be in the cats' best interest," she said. In this case, relocation "was a good thing for the cats." Kotter told me that TNR was a tough sell in small towns. It took compromise and small steps to bring people with no understanding of the concept to accept it, she said. Once a feral cat overpopulation problem arose, it was difficult for many people to understand why they didn't simply get rid of the cats. If killing them was not acceptable, then moving them certainly was. Taking them away and then bringing them back didn't make sense. Indeed, bringing back the same cats that were causing problems—now sterilized, vaccinated, and healthy—seemed to be the height of folly to many people.

256   **"It's all the rage . . . And it doesn't work":** Ted Williams, "Felines Fatales," *Audubon* magazine, September-October 2009.

256   **"neither endorses nor opposes . . .":** American Veterinary Medical Association, "AVMA Policy: Free-Roaming Abandoned and Feral Cats," revised June 2009, www.avma.org/issues/policy/animal_welfare/feral_cats.asp.

257   **If every pet vet volunteered:** Most don't volunteer, or if they do, it is for one-time or occasional sterilization campaigns. The median wage for all vets in 2008 was about $80,000, according to the Bureau of Labor Statistics. Most of them do not like to work for free. Spaying females normally costs $60 to $200, and castrating males from $40 to $100. Operating rooms might cost a surgical vet $200 an hour. The biggest problem TNR projects have is finding vets who will perform these surgeries at a discount, at cost, or for free.

257   **cheaper to trap-neuter-return all feral cats:** John Dunham and Associates, "The Fiscal Impact of Trap, Neuter and Return Policies in Controlling Feral Cat Populations in the United States," March 4, 2010, www.guerrillaeconomics.biz/communitycats/methodology.pdf.

257   **"The study appears to be . . . determined by the conclusion desired":** R. Scott Nolen, "Economic Study Estimates Costs of Feral Cat Control," *JAVMA News,* June 1, 2010.

257   **euthanasia costs . . . cut in half:** Brent Martin, letter to the editor, *JAVMA News,* August 1, 2010.

258   **carbon monoxide euthanasia chambers:** Jack W. Zimmerly, e-mail, August 21, 2010.

258   **thus thwarting TNR's ultimate objective:** Patrick Foley, Janet E. Foley, Julie K. Levy, and Terry Paik, "Analysis of the Impact of Trap-Neuter-Return Programs on Populations of Feral Cats," *JAVMA,* December 1, 2005. Mathematical

models indicate that 71 to 94 percent of cats in a colony must be neutered for a population decline, assuming no in-migration. A ten-year, countywide TNR effort in San Diego resulted in no population decline. A seven-year program in Alachua County, Florida, resulted in an increase. Critics call this proof that TNR doesn't work to lower populations, but Dr. Julie Levy, who was involved in both, said they didn't show failure; rather, TNR "simply needs to be practiced on a larger scale."

258   **new cats move in:** In 2002, Linda Winter of the American Bird Conservancy told the 2002 AVMA's convention that TNR advocates propagate six myths: (1) feral cat colonies die out in one or two years from attrition (it takes many years and occurs only if no new cats join); (2) the purpose of TNR is to eliminate cat colonies (proponents really want to stabilize and maintain them); (3) eradication doesn't work because cats have an "ecological niche" (remove the cats and their food, and the niche disappears); (4) cats are territorial and will prevent outside cats from joining their colony (false, according to several scientific studies); (5) well-fed cats don't kill wildlife (yes they do, for practice, habit, or recreation if not for food); (6) TNR is more humane than euthanasia (TNR prolongs traumatic, disease-filled lives).

258   **"I got the same line. . . . It's rubbish":** T. Williams, "Felines Fatales."

258   **"Feral cats . . . live healthy, natural lives":** Alley Cat Allies, "Truth Cards," 2009, available from www.alleycat.org.

259   **"Unfortunately, most of these cats will suffer . . .":** American Veterinary Medical Association, "AVMA Policy."

259   **killing birds and small animals:** False claims by TNR advocates go unchallenged by scientists, wrote three biologists in a 2009 article, "perhaps in part because TNR has been approached largely as an animal welfare issue instead of being recognized as a broad environmental issue with a range of impacts on species conservation, the physical environment, and human health. Conservation scientists and advocates must properly identify the environmental implications of feral cat management and actively engage this issue to bring scientific information to the attention of policy makers." Travis Longcore, Catherine Rich, and Lauren M. Sullivan, "Critical Assessment of Claims Regarding Management of Feral Cats by Trap-Neuter-Return," *Conservation Biology* 23 (2009): 887–94.

259   **"These free-roaming abandoned and feral cats . . .":** American Veterinary Medical Association, "AVMA Policy."

259   **"Wild animals are . . . maimed, mauled, dismembered":** David A. Jessup, "The Welfare of Feral Cats and Wildlife," *JAVMA* 225, no. 9 (2004): 1378.

260   **invasive species on the planet:** Not long ago, I attended a garden party at an old farm in upstate New York, where guests helped themselves to wine and a luncheon buffet. It was a jolly gathering, with much laughing and talking as people took places around outdoor tables. Then, one by one, they fell silent. The attention of, first, one guest, then another and another, was drawn to a spot on the lawn, not one hundred feet away, near a flower bed. There a chipmunk went about its business unaware of a black and white cat slowly coming up from behind in a stalking crouch. It was a sunny June afternoon, but the merriment

evaporated as attention riveted to the drama in the grass. The cat moved in. The chipmunk finally saw it, but too late. "Oh my God," a woman gasped. The cat pounced on the little rodent, then backed up and watched. The chipmunk, seemingly disoriented, made a dash for the flower bed. The cat cut it off. The chipmunk veered sideways. The cat leapt into its path and pounced again. This time the chipmunk appeared hurt. The cat pawed it as if it were a ball of string. Finally, a guest got up and ran toward the two creatures. The cat fled in the direction of the barn, its home. The chipmunk, hurt but still mobile, made it to the flower bed and into its hole.

260   **likened cat predation . . . to the overuse of pesticides:** Pamela Jo Hatley, "Will Feral Cats Silence Spring in Your Town?" May 2004, www.pamelajohatley.com/Articles/ABA.pdf.

260   **"TNR is a symptom of the gross ecological illiteracy . . .":** T. Williams, "Felines Fatales."

261   **two very different worlds:** Col. Paul L. Barrows, e-mail, September 14, 2002.

262   **"few veterinarians know anything beyond the Discovery Channel . . .":** Colin M. Gillin, e-mail, August 19, 2010.

263   **"flawed data and faulty logic":** Alley Cat Allies, "Tell City Council: We Want Trap-Neuter-Return Back!" quoted in The Foothills Forum, www.thefoothillsforum.com/forum/viewtopic.php?f=19&t=5712, posting February 12, 2010.

263   **"From a wildlife agency perspective . . . as illegal as poisoning":** Jessup, "Welfare of Feral Cats," p. 1381.

263   **After his 1993 study:** J. S. Coleman and S. A. Temple, "Rural Residents' Free-Ranging Domestic Cats: A Survey," *Wildlife Society Bulletin* 21: 381–90.

264   **"Questions regarding the value or inutility of the domestic cat . . .":** Edward Howe Forbush, *The Domestic Cat: Bird Killer, Mouser and Destroyer of Wild Life, Means of Utilizing and Controlling It* (Boston: Commonwealth of Massachusetts, State Board of Agriculture, 1916), p. 3.

264   **professional sniper was hired:** T. Gilbert Pearson, *Bird-Lore Magazine,* July-August 1910, p. 174.

264   **"We killed every cat that was found . . .":** Hornaday, *Our Vanishing Wild Life,* p. 73.

265   **shooting feral cats:** Trudy Sharp and Glen Saunders, *Ground Shooting of Feral Cats* (Sydney: New South Wales Department of Primary Industries, January 10, 2004), www.dpi.nsw.gov.au/__data/assets/pdf_file/0003/57234/cat-001.pdf.

265   **shooting as a humane method:** American Veterinary Medical Association, AVMA Guidelines on Euthanasia, June 2007, www.avma.org/issues/animal_welfare/euthanasia.pdf, p. 13.

265   **"It reflects the attitudes of people . . .":** Kate Murphy, "Judge Declares a Mistrial in Texas Cat Killing Case," *New York Times,* November 17, 2007.

265   **Cats hunt mainly with their ears:** Dennis C. Turner and Patrick Bateson, *The Domestic Cat: The Biology of Its Behavior* (1988; repr., Cambridge: Cambridge University Press, 2000), p. 152.

267   **"most serious enemies of the bobwhite quail":** Herbert L. Stoddard, *The Bobwhite Quail: Its Habits, Preservation and Increase* (Washington, DC: U.S.

Biological Survey, 1931), p. 8. Stoddard was a friend of Aldo Leopold and a pioneering conservationist who reintroduced regular woods burning to maintain the pine-wiregrass landscape much as Indians had done as a management tool. At the time, his ideas were controversial because they contradicted prevailing campaigns for fire suppression. But he showed that burning benefited the trees and enhanced habitat for quail, in part by reducing predator hideouts. He went on to help found the Tall Timbers Research Station, which was devoted to the study of fire ecology.

267 **hear baby chicks pecking:** Stoddard, *Bobwhite Quail,* p. 190.

EPILOGUE

270 **full of places to hide and reproduce:** In a 2006 interview, Ed Carrow, of Orlando Critter Control, told me: "A raccoon lives in a hole in a dead tree. So do I, only my dead tree has been cut into lumber and turned into a house, and that house is full of holes. It can hold a lot more raccoons than your average dead tree in the [nearby] Ocala National Forest." Garbage cans and bird feeders provide food. Air-conditioning unit drip trays are a handy source of water.

270 **conflicts would mount:** David Foster et al., "Wildlife Dynamics in the Changing New England Landscape," *Journal of Biogeography* 29 (2002): 1351.

271 **"By this time tomorrow . . . tumble into extinction":** Tom Knudson, "Green Machine: Mission Adrift in a Frenzy of Fund Raising," *Sacramento Bee,* April 23, 2001. This Rainforest Alliance pitch was deconstructed by Pulitzer Prize–winning journalist Tom Knudson: "Fact: No one knows how rapidly species are going extinct. The Alliance's figure is an extreme estimate that counts tropical beetles and other insects—including ones not yet known to science—in its definition of wildlife."

272 **species . . . known to be threatened:** International Union for Conservation of Nature, "The IUCN Red List of Threatened Species," www.iucnredlist.org/, table 2.

272 **U.S. Fish and Wildlife Service . . . endangered species list:** U.S. Fish and Wildlife Service, "Endangered Species Program," www.fws.gov/endangered/.

274 **"It would be wonderful if we could all get along . . .":** Michael Hutchins, "Animal Rights and Conservation," *Conservation Biology* 22, no. 4 (2008): 815–16.

275 **"What we know . . . a major train wreck for deer-human conflicts":** Terry Messmer, e-mail, November 10, 2010.

276 **selling the venison at local farmers' markets:** Bryon P. Shissler, e-mail, August 14, 2007.

277 **wild venison is "free-range":** Steve Rinella, "Locavore, Get Your Gun," *New York Times,* December 14, 2007.

278 **a diverse group:** Jon P. Beckmann et al., *Safe Passages: Highways, Wildlife, and Habitat Connectivity* (Washington, DC: Island Press, 2010).

280 **"Nutria-Palooza":** Anna Jane Grossman, "Nutria-Palooza: Is Their Pest Your Clean Conscience?" *New York Times,* November 18, 2010.

281 **"why not make something beautiful out of them":** Ibid.

282 **euthanizing, kill-trapping—and shooting:** Aaron M. Hildreth, Stephen M.

Vantassel, and Scott E. Hygnstrom, *Feral Cats and Their Management* (Lincoln: University of Nebraska Extension, 2010), p. 5.

282   **"barbaric and utterly disturbing"**: Alley Cat Allies, "Alley Cat Allies Fires Back at the University of Nebraska," *Alley Cat Allies E-News,* December 2010.

282   **"biased" and "thinly veiled advocacy"**: Best Friends Animal Society news release, "Nebraska Circular Advocating Killing Cats Based on Poor Science, Best Friends Says," December 3, 2010.

282   **"must-read"**: American Bird Conservancy, "New Report Puts Economic Impact of Feral Cat Predation on Birds at $17 Billion," media release, December 1, 2010, www.abcbirds.org/newsandreports/releases/101208.html.

282   **"The political power of wildlife advocates . . ."**: T. Williams, "Felines Fatales."

282   **coyote population in greater Chicago**: Stanley D. Gehrt, *Urban Coyote Ecology and Management: The Cook County, Illinois, Coyote Project,* Bulletin 929 (Columbus: Ohio State University Extension, 2006).

282   **"It's not just us encroaching . . . they're encroaching on us"**: Sam Dolnick, "Coyote Attacks Put a Suburb on the Alert," *New York Times,* July 2, 2010.

283   **"we'll kill you"**: Rob Erickson, interview, July 2010, and Bob Noonan, e-mail, July 5, 2010.

283   **FBI's investigation was "ongoing"**: Tom Meloni, interview, October 21, 2010.

283   **"full control techniques . . ."**: "Coyote Policy: City of Wheaton," November 15, 2010, www.wheaton.il.us/WorkArea/DownloadAsset.aspx?id=6066, p. 12.

284   **turning out locavores**: Jessica Prentice coined the word in 2005 to challenge San Francisco Bay Area residents to eat things grown in their own "foodshed," or within a hundred-mile radius.

284   **"Once upon a time . . ."**: Brian Donahue, *Reclaiming the Commons: Community Farms and Forests in a New England Town* (New Haven: Yale University Press, 1999), p. 2.

284   **"It is good for children . . ."**: Brian Donahue, interview, 2005.

285   **"Do the residents of Park Avenue want to look out the window at vegetables?"**: William E. Geist, " 'Undesirables' on Park Avenue," *New York Times,* February 28, 1984.

287   **"Angelo hunts deer . . ."**: Michael Pollan, *The Omnivore's Dilemma: A Natural History of Four Meals* (New York: Penguin Press, 2006), p. 338.

290   **"As long as the global consequences of consumption are ignored . . ."**: Mary M. Berlik, David B. Kittredge, and David R. Foster, *The Illusion of Preservation: A Global Environmental Argument for the Local Production of Natural Resources* (Petersham, MA: Harvard Forest, 2002).

290   **"vision" for managing**: David R. Foster et al., *Wildlands and Woodlands: A Vision for the Forests of Massachusetts* (Petersham, MA: Harvard Forest, 2005).

291   **rare second chance**: Ibid.

BIBLIOGRAPHY

Achenbach, Joel. *The Grand Idea*. New York: Simon & Schuster, 2004.

Agnew, Eleanor. *Back from the Land: How Young Americans Went to Nature in the 1970s, and Why They Came Back*. Chicago: Ivan R. Dee, 2004.

Albion, Robert. *Forests and Sea Power: The Timber Problem of the Royal Navy, 1652–1862*. Cambridge, MA: Harvard University Press, 1926.

Ambrose, Stephen E. *Undaunted Courage: Meriwether Lewis, Thomas Jefferson, and the Opening of the American West*. New York: Simon & Schuster, 1996.

American Pet Products Manufacturers Association. *2010–2011 APPMA National Pet Owners Survey*. Greenwich, CT: American Pet Products Manufacturers Association, 2011.

Baker, B. W., and E. P. Hill. *Wild Mammals of North America: Biology, Management and Conservation*. 2nd ed. Baltimore: Johns Hopkins University Press, 2003.

Beckmann, Jon P., Anthony P. Clevenger, Marcel P. Huijser, and Jodi A. Hilty. *Safe Passages: Highways, Wildlife, and Habitat Connectivity*. Washington, DC: Island Press, 2010.

Beckmann, Jon P., and Carl W. Lackey. "Carnivores, Urban Landscapes, and Longitudinal Studies: A Case History of Black Bears." *Human-Wildlife Conflicts* 2 (Fall 2008): 168–74.

Belanger, Dian, and Adrian Kinnane. *Managing American Wildlife: A History of the International Association of Fish and Wildlife Agencies*. Rockville, MD: Montrose Press, 2002.

Belanger, Pamela J. *Inventing Acadia: Artists and Tourists at Mount Desert*. Rockland, ME: Farnsworth Art Museum, 1999.

Berkeley, Ellen Perry. *TNR: Past, Present and Future: A History of the Trap-Neuter-Return Movement*. Washington, DC: Alley Cat Allies, 2004.

Berlik, Mary M., David B. Kittredge, and David R. Foster. *The Illusion of Preservation: A Global Environmental Argument for the Local Production of Natural Resources*. Petersham, MA: Harvard Forest, 2002.

Botkin, Daniel B. *Discordant Harmonies: A New Ecology for the Twenty-first Century.* New York: Oxford University Press, 1990.

Brinkley, Douglas. *The Wilderness Warrior: Theodore Roosevelt and the Crusade for America.* New York: HarperCollins, 2009.

Brooks, David. *Bobos in Paradise: The New Upper Class and How They Got There.* New York: Simon & Schuster, 2000.

Bruegmann, Robert. *Sprawl: A Compact History.* Chicago: University of Chicago Press, 2005.

Bunker, Nick. *Making Haste from Babylon: The Mayflower Pilgrims and Their World.* New York: Alfred A. Knopf, 2010.

Bunting, W. H. *A Day's Work: A Sampler of Historic Maine Photographs, 1860–1920.* Gardiner, ME: Tilbury House, 1997.

Carson, Rachel. *Silent Spring.* Cambridge, MA: Riverside Press, 1962.

Cartmill, Matt. *A View to Death in the Morning: Hunting and Nature Through History.* Cambridge, MA: Harvard University Press, 1993.

Catton, Bruce. *Michigan: A History.* New York: W. W. Norton, 1976.

Conkling, Philip W. *Islands in Time: A Natural and Human History of the Islands of Maine.* Camden, ME: Down East Books, 1981.

Conover, Michael R. *Resolving Human-Wildlife Conflicts: The Science of Wildlife Damage Management.* Boca Raton: Lewis Publishers, 2002.

Conover, M. R., W. C. Pitt, K. K. Kessler, T. J. DuBow, and W. A. Sanborn. "Review of Human Injuries, Illnesses, and Economic Losses Caused by Wildlife in the United States." *Wildlife Society Bulletin* 23, no. 3 (1995): 407–14.

Cronon, William. *Changes in the Land: Indians, Colonists, and the Ecology of New England.* New York: Hill and Wang, 1983.

———. *Nature's Metropolis: Chicago and the Great West.* New York: W. W. Norton, 1991.

———. *Uncommon Ground: Rethinking the Human Place in Nature.* New York: W. W. Norton, 1996.

Curtis, Paul D., and Kristi L. Sullivan. *White-Tailed Deer.* Wildlife Damage Management Fact Sheet Series. Ithaca, NY: Cornell University Wildlife Publications, 2006.

Dempsey, Dave. *Ruin and Recovery: Michigan's Rise as a Conservation Leader.* Ann Arbor: University of Michigan Press, 2001.

D'Este, Carlos. *Patton: A Genius for War.* New York: HarperCollins, 1995.

DeStefano, Stephen. *Coyote at the Kitchen Door: Living with Wildlife in Suburbia.* Cambridge, MA: Harvard University Press, 2010.

Dickmann, Donald I., and Larry A. Leefers. *The Forests of Michigan.* Ann Arbor: University of Michigan Press, 2003.

Dickson, James G., ed. *The Wild Turkey: Biology and Management.* Mechanicsburg, PA: Stackpole Books, 1992.

Dizard, Jan E. *Going Wild: Hunting, Animal Rights, and the Contested Meaning of Nature*. Amherst: University of Massachusetts Press, 1999.

Dolin, Eric Jay. *Fur, Fortune, and Empire: The Epic History of the Fur Trade in America*. New York: W. W. Norton, 2010.

Donahue, Brian. *The Great Meadow: Farmers and the Land in Colonial Concord*. New Haven: Yale University Press, 2004.

———. *Reclaiming the Commons: Community Farms and Forests in a New England Town*. New Haven: Yale University Press, 1999.

Dunlap, Thomas R. *Saving America's Wildlife: Ecology and the American Mind, 1850–1990*. Princeton: Princeton University Press, 1988.

Dunn, Erica H., and Diane L. Tessaglia-Hymes. *Birds at Your Feeder: A Guide to Feeding Habitats, Behavior, Distribution and Abundance*. 1999. Reprint, New York: W. W. Norton, 2001.

Du Toit, Johan T. "Standardizing the Data on Wildlife-Vehicle Collisions." *Human-Wildlife Conflicts* 2, no. 1 (2008): 5–8.

Eliot, Charles W., II. *The Future of Mount Desert Island*. Bar Harbor, ME: Bar Harbor Village Improvement Association, 1928.

Emerson, George B. *Report on the Trees and Shrubs Growing Naturally in the Forests of Massachusetts*. Springfield, MA: Botanical Survey, 1923.

Environmental Protection Agency. *2008 Report on the Environment*. Washington, DC: Center for Environmental Assessment, 2008. http://cfpub.epa.gov/eroe/index.cfm?fuseaction=list.listBySubTopic&ch=46&s=343.

Fedkiw, John, Douglas W. MacCleery, and V. Alaric Sample. *Pathway to Sustainability: Defining the Bounds on Forest Management*. Durham, NC: Forest Historical Society, 2004.

Foglesong, Richard E. *Married to the Mouse: Walt Disney World and Orlando*. New Haven: Yale University Press, 2001.

Forbush, Edward Howe. *The Domestic Cat: Bird Killer, Mouser and Destroyer of Wild Life; Means of Utilizing and Controlling It*. Boston: Commonwealth of Massachusetts, State Board of Agriculture, 1916.

Forman, Richard T. T., Daniel Sperling, John A. Bissonette, Anthony P. Clevenger, Carol D. Cutshall, Virginia H. Dale, Lenore Fahrig, et al. *Road Ecology: Science and Solutions*. Washington, DC: Island Press, 2003.

Foster, David R. *Thoreau's Country: Journey Through a Transformed Landscape*. Cambridge, MA: Harvard University Press, 1999.

Foster, David R., and John D. Aber. *Forests in Time: The Environmental Consequences of 1,000 Years of Change in New England*. New Haven: Yale University Press, 2004.

Foster, David R., Brian M. Donahue, David B. Kittredge, Kathy Fallon Lambert, Malcolm I. Hunter, Brian R. Hall, Lloyd C. Irland, et al. *Wildlands and Woodlands: A Vision for the New England Landscape*. Petersham, MA: Harvard Forest, 2010.

Foster, David R., David B. Kittredge, Brian Donahue, Glenn Motzkin, David Orwig, Aaron M. Ellison, Brian R. Hall, Betsy Colburn, and Anthony D'Amato. *Wildlands and Woodlands: A Vision for the Forests of Massachusetts.* Petersham, MA: Harvard Forest, 2005.

Foster, David, Glenn Motzkin, Debra Bernardos, and James Cardoza. "Wildlife Dynamics in the Changing New England Landscape." *Journal of Biogeography* 29 (2002): 1337–57.

Frye, Bob. *Deer Wars: Science, Tradition, and the Battle over Managing Whitetails in Pennsylvania.* 1967. Reprint, University Park: Pennsylvania State University Press, 2006.

Gehrt, Stanley D. *Urban Coyote Ecology and Management: The Cook County, Illinois, Coyote Project.* Bulletin 929. Columbus: Ohio State University Extension, 2006.

Geist, Valerius. "Triumph of the Commons: The North American Model of Wildlife Conservation as Means of Creating Wealth and Protecting Public Health While Generating Biodiversity." *Wild Lands Advocate* 12, no. 6 (2006): 5–11.

Gottdiener, Mark. *The Theming of America: American Dreams, Media Fantasies, and Themed Environments.* Boulder, CO: Westview Press, 2001.

Graham, Frank, Jr. *Man's Dominion: The Story of Conservation in America.* New York: M. Evans, 1971.

Grunwald, Michael. *The Swamp: The Everglades, Florida, and the Politics of Paradise.* New York: Simon & Schuster, 2006.

Hall, H. Dale. *2006 National Survey of Fishing, Hunting, and Wildlife-Associated Recreation.* Washington, DC: U.S. Fish and Wildlife Service, 2006.

Halls, Lowell K., Richard E. McCabe, and Lawrence R. Jahn. *White-Tailed Deer: Ecology and Management.* Washington, DC: Wildlife Management Institute, 1984.

Hamm, Dale, and David Bakke. *The Last of the Market Hunters.* Carbondale: Southern Illinois University Press, 1996.

Hanson, Harold C. *The Giant Canada Goose.* 1965. Reprint, Carbondale: Southern Illinois University Press, 1997.

Harrison, Jim. *The Woman Lit by Fireflies.* New York: Grove Press, 1990.

Hays, Samuel P. *Conservation and the Gospel of Efficiency: The Progressive Conservation Movement, 1890–1920.* Cambridge, MA: Harvard University Press, 1959.

Henderson, Junius, and Elberta Louise Craig. *Economic Mammalogy.* Springfield, IL: Charles C. Thomas, 1932.

Hildreth, Aaron M., Stephen M. Vantassel, and Scott E. Hygnstrom. *Feral Cats and Their Management.* Lincoln: University of Nebraska Extension, 2010.

Hogan, Matt. "Migratory Bird Hunting and Permits; Regulations for Managing Resident Canada Goose Populations; Final Rule." *Federal Register* 71, no. 154 (August 10, 2006).

Hornaday, William T. *Our Vanishing Wild Life: Its Extermination and Preservation.* New York: New York Zoological Society, 1913.

International Institute for Strategic Studies. *The Military Balance 2011*. New York: Taylor and Francis, 2011.

Irland, Lloyd C. *The Northeast's Changing Forest*. Cambridge, MA: Harvard University Press, 1999.

Jackson, Kenneth T. *Crabgrass Frontier: The Suburbanization of the United States*. New York: Oxford University Press, 1985.

Jacoby, Karl. *Crimes Against Nature: Squatters, Poachers, Thieves, and the Hidden History of American Conservation*. Berkeley: University of California Press, 2001.

Jenkins, Virginia Scott. *The Lawn: A History of an American Obsession*. Washington, DC: Smithsonian Institution Press, 1994.

Jennings, Francis. *The Invasion of America: Indians, Colonialism, and the Cant of Conquest*. Chapel Hill: University of North Carolina Press, 1975.

Jessup, David A. "The Welfare of Feral Cats and Wildlife." *JAVMA* 225, no. 9 (2004): 1377–83.

Johnson, Edward. *Johnson's Wonder-Working Providence*. 1654. Reprint, New York: Barnes and Noble, 1910.

Johnson, Kenneth M. *The Rural Rebound*. Reports on America. Washington, DC: Population Reference Bureau, August 1999.

Kalish, Mildred Armstrong. *Little Heathens: Hard Times and High Spirits on an Iowa Farm During the Great Depression*. New York: Bantam, 2007.

Kellogg, Royal S. *The Timber Supply of the United States*. Circular 166. Washington, DC: U.S. Forest Service, 1909.

Kirkpatrick, Jay F., and John W. Turner Jr. "Urban Deer Contraception: The Seven Stages of Grief." *Wildlife Society Bulletin* 25, no. 2 (1997): 515–19.

Kokel, Ron W., and Jon Andrew. *Draft Environmental Impact Statement: Resident Canada Goose Management*. Washington, DC: U.S. Fish and Wildlife Service, 2002.

Krech, Shepard, III. *The Ecological Indian: Myth and History*. New York: W. W. Norton, 1999.

Kunstler, James Howard. *The Geography of Nowhere: The Rise and Decline of America's Man-Made Landscape*. New York: Simon & Schuster, 1993.

Latham, Roger Earl, Jan Beyea, Merlin Benner, Cindy Adams Dunn, Mary Ann Fajvan, Ronald R. Freed, Marrett Grund, Stephen B. Horsley, Ann Fowler Rhoads, and Bryon P. Shissler. *Managing White-Tailed Deer in Forest Habitat from an Ecosystem Perspective: Pennsylvania Case Study*. Harrisburg: Audubon Pennsylvania and Pennsylvania Habitat Alliance, 2005.

Leopold, Aldo. *A Sand County Almanac, with Essays on Conservation from Round River*. 1949. Reprint, New York: Oxford University Press, 1966.

Levy, Julie K., and P. Cynda Crawford. "Humane Strategies for Controlling Feral Cat Populations." *JAVMA* 225, no. 9 (2004): 1354–60.

Longcore, Travis, Catherine Rich, and Lauren M. Sullivan. "Critical Assessment of Claims Regarding Management of Feral Cats by Trap-Neuter-Return." *Conservation Biology* 23 (2009): 887–94.

Louv, Richard. *Last Child in the Woods: Saving Our Children from Nature-Deficit Disorder.* Chapel Hill, NC: Algonquin Books, 2005.

———. *The Nature Principle: Human Restoration and the End of Nature-Deficit Disorder.* Chapel Hill, NC: Algonquin Books, 2011.

Lund, Thomas A. *American Wildlife Law.* Berkeley: University of California Press, 1980.

Lutts, Ralph H. *The Nature Fakers: Wildlife, Science and Sentiment.* Charlottesville: University Press of Virginia, 1990.

MacCleery, Douglas W. *American Forests: A History of Resiliency and Recovery.* Durham, NC: Forest History Society, 2002.

———. *What on Earth Have We Done to Our Forests? A Brief Overview on the Condition and Trends of U.S. Forests.* Washington, DC: U.S. Forest Service, 1992.

Mann, Charles C. *1491: New Revelations of the Americas Before Columbus.* New York: Alfred A. Knopf, 2005.

———. *1493: Uncovering the New World Columbus Created.* New York: Alfred A. Knopf, 2011.

Marsh, George Perkins. *Man and Nature; or, Physical Geography as Modified by Human Action.* 1864. Reprint, Seattle: University of Washington Press, 2003.

Martin, Clara Barnes. *Mount Desert on the Coast of Maine.* Portland, ME: Loring, Short and Harmon, 1871.

Matthiessen, Peter. *Wildlife in America.* 1959. Reprint, New York: Penguin Books USA, 1987.

McDonald, J. Scott, and Karl V. Miller. *A History of White-Tailed Deer Restocking in the United States, 1878 to 2004.* Athens, GA: Quality Deer Management Association and D. B. Warnell School of Forest Resources, 2004.

McKibben, Bill. *The End of Nature.* New York: Random House, 1989.

McNichol, Dan. *Paving the Way.* Lanham, MD: National Asphalt Pavement Association, 2005.

———. *The Roads That Built America: The Incredible Story of the U.S. Interstate System.* New York: Sterling, 2006.

McShea, William J., H. Brian Underwood, and John H. Rappole. *The Science of Overabundance: Deer Ecology and Population Management.* Washington, DC: Smithsonian Institution Press, 1997.

Miniter, Frank. *The Politically Incorrect Guide to Hunting.* Washington, DC: Regnery, 2007.

Mitman, Gregg. *Reel Nature: America's Romance with Wildlife on Film.* Cambridge, MA: Harvard University Press, 1999.

Morison, Samuel Eliot. *The Story of Mount Desert Island.* Boston: Little, Brown, 1960.

Morton, Thomas. *New English Canaan.* Amsterdam, Netherlands, 1637.

Mowbray, T. B., C. R. Ely, J. S. Sedinger, and R. E. Trost. *Canada Goose: Branta canadensis.* Birds of North America 682. Philadelphia: Birds of North America, 2002.

Nash, Roderick Frazier. *Wilderness and the American Mind.* 1967. Reprint, New Haven: Yale University Press, 1982.

Organ, J. F., R. F. Gotie, T. A. Decker, and G. R. Batcheller. "A Case Study in the Sustained Use of Wildlife: The Management of Beaver in the Northeastern United States." In *Enhancing Sustainability: Resources for Our Future,* SUI Technical Series 1. Edited by H. A. van der Linde and M. H. Danskin. Cambridge: International Union for Conservation of Nature, 1998.

Paisley, Clifton. *From Cotton to Quail: An Agricultural Chronicle of Leon County, Florida, 1860–1967.* Tallahassee: University Presses of Florida, 1981.

———. *The Red Hills of Florida, 1528–1865.* Tuscaloosa: University of Alabama Press, 1989.

Palmer, Chris. *Shooting in the Wild: An Insider's Account of Making Movies in the Animal Kingdom.* San Francisco: Sierra Club Books, 2010.

Partridge, Bellamy. *Going, Going, Gone!* New York: E. P. Dutton, 1958.

Peterson, Eugene T. "The History of Wildlife Conservation in Michigan, 1859–1921." Ph.D. diss., University of Michigan, 1952.

Philbrick, Nathaniel. *Mayflower: A Story of Courage, Community, and War.* New York: Penguin Group, 2006.

Phillips, Paul Chrisler. *The Fur Trade.* Norman: University of Oklahoma Press, 1961.

Pollan, Michael. *The Omnivore's Dilemma: A Natural History of Four Meals.* New York: Penguin Press, 2006.

———. *Second Nature: A Gardener's Education.* New York: Grove/Atlantic, 1991.

Posewitz, Jim. *Beyond Fair Chase.* Guilford, CT: Globe Pequot Press, 2002.

———. *Inherit the Hunt: A Journey into the Heart of American Hunting.* Guilford, CT: Globe Pequot Press, 1999.

Reiger, John F. *American Sportsmen and the Origins of Conservation.* Corvallis: Oregon State University Press, 2001.

Roberts, Ann Rockefeller. *Mr. Rockefeller's Roads: The Untold Story of Acadia's Carriage Roads and Their Creator.* Camden, ME: Down East Books, 1990.

Rome, Adam. *The Bulldozer in the Countryside: Suburban Sprawl and the Rise of American Environmentalism.* Cambridge: Cambridge University Press, 2001.

Roths, Jaylene. *A History of Mount Desert Island Agriculture.* Mount Desert, ME: Mount Desert Island Historical Society, 2005.

Sanderson, Virginia Somes. *The Living Past: Being the Story of Somesville, Mount Desert, Maine, and Its Relationship with Other Areas of the Island.* Mount Desert, ME: Beech Hill, 1982.

Sanger, David, and Harald E. L. Prins. *An Island in Time: Three Thousand Years of Cultural Exchange on Mount Desert Island.* Bar Harbor, ME: Robert Abbe Museum, 1989.

Sargent, Charles Sprague. *Report on the Forests of North America (Exclusive of Mexico).* Washington, DC: U.S. Census, 1884.

Shabecoff, Philip. *A Fierce Green Fire: The American Environmental Movement*. Washington, DC: Island Press, 1993.

Shissler, Bryon P. *Deer Management Plan for Lower Makefield Twp*. Fort Hill, PA: Natural Resource Consultants, 2007.

Shorto, Russell. *The Island at the Center of the World*. New York: Doubleday, 2004.

Singer, Peter. *Animal Liberation*. New York: Random House, 1975.

Smith, Andrew W. *The Turkey: An American Story*. Chicago: University of Illinois Press, 2006.

Smith, Brad W., Patrick D. Miles, Charles H. Perry, and Scott A. Pugh, technical coordinators. *Forest Resources of the United States, 2007*. Washington, DC: U.S. Forest Service, 2007.

Steinberg, Ted. *Down to Earth: Nature's Role in American History*. New York: Oxford University Press, 2002.

St. Germain, Tom, and Jay Saunders. *Trails of History: The Story of Mount Desert Island's Paths from Norumbega to Acadia*. Bar Harbor, ME: Parkman Publications, 1993.

Stoddard, Herbert L. *The Bobwhite Quail: Its Habits, Preservation and Increase*. Washington, DC: U.S. Bureau of Biological Survey, 1931.

Stommel, Henry, and Elizabeth Stommel. *Volcano Weather: The Story of 1816, the Year Without a Summer*. Newport, RI: Seven Seas Press, 1983.

Trefethen, James B. *An American Crusade for Wildlife*. New York: Winchester Press, 1975.

Turner, Dennis C., and Patrick Bateson, *The Domestic Cat: The Biology of Its Behavior*. 1988. Reprint, Cambridge: Cambridge University Press, 2000.

Walsh, Harry M. *The Outlaw Gunner*. Centreville, MD: Tidewater, 1971.

Wegner, Robert. *Deer and Deer Hunting: The Serious Hunter's Guide*. Mechanicsburg, PA: Stackpole Books, 1984.

———. *Legendary Deerslayers*. Iola, WI: Krause Publications, 2004.

Whitney, Gordon G., and William C. Davis. "Thoreau and the Forest History of Concord, Massachusetts." *Journal of Forest History* 30 (April 1986): 70–81.

Williams, Michael. *Americans and Their Forests: A Historical Geography*. Cambridge: Cambridge University Press, 1989.

———. *Deforesting the Earth: From Prehistory to Global Crisis*. Chicago: University of Chicago Press, 2006.

Williams, Nigel. *From Wimbledon to Waco*. London: Faber and Faber, 1995.

Wilmerding, John. *The Artist's Mount Desert: American Painters on the Maine Coast*. Princeton: Princeton University Press, 1994.

About the Author

JIM STERBA has been a foreign correspondent and national affairs reporter for more than four decades for the *Wall Street Journal* and *New York Times*. He is the author of *Frankie's Place: A Love Story*, about summers in Maine with his wife, the author Frances FitzGerald.

Printed in the United States
by Baker & Taylor Publisher Services